THE INTREPID TRAVELER'S
COMPLETE DESK REFERENCE

The Intrepid Traveler's Complete Desk Reference

Sally Scanlon

Kelly Monaghan

THE INTREPID TRAVELER'S
COMPLETE DESK REFERENCE

Second edition

Cover art by Fuszion Art + Design

For information contact
The Intrepid Traveler
P.O. Box 438
New York, NY 10034
http://www.intrepidtraveler.com

ISBN 1-887140-06-9
LOC 97-70113

Publisher's Cataloging in Publication Data
Prepared by Sanford Berman, Head Cataloger, Hennepin County Library,
Minnetonka, MN.
Scanlon, Sally
    The Intrepid Traveler's complete desk reference.
By Sally Scanlon and Kelly Monaghan. New York: The Intrepid Traveler,
copyright 1998.
    PARTIAL CONTENTS: Airport, airline, country & currency codes. —
Industry contacts & information sources. —Reference section and bibliog-
raphy. Getting passports & visas. Time zones at a glance. Glossary of travel-
related terms & abbreviations.
    1. Travel—Information services—Directories. 2. Tourist trade—Infor-
mation services—Directories. 3. Travel—Dictionaries. 4. Tourist trade—
Dictionaries. 5. Travel—Bibliography. 6. Tourist trade—Bibliography. 7.
Countries—Codes. 8. Airlines—Codes. 9. Airports—Codes. 10. Money—
Codes. 11. Time zones. 12. Passports. 13. Visas.
    I. Intrepid Traveler. II. Title. III. Title: Traveler's complete desk ref-
erence. IV. Monaghan, Kelly.
    910.2

DEDICATION

This book is respectfully dedicated to the independent, outside agent — the future of the travel industry.

Table of Contents

Introduction

This book grew out of my efforts to learn the travel business as an outside sales rep and independent contractor. There were numerous codes to learn so I could navigate the airline computerized reservation service available through on-line services like CompuServe. There were unfamiliar terms and jargon to master so I could converse fluently with reservationists and suppliers. There was information to gather so I could serve my clients better.

While the learning process is always enjoyable, I found myself frequently frustrated by the time it took to put my hands on just the piece of information I needed. I searched through the growing pile of industry references in my office. I spent time on the phone tracking down numbers and addresses. I launched myself into cyberspace to get my questions answered. If only there was a handy, one-stop reference that would give me the information I needed quickly, when I needed it.

If necessity is the mother of invention, then frustration is its midwife. Out of my annoyance grew the book you now hold in your hands. Sally Scanlon and I have designed it to help you avoid the glitches that I experienced when I first started out and to save you time as you begin to navigate the exciting world of selling travel.

The Intrepid Traveler's Complete Desk Reference is conceived primarily as a companion piece to my book, *Home-Based Travel Agent: How To Cash In On The Exciting NEW World Of Travel Marketing*. That means it is dedicated to the beginner. However, even experienced travel agents will find this a handy guide to have on their desk, near the CRT and the phone, ready to provide the code to that out-of-the-way destination or the toll-free number of an unfamiliar supplier. The book should also offer those who experience the travel industry as customers a window into this exciting world. It will allow them to decipher the gibberish on their airline tickets and itineraries and help them better understand the special terms and jargon used in brochures and in the ever-present fine print. Not incidentally, it will assist them as they make their own travel arrangements electronically via the Internet.

The Intrepid Traveler's Complete Desk Reference is, like Caesar's Gaul, divided into three parts. The first is dedicated to the codes that make researching fares and schedules a breeze. In *Home-Based Travel Agent*, I explain how to use these codes in easySABRE to quickly narrow down your search for the best deal for yourself or your clients. Of course, you will also use these codes if you are building an itinerary on a dedicated CRS. Therefore, with the more experienced agent in mind, we have included rental car and hotel codes too, as well as the less frequently used country and currency codes.

Part Two presents a cornucopia of toll-free phone numbers which give you access to both travel industry suppliers and a wealth of free travel information. Also included are listings of travel industry organizations and consortiums. New to this second edition is a listing of web site addresses of particular interest to travel agents.

The reference section, Part Three, will help answer frequently asked questions by deciphering industry jargon, acronyms, and frequently used CRS abbreviations. Also here you will find an extensive bibliography pointing you towards innumerable sources of information that can deepen your knowledge of both the travel industry and the many exciting destinations it serves.

Kelly Monaghan
New York City

Part One:

Airport
Airline
Country
&
Currency
Codes

About the Codes

This section contains information about the primary codes used in the various computerized reservations systems (CRS) to identify cities, airports, airlines and other suppliers. These codes are universal, that is, they are the same no matter which CRS you happen to be using. They serve the dual purpose of making the CRSs faster and more efficient, by sharply reducing the chances of confusion or error.

You will turn to this section in one of two situations: You need to find the proper code for a destination or a carrier or you are confronted with an unfamiliar code and need to know what it stands for. With that in mind, this section has been arranged as follows:

Domestic Airports. Here are listed, alphabetically by city name, destinations in the United States (including Puerto Rico, the Virgin Islands, American Samoa, and Guam) and Canada and the universal three-letter codes used to uniquely identify them. We have used the standard two-letter abbreviations for states and provinces, which are listed at the end of this introduction. When you are constructing a domestic itinerary, you will find the codes you need here.

International Airports. Here are listed, alphabetically by city name, destinations outside the United States and Canada along with their unique three-letter codes. When you are constructing an international itinerary, you will find the codes you need here.

Airport Codes. Until you begin to learn airport codes by heart you will find yourself confronted with unfamiliar codes. Even after you have been in the business for years, you will find that you are constantly bumping into unfamiliar codes. Here are listed, alphabetically by code, all the airports included in Domestic Airports and International Airports. When confronted with an unfamiliar airport code, this listing will identify the airport.

Airlines. Here are listed, alphabetically by airline, all the world's scheduled passenger carriers and their codes. Like airports, all airlines are identified by a unique code. As we write this, airlines are identified by two-digit alphanumeric codes, that is, some combination of letters and numbers (e.g. AA or N9). Because the two-digit format limits the possible number of codes, the industry has created a new three-digit code system for airlines. At some point in the not-too-far-distant future, the industry will switch over from the old two-digit codes to the new three-digit codes. Consequently, we have listed both codes for each airline. When the switch takes place, you'll be ready. Note that some airlines have not yet been assigned three-digit codes.

Airline Codes. Just as you will see unfamiliar airport codes, you will find unfamiliar airline codes cropping up on itineraries and CRS screens. Here we have listed, alphabetically by code, both the two- and three-digit airline codes and the airlines to which they correspond. When confronted with an unfamiliar airline code, this listing will identify the airline.

Hotels and Rental Cars. The major car rental firms and a growing number of hotel chains have their own CRS codes which allow you to book them directly through the CRS. Here are listed, alphabetically by company name, the major car rental firms and hotels and their unique CRS codes.

Hotel and Rental Car Codes. Here are listed, alphabetically by code, the codes used for hotels and rental cars and the companies which they identify.

Countries and Currencies. There is a growing trend toward international standardization in abbreviations. Here we have listed, alphabetically by country, the nations of the world. For each, we have provided the two-letter country abbreviation, the complete name of the currency used in that country, and the three-digit code for that currency.

Country and Currency Codes. Here we have listed, alphabetically by code, the two-digit country codes and the three-digit currency codes. Use this listing when you need to decipher an unfamiliar country or currency code.

Please note that codes change. This is especially true of airport and airline codes. Airports close, open or have their designation changed. Airlines start up and go out of business. All CRSs let you query the system to find a code for an airport or carrier or decipher a new or unfamiliar code.

U.S. State & Territory Abbreviations

AK	Alaska	HI	Hawaii
AL	Alabama	IA	Iowa
AR	Arkansas	ID	Idaho
AS	American Samoa	IL	Illinois
AZ	Arizona	IN	Indiana
CA	California	KS	Kansas
CO	Colorado	KY	Kentucky
CT	Connecticut	LA	Louisiana
DC	District of Columbia	MA	Massachusetts
DE	Delaware	MD	Maryland
FL	Florida	ME	Maine
GA	Georgia	MI	Michigan
GU	Guam	MN	Minnesota

MO	Missouri	PR	Puerto Rico
MS	Mississippi	RI	Rhode Island
MT	Montana	SC	South Carolina
NC	North Carolina	SD	South Dakota
ND	North Dakota	TN	Tennessee
NE	Nebraska	TX	Texas
NH	New Hampshire	UT	Utah
NJ	New Jersey	VA	Virginia
NM	New Mexico	VI	Virgin Islands
NV	Nevada	VT	Vermont
NY	New York	WA	Washington
OH	Ohio	WI	Wisconsin
OK	Oklahoma	WV	West Virginia
OR	Oregon	WY	Wyoming
PA	Pennsylvania		

Canadian Province Abbreviations

AB	Alberta	NT	Northwest Territories
BC	British Columbia	ON	Ontario
MB	Manitoba	PE	Prince Edward Island
NB	New Brunswick	PQ	Quebec
NF	Newfoundland	SK	Saskatchewan
NS	Nova Scotia	YK	Yukon Territory

Domestic Airports

Aberdeen, SD	ABR	Atikokan, OT	YIB
Abilene, TX	ABI	Atka, AK	AKB
Adak Island, AK	ADK	Atlanta, GA	ATL
Aguadilla, PR	BQN	Atlantic City (Intl), NJ	ACY
Akhiok, AK	AKK	Atlantic City, NJ	AIY
Akiachak, AK	KKI	Atmautluak, AK	ATT
Akiak, AK	AKI	Atqasuk, AK	ATK
Akron/Canton, OH	CAK	Attawapiskat, OT	YAT
Akulivik, QU	AKV	Augusta, GA	AGS
Akutan, AK	KQA	Augusta, ME	AUG
Alakanuk, AK	AUK	Aupaluk, QU	YPJ
Alamogordo, NM	ALM	Austin, TX	AUS
Alamosa, CO	ALS	Bagotville, QU	YBG
Albany, GA	ABY	Baie Comeau, QU	YBC
Albany, NY	ALB	Baker Lake, NT	YBK
Albany, OR	CVO	Bakersfield, CA	BFL
Albuquerque, NM	ABQ	Baltimore, MD	BWI
Aleknagik, AK	WKK	Banff, AB	YBA
Aleneva, AK	AED	Bangor, ME	BGR
Alexandria, LA	ESF	Bar Harbor, ME	BHB
Alitak, AK	ALZ	Barrow, AK	BRW
Allakaket, AK	AET	Barter Island, AK	BTI
Allentown, PA	ABE	Bathurst, NB	ZBF
Alliance, NE	AIA	Baton Rouge, LA	BTR
Alma, QU	YTF	Battle Creek, MI	BTL
Alpena, MI	APN	Bay City, MI	MBS
Altoona, PA	AOO	Bearskin Lake, OT	XBE
Amarillo, TX	AMA	Beaumont, TX	BPT
Ambler, AK	ABL	Beaver, AK	WBQ
Amook, AK	AOS	Beckley, WV	BKW
Anacortes, WA	OTS	Bedwell Harbour, BC	YBW
Anaheim, CA	ANA	Bella Bella, BC	ZEL
Anahim Lake, BC	YAA	Bella Coola, BC	QBC
Anaktuvuk, AK	AKP	Bellefonte, PA	PSB
Anchorage, AK	ANC	Bellingham, WA	BLI
Angling Lake, OT	YAX	Bemidji, MN	BJI
Angoon, AK	AGN	Bend/Redmond, OR	RDM
Aniak, AK	ANI	Benton Harbor, MI	BEH
Anvik, AK	ANV	Berens River, MB	YBV
Appleton, WI	ATW	Bethel, AK	BET
Arcata, CA	ACV	Bethlehem, PA	ABE
Arctic Bay, NT	YAB	Bettles, AK	BTT
Arctic Village, AK	ARC	Big Trout Lake, OT	YTL
Arviat, NT	YEK	Billings, MT	BIL
Asheville, NC	AVL	Binghamton, NY	BGM
Ashland, KY	HTS	Birch Creek, AK	KBC
Aspen, CO	ASE	Birmingham, AL	BHM
Athens, GA	AHN	Bismarck, ND	BIS

Black Tickle, NF	YBI	Chadron, NE	CDR
Blakely Island, WA	BYW	Chalkyitsik, AK	CIK
Blanc Sablon, QU	YBX	Champaign, IL	CMI
Block Island, RI	BID	Chapleau, OT	YLD
Bloomington, IN	BMG	Charleston, SC	CHS
Bloomington/Normal, IL	BMI	Charleston, WV	CRW
Bluefield/Princeton, WV	BLF	Charlo, NB	YCL
Boise, ID	BOI	Charlotte, NC	CLT
Boston, MA	BOS	Charlottesville, VA	CHO
Boulder City, NV	BLD	Charlottetown, NF	YHG
Boundary, AK	BYA	Charlottetown, PE	YYG
Bozeman, MT	BZN	Chatham, NB	YCH
Bradenton, FL	SRQ	Chattanooga, TN	CHA
Bradford, PA	BFD	Chefornak, AK	CYF
Brainerd, MN	BRD	Chesterfield Inlet, NT	YCS
Brandon, MB	YBR	Chevak, AK	VAK
Branson, MO	ZBX	Chevery, QU	YHR
Brevig Mission, AK	KTS	Cheyenne, WY	CYS
Bridgeport, CT	BDR	Chibougamau, QU	YMT
Bristol, VA	TRI	Chicago (Meigs), IL	CGX
Brochet, MB	YBT	Chicago (Metro), IL	CHI
Broughton Island, NT	YVM	Chicago (Midway), IL	MDW
Brownsville, TX	BRO	Chicago (O'Hare), IL	ORD
Brownwood, TX	BWD	Chicago (Pal Waukee), IL	PWK
Brunswick, GA	BQK	Chicken, AK	CKX
Bryan, TX	CFD	Chico, CA	CIC
Bryce Canyon, UT	BCE	Chignik, AK	KCL
Buckland, AK	BKC	Chino, CA	CNO
Buffalo, NY	BUF	Chisana, AK	CZN
Bullhead City, AZ	BHC	Chisasibi, QU	YKU
Burbank, CA	BUR	Chisholm, MN	HIB
Burlington, IA	BRL	Chuathbaluk, AK	CHU
Burlington, VT	BTV	Churchill Falls, NF	ZUM
Butte, MT	BTM	Churchill, MB	YYQ
Calgary (Intl), AB	YYC	Cincinnati (Municipal), OH	LUK
Cambridge Bay, NT	YCB	Cincinnati, OH	CVG
Campbell River, BC	YBL	Circle, AK	IRC
Candle, AK	CDL	Circle Hot Springs, AK	CHP
Cape Dorset, NT	YTE	Clarks Point, AK	CLP
Cape Girardeau, MO	CGI	Clarksburg, WV	CKB
Cape Lisburne, AK	LUR	Cleveland, OH	CLE
Cape Newenham, AK	EHM	Clovis, NM	CVN
Carlsbad, CA	CLD	Clyde River, NT	YCY
Carlsbad, NM	CNM	Cochrane, OT	YCN
Carmel, CA	MRY	Cody, WY	COD
Cartwright, NF	YRF	Coeur D'Alene, ID	COE
Casper, WY	CPR	Coffman Cove, AK	KCC
Castlegar, BC	YCG	Cold Bay, AK	CDB
Cat Lake, OT	YAC	College Station, TX	CLL
Catalina Island, CA	AVX	Colorado Springs, CO	COS
Cedar City, UT	CDC	Columbia, MO	COU
Cedar Rapids/Iowa City, IA	CID	Columbia, SC	CAE
Center Island, WA	CWS	Columbus, GA	CSG
Central, AK	CEM	Columbus, MS	UBS

Columbus, OH	CMH	Duluth, MN/Superior, WI	DLH
Columbus/Strkvl/W. Pt., MS	GTR	Durango, CO	DRO
Colville Lake, NT	YCK	Durham, NC	RDU
Comox, BC	YQQ	Dutch Harbor, AK	DUT
Coral Harbour, NT	YZS	Eagle, AK	EAA
Cordova, AK	CDV	Earlton, OT	YXR
Corpus Christi, TX	CRP	East Hampton, NY	HTO
Cortez, CO	CEZ	East Main, QU	ZEM
Craig, AK	CGA	Easton, PA	ABE
Cranbrook, BC	YXC	Eastsound, WA	ESD
Crescent City, CA	CEC	Eau Claire, WI	EAU
Crested Butte, CO	CSE	Edmonton (Intl), AB	YEG
Crooked Creek, AK	CKD	Edmonton (Metro), AB	YEA
Cross Lake, MB	YCR	Edmonton (Muni), AB	YXD
Cube Cove, AK	CUW	Edmonton (Namao), AB	YED
Culebra, PR	CPX	Edna Bay, AK	EDA
Cumberland, MD	CBE	Eek, AK	EEK
Dallas/Ft. Worth (Intl), TX	DFW	Egegik, AK	EGX
Dallas/Ft. Worth (Love), TX	DAL	Ekuk, AK	KKU
Dauphin, MB	YDN	Ekwok, AK	KEK
Davenport, IA	DVN	El Centro/Imperial, CA	IPL
Davis Inlet, NF	YDI	El Dorado, AR	ELD
Dawson City, YT	YDA	El Paso, TX	ELP
Dawson Creek, BC	YDQ	Elfin Cove, AK	ELV
Dayton, OH	DAY	Elim, AK	ELI
Daytona Beach, FL	DAB	Elko, NV	EKO
Dean River, BC	YRD	Elliot Lake, OT	YEL
Dease Lake, BC	YDL	Elmira/Corning, NY	ELM
Decatur, IL	DEC	Ely, NV	ELY
Decatur Island, WA	DTR	Emmonak, AK	EMK
Deer Lake, NF	YDF	Enid, OK	WDG
Deer Lake, OT	YVZ	Erie, PA	ERI
Deering, AK	DRG	Escanaba, MI	ESC
Del Rio, TX	DRT	Eugene, OR	EUG
Deline, NT	YWJ	Eureka/Arcata, CA	ACV
Delta Junction, AK	DJN	Evansville, IN	EVV
Deming, NM	DMN	Excursion Inlet, AK	EXI
Denver, CO	DEN	Fairbanks, AK	FAI
Des Moines, IA	DSM	Fajardo, PR	FAJ
Desolation Sound, BC	YDS	Fall River/New Bedford, MA	EWB
Detroit (City), MI	DET	False Island, AK	FAK
Detroit (Metro), MI	DTT	False Pass, AK	KFP
Detroit (Wayne Cty), MI	DTW	Fargo, ND	FAR
Devils Lake, ND	DVL	Farmingdale (Republic), NY	FRG
Dickenson, ND	DIK	Farmington, NM	FMN
Dillingham, AK	DLG	Fayetteville, AR	FYV
Diomede Island, AK	DIO	Fayetteville, NC	FAY
Dodge City, KS	DDC	Fishers Island, NY	FID
Dolomi, AK	DLO	Flagstaff, AZ	FLG
Dora Bay, AK	DOF	Flat, AK	FLT
Dothan, AL	DHN	Flin Flon, MB	YFO
Dryden, OT	YHD	Flint, MI	FNT
DuBois, PA	DUJ	Florence, AL	MSL
Dubuque, IA	DBQ	Florence, SC	FLO

Fond du Lac, SA	ZFD	Grand Canyon, AZ	GCN
Fort Albany, OT	YFA	Grand Forks, ND	GFK
Fort Chipewyan, AB	YPY	Grand Island, NE	GRI
Fort Collins/Loveland, CO	FNL	Grand Junction, CO	GJT
Fort Dodge, IA	FOD	Grand Rapids, MI	GRR
Fort Francis, OT	YAG	Grand Rapids, MN	GPZ
Fort Good Hope, NT	YGH	Grande Prairie, AB	YQU
Fort Hope, OT	YFH	Grayling, AK	KGX
Fort Huachuca/Sierra Vista, AZ	FHU	Great Bend, KS	GBD
Fort Lauderdale, FL	FLL	Great Falls, MT	GTF
Fort McMurray, AB	YMM	Green Bay, WI	GRB
Fort Myers, FL	FMY	Greensboro/H.Pt/	
Fort Myers (Regional), FL	RSW	Winston-Salem, NC	GSO
Fort Nelson, BC	YYE	Greenville, MS	GLH
Fort Resolution, NT	YFR	Greenville, NC	PGV
Fort Severn, OT	YER	Greenville/Spartanburg, SC	GSP
Fort Simpson, NT	YFS	Grise Fiord, NT	YGZ
Fort Smith, AR	FSM	Guam, GU	GUM
Fort Smith, NT	YSM	Gulfport/Biloxi, MS	GPT
Fort St. John, BC	YXJ	Gunnison, CO	GUC
Fort Wayne, IN	FWA	Gustavus, AK	GST
Fort Worth, TX	DFW	Hagerstown, MD	HGR
Fort Yukon, AK	FYU	Haines, AK	HNS
Fox Harbour, NF	YFX	Halifax (Intl), NS	YHZ
Franklin, PA	FKL	Hall Beach, NT	YUX
Fredericton, NB	YFC	Hamilton, OT	YHM
Frenchville, ME	WFK	Hampton/Newport News/	
Fresno, CA	FAT	Wmsbrg, VA	PHF
Friday Harbor, WA	FRD	Hana, Maui, HI	HNM
Gainesville, FL	GNV	Hancock, MI	CMX
Galena, AK	GAL	Harlingen, TX	HRL
Gallup, NM	GUP	Harrisburg (Intl), PA	MDT
Gambell, AK	GAM	Harrisburg, PA	HAR
Gander, NF	YQX	Harrison, AR	HRO
Ganges Harbor, BC	YGG	Hartford, CT	BDL
Garden City, KS	GCK	Hartford, CT/Springfield,MA	HFD
Gaspe, QU	YGP	Hattiesburg, MS	HBG
Gatineau/Hull, QU	YND	Havasupai, AZ	HAE
Geraldton, OT	YGQ	Havre, MT	HVR
Gethsemani, QU	ZGS	Havre St. Pierre, QU	YGV
Gillam, MB	YGX	Hay River, NT	YHY
Gillette, WY	GCC	Hays, KS	HYS
Gillies Bay, BC	YGB	Healy Lake, AK	HKB
Gjoa Haven, NT	YHK	Hearst, OT	YHF
Gladewater/Kilgore/		Helena, MT	HLN
Longview, TX	GGG	Hibbing/Chisolm, MN	HIB
Glasgow, MT	GGW	Hickory, NC	HKY
Glendive, MT	GDV	High Level, AB	YOJ
Gods Narrows, MB	YGO	Hilo, Hawaii, HI	ITO
Gods River, MB	ZGI	Hilton Head Island, SC	HHH
Golovin, AK	GLV	Hobart Bay, AK	HBH
Goodnews Bay, AK	GNU	Hobbs, NM	HOB
Goose Bay, NF	YYR	Hollis, AK	HYL
Gore Bay, OT	YZE	Holman Island, NT	YHI

Holy Cross, AK	HCR	Kahului, HI	OGG
Homer, AK	HOM	Kake, AK	KAE
Honolulu (Oahu) HI	HNL	Kakhonak, AK	KNK
Hoolehua (Molokai), HI	MKK	Kalamazoo, MI	AZO
Hoonah, AK	HNH	Kalaupapa, HI	LUP
Hooper Bay, AK	HPB	Kalispell/Glacier Natl Pk, MT	FCA
Hopedale, NF	YHO	Kalskag, AK	KLG
Hornepayne, OT	YHN	Kaltag, AK	KAL
Hot Springs, AR	HOT	Kamloops, BC	YKA
Houston (Ellington), TX	EFD	Kamuela, HI	MUE
Houston (Hobby), TX	HOU	Kangiqsujuaq, QU	YWB
Houston (Intercontinental), TX	IAH	Kangirsuk, QU	YKG
Hughes, AK	HUS	Kansas City (Downtown), MO	MKC
Huntington, WV/Ashland, KY	HTS	Kansas City (Intl), MO	MCI
Huntsville/Decatur, AL	HSV	Kapalua, Maui, HI	JHM
Huron, SD	HON	Kapuskasing, OT	YYU
Huslia, AK	HSL	Karluk, AK	KYK
Hyannis, MA	HYA	Kasaan, AK	KXA
Hydaburg, AK	HYG	Kasabonika, OT	XKS
Hyder, AK	WHD	Kaschechewan, OT	ZKE
Idaho Falls, ID	IDA	Kasigluk, AK	KUK
Igiugig, AK	IGG	Kauai Is. (Lihue), HI	LIH
Igloolik, NT	YGT	Kayenta, AZ	MVM
Iles de la Madeleine, QU	YGR	Keene, NH/Brattleboro, VT	EEN
Iliamna, AK	ILI	Kegaska, QU	ZKG
Imperial, CA	IPL	Kelowna, BC	YLW
Indianapolis, IN	IND	Kenai, AK	ENA
Int'l Falls, MN	INL	Kenmore Air Harbor, WA	KEH
Inukjuak, QU	YPH	Kenora, OT	YQK
Inuvik, NT	YEV	Ketchikan, AK	KTN
Inyokern, CA	IYK	Key West, FL	EYW
Iowa City, IA	IOW	Kiana, AK	IAN
Iqaluit, NT	YFB	Kilgore, TX	GGG
Iron Mountain, MI	IMT	Killeen, TX	ILE
Ironwood, MI	IWD	Kimmirut, NT	YLC
Island Lake, MB	YIV	King Cove, AK	KVC
Islip (Macarthur), NY	ISP	King Salmon, AK	AKN
Ithaca, NY	ITH	Kingfisher Lake, OT	KIF
Ivanof Bay, AK	KIB	Kingman, AZ	IGM
Ivujivik, QU	YIK	Kingsport, TN	TRI
Jackson Hole, WY	JAC	Kingston, OT	YGK
Jackson, MS	JAN	Kinston, NC	ISO
Jackson, TN	MKL	Kipnuk, AK	KPN
Jacksonville, FL	JAX	Kirkland Lake, OT	YKX
Jacksonville, NC	OAJ	Kirksville, MO	IRK
Jamestown, ND	JMS	Kitoi Bay, AK	KKB
Jamestown, NY	JHW	Kivalina, AK	KVL
Jefferson City, MO	JEF	Klamath Falls, OR	LMT
Johnson City, NY	BGM	Klawock, AK	KLW
Johnson City, TN	TRI	Knoxville, TN	TYS
Johnstown, PA	JST	Kobuk, AK	OBU
Jonesboro, AR	JBR	Kodiak, AK	ADQ
Joplin, MO	JLN	Kona, Hawaii, HI	KOA
Juneau, AK	JNU	Kongiganak, AK	KKH

Kotlik, AK	KOT	Lopez Island, WA	LPS
Kotzebue, AK	OTZ	Los Alamos, NM	LAM
Koyuk, AK	KKA	Los Angeles (Intl), CA	LAX
Koyukuk, AK	KYU	Los Angeles (Van Nuys), CA	VNY
Kuujjuaq, QU	YVP	Louisville, KY	SDF
Kuujjuarapik, QU	YGW	Lovell, WY	POY
Kwethluk, AK	KWT	Lubbock, TX	LBB
Kwigillingok, AK	KWK	Ludington, MI	LDM
La Crosse WI/Winona, MN	LSE	Lufkin, TX	OCH
La Grande, QU	YGL	Lynchburg, VA	LYH
La Ronge, SA	YVC	Lynn Lake, MB	YYL
La Tabatiere, QU	ZLT	Mackinac Island, MI	MCD
Lac Brochet, MB	XLB	Macon, GA	MCN
Lafayette, IN	LAF	Madison, WI	MSN
Lafayette, LA	LFT	Makkovik, NF	YMN
Lake Charles, LA	LCH	Manchester, NH	MHT
Lake Harbour, NT	YLC	Manhattan, KS	MHK
Lake Havasu City, AZ	HII	Manistee, MI	MBL
Lake Minchumina, AK	LMA	Manley Hot Springs, AK	MLY
Lake Placid, NY	LKP	Manokotak, AK	KMO
Lake Tahoe, CA	TVL	Marathon, FL	MTH
Lanai City, HI	LNY	Marietta/Parkersburg, WV	PKB
Lancaster, PA	LNS	Marion, IL	MWA
Lansdowne House, OT	YLH	Marquette, MI	MQT
Lansing, MI	LAN	Marshall, AK	MLL
Laramie, WY	LAR	Martha's Vineyard, MA	MVY
Laredo, TX	LRD	Martinsburg, WV	MRB
Larsen Bay, AK	KLN	Mary's Harbour, NF	YMH
Las Cruces, NM	LRU	Mason City, IA	MCW
Las Vegas (Henderson), NV	HSH	Massena, NY	MSS
Las Vegas (N. Terminal), NV	VGT	Mattoon, IL	MTO
Las Vegas, NV	LAS	Mayaguez, PR	MAZ
Latrobe, PA	LBE	McAllen, TX	MFE
Laurel (Hattiesburg), MS	PIB	McCook, NE	MCK
Lawton, OK	LAW	McGrath, AK	MCG
Leaf Rapids, MB	YLR	Medford, OR	MFR
Lebel-Sur-Quevillion, QU	YLS	Medicine Hat, AB	YXH
Lethbridge, AB	YQL	Mekoryuk, AK	MYU
Levelock, AK	KLL	Melbourne, FL	MLB
Lewisburg/Greenbrier		Memphis, TN	MEM
Valley, WV	LWB	Merced, CA	MCE
Lewiston, ID	LWS	Meridian, MS	MEI
Lewiston/Auburn, ME	LEW	Metlakatia, AK	MTM
Lewistown, MT	LWT	Meyers Chuck, AK	WMK
Lexington, KY	LEX	Miami (Intl), FL	MIA
Liberal, KS	LBL	Midland/Odessa, TX	MAF
Lime Village, AK	LVD	Miles City, MT	MLS
Lincoln, NE	LNK	Milwaukee, WI	MKE
Little Rock, AR	LIT	Minneapolis/St. Paul, MN	MSP
Lloydminster, AB	YLL	Minot, ND	MOT
London, OT	YXU	Minto, AK	MNT
Long Beach, CA	LGB	Mission, TX	MFE
Long Island, AK	LIJ	Missoula, MT	MSO
Longview, TX	GGG	Moab, UT	CNY

Mobile AL/Pascagoula, MS	MOB	Newtok, AK	WWT
Modesto, CA	MOD	Nightmute, AK	NME
Moline, IL	MLI	Nikolai, AK	NIB
Moncton, NB	YQM	Nikolski, AK	IKO
Monroe, LA	MLU	Noatak, AK	WTK
Mont Joli, QU	YYY	Nome, AK	OME
Monterey/Carmel, CA	MRY	Nondalton, AK	NNL
Montgomery, AL	MGM	Noorvik, AK	ORV
Montpelier/Barre, VT	MPV	Norfolk, NE	OFK
Montreal (Dorval), QU	YUL	Norfolk, VA	ORF
Montreal (Metro), QU	YMQ	Norman Wells, NT	YVQ
Montreal (Mirabel), QU	YMX	North Bay, OT	YYB
Montrose, CO	MTJ	North Bend, OR	OTH
Moosonee, OT	YMO	North Platte, NE	LBF
Morgantown, WV	MGW	North Spirit Lake, OT	YNO
Moser Bay, AK	KMY	Norway House, MB	YNE
Moses Lake, WA	MWH	Nuiqsut, AK	NUI
Mount Vernon, IL	MVN	Nulato, AK	NUL
Mountain Home, AR	WMH	Nunapitchuk, AK	NUP
Mountain Village, AK	MOU	Oak Harbor, WA	ODW
Muscle Shoals, AL	MSL	Oakland, CA	OAK
Muskegon, MI	MKG	Ofu Island, AS	OFU
Muskrat Dam, OT	MSA	Ogdensburg, NY	OGS
Myrtle Beach, SC	MYR	Oil City, PA	OIL
Nain, NF	YDP	Oklahoma City, OK	OKC
Naknek, AK	NNK	Old Crow, YT	YOC
Nanaimo, BC	YCD	Old Harbour, AK	OLH
Nanaimo (Harbour), BC	ZNA	Olga Bay, AK	KOY
Nanisivik, NT	YSR	Omaha, NE	OMA
Nantucket, MA	ACK	Ontario, CA	ONT
Napaiskak, AK	PKA	Opapamiska Lake, OT	YBS
Napakiak, AK	WNA	Orange County/Santa Ana, CA	SNA
Naples, FL	APF	Orlando (Herndon), FL	ORL
Nashville, TN	BNA	Orlando (Intl), FL	MCO
Natashquan, QU	YNA	Oshkosh, WI	OSH
Naukiti, AK	NKI	Ottawa (Intl), OT	YOW
Nelson Lagoon, AK	NLG	Ottawa (Rockcliffe), OT	YRO
Nemiscau, QU	YNS	Ottumwa, IA	OTM
New Bern, NC	EWN	Ouzinkie, AK	KOZ
New Haven, CT	HVN	Owensboro, KY	OWB
New London/Groton, CT	GON	Oxford House, MB	YOH
New Orleans, LA	MSY	Oxnard, CA	OXR
New Stuyahok, AK	KNW	Paducah, KY	PAH
New York (Dntwn H/P), NY	JRB	Page, AZ	PGA
New York (E34th St. H/P), NY	TSS	Pago Pago, AS	PPG
New York (E60th St H/P), NY	JRE	Pakuashipi, QU	YIF
New York (Kennedy), NY	JFK	Palm Springs, CA	PSP
New York (La Guardia), NY	LGA	Palmdale/Lancaster, CA	PMD
New York (Marine Air Term.), NY	QNY	Panama City, FL	PFN
New York (Metro), NY	NYC	Pangnirtung, NT	YXP
New York (W30th St. H/P), NY	JRA	Parkersburg, WV	PKB
Newark, NJ/New York, NY	EWR	Parks, AK	KPK
Newburgh (Stewart), NY	SWF	Pascagoula, MS	PGL
Newport News/Wmsbg., VA	PHF	Pasco, WA	PSC

Paulatuk, NT	YPC	Powell River, BC	YPW
Peace River, AB	YPE	Prescott, AZ	PRC
Peawanuk, OT	YPO	Presque Isle, ME	PQI
Pedro Bay, AK	PDB	Prince Albert, SA	YPA
Pelican, AK	PEC	Prince George, BC	YXS
Pellston, MI	PLN	Prince Rupert, BC	YPR
Pembroke, OT	YTA	Prince Rupert (Seal Cove), BC	ZSW
Pender Harbor, BC	YPT	Princeville, Kauai, HI	HPV
Pendleton, OR	PDT	Providence, RI	PVD
Pensacola, FL	PNS	Provincetown, MA	PVC
Penticton, BC	YYF	Prudhoe Bay/Deadhorse, AK	SCC
Peoria, IL	PIA	Pueblo, CO	PUB
Perryville, AK	KPV	Pukatawagan, MB	XPK
Petersburg, AK	PSG	Pullman, WA	PUW
Philadelphia (Intl), PA	PHL	Qualicum, BC	XQU
Philipsburg, PA	PSB	Quaqtaq, QU	YQC
Phoenix, AZ	PHX	Quebec, QU	YQB
Pickle Lake, OT	YPL	Quesnel, BC	YQZ
Pierre, SD	PIR	Quincy, IL	UIN
Pikangikum, OT	YPM	Quinhagak, AK	KWN
Pilot Point, AK	PIP	Rae Lakes, NT	YRA
Pilot Point (Ugashik), AK	UGB	Rainbow Lake, AB	YOP
Pilot Station, AK	PQS	Raleigh/Durham, NC	RDU
Pinehurst, NC	SOP	Rampart, AK	RMP
Pittsburgh, PA	PIT	Rankin Inlet, NT	YRT
Platinum, AK	PTU	Rapid City, SD	RAP
Plattsburgh, NY	PLB	Reading, PA	RDG
Pocatello, ID	PIH	Red Devil, AK	RDV
Point Baker, AK	KPB	Red Lake, OT	YRL
Point Hope, AK	PHO	Red Sucker Lake, MB	YRS
Point Lay, AK	PIZ	Redding, CA	RDD
Points North Landing, SA	YNL	Regina, SA	YQR
Ponca City, OK	PNC	Reno, NV	RNO
Ponce, PR	PSE	Repluse Bay, NT	YUT
Pond Inlet, NT	YIO	Resolute, NT	YRB
Port Alberni, BC	YPB	Rhinelander, WI	RHI
Port Alexander, AK	PTD	Richmond/Wmsbrg, VA	RIC
Port Alsworth, AK	PTA	Rigolet, NF	YRG
Port Angeles, WA	CLM	Rimouski, QU	YXK
Port Bailey, AK	KPY	Riverside, CA	RAL
Port Clarence, AK	KPC	Riverton, WY	RIW
Port Hardy, BC	YZT	Roanoke, VA	ROA
Port Heiden, AK	PTH	Roberval, QU	YRJ
Port Hope Simpson, NF	YHA	Roche Harbor, WA	RCE
Port Lions, AK	ORI	Rochester, MN	RST
Port Menier, QU	YPN	Rochester, NY	ROC
Port Moller, AK	PML	Rock Springs, WY	RKS
Port Protection, AK	PPV	Rockford, IL	RFD
Port Williams, AK	KPR	Rockland, ME	RKD
Portage Creek, AK	PCA	Rocky Mount/Wilson, NC	RWI
Portland, ME	PWM	Rosario, WA	RSJ
Portland, OR	PDX	Roswell, NM	ROW
Postville, NF	YSO	Round Lake, OT	ZRJ
Poughkeepsie, NY	POU	Rouyn, QU	YUY

Ruby, AK	RBY	Sheldon Point, AK	SXP
Ruidoso, NM	RUI	Sheridan, WY	SHR
Russian Mission, AK	RSH	Shishmaref, AK	SHH
Rutland, VT	RUT	Show Low, AZ	SOW
Sachigo Lake, OT	ZPB	Shreveport, LA	SHV
Sachs Harbour, NT	YSY	Shungnak, AK	SHG
Sacramento (Metro), CA	SMF	Sidney, NE	SNY
Saginaw/Bay City/Midland, MI	MBS	Silver City, NM	SVC
Salem, OR	SLE	Sioux City, IA	SUX
Salina, KS	SLN	Sioux Falls, SD	FSD
Salisbury, MD	SBY	Sioux Lookout, OT	YXL
Salluit, QU	YZG	Sitka, AK	SIT
Salmon Arm, BC	YSN	Skagway, AK	SGY
Salt Lake City, UT	SLC	Sleetmute, AK	SLQ
San Angelo, TX	SJT	Smith Cove, AK	SCJ
San Antonio, TX	SAT	Smithers, BC	YYD
San Diego (Brown Field), CA	SDM	South Bend, IN	SBN
San Diego (Lindberg), CA	SAN	South Indian Lake, MB	XSI
San Diego (Montgomery), CA	MYF	South Naknek, AK	WSN
San Francisco, CA	SFO	Spencer, IA	SPW
San Jose, CA	SJC	Spokane, WA	GEG
San Juan (Isla Grand), PR	SIG	Springfield, IL	SPI
San Juan (Munoz Marin), PR	SJU	Springfield, MA	BDL
San Luis Obispo, CA	SBP	Springfield, MO	SGF
Sand Point, AK	SDP	St. Anthony, NF	YAY
Sandspit, BC	YZP	St. Cloud, MN	STC
Sandy Lake, OT	ZSJ	St. Croix, VI	STX
Sankiluaq, NT	YSK	St. George Island, AK	STG
Santa Barbara, CA	SBA	St. George, UT	SGU
Santa Fe, NM	SAF	St. John, NB	YSJ
Santa Maria, CA	SMX	St. Johns, NF	YYT
Santa Rosa, CA	STS	St. Leonard, NB	YSL
Saranac Lake, NY	SLK	St. Louis (Lambert), MO	STL
Sarasota/Bradenton, FL	SRQ	St. Mary's, AK	KSM
Saskatoon, SA	YXE	St. Michael, AK	SMK
Sault Ste. Marie (Chippewa), MI	CIU	St. Paul Island, AK	SNP
Sault Ste. Marie (Metro), MI	SSM	St. Paul, MN	MSP
Sault Ste. Marie, OT	YAM	St. Petersburg/Clearwater, FL	PIE
Savannah, GA	SAV	St. Thomas, VI	STT
Savoonga, AK	SVA	State College, PA	SCE
Scammon Bay, AK	SCM	Staunton (Shenandoah	
Schefferville, QU	YKL	Valley), VA	SHD
Scottsbluff, NE	BFF	Ste. Therese Point, MB	YST
Scranton, PA	AVP	Steamboat Springs, CO	SBS
Seal Bay, AK	SYB	Stebbins, AK	WBB
Seattle/Tacoma, WA	SEA	Stephenville, NF	YJT
Sechelt, BC	YHS	Sterling/Rock Falls, IL	SQI
Selawik, AK	WLK	Stevens Point, WI	STE
Sept-Iles, QU	YZV	Stevens Village, AK	SVS
Seward, AK	SWD	Stockton, CA	SCK
Shageluk, AK	SHX	Stony Rapids, SA	YSF
Shaktoolik, AK	SKK	Stony River, AK	SRV
Shamattawa, MB	ZTM	Stuart Island, BC	YRR
Sheffield, AL	MSL	Sudbury, OT	YSB

Sugarland, TX	SGR	Umiujaq, QU	YUD
Summer Beaver, OT	SUR	Unalakleet, AK	UNK
Sun Valley, ID	SUN	Uranium City, SA	YBE
Superior, WI	SUW	Utica, New York	UCA
Swan River, MB	YSE	Utopia Creek, AK	UTO
Sydney, NS	YQY	Vail (Eagle County), CO	EGE
Syracuse, NY	SYR	Vail (Stolport), CO	WHR
Tacoma, WA	SEA	Val D'Or, QU	YVO
Takotna, AK	TCT	Valdez, AK	VDZ
Tallahassee, FL	TLH	Valdosta, GA	VLD
Taloyoak, NT	YYH	Vancouver (Intl), BC	YVR
Tampa/St. Pete., FL	TPA	Venetie, AK	VEE
Tanana, AK	TAL	Vernal, UT	VEL
Tasiujuaq, QU	YTQ	Vicksburg, MS	VKS
Tatalina, AK	TLJ	Victoria (Inner Harbour), BC	YWH
Tau, AS	TAV	Victoria (Intl), BC	YYJ
Teller, AK	TLA	Victoria, TX	VCT
Telluride, CO	TEX	Vieques, PR	VQS
Tenakee Springs, AK	TKE	Visalia, CA	VIS
Terrace, BC	YXT	Wabush, NF	YWK
Terre Haute, IN	HUF	Waco, TX	ACT
Tetlin, AK	TEH	Wainwright, AK	AIN
Texarkana, AR	TXK	Wales, AK	WAA
The Pas, MB	YQD	Walla Walla, WA	ALW
Thief River Falls, MN	TVF	Washington (Dulles), DC	IAD
Thompson, MB	YTH	Washington (Metro), DC	WAS
Thorne Bay, AK	KTB	Washington (National), DC	DCA
Thunder Bay, OT	YQT	Waskaganish, QU	YKQ
Timmins, OT	YTS	Waterfall, AK	KWF
Tin City, AK	TNC	Waterloo, IA	ALO
Tofino, BC	YAZ	Watertown, NY	ART
Togiak, AK	TOG	Watertown, SD	ATY
Tok, AK	TKJ	Watson Lake, YT	YQH
Toksook Bay, AK	OOK	Wausau, WI	AUW
Toledo, OH	TOL	Wausau (Wisc. Cntl.), WI	CWA
Topeka, KS	TOP	Wawa, OT	YXZ
Toronto (Metro), OT	YTO	Webequie, OT	YWP
Toronto (Pearson), OT	YYZ	Wemindji, QU	YNC
Toronto (Toronto Is.), OT	YTZ	Wenatchee, WA	EAT
Traverse City, MI	TVC	West Palm Beach, FL	PBI
Trenton, NJ	TTN	West Point, AK	KWP
Tri-City Airport, TN	TRI	Westerly, RI	WST
Tucson, AZ	TUS	Westsound, WA	WSX
Tuktoyaktuk, NT	YUB	Whale Cove, NT	YXN
Tulsa, OK	TUL	Whale Pass, AK	WWP
Tuluksak, AK	TLT	Wheeling, WV	HLG
Tuntutuliak, AK	WTL	White Mountain, AK	WMO
Tununak, AK	TNK	White Plains, NY	HPN
Tupelo, MS	TUP	Whitehorse, YT	YXY
Tuscaloosa, AL	TCL	Wichita Falls, TX	SPS
Twin Falls, ID	TWF	Wichita, KS	ICT
Twin Hills, AK	TWA	Wilkes-Barre/Scranton, PA	AVP
Tyler, TX	TYR	Williams Lake, BC	YWL
Uganik, AK	UGI	Williamsport, PA	IPT

Williston, ND	ISN	Wrangell, AK	WRG
Wilmington, DE	ILG	Wunnummin Lake, OT	WNN
Wilmington, NC	ILM	Yakima, WA	YKM
Windsor, OT	YQG	Yakutat, AK	YAK
Winnipeg, MB	YWG	Yankton, SD	YKN
Winona, MN	ONA	Yarmouth, NS	YQI
Winston-Salem (Smith-		Yellowknife, NT	YZF
Reynolds), NC	INT	York, PA	THV
Wolf Point, MT	OLF	Youngstown, OH	YNG
Wollaston Lake, SA	ZWL	Yuma, AZ	YUM
Worcester, MA	ORH	Zachar Bay, AK	KZB
Worland, WY	WRL		

International Airports

Aalborg, Denmark	AAL		Al Ghaydah, Yemen	AAY
Aalesund, Norway	AES		Al Hoceima, Morocco	AHU
Aarhus, Denmark	AAR		Al-Baha, Saudi Arabia	ABT
Abaiang, Kiribati	ABF		Al-Fujairah, UAE	FJR
Abemama, Kiribati	AEA		Albany, Australia	ALH
Aberdeen, Scotland	ABZ		Albuq, Yemen	BUK
Abha, Saudi Arabia	AHB		Albury, Australia	ABX
Abidjan, Cote D'lvoire	ABJ		Alderney, Channel Islands, UK	ACI
Abu Dhabi, UAE	AUH		Aleppo, Syria	ALP
Abu Simbel, Egypt	ABS		Alexander Bay, South Africa	ALJ
Abuja, Nigeria	ABV		Alexandria, Egypt	ALY
Acapulco, Mexico	ACA		Alexandroupolis, Greece	AXD
Accra, Ghana	ACC		Alghero, Italy	AHO
Adana, Turkey	ADA		Algiers, Algeria	ALG
Addis Ababa, Ethiopia	ADD		Alicante, Spain	ALC
Adelaide, Australia	ADL		Alice Springs, Australia	ASP
Aden, Yemen	ADE		Almaty, Kazakstan	ALA
Adler/Sochi, Russia	AER		Almeria, Spain	LEI
Adrar, Algeria	AZR		Alor Setar, Malaysia	AOR
Agadir, Morocco	AGA		Alotau, Papua New Guinea	GUR
Agartala, India	IXA		Alta Floresta, Brazil	AFL
Agatti Island, India	AGX		Alta, Norway	ALF
Agaun, Papua New Guinea	AUP		Altamira, Brazil	ATM
Agen, France	AGF		Altay, China	AAT
Agra, India	AGR		Altenrhein, Switzerland	ACH
Aguascalientes, Mexico	AGU		Amami O Shima, Japan	ASJ
Aguni, Japan	AGJ		Amazon Bay, Papua New Guinea	AZB
Ahmedabad, India	AMD		Ambanja, Madagascar	IVA
Ahuas, Honduras	AHS		Ambatomainty, Madagascar	AMY
Ahwaz, Iran	AWZ		Ambatondrazaka, Madagascar	WAM
Ailuk, Marshall Islands	AIM		Ambon, Indonesia	AMQ
Aioun El Atrouss, Mauritania	AEO		Amboseli, Kenya	ASV
Airok, Marshall Islands	AIC		Ambunti, Papua New Guinea	AUJ
Aitape, Papua New Guinea	ATP		Amman, Jordan	AMM
Aitutaki, Cook Islands	AIT		Amritsar, India	ATQ
Aiyura, Papua New Guinea	AYU		Amsterdam, Netherlands	AMS
Ajaccio, Corsica, France	AJA		Anaa, Fr. Polynesia	AAA
Akieni, Gabon	AKE		Anadyr, Russia	DYR
Akita, Japan	AXT		Anapa, Russia	AAQ
Akmola, Kazakstan	TSE		Ancona, Italy	AOI
Aksu, China	AKU		Andenes, Norway	ANX
Aktau. Kazakstan	SCO		Andizan, Uzbekistan	AZN
Aktyubinsk, Kazakstan	AKX		Andorra La Vella, Andorra	ALV
Akureyri, Iceland	AEY		Andros Island, Bahamas	ASD
Al Ain, UAE	AAN		Anegada, BVI	NGD
Al Arish, Egypt	AAC		Aneityum, Vanuatu	AUY

Angouleme, France	ANG	Astypalaia Is., Greece	JTY
Anguganak, Papua New Guinea	AKG	Asuncion, Paraguay	ASU
Anguilla, West Indies	AXA	Aswan, Egypt	ASW
Aniwa, Vanatu	AWD	Ataq, Yemen	AXK
Ankara (Esenboga), Turkey	ESB	Atar, Mauritania	ATR
Ankara, Turkey	ANK	Athens, Greece	ATH
Ankavandra, Madagascar	JVA	Atiu, Cook Islands	AIU
Annaba, Algeria	AAE	Attopeu, Laos	AOU
Annecy, France	NCY	Atuona, Fr. Polynesia	AUQ
Anqing, China	AQG	Atyrau, Kazakstan	GUW
Antalaha, Madagascar	ANM	Auckland, New Zealand	AKL
Antalya, Turkey	AYT	Augsburg, Germany	AGB
Antananarivo, Madagascar	TNR	Auki, Solomon Islands	AKS
Antigua, West Indies	ANU	Aumo, Papua New Guinea	AUV
Antofagasta, Chile	ANF	Aur, Marshall Islands	AUL
Antosohihy, Madagascar	WAI	Aurangabad, India	IXU
Antsalova, Madagascar	WAQ	Aurillac, France	AUR
Antsiranana, Madagascar	DIE	Aurukun Mission, Australia	AUU
Antwerp, Belgium	ANR	Avignon, France	AVN
Aomori, Japan	AOJ	Avu Avu, Solomon Islands	AVU
Apartado, Colombia	APO	Axum, Ethiopia	AXU
Apia (Fagali I.), Western Samoa	FGI	Ayacucho, Peru	AYP
Apia, Western Samoa	APW	Ayers Rock, Australia	AYQ
Aqaba, Jordan	AQJ	Bacolod, Philippines	BCD
Aracaju, Brazil	AJU	Badajoz, Spain	BJZ
Aracatuba, Brazil	ARU	Bagdogra, India	IXB
Arad, Romania	ARW	Bage, RS, Brazil	BGX
Aragip, Papua New Guinea	ARP	Baghdad, Iraq	BGW
Araguaina, Brazil	AUX	Baghdad (Saddam), Iraq	SDA
Aranuka, Kiribati	AAK	Baguio, Philippines	BAG
Arar, Saudi Arabia	RAE	Bahar Dar, Ethiopia	BJR
Arauca, Colombia	AUC	Bahawalpur, Pakistan	BHV
Arawa, Papua New Guinea	RAW	Bahia Blanca, Argentina	BHI
Arba Mintch, Ethiopia	AMH	Bahia Pinas, Panama	BFG
Ardabil, Iran	ADU	Bahia Solano, Colombia	BSC
Arequipa, Peru	AQP	Bahrain, Bahrain	BAH
Arica, Chile	ARI	Baia Mare, Romania	BAY
Arkalyk, Kazakstan	AYK	Baimuru, Papua New Guinea	VMU
Arkhangelsk, Russia	ARH	Bakalalan, Malaysia	BKM
Armenia, Colombia	AXM	Baku, Azerbaijan	BAK
Armidale, Australia	ARM	Balhash, Kazakstan	BXH
Arorae Is, Kiribati	AIS	Bali, Papua New Guinea	BAJ
Arthur's Town, Bahamas	ATC	Balikpapan, Indonesia	BPN
Aruba, Aruba	AUA	Balimo, Papua New Guinea	OPU
Arvidsjaur, Sweden	AJR	Ballina, Australia	BNK
Asahikawa, Japan	AKJ	Balmaceda, Chile	BBA
Asapa, Papua New Guinea	APP	Bamaga, Australia	ABM
Ascension, Bolivia	ASC	Bamako, Mali	BKO
Ashkhabad, Turkmenistan	ASB	Bambu, Papua New Guinea	BCP
Asmara, Eritrea	ASM	Ban Me Thuot, Vietnam	BMV
Asosa, Ethiopia	ASO	Banda Aceh, Indonesia	BTJ
Assab, Eritrea	ASA	Bandar Abbas, Iran	BND
Astrakhan, Russia	ASF	Bandar Lampung, Indonesia	TKG
Asturias, Spain	OVD	Bandar Lengeh, Iran	BDH

Bandar Seri Begawan, Brunei		Bejaia, Algeria	BJA
Darussalam	BWN	Belaga, Malaysia	BLG
Bandung, Indonesia	BDO	Belem, Brazil	BEL
Bangalore, India	BLR	Belep Is., New Caledonia	BMY
Bangkok, Thailand	BKK	Belfast (City), N. Ireland, UK	BHD
Bangui, Cen. African Republic	BGF	Belfast (Intl), N. Ireland, UK	BFS
Banjarmasin, Indonesia	BDJ	Belgrade, Yugoslavia	BEG
Banjul, Gambia	BJL	Belize City, Belize	BZE
Bannu, Pakistan	BNP	Belize City (Municipal), Belize	TZA
Baoshan, China	BSD	Bellavista, Peru	BLP
Baotou, China	BAV	Bellona Is., Solomon Islands	BNY
Baracoa, Cuba	BCA	Belo Horizonte (Confins), Brazil	CNF
Barakoma, Solomon Islands	VEV	Belo Horizonte (Metro), Brazil	BHZ
Barbuda, West Indies	BBQ	Belo Horizonte (Pampulha),	
Barcaldine, Australia	BCI	Brazil	PLU
Barcelona, Spain	BCN	Beloreck, Russia	BCX
Barcelona, Venezuela	BLA	Benbecula, Scotland, UK	BEB
Bardufoss, Norway	BDU	Benghazi, Libya	BEN
Bari, Italy	BRI	Bengkulu, Indonesia	BKS
Bario, Malaysia	BBN	Benguela, Angola	BUG
Barisal, Bangladesh	BZL	Benin City, Nigeria	BNI
Barnaul, Russia	BAX	Berau, Indonesia	BEJ
Barquisimeto, Venezuela	BRM	Berbera, Somalia	BBO
Barra Colorado, Costa Rica	BCL	Berdyansk, Ukraine	ERD
Barra Do Garcas, Brazil	BPG	Bergen, Norway	BGO
Barra, Scotland, UK	BRR	Bergerac, France	EGC
Barrancabermeja, Colombia	EJA	Berlevag, Norway	BVG
Barranquilla, Colombia	BAQ	Berlin (Metro), Germany	BER
Barreiras, Brazil	BRA	Berlin (Schoenefeld), Germany	SXF
Barrow Island, Australia	BWB	Berlin (Tegel), Germany	TXL
Basankusu, Zaire	BSU	Berlin (Tempelhof), Germany	THF
Basel, Switzerland	BSL	Bermuda, Atlantic Ocean	BDA
Basse-Terre, Guadeloupe	BBR	Bern, Switzerland	BRN
Bastia, Corsica, France	BIA	Beru, Kiribati	BEZ
Bata, Equatorial Guinea	BSG	Besalampy, Madagascar	BPY
Batam, Indonesia	BXM	Beziers, France	BZR
Bathurst, Australia	BHS	Bhadrapur, Nepal	BDP
Bathurst Is., Australia	BRT	Bhairawa, Nepal	BWA
Batman, Turkey	BAL	Bhamo, Myanmar	BMO
Batsfjord, Norway	BJF	Bharatpur, Nepal	BHR
Battambang, Cambodia	BBM	Bhavnagar, India	BHU
Batumi, Georgia	BUS	Bhopal, India	BHO
Bauru, Brazil	BAU	Bhubaneswar, India	BBI
Bayamo, Cuba	BYM	Bhuj, India	BHJ
Bayreuth, Germany	BYU	Biak, Indonesia	BIK
Bechar, Algeria	CBH	Bialla, Papua New Guinea	BAA
Bedourie, Australia	BEU	Biarritz, France	BIQ
Beef Island, BVI	EIS	Big Creek, Belize	BGK
Beica, Ethiopia	BEI	Bikini Atoll, Marshall Islands	BII
Beihai, China	BHY	Bilbao, Spain	BIO
Beijing (Capital), China	PEK	Billund, Denmark	BLL
Beijing, China	BJS	Bima, Indonesia	BMU
Beira, Mozambique	BEW	Bimini, Bahamas	BIM
Beirut, Lebanon	BEY	Biniguni, Papua New Guinea	XBN

Bintulu, Malaysia	BTU	Bremen, Germany	BRE
Biratnagar, Nepal	BIR	Brest, Belarus	BQT
Birdsville, Australia	BVI	Brest, France	BES
Birmingham, England, UK	BHX	Brewarrina, Australia	BWQ
Bisha, Saudi Arabia	BHH	Bridgetown, Barbados	BGI
Bishkek, Kyrgyzstan	FRU	Brindisi, Italy	BDS
Biskra, Algeria	BSK	Brisbane, Australia	BNE
Bissau, Guinea Bissau	OXB	Bristol, England, UK	BRS
Bitam, Gabon	BMM	Brive-La-Gaillarde, France	BVE
Blackall, Australia	BKQ	Brize Norton, England, UK	BZZ
Blackpool, England, UK	BLK	Brno, Czech Rep.	BRQ
Blackwater, Australia	BLT	Broken Hill, Australia	BHQ
Blagoveschensk, Russia	BQS	Bronnoysund, Norway	BNN
Blantyre, Malawi	BLZ	Broome, Australia	BME
Blenheim, New Zealand	BHE	Brus Laguna, Honduras	BHG
Bloemfontein, South Africa	BFN	Brussels, Belgium	BRU
Bluefields, Nicaragua	BEF	Bubaque, Guinea-Bissau	BQE
Blumenau, Brazil	BNU	Bucaramanga, Colombia	BGA
Boa Vista, Brazil	BVB	Bucharest (Baneasa), Romania	BBU
Boa Vista, Cape Verde Islands	BVC	Bucharest (Metro), Romania	BUH
Boang, Papua New Guinea	BOV	Bucharest (Otopeni), Romania	OTP
Bocas Del Toro, Panama	BOC	Budapest, Hungary	BUD
Bodo, Norway	BOO	Buenos Aires (Metro), Argentina	BUE
Bodrum, Turkey	BXN	Buenos Aires (Newbery),	
Boende, Zaire	BNB	Argentina	AEP
Bogota, Colombia	BOG	Buenos Aires (Pistarini),	
Bol, Croatia	BWK	Argentina	EZE
Bologna, Italy	BLQ	Buin, Papua New Guinea	UBI
Bom Jesus Da Lapa, Brazil	LAZ	Bujumbura, Burundi	BJM
Bombay, India	BOM	Buka, Papua New Guinea	BUA
Bonaire, Neth. Antilles	BON	Bukhara, Uzbekistan	BHK
Bonanza, Nicaragua	BZA	Bulawayo, Zimbabwe	BUQ
Bonn, Germany	BNJ	Bulolo, Papua New Guinea	BUL
Bora Bora, Fr. Polynesia	BOB	Bumba, Zaire	BMB
Borama, Somalia	BXX	Bundaberg, Australia	BDB
Bordeaux, France	BOD	Bunia, Zaire	BUX
Bordj Badji Mokhtar, Algeria	BMW	Bunsil, Papua New Guinea	BXZ
Borlange, Sweden	BLE	Burao, Somalia	BUO
Bornholm, Denmark	RNN	Bureta, Fiji	LEV
Borroloola, Australia	BOX	Buri Ram, Thailand	BFV
Bossaso, Somalia	BSA	Burketown, Australia	BUC
Bouake, Cote D'Ivoire	BYK	Burnie, Australia	BWT
Boulia, Australia	BQL	Bushehr, Iran	BUZ
Bourgas, Bulgaria	BOJ	Busuanga, Philippines	USU
Bourke, Australia	BRK	Butaritari, Kiribati	BBG
Bournemouth, England, UK	BOH	Butuan, Philippines	BXU
Bradford, England, UK	BRF	Cabinda, Angola	CAB
Braganca, Portugal	BGC	Cacoal, Brazil	OAL
Brampton Is., Australia	BMP	Caen, France	CFR
Brasilia, Brazil	BSB	Cagayan de Oro, Philippines	CGY
Bratislava, Slovakia	BTS	Cagliari, Italy	CAG
Bratsk, Russia	BTK	Cairns, Australia	CNS
Brava, Cape Verde Islands	BVR	Cairo, Egypt	CAI
Brazzaville, Congo	BZV	Cajamarca, Peru	CJA

Calabar, Nigeria	CBQ	Chachapoyas, Peru	CHH
Calama, Chile	CJC	Chah-Bahar, Iran	ZBR
Calcutta, India	CCU	Chandigarh, India	IXC
Cali, Colombia	CLO	Changchun, China	CGQ
Calicut, India	CCJ	Changde, China	CGD
Calvi, Corsica, France	CLY	Changsha, China	CSX
Camaguey, Cuba	CMW	Changuinola, Panama	CHX
Cambridge, England, UK	CBG	Changzhou, China	CZX
Campbeltown, Scotland, UK	CAL	Chania, Crete, Greece	CHQ
Campeche, Mexico	CPE	Chaoyang, China	CHG
Campina Grande, Brazil	CPV	Chapeco, Brazil	XAP
Campinas, Brazil	CPQ	Charleroi, Belgium	CRL
Campo Grande, Brazil	CGR	Charleville, Australia	CTL
Campos, Brazil	CAW	Chatham Island, New Zealand	CHT
Canaima, Venezuela	CAJ	Cheju, Korea	CJU
Canberra, Australia	CBR	Chelyabinsk, Russia	CEK
Cancun, Mexico	CUN	Chengdu, China	CTU
Cannes, France	CEQ	Chennai/Madras, India	MAA
Canouan Is., Windward Islands	CIW	Cherbourg, France	CER
Canton, China	CAN	Chetumal, Mexico	CTM
Canton Island, Kiribati	CIS	Chiang Mai, Thailand	CNX
Cap Haitien, Haiti	CAP	Chiang Rai, Thailand	CEI
Cap Skirring, Senegal	CSK	Chiayi, Taiwan	CYI
Cape Gloucester, Papua New		Chichen Itza, Mexico	CZA
Guinea	CGC	Chiclayo, Peru	CIX
Cape Orford, Papua New Guinea	CPI	Chigorodo, Colombia	IGO
Cape Town, South Africa	CPT	Chihuahua, Mexico	CUU
Cape Vogel, Papua New Guinea	CVL	Chimbote, Peru	CHM
Capurgana, Colombia	CPB	Chinju, Korea	HIN
Caracas, Venezuela	CCS	Chios, Greece	JKH
Carajas, Brazil	CKS	Chita, Russia	HTA
Caravelas, Brazil	CRQ	Chitral, Pakistan	CJL
Cardiff, Wales, UK	CWL	Chitre, Panama	CTD
Carnarvon, Australia	CVQ	Chittagong, Bangladesh	CGP
Carriacou Is., Grenada	CRU	Choiseul Bay, Solomon Islands	CHY
Carrillo, Costa Rica	RIK	Chongqing, China	CKG
Cartagena, Colombia	CTG	Chos Malal, Argentina	HOS
Casablanca (Anfa), Morocco	CAS	Christchurch, New Zealand	CHC
Casablanca (Mohamed V),		Christmas Is., Indian Ocean	XCH
Morocco	CMN	Christmas Is., Kiribati	CXI
Cascavel, Brazil	CAC	Chub Cay, Bahamas	CCZ
Casino, Australia	CSI	Cicia, Fiji	ICI
Castres, France	DCM	Ciego De Avila, Cuba	AVI
Catamarca, Argentina	CTC	Ciudad Bolivar, Venezuela	CBL
Catania, Italy	CTA	Ciudad Del Carmen, Mexico	CME
Caticlan, Philippines	MPH	Ciudad Del Este, Paraguay	AGT
Caucasia, Colombia	CAQ	Ciudad Juarez, Mexico	CJS
Caxias Do Sul, Brazil	CXJ	Ciudad Obregon, Mexico	CEN
Caye Caulker, Belize	CUK	Ciudad Victoria, Mexico	CVM
Cayenne, Fr. Guiana	CAY	Clermont-Ferrand, France	CFE
Cayman Brac Is., West Indies	CYB	Cleve, Australia	CVC
Cayo Coco, Cuba	CCC	Cloncurry, Australia	CNJ
Cebu, Philippines	CEB	Club Makokola, Malawi	CMK
Ceduna, Australia	CED	Cluj, Romania	CLJ

Cobar, Australia	CAZ	Cue, Australia	CUY
Cobija, Bolivia	CIJ	Cuenca, Ecuador	CUE
Cochabamba, Bolivia	CBB	Cuiaba, Brazil	CGB
Cochin, India	COK	Culiacan, Mexico	CUL
Cocos-Keeling Is., Indian Ocean	CCK	Culion, Philippines	CUJ
Coen, Australia	CUQ	Cumana, Venezuela	CUM
Coffs Harbour, Australia	CFS	Cunnamulla, Australia	CMA
Coimbatore, India	CJB	Curaçao, Neth. Antilles	CUR
Colima, Mexico	CLQ	Curitiba, Brazil	CWB
Cologne/Bonn, Germany	CGN	Cuzco, Peru	CUZ
Colombo, Sri Lanka	CMB	Da Nang, Viet Nam	DAD
Colon, Panama	ONX	Dakar, Senegal	DKR
Colonia, Uruguay	CYR	Dakhla, Morocco	VIL
Comodoro Rivadavia, Argentina	CRD	Dalaman, Turkey	DLM
Conakry, Guinea	CKY	Dalat, Viet Nam	DLI
Conceicao Do Araguaia, Brazil	CDJ	Dalbandin, Pakistan	DBA
Concepcion, Chile	CCP	Dali City, China	DLU
Concordia, Argentina	COC	Dalian, China	DLC
Condoto, Colombia	COG	Damascus, Syria	DAM
Connaught, Ireland	NOC	Dandong, China	DDG
Constanta, Romania	CND	Dangriga, Belize	DGA
Constantine, Algeria	CZL	Dar Es Salaam, Tanzania	DAR
Contadora, Panama	OTD	Daru, Papua New Guinea	DAU
Coober Pedy, Australia	CPD	Darwin, Australia	DRW
Cooktown, Australia	CTN	Davao, Philippines	DVO
Cooma, Australia	OOM	David, Panama	DAV
Coonabarabran, Australia	COJ	Dawe, Myanmar	TVY
Coonamble, Australia	CNB	Daxian, China	DAX
Cootamundra, Australia	CMD	Daydream Is., Australia	DDI
Copenhagen, Denmark	CPH	Dayong, China	DYG
Copenhagen-Roskilde, Denmark	RKE	Deadman's Cay, Bahamas	LGI
Copiapo, Chile	CPO	Deauville, France	DOL
Cordoba, Argentina	COR	Debra Marcos, Ethiopia	DBM
Cork, Ireland	ORK	Debra Tabor, Ethiopia	DBT
Corn Is., Nicaragua	RNI	Deirezzor, Syria	DEZ
Coro, Venezuela	CZE	Delhi, India	DEL
Corozal, Belize	CZH	Dembidollo, Ethiopia	DEM
Corrientes, Argentina	CNQ	Denham, Australia	DNM
Corumba, Brazil	CMG	Denizli, Turkey	DNZ
Corvo Island, Portugal	CVU	Denpasar, Indonesia	DPS
Cotabato, Philippines	CBO	Dera Ghazi Khan, Pakistan	DEA
Coto 47, Costa Rica	OTR	Dera Ismail Khan, Pakistan	DSK
Cotonou, Benin	COO	Derby, Australia	DRB
Cowarie, Australia	CWR	Derim, Papua New Guinea	DER
Cowra, Australia	CWT	Dessie, Ethiopia	DSE
Cox's Bazar, Bangladesh	CXB	Devonport, Australia	DPO
Cozumel, Mexico	CZM	Dhahran, Saudi Arabia	DHA
Craig Cove, Vanuatu	CCV	Dhaka, Bangladesh	DAC
Crisciuma, Brazil	CCM	Dhangarhi, Nepal	DHI
Crooked Is., Bahamas	CRI	Dibaa, Oman	BYB
Crotone, Italy	CRV	Dibrugarh, India	DIB
Cruzeiro Do Sul, Brazil	CZS	Dien-Bien-Phu, Viet Nam	DIN
Cucuta, Colombia	CUC	Dijon, France	DIJ
Cudal, Australia	CUG	Dili, Indonesia	DIL

Dillons Bay, Vanuatu	DLY	El Salvador, Chile	ESR
Dimapur, India	DMU	El Yopal, Colombia	EYP
Dinard, France	DNR	Elat, Israel	ETH
Dipolog, Philippines	DPL	Elazig, Turkey	EZS
Dire Dawa, Ethiopia	DIR	Elba Island, Italy	EBA
Diu, India	DIU	Elista, Russia	ESL
Divinopolis, Brazil	DIQ	Emae, Vanuatu	EAE
Diyarbakir, Turkey	DIY	Embessa, Papua New Guinea	EMS
Djanet, Algeria	DJG	Emirau, Papua New Guinea	EMI
Djerba, Tunisia	DJE	Emo, Papua New Guinea	EMO
Djibouti, Djibouti	JIB	Enewetok, Marshall Islands	ENT
Dnepropetrovsk, Ukraine	DNK	Enontekio, Finland	ENF
Dobo, Indonesia	DOB	Enschede, Netherlands	ENS
Dodoima, Papua New Guinea	DDM	Entebbe/Kampala, Uganda	EBB
Dolpa, Nepal	DOP	Enugu, Nigeria	ENU
Dominica (Cane), West Indies	DCF	Epinal, France	EPL
Dominica, West Indies	DOM	Ercan, Cyprus	ECN
Donegal, Ireland	CFN	Erechim, Brazil	ERM
Donetsk, Ukraine	DOK	Erfurt, Germany	ERF
Dongola, Sudan	DOG	Erigavo, Somalia	ERA
Doomadgee Mission, Australia	DMD	Errachidia, Morocco	ERH
Dortmund, Germany	DTM	Erzincan, Turkey	ERC
Douala, Cameroon	DLA	Erzurum, Turkey	ERZ
Dourados, Brazil	DOU	Esa'Ala, Papua New Guinea	ESA
Dresden, Germany	DRS	Esbjerg, Denmark	EBJ
Dubai, UAE	DXB	Esmeraldas, Ecuador	ESM
Dubbo, Australia	DBO	Esperance, Australia	EPR
Dublin, Ireland	DUB	Espirtu Santo, Vanuatu	SON
Dubrovnik, Croatia	DBV	Esquel, Argentina	EQS
Duesseldorf, Germany	DUS	Essen, Germany	ESS
Dumaguete, Philippines	DGT	Eua, Tonga	EUA
Dundee, Scotland, UK	DND	Evenes, Norway	EVE
Dundo, Angola	DUE	Exeter, England, UK	EXT
Dunedin, New Zealand	DUD	Fagernes, Norway	VDB
Dunhuang, China	DNH	Faisalabad, Pakistan	LYP
Dunk Is., Australia	DKI	Fakarava, Fr. Polynesia	FAV
Durango, Mexico	DGO	Fane, Papua New Guinea	FNE
Durban, South Africa	DUR	Farafangana, Madagascar	RVA
Dushanbe, Tajikistan	DYU	Faro, Portugal	FAO
Dzaoudzi, Mayotte	DZA	Faroe Islands, Denmark	FAE
East London, South Africa	ELS	Farsund, Norway	FAN
East Midlands, England, UK	EMA	Fera Is., Solomon Islands	FRE
Easter Island, Chile	IPC	Fergana, Uzbekistan	FEG
Ebon, Marshall Islands	EBO	Fernando de Noronha, Brazil	FEN
Edinburgh, Scotland, UK	EDI	Fez, Morocco	FEZ
Edward River, Australia	EDR	Fianarantsoa, Madagascar	WFI
Egilsstadir, Iceland	EGS	Figari, France	FSC
Eia, Papua New Guinea	EIA	Finschhafen, Papua New Guinea	FIN
Eindhoven, Netherlands	EIN	Flateyri, Iceland	FLI
Ekaterinburg, Russia	SVX	Flinders Is., Australia	FLS
Ekibastuz, Kazakstan	EKB	Florence, Italy	FLR
El Golea, Algeria	ELG	Florencia, Colombia	FLA
El Oued, Algeria	ELU	Flores, Guatemala	FRS
El Real, Panama	ELE	Florianopolis, Brazil	FLN

Floro, Norway	FRO	George Town, Bahamas	GGT
Forbes, Australia	FRB	Georgetown, Guyana	GEO
Forde, Norway	FDE	Geraldton, Australia	GET
Formosa, Argentina	FMA	Gewoya, Papua New Guinea	GEW
Fort Dauphin, Madagascar	FTU	Ghardaia, Algeria	GHA
Fort De France, Martinique	FDF	Ghimbi, Ethiopia	GHD
Fortaleza, Brazil	FOR	Gibraltar, Gibraltar	GIB
Franca, Brazil	FRC	Gilgit, Pakistan	GIL
Franceville, Gabon	MVB	Gisborne, New Zealand	GIS
Francisco Beltrao, Brazil	FBE	Gizan, Saudi Arabia	GIZ
Francistown, Botswana	FRW	Gizo, Solomon Islands	GZO
Frankfurt, Germany	FRA	Gladstone, Australia	GLT
Freeport, Bahamas	FPO	Glasgow (Prestwick), Scotland,	
Freetown, Sierra Leone	FNA	UK	PIK
Freida River, Papua New Guinea	FAQ	Glasgow, Scotland, UK	GLA
Friedrichshafen, Germany	FDH	Glen Innes, Australia	GLI
Fuerteventura,Spain	FUE	Goa, India	GOI
Fukue, Japan	FUJ	Goba, Ethiopia	GOB
Fukuoka, Japan	FUK	Gode/Iddidole, Ethiopia	GDE
Fukushima, Japan	FKS	Goiania, Brazil	GYN
Funafuti Atol, Tuvalu	FUN	Gold Coast, Australia	OOL
Funchal, Portugal	FNC	Golfito, Costa Rica	GLF
Futuna Island, Vanuatu	FTA	Golmud, China	GOQ
Futuna, Wallis & Futuna Is.	FUT	Goma, Zaire	GOM
Fuzhou, China	FOC	Gonalia, Papua New Guinea	GOE
Gaborone, Botswana	GBE	Gondar, Ethiopia	GDQ
Gallivare, Sweden	GEV	Gora, Papua New Guinea	GOC
Galway, Ireland	GWY	Gore, Ethiopia	GOR
Gamba, Gabon	GAX	Goroka, Papua New Guinea	GKA
Gambela, Ethiopia	GMB	Gorontalo, Indonesia	GTO
Gambier Is., Fr. Polynesia	GMR	Gothenburg, Sweden	GOT
Gan Island, Maldives	GAN	Goundam, Mali	GUD
Ganzhou, China	KOW	Gove, Australia	GOV
Gao, Mali	GAQ	Governador Valadares, Brazil	GVR
Garachine, Panama	GHE	Governors Harbour, Bahamas	GHB
Garaina, Papua New Guinea	GAR	Gozo, Malta	GZM
Garasa, Papua New Guinea	GRL	Graciosa Is., Portugal	GRW
Garden Point, Australia	GPN	Grafton, Australia	GFN
Gasmata Is., Papua New Guinea	GMI	Gran Canaria, Spain	LPA
Gassim, Saudi Arabia	ELQ	Granada, Spain	GRX
Gaua, Vanuatu	ZGU	Grand Bahama Island, Bahamas	GBI
Gauhati, India	GAU	Grand Cayman, Cayman Islands	GCM
Gavle, Sweden	GVX	Grand Turk Is., Turks & Caicos	GDT
Gaziantep, Turkey	GZT	Graz, Austria	GRZ
Gbadolite, Zaire	BDT	Great Harbour Cay, Bahamas	GHC
Gdansk, Poland	GDN	Great Keppel Is., Australia	GKL
Geilo, Norway	DLD	Green River, Papua New Guinea	GVI
Gelendzik, Russia	GDZ	Grenada, Windward Islands	GND
Gemena, Zaire	GMA	Grenoble, France	GNB
General Roca, Argentina	GNR	Griffith, Australia	GFF
General Santos, Philippines	GES	Groennedal, Greenland	JGR
Geneva, Switzerland	GVA	Groningen, Netherlands	GRQ
Genoa, Italy	GOA	Groote Is., Australia	GTE
George, South Africa	GRJ	Guadalajara, Mexico	GDL

Guadeloupe, Leeward Islands	BBR	Haugesund, Norway	HAU
Guanaja, Honduras	GJA	Havana, Cuba	HAV
Guanambi, Brazil	GNM	Hay, Australia	HXX
Guangzhou, China	CAN	Hayfield, Papua New Guinea	HYF
Guantanamo, Cuba	GAO	Hayman Is., Australia	HIS
Guapi, Colombia	GPI	Hefei, China	HFE
Guarapari, Brazil	GUZ	Heho, Myanmar	HEH
Guasopa, Papua New Guinea	GAZ	Heidelberg, Germany	HDB
Guatemala City, Guatemala	GUA	Heihe, China	HEK
Guayaquil, Ecuador	GYE	Helgoland, Germany	HGL
Guayaramerin, Bolivia	GYA	Helsingborg, Sweden	AGH
Guaymas, Mexico	GYM	Helsinki, Finland	HEL
Guernsey, Channel Islands, UK	GCI	Hemavan, Sweden	HMV
Guerrero Negro, Mexico	GUB	Heraklion, Greece	HER
Guilin, China	KWL	Heringsdorf, Germany	HDF
Guiyang, China	KWE	Hermosillo, Mexico	HMO
Gunnedah, Australia	GUH	Hervey Bay, Australia	HVB
Gurayat, Saudi Arabia	URY	Hiroshima, Japan	HIJ
Gurupi, Brazil	GRP	Ho Chi Minh, Viet Nam	SGN
Gwadar, Pakistan	GWD	Hobart, Australia	HBA
Gwalior, India	GWL	Hodeidah, Yemen	HOD
Gyandzha, Azerbaijan	KVD	Hoedspruit, South Africa	HDS
Gyourmi, Armenia	LWN	Hof, Germany	HOQ
Ha'apai, Tonga	HPA	Hofuf, Saudi Arabia	HOF
Hachijo Jima, Japan	HAC	Hohhot, China	HET
Hafr Albatin, Saudi Arabia	HBT	Hokitika, New Zealand	HKK
Hagfors, Sweden	HFS	Holguin, Cuba	HOG
Hahn, Germany	HHN	Hong Kong, Hong Kong	HKG
Haifa, Israel	HFA	Honiara, Solomon Islands	HIR
Haikou, China	HAK	Honningsvag, Norway	HVG
Hail, Saudi Arabia	HAS	Hooker Creek, Australia	HOK
Hailar, China	HLD	Hornafjordur, Iceland	HFN
Haiphong, Viet Nam	HPH	Horta, Portugal	HOR
Hakodate, Japan	HKD	Hoskins, Papua New Guinea	HKN
Halmstad, Sweden	HAD	Hotan, China	HTN
Hamburg, Germany	HAM	Houeisay, Laos	HOE
Hamilton, Bermuda	BDA	Hua Hin, Thailand	HHQ
Hamilton Is., Australia	HTI	Huahine Is., Fr. Polynesia	HUH
Hamilton, New Zealand	HLZ	Hualien, Taiwan	HUN
Hammerfest, Norway	HFT	Huambo, Angola	NOV
Hangzhou, China	HGH	Huanghua, China	HHA
Hanimaadhoo, Maldives	HAQ	Huangyan, China	HYN
Hanoi, Viet Nam	HAN	Huanuco, Peru	HUU
Hanover, Germany	HAJ	Huatulco, Mexico	HUX
Hanzhong, China	HZG	Hudiksvall, Sweden	HUV
Hao Is., Fr. Polynesia	HOI	Hue, Viet Nam	HUI
Harare, Zimbabwe	HRE	Hughenden, Australia	HGD
Harbin, China	HRB	Hultsfred, Sweden	HLF
Harbour Island, Bahamas	HBI	Humberside, England, UK	HUY
Hargeisa, Somalia	HGA	Humera, Ethiopia	HUE
Hassi Messaoud, Algeria	HME	Hurghada, Egypt	HRG
Hasvik, Norway	HAA	Husavik, Iceland	HZK
Hat Yai, Thailand	HDY	Hwange Nat'l Park, Zimbabwe	HWN
Hateruma, Japan	HTR	Hyderabad, India	HYD

Hyderabad, Pakistan	HDD	Istanbul, Turkey	IST
Iasi, Romania	IAS	Itabuna, Brazil	ITN
Ibague, Colombia	IBE	Itaituba, Brazil	ITB
Ibiza, Spain	IBZ	Itokama, Papua New Guinea	ITK
Iboki, Papua New Guinea	IBI	Ivalo, Finland	IVL
Idre, Sweden	IDB	Ivano-Frankovsk, Ukraine	IFO
Iguassu Falls, Brazil	IGU	Iwami, Japan	IWJ
Iguazu, Argentina	IGR	Ixtapa/Zihautenejo, Mexico	ZIH
Ihu, Papua New Guinea	IHU	Izmir (Adnan Mend), Turkey	ADB
Ikaria Island, Greece	JIK	Izmir (Cigli), Turkey	IGL
Iki, Japan	IKI	Izmir (Metro), Turkey	IZM
Ile Des Pins, New Caledonia	ILP	Izumo, Japan	IZO
Ilheus, Brazil	IOS	Jabot, Marshall Islands	JAT
Illizi, Algeria	VVZ	Jacobabad, Pakistan	JAG
Ilo, Peru	ILQ	Jacquinot Bay, Papua New	
Iloilo, Philippines	ILO	Guinea	JAQ
Ilulissat, Greenland	JAV	Jagdalpur, India	JGB
Imperatriz, Brazil	IMP	Jaipur, India	JAI
Impfondol, Congo	ION	Jakarta (Halim), Indonesia	HLP
Imphal, India	IMF	Jakarta (Metro), Indonesia	JKT
In Amenas, Algeria	IAM	Jakarta (Soekarno), Indonesia	CGK
In Salah, Algeria	INZ	Jaluit Is., Marshall Islands	UIT
Inagua, Bahamas	IGA	Jambi, Indonesia	DJB
Indagen, Papua New Guinea	IDN	Jammu, India	IXJ
Indaselassie, Ethiopia	SHC	Jamnagar, India	JGA
Indore, India	IDR	Janakpur, Nepal	JKR
Ine, Marshall Islands	IMI	Jaque, Panama	JQE
Inisheer, Ireland	INQ	Jayapura, Indonesia	DJJ
Inishmaan, Ireland	IIA	Jeddah, Saudi Arabia	JED
Inishmore, Ireland	IOR	Jeh, Marshall Islands	JEJ
Innsbruck, Austria	INN	Jerez de la Frontera, Spain	XRY
Invercargill, New Zealand	IVC	Jersey, Channel Islands, UK	JER
Inverell, Australia	IVR	Jerusalem, Israel	JRS
Inverness, Scotland, UK	INV	Jessore, Bangladesh	JSR
Ioannina, Greece	IOA	Ji-Parana, Brazil	JPR
Iokea, Papua New Guinea	IOK	Jiamusi, China	JMU
Ioma, Papua New Guinea	IOP	Jijel, Algeria	GJL
Ipatinga, Brazil	IPN	Jilin, China	JIL
Ipiales, Colombia	IPI	Jimma, Ethiopia	JIM
Ipoh, Malaysia	IPH	Jinan, China	TNA
Ipota, Vanuatu	IPA	Jingdezhen, China	JDZ
Iquique, Chile	IQQ	Jinghong, China	JHG
Iquitos, Peru	IQT	Jinka, Ethiopa	BCO
Irkutsk, Russia	IKT	Jinzhou, China	JNZ
Isafjordur, Iceland	IFJ	Jiujiang, China	JIU
Isfahan, Iran	IFN	Jiwani, Pakistan	JIW
Ishigaki, Japan	ISG	Joacaba, Brazil	JCB
Isiro, Zaire	IRP	Joao Pessoa, Brazil	JPA
Islamabad, Pakistan	ISB	Jodhpur, India	JDH
Islay, Scotland, UK	ILY	Joensuu, Finland	JOE
Isle of Man, UK	IOM	Johannesburg, South Africa	JNB
Isle of Skye, Scotland, UK	SKL	Johnston Island, Pacific Ocean	JON
Isles of Scilly (St. Marys), UK	ISC	Johor Bahru, Malaysia	JHB
Isles of Scilly (Tresco), UK	TSO	Joinville, Brazil	JOI

Jomsom, Nepal	JMO	Karpathos, Greece	AOK
Jonkoping, Sweden	JKG	Karratha, Australia	KTA
Jorhat, India	JRH	Kars, Turkey	KSY
Jos, Nigeria	JOS	Karshi, Uzbekistan	KSQ
Jouf, Saudi Arabia	AJF	Karumba, Australia	KRB
Juanjui, Peru	JJI	Karup, Denmark	KRP
Juazeiro Do Norte, Brazil	JDO	Kasane, Botswana	BBK
Juiz De Fora, Brazil	JDF	Kashi, China	KHG
Jujuy, Argentina	JUJ	Kasos Island, Greece	KSJ
Julia Creek, Australia	JCK	Kastelorizo, Greece	KZS
Juliaca, Peru	JUL	Kastoria, Greece	KSO
Jumla, Nepal	JUM	Katherine, Australia	KTR
Juzhou, China	JUZ	Kathmandu, Nepal	KTM
Jyvaskyla, Finland	JYV	Katowice, Poland	KTW
Kaadedhdhoo, Maldives	KDM	Kaukura Atoll, Fr. Polynesia	KKR
Kaben, Marshall Islands	KBT	Kaunas, Lithuania	KUN
Kabul, Afghanistan	KBL	Kavala, Greece	KVA
Kabwum, Papua New Guinea	KBM	Kavieng, Papua New Guinea	KVG
Kadhdhoo, Maldives	KDO	Kawito, Papua New Guinea	KWO
Kaduna, Nigeria	KAD	Kawthaung, Myanmar	KAW
Kagau, Solomon Islands	KGE	Kayes, Mali	KYS
Kagoshima, Japan	KOJ	Kayseri, Turkey	ASR
Kahramanmaras, Turkey	KCM	Kazan, Russia	KZN
Kaintiba, Papua New Guinea	KZF	Keetmanshoop, Namibia	KMP
Kaiserslauter, Germany	KLT	Kefallinia, Greece	EFL
Kaitaia, New Zealand	KAT	Kemerovo, Russia	KEJ
Kajaani, Finland	KAJ	Kemi/Tornio, Finland	KEM
Kalamata, Greece	KLX	Kempsey, Australia	KPS
Kalbarri, Australia	KAX	Kendari, Indonesia	KDI
Kalemie, Zaire	FMI	Kengtung, Myanmar	KET
Kalemyo, Myanmar	KMV	Kenieba, Mali	KNZ
Kalgoorlie, Australia	KGI	Kerama, Japan	KJP
Kalibo, Philippines	KLO	Kerema, Papua New Guinea	KMA
Kaliningrad, Russia	KGD	Kerikeri, New Zealand	KKE
Kalkurung, Australia	KFG	Kerkyra, Greece	CFU
Kalmar, Sweden	KLR	Kerman, Iran	KER
Kameshli, Syria	KAC	Kermanshah, Iran	KSH
Kamina, Papua New Guinea	KMF	Kerry County, Ireland	KIR
Kanabea, Papua New Guinea	KEX	Kerteh, Malaysia	KTE
Kananga, Zaire	KGA	Keshad, India	IXK
Kandavu, Fiji	KDV	Khabarovsk, Russia	KHV
Kandla, India	IXY	Khajuraho, India	HJR
Kandrian, Papua New Guinea	KDR	Khamti, Myanmar	KHM
Kangerlussuaq, Greenland	SFJ	Kharkov, Ukraine	HRK
Kangnung, Korea	KAG	Khartoum, Sudan	KRT
Kano, Nigeria	KAN	Khasab, Oman	KHS
Kaohsiung, Taiwan	KHH	Khon Kaen, Thailand	KKC
Kapit, Malaysia	KPI	Khuzdar, Pakistan	KDD
Karachi, Pakistan	KHI	Kiel, Germany	KEL
Karaganda, Kazakstan	KGF	Kiev (Borispol), Ukraine	KBP
Karamay, China	KRY	Kiev (Metro), Ukraine	IEV
Karawari, Papua New Guinea	KRJ	Kiffa, Mauritania	KFA
Kariba, Zimbabwe	KAB	Kigali, Rwanda	KGL
Karlstad, Sweden	KSD	Kigoma, Tanzania	TKQ

Kikaiga Shima, Japan	KKX	Kowanyama, Australia	KWM
Kikori, Papua New Guinea	KRI	Kozani, Greece	KZI
Kili Is., Marshall Islands	KIO	Krakow, Poland	KRK
Kilimanjaro, Tanzania	JRO	Kramfors, Sweden	KRF
Kimberley, South Africa	KIM	Krasnodar, Russia	KRR
Kindu, Zaire	KND	Krasnowodsk, Turkmenistan	KRW
King Is., Australia	KNS	Krasnoyarsk, Russia	KJA
Kingscote, Australia	KGC	Kristiansand, Norway	KRS
Kingston, Jamaica	KIN	Kristianstad, Sweden	KID
Kingston (Tinson), Jamaica	KTP	Kristiansund, Norway	KSU
Kinmen, Taiwan	KNH	Kuala Lumpur, Malaysia	KUL
Kinshasa, Zaire	FIH	Kuala Terengganu, Malaysia	TGG
Kira, Papua New Guinea	KIQ	Kuantan, Malaysia	KUA
Kirakira, Solomon Islands	IRA	Kuching, Malaysia	KCH
Kirkenes, Norway	KKN	Kudat, Malaysia	KUD
Kirkwall, Scotland, UK	KOI	Kuito, Angola	SVP
Kirovograd, Ukraine	KGO	Kulu, India	KUU
Kiruna, Sweden	KRN	Kulusuk Is., Greenland	KUS
Kisangani, Zaire	FKI	Kumamoto, Japan	KMJ
Kishinev, Moldova	KIV	Kumejima, Japan	UEO
Kisumu, Kenya	KIS	Kundiawa, Papua New Guinea	CMU
Kita Kyushu, Japan	KKJ	Kunming, China	KMG
Kitadaito, Japan	KTD	Kunsan, Korea	KUV
Kitava, Papua New Guinea	KVE	Kununurra, Australia	KNX
Kithira, Greece	KIT	Kuopio, Finland	KUO
Kittila, Finland	KTT	Kupang, Indonesia	KOE
Kiunga, Papua New Guinea	UNG	Kuqa, China	KCA
Kiwayu, Kenya	KWY	Kuri, Papua New Guinea	KUQ
Klagenfurt, Austria	KLU	Kuria, Kiribati	KUC
Kleinzee, South Africa	KLZ	Kushiro, Japan	KUH
Knock, Ireland	NOC	Kuusamo, Finland	KAO
Kochi, Japan	KCZ	Kuwait, Kuwait	KWI
Koh Kong, Cambodia	KKZ	Kwajalein, Marshall Islands	KWA
Koh Samui, Thailand	USM	Kwangju, Korea	KWJ
Kokkola/Pietarsaari, Finland	KOK	Kyaukpyu, Myanmar	KYP
Kokoda, Papua New Guinea	KKD	Kyoto, Japan	KIX
Kokshetau, Kazakstan	KOV	Kyzl Orda, Kazakstan	KZO
Komatsu, Japan	KMQ	La Ceiba, Honduras	LCE
Kone, New Caledonia	KNQ	La Coruna, Spain	LCG
Konge, Papua New Guinea	KGB	La Desirade, Guadeloupe	DSD
Konya, Turkey	KYA	La Palma, Panama	PLP
Korhogo, Cote D'Ivoire	HGO	La Paz, Bolivia	LPB
Korla, China	KRL	La Paz, Mexico	LAP
Koro, Fiji	KXF	La Rioja, Argentina	IRJ
Koror, Palau	ROR	La Rochelle, France	LRH
Kos, Greece	KGS	La Serena, Chile	LSC
Kosice, Slovakia	KSC	Laayoune, Morocco	EUN
Kosrae, Micronesia	KSA	Labasa, Fiji	LBS
Kostanay, Kazakstan	KSN	Lablab, Papua New Guinea	LAB
Koszalin, Poland	OSZ	Labuan, Malaysia	LBU
Kota Bharu, Malaysia	KBR	Lae Is., Marshall Islands	LML
Kota Kinabalu, Malaysia	BKI	Lae, Papua New Guinea	LAE
Koulamoutou, Gabon	KOU	Lages, Brazil	LAJ
Koumac, New Caledonia	KOC	Lago Agrio, Ecuador	LGQ

Lagos, NIgeria	LOS	Lianyungang, China	LYG
Lahad Datu, Malaysia	LDU	Liberia, Costa Rica	LIR
Lahore, Pakistan	LHE	Libreville, Gabon	LBV
Lake Evella, Australia	LEL	Lichinga, Mozambique	VXC
Lakeba, Fiji	LKB	Lidkoping, Sweden	LDK
Lakselv, Norway	LKL	Lifou, New Caledonia	LIF
Lalibela, Ethiopia	LLI	Lightning Ridge, Australia	LHG
Lamap, Vanuatu	LPM	Lihir Island, Papua New Guinea	LNG
Lambarene, Gabon	LBQ	Lijiang City, China	LJG
Lamen Bay, Vanuatu	LNB	Likiep Is., Marshall Islands	LIK
Lamezia/Terme, Italy	SUF	Lilabari, India	IXI
Lamidanda, Nepal	LDN	Lille, France	LIL
Lampang, Thailand	LPT	Lilongwe, Malawi	LLW
Lampedusa, Italy	LMP	Lima, Peru	LIM
Lamu, Kenya	LAU	Limbang, Malaysia	LMN
Lands End, England, UK	LEQ	Limoges, France	LIG
Langkawi, Malaysia	LGK	Lindeman Is., Australia	LDC
Lannion, France	LAI	Lindi, Tanzania	LDI
Lanzarote, Spain	ACE	Linkoping, Sweden	LPI
Lanzhou, China	LHW	Linz, Austria	LNZ
Laoag, Philippines	LAO	Lisala, Zaire	LIQ
Lappeenranta, Finland	LPP	Lisbon, Portugal	LIS
Larnaca, Cyprus	LCA	Lismore, Australia	LSY
Las Palmas, Canary Islands	LPA	Liuzhou, China	LZH
Las Piedras, Venezuela	LSP	Liverpool, England, UK	LPL
Las Tunas, Cuba	VTU	Livingstone, Zambia	LVI
Lashio, Myanmar	LSH	Livramento, Brazil	LVB
Lastourville, Gabon	LTL	Lizard Is., Australia	LZR
Latakia, Syria	LTK	Ljubljana, Slovenia	LJU
Laucala Island, Fiji	LUC	Lockhart River, Australia	IRG
Launceston, Australia	LST	Lodja, Zaire	LJA
Laverton, Australia	LVO	Loen, Marshall Islands	LOF
Lawas, Malaysia	LWY	Loikaw, Myanmar	LIW
Lazaro Cardenas, Mexico	LZC	Lome, Togo	LFW
Le Havre, France	LEH	Loncopue, Argentina	LCP
Le Puy, France	LPY	London (City), England, UK	LCY
Le Touquet, France	LTQ	London (Gatwick), England, UK	LGW
Learmonth, Australia	LEA	London (Heathrow), England,	
Leeds, England, UK	LBA	UK	LHR
Legaspi, Philippines	LGP	London (Luton), England, UK	LTN
Leguizamo, Colombia	LGZ	London (Metro), England, UK	LON
Leh, India	IXL	London (Stansted), England, UK	STN
Leigh Creek, Australia	LGH	Londonderry, N. Ireland, UK	LDY
Leinster, Australia	LER	Londrina, Brazil	LDB
Leipzig, Germany	LEJ	Long Banga, Malaysia	LBP
Leknes, Norway	LKN	Long Is., Australia	HAP
Lemnos, Greece	LXS	Long Island, Bahamas	LGI
Leon, Mexico	LEN	Long Lellang, Malaysia	LGL
Leon/Guanajuato, Mexico	BJX	Long Pasia, Malaysia	GSA
Leonora, Australia	LNO	Long Semado, Malaysia	LSM
Leros, Greece	LRS	Long Seridan, Malaysia	ODN
Lese, Papua New Guinea	LNG	Long Sukang, Malaysia	LSU
Leticia, Colombia	LET	Longana, Vanuatu	LOD
Lhasa, China	LXA	Longreach, Australia	LRE

Longyearbyen, Norway	LYR	Maintirano, Madagascar	MXT
Lonorore, Vanuatu	LNE	Maio, Cape Verde Islands	MMO
Lord Howe Is., Australia	LDH	Maitland, Australia	MTL
Loreto, Mexico	LTO	Majkin, Marshall Islands	MJE
Lorient, France	LRT	Majunga, Madagascar	MJN
Los Angeles, Chile	LSQ	Majuro, Marshall Islands	MAJ
Los Cabos, Mexico	SJD	Makale, Ethiopia	MQX
Los Mochis, Mexico	LMM	Makemo, Fr. Polynesia	MKP
Losuia, Papua New Guinea	LSA	Makhachkala, Russia	MCX
Loubomo, Congo	DIS	Makin Is., Kiribati	MTK
Lourdes/Tarbes, France	LDE	Makokou, Gabon	MKU
Luanda, Angola	LAD	Makung, Taiwan	MZG
Luang Namtha, Laos	LXG	Makurdi, Nigeria	MDI
Luang Prabang, Laos	LPQ	Malabo, Equatorial Guinea	SSG
Lubang, Philippines	LBX	Malacca, Malaysia	MKZ
Lubango, Angola	SDD	Malaga, Spain	AGP
Lubumbashi, Zaire	FBM	Malalaua, Papua New Guinea	MLQ
Lucknow, India	LKO	Malang, Indonesia	MLG
Luderitz, Namibia	LUD	Malange, Angola	MEG
Luena, Angola	LUO	Malargue, Argentina	LGS
Lugano, Switzerland	LUG	Malatya, Turkey	MLX
Lukla, Nepal	LUA	Male, Maldives	MLE
Lulea, Sweden	LLA	Malekolon, Papua New Guinea	MKN
Lumi, Papua New Guinea	LMI	Malindi, Kenya	MYD
Luoyang, China	LYA	Malmo (City Hvc), Sweden	HMA
Lusaka, Zambia	LUN	Malmo (Metro), Sweden	MMA
Luxembourg, Luxembourg	LUX	Malmo (Sturup), Sweden	MMX
Luxi, China	LUM	Maloelap Is., Marshall Islands	MAV
Luxor, Egypt	LXR	Malololailai, Fiji	PTF
Luzhou, China	LZO	Maloy Harbor, Norway	QFQ
Lvov, Ukraine	LWO	Malta, Malta	MLA
Lycksele, Sweden	LYC	Man, Cote D'Ivoire	MJC
Lyon, France	LYS	Mana, Fiji	MNF
M'banza Congo, Angola	SSY	Manado, Indonesia	MDC
Maastricht, Netherlands	MST	Managua, Nicaragua	MGA
MacArthur River, Australia	MCV	Manakara, Madagascar	WVK
Macau, Macau	MFM	Mananara, Madagascar	WMR
Maceio, Brazil	MCZ	Manang, Nepal	NGX
Mackay, Australia	MKY	Mananjary, Madagascar	MNJ
Madang, Papua New Guinea	MAG	Manaus, Brazil	MAO
Madinah, Saudi Arabia	MED	Manchester, England, UK	MAN
Madras, India	MAA	Mandalay, Myanmar	MDL
Madrid, Spain	MAD	Mandritsara, Madagascar	WMA
Madurai, India	IXM	Mangaia, Cook Islands	MGS
Mae Hong Son, Thailand	HGN	Mangalore, India	IXE
Mae Sot, Thailand	MAQ	Mangrove Cay, Bahamas	MAY
Maewo, Vanuatu	MWF	Manguna, Papua New Guinea	MFO
Magadan, Russia	GDX	Manihi, Fr. Polynesia	XMH
Magdalena, Bolivia	MGD	Manihiki Is., Cook Islands	MHX
Magnitogorsk, Russia	MQF	Manila, Philippines	MNL
Mahe Is., Seychelles	SEZ	Maningrida, Australia	MNG
Mahendranagar, Nepal	XMG	Manizales, Colombia	MZL
Maiana, Kiribati	MNK	Manja, Madagascar	MJA
Maiduguri, Nigeria	MIU	Mannheim, Germany	MHG

Manus Is., Papua New Guinea	MAS
Manzanillo, Cuba	MZO
Manzanillo, Mexico	ZLO
Manzini, Swaziland	MTS
Maota, Savai'i Is., Western Samoa	MXS
Mapua, Papua New Guinea	MPU
Maputo, Mozambique	MPM
Mar Del Plata, Argentina	MDQ
Mara Lodges, Kenya	MRE
Maraba, Brazil	MAB
Maracaibo, Venezuela	MAR
Marakei, Kiribati	MZK
Maramuni, Papua New Guinea	MWI
Marau Sound, Solomon Islands	RUS
Mare, New Caledonia	MEE
Margate, South Africa	MGH
Marie Galante, Fr. Antilles	GBJ
Mariehamn, Finland	MHQ
Marilia, Brazil	MII
Maringa, Brazil	MGF
Mariupol, Ukraine	MPW
Maroantsetra, Madagascar	WMN
Maroua, Cameroon	MVR
Marrakech, Morocco	RAK
Marseille, France	MRS
Marsh Harbour, Bahamas	MHH
Marudi, Malaysia	MUR
Maryborough, Australia	MBH
Mascara, Algeria	MUW
Maseru, Lesotho	MSU
Mashad, Iran	MHD
Masirah, Oman	MSH
Mastic Point, Bahamas	MSK
Matadi, Zaire	MAT
Mataiva, Fr. Polynesia	MVT
Matamoros, Mexico	MAM
Mataram, Indonesia	AMI
Matsumoto, Japan	MMJ
Matsuyama, Japan	MYJ
Maturin, Venezuela	MUN
Mauke Is., Cook Islands	MUK
Maulmyine, Myanmar	MNU
Maumere, Indonesia	MOF
Maun, Botswana	MUB
Maupiti, Fr. Polynesia	MAU
Mauritius, Mauritius	MRU
Mayaguana, Bahamas	MYG
Mazatlan, Mexico	MZT
Mbambanakira, Solomon Islands	MBU
Mbandaka, Zaire	MDK
Mbuji-Mayi, Zaire	MJM
Medan, Indonesia	MES
Medellin (Cordova), Colombia	MDE
Medellin (Herrera), Colombia	EOH

Meekatharra, Australia	MKR
Mehamn, Norway	MEH
Meixian, China	MXZ
Mejit Is., Marshall Islands	MJB
Mekane Selam, Ethiopia	MKS
Melbourne (Essendon), Australia	MEB
Melbourne (Tullamarine), Australia	MEL
Melilla, Spain	MLN
Memanbetsu, Japan	MMB
Mendi, Ethiopia	NDM
Mendi, Papua New Guinea	MDU
Mendoza, Argentina	MDZ
Menongue, Angola	SPP
Menorca, Spain	MAH
Menyamya, Papua New Guinea	MYX
Merauke, Indonesia	MKQ
Merida, Mexico	MID
Merida, Venezuela	MRD
Merimbula, Australia	MIM
Mesalia, Papua New Guinea	MFZ
Metz, France	MZM
Metz/Nancy, France	ETZ
Mexicali, Mexico	MXL
Mexico City, Mexico	MEX
Mfuwe, Zambia	MFU
Miandrivazo, Madagascar	ZVA
Mianwali, Pakistan	MWD
Middle Caicos, Turks & Caicos	MDS
Mikkeli, Finland	MIK
Mikonos, Greece	JMK
Milan (Linate), Italy	LIN
Milan (Malpensa), Italy	MXP
Milan (Metro), Italy	MIL
Milan (Orio Al Serio), Italy	BGY
Mildura, Australia	MQL
Milford Sound, New Zealand	MFN
Mili Is., Marshall Islands	MIJ
Millingimbi, Australia	MGT
Milos, Greece	MLO
Minacu, Brazil	MQH
Minami Daito, Japan	MMD
Minatitlan, Mexico	MTT
Mineralnye Vody, Russia	MRV
Minsk, Belarus	MSQ
Miri, Malaysia	MYY
Mirpur Khas, Pakistan	MPD
Misawa, Japan	MSJ
Misima Is., Papua New Guinea	MIS
Mitiaro, Cook Islands	MOI
Mitzic, Gabon	MZC
Miyake Jima, Japan	MYE
Miyako Jima, Japan	MMY
Miyazaki, Japan	KMI

Mizan Teferi, Ethiopia	MTF	Mota Lava, Vanuatu	MTV
Mmabatho, South Africa	MBD	Motueka, New Zealand	MZP
Mo I Rana, Norway	MQN	Mouila, Gabon	MJL
Moa, Cuba	MOA	Mount Cook (Glentanner), New	
Moala, Fiji	MFJ	Zealand	GTN
Moanda, Gabon	MFF	Mount Cook, New Zealand	MON
Moanda, Zaire	MNB	Mount Gambier, Australia	MGB
Mogadishu, Somalia	MGQ	Mount Hagen, Papua New	
Mohenjo Daro, Pakistan	MJD	Guinea	HGU
Mokuti Lodge, Namibia	OKU	Mount. Isa, Australia	ISA
Molde, Norway	MOL	Mount Keith, Australia	WME
Mombasa, Kenya	MBA	Mount Magnet, Australia	MMG
Monastir, Tunisia	MIR	Mount Pleasant, Falkland Is.	MPN
Monbetsu, Japan	MBE	Moyobamba, Peru	MBP
Monclova, Mexico	LOV	Mpacha, Namibia	MPA
Mong Hsat, Myanmar	MOG	Mtwara, Tanzania	MYW
Monkey Mia, Australia	MJK	Mucuri, Brazil	MVS
Mono Is., Solomon Islands	MNY	Mudanjiang, China	MDG
Monrovia (Roberts Intl), Liberia	ROB	Mudgee, Australia	DGE
Monrovia (Sprigg Payne),		Muenster, Germany	FMO
Liberia	MLW	Mukah, Malaysia	MKM
Monte Carlo (H/P), Monaco	MCM	Mulhouse, France	BSL
Monte Dourado, Brazil	MEU	Mulhouse, France/Basel,	
Montego Bay, Jamaica	MBJ	Switzerland	MLH
Monteria, Colombia	MTR	Multan, Pakistan	MUX
Monterrey, Mexico	MTY	Mulu, Malaysia	MZV
Montes Claros, Brazil	MOC	Munda, Solomon Islands	MUA
Montevideo, Uruguay	MVD	Mundulkiri, Cambodia	MWV
Montlucon, France	MCU	Munich, Germany	MUC
Montpellier, France	MPL	Murcia, Spain	MJV
Montserrat, Montserrat	MNI	Murmansk, Russia	MMK
Moorabbin, Australia	MBW	Mus, Turkey	MSR
Moorea, Fr. Polynesia	MOZ	Muscat, Oman	MCT
Mopti, Mali	MZI	Musoma, Tanzania	MUZ
Mora, Sweden	MXX	Mussau, Papua New Guinea	MWU
Morafenobe, Madagascar	TVA	Muzaffarabad, Pakistan	MFG
Moree, Australia	MRZ	Mwanza, Tanzania	MWZ
Morelia, Mexico	MLM	Myeik, Myanmar	MGZ
Morioka, Japan	HNA	Myitkyina, Myanmar	MYT
Mornington, Australia	ONG	Mysore, India	MYQ
Moro, Papua New Guinea	MXH	Mytilene, Greece	MJT
Morombe, Madagascar	MXM	Mzuzu, Malawi	ZZU
Morondava, Madagascar	MOQ	N'Zeto, Angola	ARZ
Moroni, Comoros	YVA	Naberevnye Chelny, Russia	NBC
Moroni (Hahaya), Comoros	HAH	Nadi, Fiji	NAN
Moruya, Australia	MYA	Nadym, Russia	NYM
Moscow (Bykovo), Russia	BKA	Naga, Philippines	WNP
Moscow (Domodedovo), Russia	DME	Nagasaki, Japan	NGS
Moscow (Metro), Russia	MOW	Nagoya, Japan	NGO
Moscow (Sheremetyevo), Russia	SVO	Nagpur, India	NAG
Moscow (Vnukovo), Russia	VKO	Nairobi (Metro), Kenya	NBO
Mosjoen, Norway	MJF	Nairobi (Wilson), Kenya	WIL
Mostar, Bosnia	OMO	Nakashibetsu, Japan	SHB
Mosteiros, Cape Verde Islands	MTI	Nakhon Phanom, Thailand	KOP

Nakhon Ratchasima, Thailand	NAK	Nepalganj, Nepal	KEP
Nakhon Si Thammarat,		Neryungri, Russia	NER
Thailand	NST	Neuquen, Argentina	NQN
Namangan, Uzbekistan	NMA	Nevis, Leeward Islands	NEV
Namatanai, Papua New Guinea	ATN	New Plymouth, New Zealand	NPL
Namdrik Is., Marshall Islands	NDK	New Valley, Egypt	UVL
Namibe, Angola	MSZ	Newcastle, Australia	NTL
Nampula, Mozambique	APL	Newcastle (Belmont), Australia	BEO
Namsos, Norway	OSY	Newcastle, England, UK	NCL
Namudi, Papua New Guinea	NDI	Newman, Australia	ZNE
Nan, Thailand	NNT	Newquay, England, UK	NQY
Nanchang, China	KHN	Ngaoundere, Cameroon	NGE
Nanchong, China	NAO	Ngau Is., Fiji	NGI
Nanjing, China	NKG	Ngukurr, Australia	RPM
Nanking, China	NKG	Nha-Trang, Viet Nam	NHA
Nanking, Papua New Guinea	NKN	Niamey, Niger	NIM
Nanning, China	NNG	Niamtougou, Togo	LRL
Nanortalik, Greenland	JNN	Nice, France	NCE
Nantes, France	NTE	Nicosia, Cyprus	NIC
Nantong, China	NTG	Niigata, Japan	KIJ
Nanyang, China	NNY	Nikolaev, Ukraine	NLV
Nanyuki, Kenya	NYK	Nikunau, Kiribati	NIG
Naoro, Papua New Guinea	NOO	Nimes, France	FNI
Napier, New Zealand	NPE	Ningbo, China	NGB
Naples, Italy	NAP	Nioro, Mali	NIX
Narathiwat, Thailand	NAW	Niquelandia, Brazil	NQL
Nare, Colombia	NAR	Nissan Is., Papua New Guinea	IIS
Narrabri, Australia	NAA	Niuafo'ou, Tonga	NFO
Narrandera, Australia	NRA	Niuatoputapu, Tonga	NTT
Narsaq, Greenland	JNS	Niue Island, Niue	IUE
Narsarsuaq, Greenland	UAK	Nizhnevartovsk, Russia	NJC
Narvik, Norway	NVK	Nizhniy Novgorod, Russia	GOJ
Nassau, Bahamas	NAS	Nkayi, Congo	NKY
Nassau (Paradise Is.), Bahamas	PID	Nojabrxsk, Russia	NOJ
Nassau (SPB), Bahamas	WZY	Nonouti, Kiribati	NON
Natal, Brazil	NAT	Nordholz-Spieka, Germany	NDZ
Nauru Is., Rep. of Nauru	INU	Norfolk Is., Pacific Ocean	NLK
Navegantes, Brazil	NVT	Norilsk, Russia	NSK
Nawabshah, Pakistan	WNS	Normanton, Australia	NTN
Naxos, Greece	JNX	Norrkoping, Sweden	NRK
Ndjamena, Chad	NDJ	Norsup, Vanuatu	NUS
Ndola, Zambia	NLA	North Caicos, Turks & Caicos	NCA
Necocli, Colombia	NCI	North Eleuthera, Bahamas	ELH
Neerlerit Inaat, Greenland	CNP	Norwich, England, UK	NWI
Neftekamsk, Russia	NEF	Nosara Beach, Costa Rica	NOB
Nefteyugansk, Russia	NFG	Nossi-be, Madagascar	NOS
Neghelli, Ethiopia	EGL	Nouadhibou, Mauritania	NDB
Negril, Jamaica	NEG	Nouakchott, Mauritania	NKC
Neiva, Colombia	NVA	Noumea (Magenta), New	
Nejjo, Ethiopia	NEJ	Caledonia	GEA
Nejran, Saudi Arabia	EAM	Noumea, New Caledonia	NOU
Nelson, New Zealand	NSN	Novosibirsk, Russia	OVB
Nelspruit, South Africa	NLP	Novyj Urengoj, Russia	NUX
Nema, Mauritania	EMN	Nowata, Papua New Guinea	NWT

Nueva Gerona, Cuba	GER	Oskarshamn, Sweden	OSK
Nueva Guinea, Nicaragua	NVG	Oslo (Fornebu), Norway	FBU
Nuevo Laredo, Mexico	NLD	Oslo (Gardermoen), Norway	GEN
Nuku Hiva, Fr. Polynesia	NHV	Oslo (Metro), Norway	OSL
Nuku, Papua New Guinea	UKU	Osorno, Chile	ZOS
Nukus, Uzbekistan	NCU	Ostersund, Sweden	OSD
Numbulwar, Australia	NUB	Ostrava, Czech Rep.	OSR
Nuqui, Colombia	NQU	Otu, Colombia	OTU
Nuremberg, Germany	NUE	Ouagadougou, Burkina Faso	OUA
Nuuk, Greenland	GOH	Ouargla, Algeria	OGX
Nyaung-u, Myanmar	NYU	Ouarzazate, Morocco	OZZ
Nykoping, Sweden	NYO	Oudomxay, Laos	ODY
Nyngan, Australia	NYN	Ouesso, Congo	OUE
Oaxaca, Mexico	OAX	Oujda, Morocco	OUD
Obihiro, Japan	OBO	Oulu, Finland	OUL
Ocana, Colombia	OCV	Ouvea, New Caledonia	UVE
Ocho Rios, Jamaica	OCJ	Ovda, Israel	VDA
Odense, Denmark	ODE	Owando, Congo	FTX
Odessa, Ukraine	ODS	Oyem, Gabon	OYE
Ohrid, Macedonia	OHD	Paama, Vanuatu	PBJ
Oita, Japan	OIT	Paamiut, Greenland	JFR
Okayama, Japan	OKJ	Pacific Harbour, Fiji	PHR
Oki Island, Japan	OKI	Padang, Indonesia	PDG
Okinawa, Japan	OKA	Paderborn, Germany	PAD
Okino Erabu, Japan	OKE	Pakse, Laos	PKZ
Okondja, Gabon	OKN	Palanga, Lithuania	PLQ
Okushiri, Japan	OIR	Palangkaraya, Indonesia	PKY
Olbia, Italy	OLB	Palembang, Indonesia	PLM
Olpoi, Vanuatu	OLJ	Palenque, Mexico	PQM
Olympic Dam, Australia	OLP	Palermo, Italy	PMO
Omboue, Gabon	OMB	Palma Mallorca, Spain	PMI
Omsk, Russia	OMS	Palmar, Costa Rica	PMZ
Ondangwa, Namibia	OND	Palmas, Brazil	PMW
Ongava Game Reserve, Namibia	OGV	Palmerston N., New Zealand	PMR
Ononge, Papua New Guinea	ONB	Palu, Indonesia	PLW
Onotoa, Kiribati	OOT	Pamplona, Spain	PNA
Open Bay, Papua New Guinea	OPB	Panama City (Paitilla), Panama	PAC
Oradea, Romania	OMR	Panama City (Tocumen Intl),	
Oran, Algeria	ORN	Panama	PTY
Orange, Australia	OAG	Pangkalpinang, Indonesia	PGK
Orange (Cudal), Australia	CUG	Panjgur, Pakistan	PJG
Oranjemund, Namibia	OMD	Pantelleria, Italy	PNL
Orebro, Sweden	ORB	Papeete, Fr. Polynesia	PPT
Orenburg, Russia	REN	Paphos, Cyprus	PFO
Ormara, Pakistan	ORW	Para Chinar, Pakistan	PAJ
Ornskoldsvik, Sweden	OER	Paraburdoo, Australia	PBO
Orsk, Russia	OSW	Paramaribo, Suriname	PBM
Orsta-Volda, Norway	HOV	Paramaribo (Zorg En Hoop),	
Osaka (Itami), Japan	ITM	Suriname	ORG
Osaka (Kansai), Japan	KIX	Paraparaumu, New Zealand	PPQ
Osaka (Metro), Japan	OSA	Parasi, Solomon Islands	PRS
Osh, Kyrgyzstan	OSS	Paris (De Gaulle), France	CDG
Oshima, Japan	OIM	Paris (Metro), France	PAR
Osijek, Croatia	OSI	Paris (Orly), France	ORY

Parkes, Australia	PKE	Plettenberg Bay, South Africa	PBZ
Parma, Italy	PMF	Plymouth, England, UK	PLH
Parnaiba, B razil	PHB	Podgorica, Yugoslavia	TGD
Paro, Bhutan	PBH	Pohang, Korea	KPO
Paros, Greece	PAS	Pohnpei, Micronesia	PNI
Pasni, Pakistan	PSI	Pointe A Pitre, Guadeloupe	PTP
Passo Fundo, Brazil	PFB	Pointe Noire, Congo	PNR
Pasto, Colombia	PSO	Poitiers, France	PIS
Patna, India	PAT	Pokhara, Nepal	PKR
Patos De Minas, Brazil	POJ	Ponta Delgada, Portugal	PDL
Patras, Greece	GPA	Ponta Grossa, Brazil	PGZ
Patreksfjordur, Iceland	PFJ	Ponta Pora, Brazil	PMG
Pau, France	PUF	Pontianak, Indonesia	PNK
Paulo Afonso, Brazil	PAV	Poona, India	PNQ
Pavlodar, Kazakstan	PWQ	Popayan, Colombia	PPN
Pedro Juan Caballero, Paraguay	PJC	Popondetta, Papua New Guinea	PNP
Pekanbaru, Indonesia	PKU	Porbandar, India	PBD
Pelly Bay, NT	YUF	Pori, Finland	POR
Pelotas, Brazil	PET	Porlamar, Venezuela	PMV
Pemba, Mozambique	POL	Port Antonio, Jamaica	POT
Pemba, Tanzania	PMA	Port Au Prince, Haiti	PAP
Penang, Malaysia	PEN	Port Augusta, Australia	PUG
Penneshaw, Australia	PEA	Port Blair, India	IXZ
Penrhyn Is., Cook Islands	PYE	Port Elizabeth, South Africa	PLZ
Penzance, England, UK	PZE	Port Elizabeth, Windward	
Pereira, Colombia	PEI	Islands	BQU
Perigueux, France	PGX	Port Gentil, Gabon	POG
Perm, Russia	PEE	Port Harcourt, Nigeria	PHC
Perpignan, France	PGF	Port Hedland, Australia	PHE
Perth, Australia	PER	Port Lincoln, Australia	PLO
Perugia, Italy	PEG	Port Macquarie, Australia	PQQ
Pescara, Italy	PSR	Port Moresby, Papua New	
Peshawar, Pakistan	PEW	Guinea	POM
Petrolina, Brazil	PNZ	Port of Spain, Trinidad & Tobago	POS
Petropavlovsk, Kazakstan	PPK	Port Sudan, Sudan	PZU
Petropavlovsk-Kamchats, Russia	PKC	Port Vila, Vanuatu	VLI
Petrozavodsk, Russia	PES	Portland, Australia	PTJ
Phalaborwa, South Africa	PHW	Porto Alegre, Brazil	POA
Phaplu, Nepal	PPL	Porto Nacional, Brazil	PNB
Phitsanulok, Thailand	PHS	Porto, Portugal	OPO
Phnom Penh, Cambodia	PNH	Porto Santo, Portugal	PXO
Phrae, Thailand	PRH	Porto Seguro, Brazil	BPS
Phuket, Thailand	HKT	Porto Velho, Brazil	PVH
Pico Island, Portugal	PIX	Posadas, Argentina	PSS
Piedras Negras, Mexico	PDS	Potosi, Bolivia	POI
Pietermaritzburg, South Africa	PZB	Poum, New Caledonia	PUV
Pietersburg, South Africa	PTG	Pouso Alegre, Brazil	PPY
Pingtung, Taiwan	PIF	Poza Rica, Mexico	PAZ
Pisa, Italy	PSA	Poznan, Poland	POZ
Pituffik, Greenland	PIU	Prague, Czech Rep.	PRG
Piura, Peru	PIU	Praia, Cape Verde Islands	RAI
Placencia, Belize	PLJ	Praslin Is., Seychelles Is.	PRI
Playa Del Carmen, Mexico	PCM	Pres. Prudente, Brazil	PPB
Pleiku, Viet Nam	PXU	Preveza/Lefkas, Greece	PVK

Principe Is., Principe Is.	PCP	Rabat, Morocco	RBA
Pristina, Yugoslavia	PRN	Rabaul, Papua New Guinea	RAB
Proserpine, Australia	PPP	Rafha, Saudi Arabia	RAH
Providencia, Colombia	PVA	Rahim Yar Khan, Pakistan	RYK
Providenciales, Turks & Caicos	PLS	Raiatea, Fr. Polynesia	RFP
Pucallpa, Peru	PCL	Raipur, India	RPR
Puebla, Mexico	PBC	Rajkot, India	RAJ
Puerto Asis, Colombia	PUU	Rajshahi, Bangladesh	RJH
Puerto Ayacucho, Venezuela	PYH	Ramata, Solomon Islands	RBV
Puerto Berrio, Colombia	PBE	Ramingining, Australia	RAM
Puerto Cabezas, Nicaragua	PUZ	Ranchi, India	IXR
Puerto Carreno, Colombia	PCR	Rangiroa, Fr. Polynesia	RGI
Puerto Escondido, Mexico	PXM	Ranong, Thailand	UNN
Puerto Inirida, Colombia	PDA	Rarotonga, Cook Islands	RAR
Puerto Jiminez, Costa Rica	PJM	Ras Al Khaimah, UAE	RKT
Puerto Lempira, Honduras	PEU	Ras An Naqb, Egypt	RAF
Puerto Madryn, Argentina	PMY	Rasht, Iran	RAS
Puerto Maldonado, Peru	PEM	Rawala Kot, Pakistan	RAZ
Puerto Montt, Chile	PMC	Rebun, Japan	RBJ
Puerto Ordaz, Venezuela	PZO	Recife, Brazil	REC
Puerto Penasco, Mexico	PPE	Redcliffe, Vanuatu	RCL
Puerto Plata, Dominican Rep.	POP	Redencao, Brazil	RDC
Puerto Princesa, Philippines	PPS	Reggio Calabria, Italy	REG
Puerto Suarez, Bolivia	PSZ	Reims, France	RHE
Puerto Vallarta, Mexico	PVR	Renmark, Australia	RMK
Pula, Croatia	PUY	Rennell, Solomon Islands	RNL
Pumani, Papua New Guinea	PMN	Rennes, France	RNS
Punta Arenas, Chile	PUQ	Resistencia, Argentina	RES
Punta Cana, Dominican Rep.	PUJ	Reunion Island, Indian Ocean	RUN
Punta Del Este, Uruguay	PDP	Reus, Spain	REU
Punta Gorda, Belize	PND	Reykjavik (Domestic), Iceland	RKV
Punta Islita, Costa Rica	PBP	Reykjavik (Keflavik), Iceland	KEF
Pusan, Korea	PUS	Reykjavik (Metro), Iceland	REK
Putao, Myanmar	PBU	Reynosa, Mexico	REX
Puttaparthi, India	PUT	Rhodes, Greece	RHO
Pyongyang, N. Korea	FNJ	Ribeirao Preto, Brazil	RAO
Qaisumah, Saudi Arabia	AQI	Riberalta, Bolivia	RIB
Qiemo, China	IQM	Richards Bay, South Africa	RCB
Qingdao, China	TAO	Richmond, Australia	RCM
Qinhuangdao, China	SHP	Riga, Latvia	RIX
Qiqihar, China	NDG	Rincon de los Sauces, Argentina	RDS
Queenstown, Australia	UEE	Ringi Cove, Solomon Islands	RIN
Queenstown, New Zealand	ZQN	Rio Branco, Brazil	RBR
Quelimane, Mozambique	UEL	Rio Cuarto, Argentina	RCU
Quepos, Costa Rica	XQP	Rio De Janeiro (Dumont), Brazil	SDU
Queretaro, Mexico	QRO	Rio De Janeiro (Metro), Brazil	RIO
Quetta, Pakistan	UET	Rio de Janeriro (Intl), Brazil	GIG
Qui Nhon, Viet Nam	UIH	Rio Gallegos, Argentina	RGL
Quibdo, Colombia	UIB	Rio Grande, Argentina	RGA
Quilpie, Australia	ULP	Rio Grande, Brazil	RIG
Quimper, France	UIP	Riohacha, Colombia	RCH
Quine Hill, Vanuatu	UIQ	Rioja, Peru	RIJ
Quito, Ecuador	UIO	Rishiri, Japan	RIS
Rabaraba, Papua New Guinea	RBP	Riyadh, Saudi Arabia	RUH

Riyan Mukalla, Yemen	RIY	Sambava, Madagascar	SVB
Roanne, France	RNE	Sambu, Panama	SAX
Roatan, Honduras	RTB	Samburu, Kenya	UAS
Rock Sound, Bahamas	RSD	Samos, Greece	SMI
Rockhampton, Australia	ROK	Samsun, Turkey	SSX
Rodez, France	RDZ	San Andres Is., Colombia	ADZ
Rodrigues Island, Mauritius	RRG	San Andros, Bahamas	SAQ
Roervik, Norway	RVK	San Antonio, Venezuela	SVZ
Roma, Australia	RMA	San Borja, Bolivia	SRJ
Rome (Ciampino), Italy	CIA	San Carlos de Bariloche,	
Rome (Fiumicino), Italy	FCO	Argentina	BRC
Rome (Metro), Italy	ROM	San Carlos, Nicaragua	NCR
Rondonopolis, Brazil	ROO	San Cristobal, Ecuador	SCY
Ronneby, Sweden	RNB	San Fernando De Apure,	
Roros, Norway	RRS	Venezuela	SFD
Rosario, Argentina	ROS	San Joaquin, Bolivia	SJB
Rosh Pina, Israel	RPN	San Jose Cabo, Mexico	SJD
Rost, Norway	RET	San Jose, Costa Rica	SJO
Rostock-Laage, Germany	RLG	San Jose, Philippines	SJI
Rostov, Russia	ROV	San Juan, Argentina	UAQ
Rota, Mariana Islands	ROP	San Luis, Argentina	LUQ
Rotorua, New Zealand	ROT	San Luis Potosi, Mexico	SLP
Rotterdam, Netherlands	RTM	San Martin de los Andes,	
Rottnest Is., Australia	RTS	Argentina	CPC
Rotuma, Fiji	RTA	San Miguel, Panama	NMG
Rouen, France	URO	San Pedro, Belize	SPR
Rovaniemi, Finland	RVN	San Pedro Sula, Honduras	SAP
Roxas City, Philippines	RXS	San Rafael, Argentina	AFA
Rundu, Namibia	NDU	San Salvador, Bahamas	ZSA
Rurutu Is., Fr. Polynesia	RUR	San Salvador, El Salvador	SAL
Saarbruecken, Germany	SCN	San Sebastian, Spain	EAS
Saba, Neth. Antilles	SAB	San Tome, Venezuela	SOM
Sadah, Yemen Arab Rep.	SYE	San Vincente Del Caguan,	
Safia, Papua New Guinea	SFU	Colombia	SVI
Saidpur, Bangladesh	SPD	Sana'a, Yemen Arab Rep.	SAH
Saidu Sharif, Pakistan	SDT	Sandakan, Malaysia	SDK
Saipan, Mariana Islands	SPN	Sandane, Norway	SDN
Sakon Nakhon, Thailand	SNO	Sandefjord, Norway	TRF
Sal, Cape Verde Islands	SID	Sandnessjoen, Norway	SSJ
Salalah, Oman	SLL	Sanliurfa, Turkey	SFQ
Salamanca, Spain	SLM	Santa Ana, Solomon Islands	NNB
Salamo, Papua New Guinea	SAM	Santa Cruz Do Sul, Brazil	CSU
Sale, Australia	SXE	Santa Cruz Is., Solomon Islands	SCZ
Salehard, Russia	SLY	Santa Cruz La Palma, Spain	SPC
Salina Cruz, Mexico	SCX	Santa Cruz (Trompillo), Bolivia	SRZ
Salt Cay, Turks & Caicos	SLX	Santa Cruz (Viru Viru), Bolivia	VVI
Salta, Argentina	SLA	Santa Elena, Venezuela	SNV
Saltillo, Mexico	SLW	Santa Fe, Argentina	SFN
Salvador, Brazil	SSA	Santa Maria, Brazil	RIA
Salzburg, Austria	SZG	Santa Maria, Portugal	SMA
Sam Neua, Laos	NEU	Santa Marta, Colombia	SMR
Samara, Russia	KUF	Santa Rosa, Argentina	RSA
Samarinda, Indonesia	SRI	Santa Rosa, Brazil	SRA
Samarkand, Uzbekistan	SKD	Santa Terezinha, Brazil	STZ

Santana Do Araguaia, Brazil	CMP	Sendai, Japan	SDJ
Santander, Spain	SDR	Seoul, Korea	SEL
Santarem, Brazil	STM	Seville, Spain	SVQ
Santiago, Chile	SCL	Sfax, Tunisia	SFA
Santiago, Cuba	SCU	Shanghai, China	SHA
Santiago De Compostela, Spain	SCQ	Shannon, Ireland	SNN
Santiago Del Estero, Argentina	SDE	Shantou, China	SWA
Santiago, Dominican Rep.	STI	Sharjah, UAE	SHJ
Santiago, Panama	SYP	Sharm El Sheikh, Egypt	SSH
Santo Angelo, Brazil	GEL	Sharurah, Saudi Arabia	SHW
Santo Antao, Cape Verde Islands	NTO	Shashi, China	SHS
Santo Domingo, Dominican Rep.	SDQ	Shenyang, China	SHE
Sanya, China	SYX	Shenzhen, China	SZX
Sao Felix Do Araguaia, Brazil	SXO	Shepparton, Australia	SHT
Sao Felix Do Xingu, Brazil	SXX	Shetland Is. (Lerwick),	
Sao Jorge Island, Portugal	SJZ	Scotland, UK	LWK
Sao Jose Do Rio Preto, Brazil	SJP	Shetland Is., Scotland, UK	SDZ
Sao Jose Dos Campos, Brazil	SJK	Shetland Is. (Sumburgh),	
Sao Luiz, Brazil	SLZ	Scotland, UK	LSI
Sao Nicolau, Cape Verde Islands	SNE	Shijiazhuang, China	SJW
Sao Paolo (Viracopas), Brazil	VCP	Shillavo, Ethiopia	HIL
Sao Paulo (Congonhas), Brazil	CGH	Shimkent, Kazakstan	CIT
Sao Paulo (Guarulhos), Brazil	GRU	Shiraz, Iran	SYZ
Sao Paulo (Metro), Brazil	SAO	Shonai, Japan	SYO
Sao Tome Island	TMS	Shute Harbour, Australia	JHQ
Sao Vicente, Cape Verde Islands	VXE	Sibiu, Romania	SBZ
Sapporo (Chitose), Japan	CTS	Sibu, Malaysia	SBW
Sapporo (Metro), Japan	SPK	Siem Reap, Cambodia	REP
Sapporo (Okadama), Japan	OKD	Sihanoukville, Cambodia	KOS
Sara, Vanuatu	SSR	Siirit, Turkey	SXZ
Sarajevo, Bosnia	SJJ	Sila, Papua New Guinea	SIL
Saratov, Russia	RTW	Silchar, India	IXS
Saravane, Laos	VNA	Silur, Papua New Guinea	SWR
Sary, Iran	SRY	Simao, China	SYM
Satu Mare, Romania	SUJ	Simferopol, Ukraine	SIP
Satwag, Papua New Guinea	SWG	Simikot, Nepal	IMK
Saudarkrokur, Iceland	SAK	Simla, India	SLV
Sauren, Papua New Guines	SXW	Simra, Nepal	SIF
Saurimo, Angola	VHC	Sindal, Denmark	IMK
Savannakhet, Laos	ZVK	Singapore (Changi), Singapore	SIN
Savonlinna, Finland	SVL	Singleton, Australia	SIX
Savusavu, Fiji	SVU	Sinop, Brazil	OPS
Sayaboury, Laos	ZBY	Sinop, Turkey	SIC
Scone, Australia	NSO	Sion, Switzerland	SIR
Sege, Solomon Islands	EGM	Sitia, Greece	JSH
Sehulea, Papua New Guinea	SXH	Sittwe, Myanmar	AKY
Sehwen Sharif, Pakistan	SYW	Siuna, Nicaragua	SIU
Seinajoki, Finland	SJY	Sivas, Turkey	VAS
Seiyun, Yemen	GXF	Skardu, Pakistan	KDU
Selibaby, Mauritania	SEY	Skelleftea, Sweden	SFT
Selje, Norway	QFK	Skiathos, Greece	JSI
Semarang, Indonesia	SRG	Skien, Norway	SKE
Semipalatinsk, Kazakstan	PLX	Skiros, Greece	SKU
Semporna, Malaysia	SMM	Skopje, Macedonia	SKP

Skovde, Sweden	KVB	Stornoway, Scotland, UK	SYY
Skukuza, South Africa	SZK	Storuman, Sweden	SQO
Sligo, Ireland	SXL	Strasbourg, France	SXB
Snake Bay, Australia	SNB	Strzhewoi, Russia	SWT
Socotra, Yemen	SCT	Stung Treng, Cambodia	TNX
Soderhamn, Sweden	SOO	Stuttgart, Germany	STR
Sofia, Bulgaria	SOF	Stuttgart (Main RR), Germany	ZWS
Sogamoso, Colombia	SOX	Suavanao, Solomon Islands	VAO
Sogndal, Norway	SOG	Suceava, Romania	SCV
Sokcho, Korea	SHO	Sucre, Bolivia	SRE
Sokoto, Nigeria	SKO	Sui, Pakistan	SUL
Sola, Vanuatu	SLH	Sukhothai, Thailand	THS
Solo City, Indonesia	SOC	Sukkertoppen, Greenland	JSU
Son La, Viet Nam	SQH	Sukkur, Pakistan	SKZ
Sonderborg, Denmark	SGD	Sule, Papua New Guinea	ULE
Sorkjosen, Norway	SOJ	Sun City, South Africa	NTY
Sorong, Indonesia	SOQ	Sundsvall, Sweden	SDL
South Andros, Bahamas	TZN	Sunshine Coast, Australia	MCY
South Caicos, Turks & Caicos	XSC	Sur, Oman	SUH
South Molle Is., Australia	SOI	Surabaya, Indonesia	SUB
South West Bay, Vanuatu	SWJ	Surat, India	STV
Southampton, England, UK	SOU	Surat Thani, Thailand	URT
Southern Cross, Australia	SQC	Surgut, Russia	SGC
Soyo, Angola	SZA	Surkhet, Nepal	SKH
Split, Croatia	SPU	Suva, Fiji	SUV
Spring Point, Bahamas	AXP	Sveg, Sweden	EVG
Springbok, South Africa	SBU	Svolvaer, Norway	SVJ
Srinagar, India	SXR	Swakopmund, Namibia	SWP
St. Barthelemy, Guadeloupe	SBH	Sydney, Australia	SYD
St. Brieuc, France	SBK	Sydney (Palm Beach), Australia	LBH
St. Etienne, France	EBU	Sydney (Rose Bay), Australia	RSE
St. Eustatius, Neth. Antilles	EUX	Sylhet, Bangladesh	ZYL
St. George, Australia	SGO	Syros, Greece	JSY
St. Kitts, St. Kitts & Nevis	SKB	Szczecin, Poland	SZZ
St. Lucia (Hewanorra), West Indies	UVF	Taba, Egypt	TCP
		Tabarka, Tunisia	TBJ
St. Lucia, West Indies	SLU	Tabatinga, Brazil	TBT
St. Maarten (Esperance), Neth. Antilles	SFG	Tabiteuea North, Kiribati	TBF
		Tabiteuea South, Kiribati	TSU
St. Maarten, Neth. Antilles	SXM	Tabora, Tanzania	TBO
St. Petersburg, Russia	LED	Tabriz, Iran	TBZ
St. Petersburg (Rzhevka), Russia	RVH	Tabubil, Papua New Guinea	TBG
St. Pierre, St. Pierre and Miquelon	FSP	Tabuk, Saudi Arabia	TUU
		Tacheng, China	TCG
St. Tropez, France	JSZ	Tachilek, Myanmar	THL
St. Vincent, Windward Islands	SVD	Tacloban, Philippines	TAC
Stavanger, Norway	SVG	Tacna, Peru	TCQ
Stavropol, Russia	STW	Taegu, Korea	TAE
Stella Maris, Bahamas	SML	Taichung, Taiwan	TXG
Stockholm (Arlanda), Sweden	ARN	Taif, Saudi Arabia	TIF
Stockholm (Metro), Sweden	STO	Tainan, Taiwan	TNN
Stockolm (Bromma), Sweden	BMA	Taipei (Chiang Kai Shek), Taiwan	TPE
Stokmarknes, Norway	SKN	Taipei (Sung Shan), Taiwan	TSA
Stord, Norway	SRP	Taitung, Taiwan	TTT

Taiyuan, China	TYN	Tennant Creek, Australia	TCA
Taiz, Yemen	TAI	Tepic, Mexico	TPQ
Takamatsu, Japan	TAK	Teptep, Papua New Guinea	TEP
Takapoto, Fr. Polynesia	TKP	Terapo, Papua New Guinea	TEO
Takaroa, Fr. Polynesia	TKX	Terceira Is., Portugal	TER
Talara, Peru	TYL	Teresina, Brazil	THE
Tallinn, Estonia	TLL	Termez, Uzbekistan	TMJ
Tamana Island, Kiribati	TMN	Ternate, Indonesia	TTE
Tamanrasset, Algeria	TMR	Terre De Haut, Guadeloupe	LSS
Tamarindo, Costa Rica	TNO	Tetabedi, Papua New Guinea	TDB
Tamatave, Madagascar	TMM	Tete, Mozambique	TET
Tambor, Costa Rica	TMU	Tetuan, Morocco	TTU
Tame, Colombia	TME	Tezpur, India	TEZ
Tampere, Finland	TMP	Thandwe, Myanmar	SNW
Tampico, Mexico	TAM	Thangool, Australia	THG
Tamworth, Australia	TMW	Thargomindah, Australia	XTG
Tan Tan, Morocco	TTA	The Bight, Bahamas	TBI
Tanegashima, Japan	TNE	Thessaloniki, Greece	SKG
Tangier, Morocco	TNG	Thira, Greece	JTR
Tanjung Pandan, Indonesia	TTR	Thisted, Denmark	TED
Tanna, Vanuatu	TAH	Thursday Is., Australia	TIS
Tapachula, Mexico	TAP	Tianjin, China	TSN
Tapini, Papua New Guinea	TPI	Tiaret, Algeria	TID
Taplejung, Nepal	TPJ	Tidjikja, Mauritania	TIY
Tarakan, Indonesia	TRK	Tiga, New Caledonia	TGJ
Taramajima, Japan	TRA	Tijuana, Mexico	TIJ
Tarapoto, Peru	TPP	Tikehau Atoll, Fr. Polynesia	TIH
Tarawa, Kiribati	TRW	Timaru, New Zealand	TIU
Taree, Australia	TRO	Timbuktu (Tombouctou), Mali	TOM
Tari, Papua New Guinea	TIZ	Timbunke, Papua New Guinea	TBE
Tarija, Bolivia	TJA	Timimoun, Algeria	TMX
Tashkent, Uzbekistan	TAS	Timisoara, Romania	TSR
Tatry/Poprad, Slovakia	TAT	Tinak Is., Marshall Islands	TIC
Taupo, New Zealand	TUO	Tindouf, Algeria	TIN
Tauranga, New Zealand	TRG	Tingo Maria, Peru	TGI
Taveuni, Fiji	TVU	Tinian, Mariana Islands	TIQ
Tawau, Malaysia	TWU	Tioman, Malaysia	TOD
Tbessa, Algeria	TEE	Tippi, Ethiopia	TIE
Tbilisi, Georgia	TBS	Tirana, Albania	TIA
Tchibanga, Gabon	TCH	Tiree, Scotland, UK	TRE
Te Anau, New Zealand	TEU	Tirgu Mures, Romania	TGM
Teesside, England, UK	MME	Tiruchirapally, India	TRZ
Tefe, Brazil	TFF	Tirupati, India	TIR
Tegucigalpa, Honduras	TGU	Tivat, Yugoslavia	TIV
Tehran, Iran	THR	Tlemsen, Algeria	TLM
Tekadu, Papua New Guinea	TKB	Tobago, Trinidad & Tobago	TAB
Tel Aviv (Jaffa), Israel	TLV	Tokat, Turkey	TJK
Tel Aviv/Jaffa (Sde Dov), Israel	SDV	Tokunoshima, Japan	TKN
Telefomin, Papua New Guinea	TFM	Tokushima, Japan	TKS
Tembagapura, Indonesia	TIM	Tokyo (Haneda), Japan	HND
Temuco, Chile	ZCO	Tokyo (Metro), Japan	TYO
Tenerife (Metro), Spain	TCI	Tokyo (Narita), Japan	NRT
Tenerife (N. Los Rodeo), Spain	TFN	Toledo, Brazil	TOW
Tenerife (Reina Sofia), Spain	TFS	Tomanggong, Malaysia	TMG

Tomsk, Russia	TOF	Tunxi, China	TXN
Tongatapu, Tonga	TBU	Turaif, Saudi Arabia	TUI
Tongoa, Vanuatu	TGH	Turbat, Pakistan	TUK
Toowoomba, Australia	TWB	Turbo, Colombia	TRB
Torreon, Mexico	TRC	Turin, Italy	TRN
Torres, Vanuatu	TOH	Turku, Finland	TKU
Torsby, Sweden	TYF	Tuticorin, India	TCR
Tortola (Road Town), BVI	RAD	Tuxtla Gutierrez, Mexico	TGZ
Tortola (Westend), BVI	TOV	Tuy Hoa, Vietnam	TBB
Tortuquero, Costa Rica	TTQ	Tyumen, Russia	TJM
Tottori, Japan	TTJ	Ube, Japan	UBJ
Touggourt, Algeria	TGR	Uberaba, Brazil	UBA
Touho, New Caledonia	TOU	Uberlandia, Brazil	UDI
Toulon, France	TLN	Ubon Ratchathani, Thailand	UBP
Toulouse, France	TLS	Udaipur, India	UDR
Tours, France	TUF	Udon Thani, Thailand	UTH
Townsville, Australia	TSV	Ufa, Russia	UFA
Toyama, Japan	TOY	Uige, Angola	UGO
Toyooka, Japan	TJH	Ujae Is., Marshall Islands	UJE
Tozeur, Tunisia	TOE	Ujung Pandang, Indonesia	UPG
Trabzon, Turkey	TZX	Ukhta, Russia	UCT
Trang, Thailand	TST	Ulan Bator, Mongolia	ULN
Trapani, Italy	TPS	Ulan-Ude, Russia	UUD
Traralgon, Australia	TGN	Ulei, Vanuatu	ULB
Treasure Cay, Bahamas	TCB	Ulgit, Mongolia	ULG
Trelew, Argentina	REL	Ulsan, Korea	USN
Trieste, Italy	TRS	Ulundi, South Africa	ULD
Trinidad, Bolivia	TDD	Umea, Sweden	UME
Tripoli, Libya	TIP	Umtata, South Africa	UTT
Trivandrum, India	TRV	Union Island, St. Vincent	UNI
Trollhattan, Sweden	THN	Unst, Shetland Is., Scotland, UK	UNT
Trombetas, Brazil	TMT	Upernavik, Greenland	JUV
Tromso, Norway	TOS	Upington, South Africa	UTN
Trondheim, Norway	TRD	Uraj, Russia	URJ
Trujillo, Honduras	TJI	Uralsk, Kazakstan	URA
Trujillo, Peru	TRU	Urgench, Uzbekistan	UGC
Truk, Micronesia	TKK	Urmieh, Iran	OMH
Tsaratanana, Madagascar	TTS	Urrao, Colombia	URR
Tshikapa, Zaire	TSH	Uruapan, Mexico	UPN
Tsiroanomandidy, Madagascar	WTS	Uruguaiana, Brazil	URG
Tsumeb, Namibia	TSB	Urumqi, China	URC
Tsushima, Japan	TSJ	Useless Loop, Australia	USL
Tubuai, Fr. Polynesia	TUB	Ushuaia, Argentina	USH
Tucuma, Brazil	TUZ	Ust-Ilimsk, Russia	UIK
Tucuman, Argentina	TUC	Ust-Kamenogorsk, Kazakstan	UKK
Tucurui, Brazil	TUR	Utapao, Thailand	UTP
Tufi, Papua New Guinea	TFI	Utila, Honduras	UII
Tuguegarao, Philippines	TUG	Utirik Is., Marshall Islands	UTK
Tulear, Madagascar	TLE	Uummannaq, Greenland	UMD
Tum, Ethiopia	TUJ	Uvol, Papua New Guinea	UVO
Tumaco, Colombia	TCO	Vaasa, Finland	VAA
Tumbes, Peru	TBP	Vadodara, India	BDQ
Tumling Tar, Nepal	TMI	Vadso, Norway	VDS
Tunis, Tunisia	TUN	Vaeroy, Norway	VRY

Valdivia, Chile	ZAL	Waco Kungo, Angola	CEO
Valencia, Spain	VLC	Wadi-Ad-Dawasir, Saudi Arabia	WAE
Valencia, Venezuela	VLN	Wagga Wagga, Australia	WGA
Valesdir, Vanuatu	VLS	Waingapu, Indonesia	WGP
Valladolid, Spain	VLL	Wairoa, New Zealand	WIR
Valledupar, Colombia	VUP	Wakkanai, Japan	WKJ
Valverde, Spain	VDE	Walaha, Vanuatu	WLH
Van, Turkey	VAN	Walgett, Australia	WGE
Vanimo, Papua New Guinea	VAI	Walker's Cay, Bahamas	WKR
Vanuabalavu, Fiji	VBV	Wallis Is., Wallis & Futuna	
Varadero, Cuba	VRA	Islands	WLS
Varanasi, India	VNS	Walvis Bay, Namibia	WVB
Vardoe, Norway	VAW	Wanaka, New Zealand	WKA
Varginha, Brazil	VAG	Wanganui, New Zealand	WAG
Varkaus, Finland	VRK	Wangerooge, Germany	AGE
Varna, Bulgaria	VAR	Wanigela, Papua New Guinea	AGL
Vasteras, Sweden	VST	Wanxian, China	WXN
Vava'u, Tonga	VAV	Wapenamanda, Papua New	
Vaxjo, Sweden	VXO	Guinea	WBM
Venice, Italy	VCE	Warsaw, Poland	WAW
Veracruz, Mexico	VER	Waspam, Nicaragua	WSP
Verona, Italy	VRN	Wasu, Papua New Guinea	WSU
Vestmannaeyjar, Iceland	VEY	Waterford, Ireland	WAT
Victoria Falls, Zimbabwe	VFA	Wau, Papua New Guinea	WUG
Victoria R. Downs, Australia	VCD	Wedau, Papua New Guinea	WED
Videira, Brazil	VIA	Wedjh, Saudi Arabia	EJH
Viedma, Argentina	VDM	Weifang, China	WEF
Vienna, Austria	VIE	Weihai, China	WEH
Vientiane, Laos	VTE	Weipa, Australia	WEI
Vigo, Spain	VGO	Wellington, New Zealand	WLG
Vila Rica, Brazil	VLP	Wenzhou, China	WNZ
Vilhelmina, Sweden	VHM	West End, Bahamas	WTD
Vilhena, Brazil	BVH	West Wyalong, Australia	WWY
Villa Gesell, Argentina	VLG	Westerland, Germany	GWT
Villa Mercedes, Argentina	VME	Westport, New Zealand	WSZ
Villahermosa, Mexico	VSA	Westray, Scotland, UK	WRY
Villavicencio, Colombia	VVC	Wewak, Papua New Guinea	WWK
Vilnius, Lithuania	VNO	Whakatane, New Zealand	WHK
Vinh City, Vietnam	VII	Whangarei, New Zealand	WRE
Virac, Philippines	VRC	Whyalla, Australia	WYA
Virgin Gorda, BVI	VIJ	Wick, Scotland, UK	WIC
Viru, Solomon Islands	VIU	Wilhelmshaven, Germany	WVN
Visby, Sweden	VBY	Wiluna, Australia	WUN
Vishakhapatnam, India	VTZ	Windhoek (Eros), Namibia	ERS
Vitoria Da Conquista, Brazil	VDC	Windhoek (Intl), Namibia	WDH
Vitoria, Spain	VIT	Windorah, Australia	WNR
Vivigani, Papua New Guinea	VIV	Winton, Australia	WIN
Vladikavkaz, Russia	OGZ	Witu, Papua New Guinea	WIU
Vladivostok, Russia	VVO	Woitape Is., Papua New Guinea	WTP
Vohemar, Madagascar	VOH	Woja, Marshall Islands	WJA
Vojens, Denmark	SKS	Wollogorang, Australia	WLL
Volgograd, Russia	VOG	Woomera, Australia	UMR
Vologda, Russia	VGD	Wotho, Marshall Islands	WTO
Voronezh, Russia	VOZ	Wotje Is., Marshall Islands	WTE

Wroclaw, Poland	WRO	Yining, China	YIN
Wudinna, Australia	WUD	Yiwu, China	YIW
Wuhan, China	WUH	Yogyakarta, Indonesia	JOG
Wuyishan, China	WUS	Yola, Nigeria	YOL
Wuzhou, China	WUZ	Yonago, Japan	YGJ
Wyndham, Australia	WYN	Yonaguni Jima, Japan	OGN
Xayabury, Laos	XAY	Yorke Is., Australia	OKR
Xi An (Xianyang), China	XIY	Yoronjima, Japan	RNJ
Xi An (Xiguan), China	SIA	Yosu, Korea	RSU
Xiamen, China	XMN	Young, Australia	NGA
Xiangfan, China	XFN	Yule Is., Papua New Guinea	RKU
Xichang, China	XIC	Yulin, China	UYN
Xieng Khouang, Laos	XKH	Yurimaguas, Peru	YMS
Xining, China	XNN	Yuzhno-Sakhalinsk, Russia	UUS
Yakushima, Japan	KUM	Zacatecas, Mexico	ZCL
Yakutsk, Russia	YKS	Zadar, Croatia	ZAD
Yalumet, Papua New Guinea	KYX	Zagreb, Croatia	ZAG
Yamagata, Japan	GAJ	Zahedan, Iran	ZAH
Yan'an, China	ENY	Zakinthos Is., Greece	ZTH
Yanbo, Saudi Arabia	YNB	Zamboanga, Philippines	ZAM
Yandina, Solomon Islands	XYA	Zanzibar, Tanzania	ZNZ
Yangon, Myanmar	RGN	Zaporozhye, Ukraine	OZH
Yanji, China	YNJ	Zaragoza, Spain	ZAZ
Yantai, China	YNT	Zhambyl, Kazakstan	ZHA
Yaounde, Cameroon	YAO	Zhanjiang, China	ZHA
Yap, Micronesia	YAP	Zhaotong, China	ZAT
Yapsiei, Papua New Guinea	KPE	Zhengzhou, China	CGO
Yazd, Iran	AZD	Zhezkazgan, Kazakstan	DZN
Yechon, Korea	YEC	Zhob, Pakistan	PZH
Yelimane, Mali	EYL	Zhuhai, China	ZUH
Yerevan, Armenia	EVN	Ziguinchor, Senegal	ZIG
Yibin, China	YBP	Zouerate, Mauritania	OUZ
Yichang, China	YIH	Zurich, Switzerland	ZRH
Yinchuan, China	INC		

Airport Codes

AAA	Anaa, Fr. Polynesia		Argentina
AAC	Al Arish, Egypt	AER	Adler/Sochi, Russia
AAE	Annaba, Algeria	AES	Aalesund, Norway
AAK	Aranuka, Kiribati	AET	Allakaket, AK
AAL	Aalborg, Denmark	AEY	Akureyri, Iceland
AAN	Al Ain, UAE	AFA	San Rafael, Argentina
AAQ	Anapa, Russia	AFL	Alta Floresta, Brazil
AAR	Aarhus, Denmark	AGA	Agadir, Morocco
AAT	Altay, China	AGB	Augsburg, Germany
AAY	Al Ghaydah, Yemen	AGE	Wangerooge, Germany
ABE	Allentown/Bethlehem/	AGF	Agen, France
	Easton, PA	AGH	Helsingborg, Sweden
ABF	Abaiang, Kiribati	AGJ	Aguni, Japan
ABI	Abilene, TX	AGL	Wanigela, Papua New
ABJ	Abidjan, Cote D'lvoire		Guinea
ABL	Ambler, AK	AGN	Angoon, AK
ABM	Bamaga, Australia	AGP	Malaga, Spain
ABQ	Albuquerque, NM	AGR	Agra, India
ABR	Aberdeen, SD	AGS	Augusta, GA
ABS	Abu Simbel, Egypt	AGT	Ciudad Del Este, Paraguay
ABT	Al-Baha, Saudi Arabia	AGU	Aguascalientes, Mexico
ABV	Abuja, Nigeria	AGX	Agatti Island, India
ABX	Albury, Australia	AHB	Abha, Saudi Arabia
ABY	Albany, GA	AHN	Athens, GA
ABZ	Aberdeen, Scotland	AHO	Alghero, Italy
ACA	Acapulco, Mexico	AHS	Ahuas, Honduras
ACC	Accra, Ghana	AHU	Al Hoceima, Morocco
ACE	Lanzarote, Spain	AIA	Alliance, NE
ACH	Altenrhein, Switzerland	AIC	Airok, Marshall Islands
ACI	Alderney, Channel Islands,	AIM	Ailuk, Marshall Islands
	UK	AIN	Wainwright, AK
ACK	Nantucket, MA	AIS	Arorae Is, Kiribati
ACT	Waco, TX	AIT	Aitutaki, Cook Islands
ACV	Eureka/Arcata, CA	AIU	Atiu, Cook Islands
ACY	Atlantic City (Intl), NJ	AIY	Atlantic City, NJ
ADA	Adana, Turkey	AJA	Ajaccio, Corsica, France
ADB	Izmir (Adnan Mend), Turkey	AJF	Jouf, Saudi Arabia
ADD	Addis Ababa, Ethiopia	AJR	Arvidsjaur, Sweden
ADE	Aden, Yemen	AJU	Aracaju, Brazil
ADK	Adak Island, AK	AKB	Atka, AK
ADL	Adelaide, Australia	AKE	Akieni, Gabon
ADQ	Kodiak, AK	AKG	Anguganak, Papua New
ADU	Ardabil, Iran		Guinea
ADZ	San Andres Is., Colombia	AKI	Akiak, AK
AEA	Abemama, Kiribati	AKJ	Asahikawa, Japan
AED	Aleneva, AK	AKK	Akhiok, AK
AEO	Aioun El Atrouss, Mauritania	AKL	Auckland, New Zealand
AEP	Buenos Aires (Newbery),	AKN	King Salmon, AK

AKP	Anaktuvuk, AK	AQI	Qaisumah, Saudi Arabia
AKS	Auki, Solomon Islands	AQJ	Aqaba, Jordan
AKU	Aksu, China	AQP	Arequipa, Peru
AKV	Akulivik, QU	ARC	Arctic Village, AK
AKX	Aktyubinsk, Kazakstan	ARH	Arkhangelsk, Russia
AKY	Sittwe, Myanmar	ARI	Arica, Chile
ALA	Almaty, Kazakstan	ARM	Armidale, Australia
ALB	Albany, NY	ARN	Stockholm (Arlanda), Sweden
ALC	Alicante, Spain	ARP	Aragip, Papua New Guinea
ALF	Alta, Norway	ART	Watertown, NY
ALG	Algiers, Algeria	ARU	Aracatuba, Brazil
ALH	Albany, Australia	ARW	Arad, Romania
ALJ	Alexander Bay, South Africa	ARZ	N'Zeto, Angola
ALM	Alamogordo, NM	ASA	Assab, Eritrea
ALO	Waterloo, IA	ASB	Ashkhabad, Turkmenistan
ALP	Aleppo, Syria	ASC	Ascension, Bolivia
ALS	Alamosa, CO	ASD	Andros Island, Bahamas
ALV	Andorra La Vella, Andorra	ASE	Aspen, CO
ALW	Walla Walla, WA	ASF	Astrakhan, Russia
ALY	Alexandria, Egypt	ASJ	Amami O Shima, Japan
ALZ	Alitak, AK	ASM	Asmara, Eritrea
AMA	Amarillo, TX	ASO	Asosa, Ethiopia
AMD	Ahmedabad, India	ASP	Alice Springs, Australia
AMH	Arba Mintch, Ethiopia	ASR	Kayseri, Turkey
AMI	Mataram, Indonesia	ASU	Asuncion, Paraguay
AMM	Amman, Jordan	ASV	Amboseli, Kenya
AMQ	Ambon, Indonesia	ASW	Aswan, Egypt
AMS	Amsterdam, Netherlands	ATC	Arthur's Town, Bahamas
AMY	Ambatomainty, Madagascar	ATH	Athens, Greece
ANA	Anaheim, CA	ATK	Atqasuk, AK
ANC	Anchorage, AK	ATL	Atlanta, GA
ANF	Antofagasta, Chile	ATM	Altamira, Brazil
ANG	Angouleme, France	ATN	Namatanai, Papua New Guinea
ANI	Aniak, AK	ATP	Aitape, Papua New Guinea
ANK	Ankara, Turkey	ATQ	Amritsar, India
ANM	Antalaha, Madagascar	ATR	Atar, Mauritania
ANR	Antwerp, Belgium	ATT	Atmautluak, AK
ANU	Antigua, West Indies	ATW	Appleton, WI
ANV	Anvik, AK	ATY	Watertown, SD
ANX	Andenes, Norway	AUA	Aruba, Aruba
AOI	Ancona, Italy	AUC	Arauca, Colombia
AOJ	Aomori, Japan	AUG	Augusta, ME
AOK	Karpathos, Greece	AUH	Abu Dhabi, UAE
AOO	Altoona, PA	AUJ	Ambunti, Papua New Guinea
AOR	Alor Setar, Malaysia	AUK	Alakanuk, AK
AOS	Amook, AK	AUL	Aur, Marshall Islands
AOU	Attopeu, Laos	AUP	Agaun, Papua New Guinea
APF	Naples, FL	AUQ	Atuona, Fr. Polynesia
APL	Nampula, Mozambique	AUR	Aurillac, France
APN	Alpena, MI	AUS	Austin, TX
APO	Apartado, Colombia	AUU	Aurukun Mission, Australia
APP	Asapa, Papua New Guinea	AUV	Aumo, Papua New Guinea
APW	Apia, Western Samoa	AUW	Wausau, WI
AQG	Anqing, China		

AUX	Araguaina, Brazil	BCL	Barra Colorado, Costa Rica
AUY	Aneityum, Vanuatu	BCN	Barcelona, Spain
AVI	Ciego De Avila, Cuba	BCO	Jinka, Ethiopa
AVL	Asheville, NC	BCP	Bambu, Papua New Guinea
AVN	Avignon, France	BCX	Beloreck, Russia
AVP	Wilkes-Barre/Scranton, PA	BDA	Hamilton, Bermuda
AVU	Avu Avu, Solomon Islands	BDB	Bundaberg, Australia
AVX	Catalina Island, CA	BDH	Bandar Lengeh, Iran
AWD	Aniwa, Vanatu	BDJ	Banjarmasin, Indonesia
AWZ	Ahwaz, Iran	BDL	Hartford, CT/Springfield, MA
AXA	Anguilla, West Indies	BDO	Bandung, Indonesia
AXD	Alexandroupolis, Greece	BDP	Bhadrapur, Nepal
AXK	Ataq, Yemen	BDQ	Vadodara, India
AXM	Armenia, Colombia	BDR	Bridgeport, CT
AXP	Spring Point, Bahamas	BDS	Brindisi, Italy
AXT	Akita, Japan	BDT	Gbadolite, Zaire
AXU	Axum, Ethiopia	BDU	Bardufoss, Norway
AYK	Arkalyk, Kazakstan	BEB	Benbecula, Scotland, UK
AYP	Ayacucho, Peru	BEF	Bluefields, Nicaragua
AYQ	Ayers Rock, Australia	BEG	Belgrade, Yugoslavia
AYT	Antalya, Turkey	BEH	Benton Harbor, MI
AYU	Aiyura, Papua New Guinea	BEI	Beica, Ethiopia
AZB	Amazon Bay, Papua New Guinea	BEJ	Berau, Indonesia
		BEL	Belem, Brazil
AZD	Yazd, Iran	BEN	Benghazi, Libya
AZN	Andizan, Uzbekistan	BEO	Newcastle (Belmont), Australia
AZO	Kalamazoo, MI		
AZR	Adrar, Algeria	BER	Berlin (Metro), Germany
BAA	Bialla, Papua New Guinea	BES	Brest, France
BAG	Baguio, Philippines	BET	Bethel, AK
BAH	Bahrain, Bahrain	BEU	Bedourie, Australia
BAJ	Bali, Papua New Guinea	BEW	Beira, Mozambique
BAK	Baku, Azerbaijan	BEY	Beirut, Lebanon
BAL	Batman, Turkey	BEZ	Beru, Kiribati
BAQ	Barranquilla, Colombia	BFD	Bradford, PA
BAU	Bauru, Brazil	BFF	Scottsbluff, NE
BAV	Baotou, China	BFG	Bahia Pinas, Panama
BAX	Barnaul, Russia	BFL	Bakersfield, CA
BAY	Baia Mare, Romania	BFN	Bloemfontein, South Africa
BBA	Balmaceda, Chile	BFS	Belfast (Intl), N. Ireland, UK
BBG	Butaritari, Kiribati	BFV	Buri Ram, Thailand
BBI	Bhubaneswar, India	BGA	Bucaramanga, Colombia
BBK	Kasane, Botswana	BGC	Braganca, Portugal
BBM	Battambang, Cambodia	BGF	Bangui, Cen. African Republic
BBN	Bario, Malaysia		
BBO	Berbera, Somalia	BGI	Bridgetown, Barbados
BBQ	Barbuda, West Indies	BGK	Big Creek, Belize
BBR	Basse-Terre, Guadeloupe	BGM	Binghamton, NY
BBU	Bucharest (Baneasa), Romania	BGM	Johnson City, NY
		BGO	Bergen, Norway
BCA	Baracoa, Cuba	BGR	Bangor, ME
BCD	Bacolod, Philippines	BGW	Baghdad, Iraq
BCE	Bryce Canyon, UT	BGX	Bage, RS, Brazil
BCI	Barcaldine, Australia	BGY	Milan (Orio Al Serio), Italy

BHB	Bar Harbor, ME	BLK	Blackpool, England, UK
BHC	Bullhead City, AZ	BLL	Billund, Denmark
BHD	Belfast (City), N. Ireland, UK	BLP	Bellavista, Peru
BHE	Blenheim, New Zealand	BLQ	Bologna, Italy
BHG	Brus Laguna, Honduras	BLR	Bangalore, India
BHH	Bisha, Saudi Arabia	BLT	Blackwater, Australia
BHI	Bahia Blanca, Argentina	BLZ	Blantyre, Malawi
BHJ	Bhuj, India	BMA	Stockolm (Bromma), Sweden
BHK	Bukhara, Uzbekistan	BMB	Bumba, Zaire
BHM	Birmingham, AL	BME	Broome, Australia
BHO	Bhopal, India	BMG	Bloomington, IN
BHQ	Broken Hill, Australia	BMI	Bloomington/Normal, IL
BHR	Bharatpur, Nepal	BMM	Bitam, Gabon
BHS	Bathurst, Australia	BMO	Bhamo, Myanmar
BHU	Bhavnagar, India	BMP	Brampton Is., Australia
BHV	Bahawalpur, Pakistan	BMU	Bima, Indonesia
BHX	Birmingham, England, UK	BMV	Ban Me Thuot, Vietnam
BHY	Beihai, China	BMW	Bordj Badji Mokhtar, Algeria
BHZ	Belo Horizonte (Metro), Brazil	BMY	Belep Is., New Caledonia
		BNA	Nashville, TN
BIA	Bastia, Corsica, France	BNB	Boende, Zaire
BID	Block Island, RI	BND	Bandar Abbas, Iran
BII	Bikini Atoll, Marshall Islands	BNE	Brisbane, Australia
BIK	Biak, Indonesia	BNI	Benin City, Nigeria
BIL	Billings, MT	BNJ	Bonn, Germany
BIM	Bimini, Bahamas	BNK	Ballina, Australia
BIO	Bilbao, Spain	BNN	Bronnoysund, Norway
BIQ	Biarritz, France	BNP	Bannu, Pakistan
BIR	Biratnagar, Nepal	BNU	Blumenau, Brazil
BIS	Bismarck, ND	BNY	Bellona Is., Solomon Islands
BJA	Bejaia, Algeria	BOB	Bora Bora, Fr. Polynesia
BJF	Batsfjord, Norway	BOC	Bocas Del Toro, Panama
BJI	Bemidji, MN	BOD	Bordeaux, France
BJL	Banjul, Gambia	BOG	Bogota, Colombia
BJM	Bujumbura, Burundi	BOH	Bournemouth, England, UK
BJR	Bahar Dar, Ethiopia	BOI	Boise, ID
BJS	Beijing, China	BOJ	Bourgas, Bulgaria
BJX	Leon/Guanajuato, Mexico	BOM	Bombay, India
BJZ	Badajoz, Spain	BON	Bonaire, Neth. Antilles
BKA	Moscow (Bykovo), Russia	BOO	Bodo, Norway
BKC	Buckland, AK	BOS	Boston, MA
BKI	Kota Kinabalu, Malaysia	BOV	Boang, Papua New Guinea
BKK	Bangkok, Thailand	BOX	Borroloola, Australia
BKM	Bakalalan, Malaysia	BPG	Barra Do Garcas, Brazil
BKO	Bamako, Mali	BPN	Balikpapan, Indonesia
BKQ	Blackall, Australia	BPS	Porto Seguro, Brazil
BKS	Bengkulu, Indonesia	BPT	Beaumont, TX
BKW	Beckley, WV	BPY	Besalampy, Madagascar
BLA	Barcelona, Venezuela	BQE	Bubaque, Guinea-Bissau
BLD	Boulder City, NV	BQK	Brunswick, GA
BLE	Borlange, Sweden	BQL	Boulia, Australia
BLF	Bluefield/Princeton, WV	BQN	Aguadilla, PR
BLG	Belaga, Malaysia	BQS	Blagoveschensk, Russia
BLI	Bellingham, WA	BQT	Brest, Belarus

BQU	Port Elizabeth, Windward Islands
BRA	Barreiras, Brazil
BRC	San Carlos de Bariloche, Argentina
BRD	Brainerd, MN
BRE	Bremen, Germany
BRF	Bradford, England, UK
BRI	Bari, Italy
BRK	Bourke, Australia
BRL	Burlington, IA
BRM	Barquisimeto, Venezuela
BRN	Bern, Switzerland
BRO	Brownsville, TX
BRQ	Brno, Czech Rep.
BRR	Barra, Scotland, UK
BRS	Bristol, England, UK
BRT	Bathurst Is., Australia
BRU	Brussels, Belgium
BRW	Barrow, AK
BSA	Bossaso, Somalia
BSB	Brasilia, Brazil
BSC	Bahia Solano, Colombia
BSD	Baoshan, China
BSG	Bata, Equatorial Guinea
BSK	Biskra, Algeria
BSL	Basel, Switzerland/ Mulhouse, France
BSU	Basankusu, Zaire
BTI	Barter Island, AK
BTJ	Banda Aceh, Indonesia
BTK	Bratsk, Russia
BTL	Battle Creek, MI
BTM	Butte, MT
BTR	Baton Rouge, LA
BTS	Bratislava, Slovakia
BTT	Bettles, AK
BTU	Bintulu, Malaysia
BTV	Burlington, VT
BUA	Buka, Papua New Guinea
BUC	Burketown, Australia
BUD	Budapest, Hungary
BUE	Buenos Aires (Metro), Argentina
BUF	Buffalo, NY
BUG	Benguela, Angola
BUH	Bucharest (Metro), Romania
BUK	Albuq, Yemen
BUL	Bulolo, Papua New Guinea
BUO	Burao, Somalia
BUQ	Bulawayo, Zimbabwe
BUR	Burbank, CA
BUS	Batumi, Georgia
BUX	Bunia, Zaire

BUZ	Bushehr, Iran
BVB	Boa Vista, Brazil
BVC	Boa Vista, Cape Verde Islands
BVE	Brive-La-Gaillarde, France
BVG	Berlevag, Norway
BVH	Vilhena, Brazil
BVI	Birdsville, Australia
BVR	Brava, Cape Verde Islands
BWA	Bhairawa, Nepal
BWB	Barrow Island, Australia
BWD	Brownwood, TX
BWI	Baltimore, MD
BWK	Bol, Croatia
BWN	Bandar Seri Begawan, Brunei Darussalam
BWQ	Brewarrina, Australia
BWT	Burnie, Australia
BXH	Balhash, Kazakstan
BXM	Batam, Indonesia
BXN	Bodrum, Turkey
BXU	Butuan, Philippines
BXX	Borama, Somalia
BXZ	Bunsil, Papua New Guinea
BYA	Boundary, AK
BYB	Dibaa, Oman
BYK	Bouake, Cote D'lvoire
BYM	Bayamo, Cuba
BYU	Bayreuth, Germany
BYW	Blakely Island, WA
BZA	Bonanza, Nicaragua
BZE	Belize City, Belize
BZL	Barisal, Bangladesh
BZN	Bozeman, MT
BZR	Beziers, France
BZV	Brazzaville, Congo
BZZ	Brize Norton, England, UK
CAB	Cabinda, Angola
CAC	Cascavel, Brazil
CAE	Columbia, SC
CAG	Cagliari, Italy
CAI	Cairo, Egypt
CAJ	Canaima, Venezuela
CAK	Akron/Canton, OH
CAL	Campbeltown, Scotland, UK
CAN	Guangzhou (Canton), China
CAP	Cap Haitien, Haiti
CAQ	Caucasia, Colombia
CAS	Casablanca (Anfa), Morocco
CAW	Campos, Brazil
CAY	Cayenne, Fr. Guiana
CAZ	Cobar, Australia
CBB	Cochabamba, Bolivia
CBE	Cumberland, MD

CBG	Cambridge, England, UK	CGQ	Changchun, China
CBH	Bechar, Algeria	CGR	Campo Grande, Brazil
CBL	Ciudad Bolivar, Venezuela	CGX	Chicago (Meigs), IL
CBO	Cotabato, Philippines	CGY	Cagayan de Oro, Philippines
CBQ	Calabar, Nigeria	CHA	Chattanooga, TN
CBR	Canberra, Australia	CHC	Christchurch, New Zealand
CCC	Cayo Coco, Cuba	CHG	Chaoyang, China
CCJ	Calicut, India	CHH	Chachapoyas, Peru
CCK	Cocos-Keeling Is., Indian Ocean	CHI	Chicago (Metro), IL
		CHM	Chimbote, Peru
CCM	Crisciuma, Brazil	CHO	Charlottesville, VA
CCP	Concepcion, Chile	CHP	Circle Hot Springs, AK
CCS	Caracas, Venezuela	CHQ	Chania, Crete, Greece
CCU	Calcutta, India	CHS	Charleston, SC
CCV	Craig Cove, Vanuatu	CHT	Chatham Island, New Zealand
CCZ	Chub Cay, Bahamas		
CDB	Cold Bay, AK	CHU	Chuathbaluk, AK
CDC	Cedar City, UT	CHX	Changuinola, Panama
CDG	Paris (De Gaulle), France	CHY	Choiseul Bay, Solomon Islands
CDJ	Conceicao Do Araguaia, Brazil	CIA	Rome (Ciampino), Italy
CDL	Candle, AK	CIC	Chico, CA
CDR	Chadron, NE	CID	Cedar Rapids/Iowa City, IA
CDV	Cordova, AK	CIJ	Cobija, Bolivia
CEB	Cebu, Philippines	CIK	Chalkyitsik, AK
CEC	Crescent City, CA	CIS	Canton Island, Kiribati
CED	Ceduna, Australia	CIT	Shimkent, Kazakstan
CEI	Chiang Rai, Thailand	CIU	Sault Ste. Marie (Chippewa), MI
CEK	Chelyabinsk, Russia		
CEM	Central, AK	CIW	Canouan Is., Windward Islands
CEN	Ciudad Obregon, Mexico		
CEO	Waco Kungo, Angola	CIX	Chiclayo, Peru
CEQ	Cannes, France	CJA	Cajamarca, Peru
CER	Cherbourg, France	CJB	Coimbatore, India
CEZ	Cortez, CO	CJC	Calama, Chile
CFD	Bryan, TX	CJL	Chitral, Pakistan
CFE	Clermont-Ferrand, France	CJS	Ciudad Juarez, Mexico
CFN	Donegal, Ireland	CJU	Cheju, Korea
CFR	Caen, France	CKB	Clarksburg, WV
CFS	Coffs Harbour, Australia	CKD	Crooked Creek, AK
CFU	Kerkyra, Greece	CKG	Chongqing, China
CGA	Craig, AK	CKS	Carajas, Brazil
CGB	Cuiaba, Brazil	CKX	Chicken, AK
CGC	Cape Gloucester, Papua New Guinea	CKY	Conakry, Guinea
		CLD	Carlsbad, CA
CGD	Changde, China	CLE	Cleveland, OH
CGH	Sao Paulo (Congonhas), Brazil	CLJ	Cluj, Romania
		CLL	College Station, TX
CGI	Cape Girardeau, MO	CLM	Port Angeles, WA
CGK	Jakarta (Soekarno), Indonesia	CLO	Cali, Colombia
		CLP	Clarks Point, AK
CGN	Cologne/Bonn, Germany	CLQ	Colima, Mexico
CGO	Zhengzhou, China	CLT	Charlotte, NC
CGP	Chittagong, Bangladesh	CLY	Calvi, Corsica, France

CMA	Cunnamulla, Australia		CRI	Crooked Is., Bahamas
CMB	Colombo, Sri Lanka		CRL	Charleroi, Belgium
CMD	Cootamundra, Australia		CRP	Corpus Christi, TX
CME	Ciudad Del Carmen, Mexico		CRQ	Caravelas, Brazil
CMG	Corumba, Brazil		CRU	Carriacou Is., Grenada
CMH	Columbus, OH		CRV	Crotone, Italy
CMI	Champaign, IL		CRW	Charleston, WV
CMK	Club Makokola, Malawi		CSE	Crested Butte, CO
CMN	Casablanca (Mohamed V), Morocco		CSG	Columbus, GA
			CSI	Casino, Australia
CMP	Santana Do Araguaia, Brazil		CSK	Cap Skirring, Senegal
CMU	Kundiawa, Papua New Guinea		CSU	Santa Cruz Do Sul, Brazil
			CSX	Changsha, China
CMW	Camaguey, Cuba		CTA	Catania, Italy
CMX	Hancock, MI		CTC	Catamarca, Argentina
CNB	Coonamble, Australia		CTD	Chitre, Panama
CND	Constanta, Romania		CTG	Cartagena, Colombia
CNF	Belo Horizonte (Confins), Brazil		CTL	Charleville, Australia
			CTM	Chetumal, Mexico
CNJ	Cloncurry, Australia		CTN	Cooktown, Australia
CNL	Sindal, Denmark		CTS	Sapporo (Chitose), Japan
CNM	Carlsbad, NM		CTU	Chengdu, China
CNO	Chino, CA		CUC	Cucuta, Colombia
CNP	Neerlerit Inaat, Greenland		CUE	Cuenca, Ecuador
CNQ	Corrientes, Argentina		CUG	Orange (Cudal), Australia
CNS	Cairns, Australia		CUJ	Culion, Philippines
CNX	Chiang Mai, Thailand		CUK	Caye Caulker, Belize
CNY	Moab, UT		CUL	Culiacan, Mexico
COC	Concordia, Argentina		CUM	Cumana, Venezuela
COD	Cody, WY		CUN	Cancun, Mexico
COE	Coeur D'Alene, ID		CUQ	Coen, Australia
COG	Condoto, Colombia		CUR	Curaçao, Neth. Antilles
COJ	Coonabarabran, Australia		CUU	Chihuahua, Mexico
COK	Cochin, India		CUW	Cube Cove, AK
COO	Cotonou, Benin		CUY	Cue, Australia
COR	Cordoba, Argentina		CUZ	Cuzco, Peru
COS	Colorado Springs, CO		CVC	Cleve, Australia
COU	Columbia, MO		CVG	Cincinnati, OH
CPB	Capurgana, Colombia		CVL	Cape Vogel, Papua New Guinea
CPC	San Martin de los Andes, Argentina		CVM	Ciudad Victoria, Mexico
CPD	Coober Pedy, Australia		CVN	Clovis, NM
CPE	Campeche, Mexico		CVO	Albany, OR
CPH	Copenhagen, Denmark		CVQ	Carnarvon, Australia
CPI	Cape Orford, Papua New Guinea		CVU	Corvo Island, Portugal
			CWA	Wausau (Wisc. Cntl.), WI
CPO	Copiapo, Chile		CWB	Curitiba, Brazil
CPQ	Campinas, Brazil		CWL	Cardiff, Wales, UK
CPR	Casper, WY		CWR	Cowarie, Australia
CPT	Cape Town, South Africa		CWS	Center Island, WA
CPV	Campina Grande, Brazil		CWT	Cowra, Australia
CPX	Culebra, PR		CXB	Cox's Bazar, Bangladesh
CRD	Comodoro Rivadavia, Argentina		CXI	Christmas Is., Kiribati
			CXJ	Caxias Do Sul, Brazil

CYB	Cayman Brac Is., West Indies	DIJ	Dijon, France
CYF	Chefornak, AK	DIK	Dickenson, ND
CYI	Chiayi, Taiwan	DIL	Dili, Indonesia
CYR	Colonia, Uruguay	DIN	Dien-Bien-Phu, Viet Nam
CYS	Cheyenne, WY	DIO	Diomede Island, AK
CZA	Chichen Itza, Mexico	DIQ	Divinopolis, Brazil
CZE	Coro, Venezuela	DIR	Dire Dawa, Ethiopia
CZH	Corozal, Belize	DIS	Loubomo, Congo
CZL	Constantine, Algeria	DIU	Diu, India
CZM	Cozumel, Mexico	DIY	Diyarbakir, Turkey
CZN	Chisana, AK	DJB	Jambi, Indonesia
CZS	Cruzeiro Do Sul, Brazil	DJE	Djerba, Tunisia
CZX	Changzhou, China	DJG	Djanet, Algeria
DAB	Daytona Beach, FL	DJJ	Jayapura, Indonesia
DAC	Dhaka, Bangladesh	DJN	Delta Junction, AK
DAD	Da Nang, Viet Nam	DKI	Dunk Is., Australia
DAL	Dallas/Ft. Worth (Love), TX	DKR	Dakar, Senegal
DAM	Damascus, Syria	DLA	Douala, Cameroon
DAR	Dar Es Salaam, Tanzania	DLC	Dalian, China
DAU	Daru, Papua New Guinea	DLD	Geilo, Norway
DAV	David, Panama	DLG	Dillingham, AK
DAX	Daxian, China	DLH	Duluth, MN/Superior, WI
DAY	Dayton, OH	DLI	Dalat, Viet Nam
DBA	Dalbandin, Pakistan	DLM	Dalaman, Turkey
DBM	Debra Marcos, Ethiopia	DLO	Dolomi, AK
DBO	Dubbo, Australia	DLU	Dali City, China
DBQ	Dubuque, IA	DLY	Dillons Bay, Vanuatu
DBT	Debra Tabor, Ethiopia	DMD	Doomadgee Mission,
DBV	Dubrovnik, Croatia		Australia
DCA	Washington (National), DC	DME	Moscow (Domodedovo),
DCF	Dominica (Cane), West Indies		Russia
DCM	Castres, France	DMN	Deming, NM
DDC	Dodge City, KS	DMU	Dimapur, India
DDG	Dandong, China	DND	Dundee, Scotland, UK
DDI	Daydream Is., Australia	DNH	Dunhuang, China
DDM	Dodoima, Papua New Guinea	DNK	Dnepropetrovsk, Ukraine
DEA	Dera Ghazi Khan, Pakistan	DNM	Denham, Australia
DEC	Decatur, IL	DNR	Dinard, France
DEL	Delhi, India	DNZ	Denizli, Turkey
DEM	Dembidollo, Ethiopia	DOB	Dobo, Indonesia
DEN	Denver, CO	DOF	Dora Bay, AK
DER	Derim, Papua New Guinea	DOG	Dongola, Sudan
DET	Detroit (City), MI	DOK	Donetsk, Ukraine
DEZ	Deirezzor, Syria	DOL	Deauville, France
DFW	Dallas/Ft. Worth (Intl), TX	DOM	Dominica, West Indies
DGA	Dangriga, Belize	DOP	Dolpa, Nepal
DGE	Mudgee, Australia	DOU	Dourados, Brazil
DGO	Durango, Mexico	DPL	Dipolog, Philippines
DGT	Dumaguete, Philippines	DPO	Devonport, Australia
DHA	Dhahran, Saudi Arabia	DPS	Denpasar, Indonesia
DHI	Dhangarhi, Nepal	DRB	Derby, Australia
DHN	Dothan, AL	DRG	Deering, AK
DIB	Dibrugarh, India	DRO	Durango, CO
DIE	Antsiranana, Madagascar	DRS	Dresden, Germany

DRT	Del Rio, TX		EIS	Beef Island, BVI
DRW	Darwin, Australia		EJA	Barrancabermeja, Colombia
DSD	La Desirade, Guadeloupe		EJH	Wedjh, Saudi Arabia
DSE	Dessie, Ethiopia		EKB	Ekibastuz, Kazakstan
DSK	Dera Ismail Khan, Pakistan		EKO	Elko, NV
DSM	Des Moines, IA		ELD	El Dorado, AR
DTM	Dortmund, Germany		ELE	El Real, Panama
DTR	Decatur Island, WA		ELG	El Golea, Algeria
DTT	Detroit (Metro), MI		ELH	North Eleuthera, Bahamas
DTW	Detroit (Wayne Cty), MI		ELI	Elim, AK
DUB	Dublin, Ireland		ELM	Elmira/Corning, NY
DUD	Dunedin, New Zealand		ELP	El Paso, TX
DUE	Dundo, Angola		ELQ	Gassim, Saudi Arabia
DUJ	DuBois, PA		ELS	East London, South Africa
DUR	Durban, South Africa		ELU	El Oued, Algeria
DUS	Duesseldorf, Germany		ELV	Elfin Cove, AK
DUT	Dutch Harbor, AK		ELY	Ely, NV
DVL	Devils Lake, ND		EMA	East Midlands, England, UK
DVN	Davenport, IA		EMI	Emirau, Papua New Guinea
DVO	Davao, Philippines		EMK	Emmonak, AK
DXB	Dubai, UAE		EMN	Nema, Mauritania
DYG	Dayong, China		EMO	Emo, Papua New Guinea
DYR	Anadyr, Russia		EMS	Embessa, Papua New Guinea
DYU	Dushanbe, Tajikistan		ENA	Kenai, AK
DZA	Dzaoudzi, Mayotte		ENF	Enontekio, Finland
DZN	Zhezkazgan, Kazakstan		ENS	Enschede, Netherlands
EAA	Eagle, AK		ENT	Enewetok, Marshall Islands
EAE	Emae, Vanuatu		ENU	Enugu, Nigeria
EAM	Nejran, Saudi Arabia		ENY	Yan'an, China
EAS	San Sebastian, Spain		EOH	Medellin (Herrera), Colombia
EAT	Wenatchee, WA		EPL	Epinal, France
EAU	Eau Claire, WI		EPR	Esperance, Australia
EBA	Elba Is., Italy		EQS	Esquel, Argentina
EBB	Entebbe/Kampala, Uganda		ERA	Erigavo, Somalia
EBJ	Esbjerg, Denmark		ERC	Erzincan, Turkey
EBO	Ebon, Marshall Islands		ERD	Berdyansk, Ukraine
EBU	St. Etienne, France		ERF	Erfurt, Germany
ECN	Ercan, Cyprus		ERH	Errachidia, Morocco
EDA	Edna Bay, AK		ERI	Erie, PA
EDI	Edinburgh, Scotland, UK		ERM	Erechim, Brazil
EDR	Edward River, Australia		ERS	Windhoek (Eros), Namibia
EEK	Eek, AK		ERZ	Erzurum, Turkey
EEN	Keene, NH/Brattleboro, VT		ESA	Esa'Ala, Papua New Guinea
EFD	Houston (Ellington), TX		ESB	Ankara (Esenboga), Turkey
EFL	Kefallinia, Greece		ESC	Escanaba, MI
EGC	Bergerac, France		ESD	Eastsound, WA
EGE	Vail (Eagle County), CO		ESF	Alexandria, LA
EGL	Neghelli, Ethiopia		ESL	Elista, Russia
EGM	Sege, Solomon Islands		ESM	Esmeraldas, Ecuador
EGS	Egilsstadir, Iceland		ESR	El Salvador, Chile
EGX	Egegik, AK		ESS	Essen, Germany
EHM	Cape Newenham, AK		ETH	Elat, Israel
EIA	Eia, Papua New Guinea		ETZ	Metz/Nancy, France
EIN	Eindhoven, Netherlands		EUA	Eua, Tonga

EUG	Eugene, OR	FLA	Florencia, Colombia
EUN	Laayoune, Morocco	FLG	Flagstaff, AZ
EUX	St. Eustatius, Neth. Antilles	FLI	Flateyri, Iceland
EVE	Evenes, Norway	FLL	Fort Lauderdale, FL
EVG	Sveg, Sweden	FLN	Florianopolis, Brazil
EVN	Yerevan, Armenia	FLO	Florence, SC
EVV	Evansville, IN	FLR	Florence, Italy
EWB	Fall River/New Bedford, MA	FLS	Flinders Is., Australia
EWN	New Bern, NC	FLT	Flat, AK
EWR	Newark, NJ/New York, NY	FMA	Formosa, Argentina
EXI	Excursion Inlet, AK	FMI	Kalemie, Zaire
EXT	Exeter, England, UK	FMN	Farmington, NM
EYL	Yelimane, Mali	FMO	Muenster, Germany
EYP	El Yopal, Colombia	FMY	Fort Myers, FL
EYW	Key West, FL	FNA	Freetown, Sierra Leone
EZE	Buenos Aires (Pistarini),	FNC	Funchal, Portugal
	Argentina	FNE	Fane, Papua New Guinea
EZS	Elazig, Turkey	FNI	Nimes, France
FAE	Faroe Islands, Denmark	FNJ	Pyongyang, N. Korea
FAI	Fairbanks, AK	FNL	Fort Collins/Loveland, CO
FAJ	Fajardo, PR	FNT	Flint, MI
FAK	False Island, AK	FOC	Fuzhou, China
FAN	Farsund, Norway	FOD	Fort Dodge, IA
FAO	Faro, Portugal	FOR	Fortaleza, Brazil
FAQ	Freida River, Papua New	FPO	Freeport, Bahamas
	Guinea	FRA	Frankfurt, Germany
FAR	Fargo, ND	FRB	Forbes, Australia
FAT	Fresno, CA	FRC	Franca, Brazil
FAV	Fakarava, Fr. Polynesia	FRD	Friday Harbor, WA
FAY	Fayetteville, NC	FRE	Fera Is., Solomon Islands
FBE	Francisco Beltrao, Brazil	FRG	Farmingdale (Republic), NY
FBM	Lubumbashi, Zaire	FRO	Floro, Norway
FBU	Oslo (Fornebu), Norway	FRS	Flores, Guatemala
FCA	Kalispell/Glacier Natl Pk,	FRU	Bishkek, Kyrgyzstan
	MT	FRW	Francistown, Botswana
FCO	Rome (Fiumicino), Italy	FSC	Figari, France
FDE	Forde, Norway	FSD	Sioux Falls, SD
FDF	Fort De France, Martinique	FSM	Fort Smith, AR
FDH	Friedrichshafen, Germany	FSP	St. Pierre, St. Pierre and
FEG	Fergana, Uzbekistan		Miquelon
FEN	Fernando de Noronha, Brazil	FTA	Futuna Island, Vanuatu
FEZ	Fez, Morocco	FTU	Fort Dauphin, Madagascar
FGI	Apia (Fagali I.), Western	FTX	Owando, Congo
	Samoa	FUE	Fuerteventura, Spain
FHU	Fort Huachuca/Sierra Vista,	FUJ	Fukue, Japan
	AZ	FUK	Fukuoka, Japan
FID	Fishers Island, NY	FUN	Funafuti Atol, Tuvalu
FIH	Kinshasa, Zaire	FUT	Futuna, Wallis & Futuna Is.
FIN	Finschhafen, Papua New	FWA	Fort Wayne, IN
	Guinea	FYU	Fort Yukon, AK
FJR	Al-Fujairah, UAE	FYV	Fayetteville, AR
FKI	Kisangani, Zaire	GAJ	Yamagata, Japan
FKL	Franklin, PA	GAL	Galena, AK
FKS	Fukushima, Japan	GAM	Gambell, AK

GAN	Gan Island, Maldives	GIG	Rio de Janeriro (Intl), Brazil
GAO	Guantanamo, Cuba	GIL	Gilgit, Pakistan
GAQ	Gao, Mali	GIS	Gisborne, New Zealand
GAR	Garaina, Papua New Guinea	GIZ	Gizan, Saudi Arabia
GAU	Gauhati, India	GJA	Guanaja, Honduras
GAX	Gamba, Gabon	GJL	Jijel, Algeria
GAZ	Guasopa, Papua New Guinea	GJT	Grand Junction, CO
GBD	Great Bend, KS	GKA	Goroka, Papua New Guinea
GBE	Gaborone, Botswana	GKL	Great Keppel Is., Australia
GBI	Grand Bahama Island, Bahamas	GLA	Glasgow, Scotland, UK
		GLF	Golfito, Costa Rica
GBJ	Marie Galante, Fr. Antilles	GLH	Greenville, MS
GCC	Gillette, WY	GLI	Glen Innes, Australia
GCI	Guernsey, Channel Islands, UK	GLT	Gladstone, Australia
		GLV	Golovin, AK
GCK	Garden City, KS	GMA	Gemena, Zaire
GCM	Grand Cayman, Cayman Islands	GMB	Gambela, Ethiopia
		GMI	Gasmata Is., Papua New Guinea
GCN	Grand Canyon, AZ		
GDE	Gode/Iddidole, Ethiopia	GMR	Gambier Is., Fr. Polynesia
GDL	Guadalajara, Mexico	GNB	Grenoble, France
GDN	Gdansk, Poland	GND	Grenada, Windward Islands
GDQ	Gondar, Ethiopia	GNM	Guanambi, Brazil
GDT	Grand Turk Is., Turks & Caicos	GNR	General Roca, Argentina
		GNU	Goodnews Bay, AK
GDV	Glendive, MT	GNV	Gainesville, FL
GDX	Magadan, Russia	GOA	Genoa, Italy
GDZ	Gelendzik, Russia	GOB	Goba, Ethiopia
GEA	Noumea (Magenta), New Caledonia	GOC	Gora, Papua New Guinea
		GOE	Gonalia, Papua New Guinea
GEG	Spokane, WA	GOH	Nuuk, Greenland
GEL	Santo Angelo, Brazil	GOI	Goa, India
GEN	Oslo (Gardermoen), Norway	GOJ	Nizhniy Novgorod, Russia
GEO	Georgetown, Guyana	GOM	Goma, Zaire
GER	Nueva Gerona, Cuba	GON	New London/Groton, CT
GES	General Santos, Philippines	GOQ	Golmud, China
GET	Geraldton, Australia	GOR	Gore, Ethiopia
GEV	Gallivare, Sweden	GOT	Gothenburg, Sweden
GEW	Gewoya, Papua New Guinea	GOV	Gove, Australia
GFF	Griffith, Australia	GPA	Patras, Greece
GFK	Grand Forks, ND	GPI	Guapi, Colombia
GFN	Grafton, Australia	GPN	Garden Point, Australia
GGG	Gladewater/Kilgore/ Longview, TX	GPT	Gulfport/Biloxi, MS
		GPZ	Grand Rapids, MN
GGT	George Town, Bahamas	GRB	Green Bay, WI
GGW	Glasgow, MT	GRI	Grand Island, NE
GHA	Ghardaia, Algeria	GRJ	George, South Africa
GHB	Governors Harbour, Bahamas	GRL	Garasa, Papua New Guinea
		GRP	Gurupi, Brazil
GHC	Great Harbour Cay, Bahamas	GRQ	Groningen, Netherlands
		GRR	Grand Rapids, MI
GHD	Ghimbi, Ethiopia	GRU	Sao Paulo (Guarulhos), Brazil
GHE	Garachine, Panama		
GIB	Gibraltar, Gibraltar	GRW	Graciosa Is., Portugal

GRX	Granada, Spain	HAV	Havana, Cuba
GRZ	Graz, Austria	HBA	Hobart, Australia
GSA	Long Pasia, Malaysia	HBG	Hattiesburg, MS
GSO	Greensboro/H.Pt/Win-Salem,	HBH	Hobart Bay, AK
	NC	HBI	Harbour Island, Bahamas
GSP	Greenville/Spartanburg, SC	HBT	Hafr Albatin, Saudi Arabia
GST	Gustavus, AK	HCR	Holy Cross, AK
GTE	Groote Is., Australia	HDB	Heidelberg, Germany
GTF	Great Falls, MT	HDD	Hyderabad, Pakistan
GTN	Mount Cook (Glentanner),	HDF	Heringsdorf, Germany
	New Zealand	HDS	Hoedspruit, South Africa
GTO	Gorontalo, Indonesia	HDY	Hat Yai, Thailand
GTR	Columbus/Strkvl/W. Pt., MS	HEH	Heho, Myanmar
GUA	Guatemala City, Guatemala	HEK	Heihe, China
GUB	Guerrero Negro, Mexico	HEL	Helsinki, Finland
GUC	Gunnison, CO	HER	Heraklion, Greece
GUD	Goundam, Mali	HET	Hohhot, China
GUH	Gunnedah, Australia	HFA	Haifa, Israel
GUM	Guam, GU	HFD	Hartford, CT/Springfield,MA
GUP	Gallup, NM	HFE	Hefei, China
GUR	Alotau, Papua New Guinea	HFN	Hornafjordur, Iceland
GUW	Atyrau, Kazakstan	HFS	Hagfors, Sweden
GUZ	Guarapari, Brazil	HFT	Hammerfest, Norway
GVA	Geneva, Switzerland	HGA	Hargeisa, Somalia
GVI	Green River, Papua New	HGD	Hughenden, Australia
	Guinea	HGH	Hangzhou, China
GVR	Governador Valadares, Brazil	HGL	Helgoland, Germany
GVX	Gavle, Sweden	HGN	Mae Hong Son, Thailand
GWD	Gwadar, Pakistan	HGO	Korhogo, Cote D'Ivoire
GWL	Gwalior, India	HGR	Hagerstown, MD
GWT	Westerland, Germany	HGU	Mount Hagen, Papua New
GWY	Galway, Ireland		Guinea
GXF	Seiyun, Yemen	HHA	Huanghua, China
GYA	Guayaramerin, Bolivia	HHH	Hilton Head Island, SC
GYE	Guayaquil, Ecuador	HHN	Hahn, Germany
GYM	Guaymas, Mexico	HHQ	Hua Hin, Thailand
GYN	Goiania, Brazil	HIB	Hibbing/Chisolm, MN
GZM	Gozo, Malta	HII	Lake Havasu City, AZ
GZO	Gizo, Solomon Islands	HIJ	Hiroshima, Japan
GZT	Gaziantep, Turkey	HIL	Shillavo, Ethiopia
HAA	Hasvik, Norway	HIN	Chinju, Korea
HAC	Hachijo Jima, Japan	HIR	Honiara, Solomon Islands
HAD	Halmstad, Sweden	HIS	Hayman Is., Australia
HAE	Havasupai, AZ	HJR	Khajuraho, India
HAH	Moroni (Hahaya), Comoros	HKB	Healy Lake, AK
HAJ	Hanover, Germany	HKD	Hakodate, Japan
HAK	Haikou, China	HKG	Hong Kong, Hong Kong
HAM	Hamburg, Germany	HKK	Hokitika, New Zealand
HAN	Hanoi, Viet Nam	HKN	Hoskins, Papua New Guinea
HAP	Long Is., Australia	HKT	Phuket, Thailand
HAQ	Hanimaadhoo, Maldives	HKY	Hickory, NC
HAR	Harrisburg, PA	HLD	Hailar, China
HAS	Hail, Saudi Arabia	HLF	Hultsfred, Sweden
HAU	Haugesund, Norway	HLG	Wheeling, WV

HLN	Helena, MT	HUS	Hughes, AK
HLP	Jakarta (Halim), Indonesia	HUU	Huanuco, Peru
HLZ	Hamilton, New Zealand	HUV	Hudiksvall, Sweden
HMA	Malmo (City Hvc), Sweden	HUX	Huatulco, Mexico
HME	Hassi Messaoud, Algeria	HUY	Humberside, England, UK
HMO	Hermosillo, Mexico	HVB	Hervey Bay, Australia
HMV	Hemavan, Sweden	HVG	Honningsvag, Norway
HNA	Morioka, Japan	HVN	New Haven, CT
HND	Tokyo (Haneda), Japan	HVR	Havre, MT
HNH	Hoonah, AK	HWN	Hwange Nat'l Park,
HNL	Honolulu (Oahu) HI		Zimbabwe
HNM	Hana, Maui, HI	HXX	Hay, Australia
HNS	Haines, AK	HYA	Hyannis, MA
HOB	Hobbs, NM	HYD	Hyderabad, India
HOD	Hodeidah, Yemen	HYF	Hayfield, Papua New Guinea
HOE	Houeisay, Laos	HYG	Hydaburg, AK
HOF	Hofuf, Saudi Arabia	HYL	Hollis, AK
HOG	Holguin, Cuba	HYN	Huangyan, China
HOI	Hao Is., Fr. Polynesia	HYS	Hays, KS
HOK	Hooker Creek, Australia	HZG	Hanzhong, China
HOM	Homer, AK	HZK	Husavik, Iceland
HON	Huron, SD	IAD	Washington (Dulles), DC
HOQ	Hof, Germany	IAH	Houston (Intercontinental),
HOR	Horta, Portugal		TX
HOS	Chos Malal, Argentina	IAM	In Amenas, Algeria
HOT	Hot Springs, AR	IAN	Kiana, AK
HOU	Houston (Hobby), TX	IAS	Iasi, Romania
HOV	Orsta-Volda, Norway	IBE	Ibague, Colombia
HPA	Ha'apai, Tonga	IBI	Iboki, Papua New Guinea
HPB	Hooper Bay, AK	IBZ	Ibiza, Spain
HPH	Haiphong, Viet Nam	ICI	Cicia, Fiji
HPN	White Plains, NY	ICT	Wichita, KS
HPV	Princeville, Kauai, HI	IDA	Idaho Falls, ID
HRB	Harbin, China	IDB	Idre, Sweden
HRE	Harare, Zimbabwe	IDN	Indagen, Papua New Guinea
HRG	Hurghada, Egypt	IDR	Indore, India
HRK	Kharkov, Ukraine	IEV	Kiev (Metro), Ukraine
HRL	Harlingen, TX	IFJ	Isafjordur, Iceland
HRO	Harrison, AR	IFN	Isfahan, Iran
HSH	Las Vegas (Henderson), NV	IFO	Ivano-Frankovsk, Ukraine
HSL	Huslia, AK	IGA	Inagua, Bahamas
HSV	Huntsville/Decatur, AL	IGG	Igiugig, AK
HTA	Chita, Russia	IGL	Izmir (Cigli), Turkey
HTI	Hamilton Is., Australia	IGM	Kingman, AZ
HTN	Hotan, China	IGO	Chigorodo, Colombia
HTO	East Hampton, NY	IGR	Iguazu, Argentina
HTR	Hateruma, Japan	IGU	Iguassu Falls, Brazil
HTS	Huntington, WV/Ashland,	IHU	Ihu, Papua New Guinea
	KY	IIA	Inishmaan, Ireland
HUE	Humera, Ethiopia	IIS	Nissan Is., Papua New
HUF	Terre Haute, IN		Guinea
HUH	Huahine Is., Fr. Polynesia	IKI	Iki, Japan
HUI	Hue, Viet Nam	IKO	Nikolski, AK
HUN	Hualien, Taiwan	IKT	Irkutsk, Russia

ILE	Killeen, TX	IST	Istanbul, Turkey
ILG	Wilmington, DE	ITB	Itaituba, Brazil
ILI	Iliamna, AK	ITH	Ithaca, NY
ILM	Wilmington, NC	ITK	Itokama, Papua New Guinea
ILO	Iloilo, Philippines	ITM	Osaka (Itami), Japan
ILP	Ile Des Pins, New Caledonia	ITN	Itabuna, Brazil
ILQ	Ilo, Peru	ITO	Hilo, Hawaii, HI
ILY	Islay, Scotland, UK	IUE	Niue Island, Niue
IMF	Imphal, India	IVA	Ambanja, Madagascar
IMI	Ine, Marshall Islands	IVC	Invercargill, New Zealand
IMK	Simikot, Nepal	IVL	Ivalo, Finland
IMP	Imperatriz, Brazil	IVR	Inverell, Australia
IMT	Iron Mountain, MI	IWD	Ironwood, MI
INC	Yinchuan, China	IWJ	Iwami, Japan
IND	Indianapolis, IN	IXA	Agartala, India
INL	Int'l Falls, MN	IXB	Bagdogra, India
INN	Innsbruck, Austria	IXC	Chandigarh, India
INQ	Inisheer, Ireland	IXE	Mangalore, India
INT	Winston-Salem (Smith-	IXI	Lilabari, India
	Reynolds), NC	IXJ	Jammu, India
INU	Nauru Is., Rep. of Nauru	IXK	Keshad, India
INV	Inverness, Scotland, UK	IXL	Leh, India
INZ	In Salah, Algeria	IXM	Madurai, India
IOA	Ioannina, Greece	IXR	Ranchi, India
IOK	Iokea, Papua New Guinea	IXS	Silchar, India
IOM	Isle of Man, UK	IXU	Aurangabad, India
ION	Impfondol, Congo	IXY	Kandla, India
IOP	Ioma, Papua New Guinea	IXZ	Port Blair, India
IOR	Inishmore, Ireland	IYK	Inyokern, CA
IOS	Ilheus, Brazil	IZM	Izmir (Metro), Turkey
IOW	Iowa City, IA	IZO	Izumo, Japan
IPA	Ipota, Vanuatu	JAC	Jackson Hole, WY
IPC	Easter Island, Chile	JAG	Jacobabad, Pakistan
IPH	Ipoh, Malaysia	JAI	Jaipur, India
IPI	Ipiales, Colombia	JAN	Jackson, MS
IPL	El Centro/Imperial, CA	JAQ	Jacquinot Bay, Papua New
IPN	Ipatinga, Brazil		Guinea
IPT	Williamsport, PA	JAT	Jabot, Marshall Islands
IQM	Qiemo, China	JAV	Ilulissat, Greenland
IQQ	Iquique, Chile	JAX	Jacksonville, FL
IQT	Iquitos, Peru	JBR	Jonesboro, AR
IRA	Kirakira, Solomon Islands	JCB	Joacaba, Brazil
IRC	Circle, AK	JCK	Julia Creek, Australia
IRG	Lockhart River, Australia	JDF	Juiz De Fora, Brazil
IRJ	La Rioja, Argentina	JDH	Jodhpur, India
IRK	Kirksville, MO	JDO	Juazeiro Do Norte, Brazil
IRP	Isiro, Zaire	JDZ	Jingdezhen, China
ISA	Mount. Isa, Australia	JED	Jeddah, Saudi Arabia
ISB	Islamabad, Pakistan	JEF	Jefferson City, MO
ISC	Isles of Scilly (St. Marys), UK	JEJ	Jeh, Marshall Islands
ISG	Ishigaki, Japan	JER	Jersey, Channel Islands, UK
ISN	Williston, ND	JFK	New York (Kennedy), NY
ISO	Kinston, NC	JFR	Paamiut, Greenland
ISP	Islip (Macarthur), NY	JGA	Jamnagar, India

JGB	Jagdalpur, India	JUJ	Jujuy, Argentina
JGR	Groennedal, Greenland	JUL	Juliaca, Peru
JHB	Johor Bahru, Malaysia	JUM	Jumla, Nepal
JHG	Jinghong, China	JUV	Upernavik, Greenland
JHM	Kapalua, Maui, HI	JUZ	Juzhou, China
JHQ	Shute Harbour, Australia	JVA	Ankavandra, Madagascar
JHW	Jamestown, NY	JYV	Jyvaskyla, Finland
JIB	Djibouti, Djibouti	KAB	Kariba, Zimbabwe
JIK	Ikaria Island, Greece	KAC	Kameshli, Syria
JIL	Jilin, China	KAD	Kaduna, Nigeria
JIM	Jimma, Ethiopia	KAE	Kake, AK
JIU	Jiujiang, China	KAG	Kangnung, Korea
JIW	Jiwani, Pakistan	KAJ	Kajaani, Finland
JJI	Juanjui, Peru	KAL	Kaltag, AK
JKG	Jonkoping, Sweden	KAN	Kano, Nigeria
JKH	Chios, Greece	KAO	Kuusamo, Finland
JKR	Janakpur, Nepal	KAT	Kaitaia, New Zealand
JKT	Jakarta (Metro), Indonesia	KAW	Kawthaung, Myanmar
JLN	Joplin, MO	KAX	Kalbarri, Australia
JMK	Mikonos, Greece	KBC	Birch Creek, AK
JMO	Jomsom, Nepal	KBL	Kabul, Afghanistan
JMS	Jamestown, ND	KBM	Kabwum, Papua New Guinea
JMU	Jiamusi, China	KBP	Kiev (Borispol), Ukraine
JNB	Johannesburg, South Africa	KBR	Kota Bharu, Malaysia
JNN	Nanortalik, Greenland	KBT	Kaben, Marshall Islands
JNS	Narsaq, Greenland	KCA	Kuqa, China
JNU	Juneau, AK	KCC	Coffman Cove, AK
JNX	Naxos, Greece	KCH	Kuching, Malaysia
JNZ	Jinzhou, China	KCL	Chignik, AK
JOE	Joensuu, Finland	KCM	Kahramanmaras, Turkey
JOG	Yogyakarta, Indonesia	KCZ	Kochi, Japan
JOI	Joinville, Brazil	KDD	Khuzdar, Pakistan
JON	Johnston Island, Pacific Ocean	KDI	Kendari, Indonesia
		KDM	Kaadedhdhoo, Maldives
JOS	Jos, Nigeria	KDO	Kadhdhoo, Maldives
JPA	Joao Pessoa, Brazil	KDR	Kandrian, Papua New Guinea
JPR	Ji-Parana, Brazil		
JQE	Jaque, Panama	KDU	Skardu, Pakistan
JRA	New York (W30th St. H/P), NY	KDV	Kandavu, Fiji
		KEF	Reykjavik (Keflavik), Iceland
JRB	New York (Dntwn H/P), NY	KEH	Kenmore Air Harbor, WA
JRE	New York (E60th St H/P), NY	KEJ	Kemerovo, Russia
JRH	Jorhat, India	KEK	Ekwok, AK
JRO	Kilimanjaro, Tanzania	KEL	Kiel, Germany
JRS	Jerusalem, Israel	KEM	Kemi/Tornio, Finland
JSH	Sitia, Greece	KEP	Nepalganj, Nepal
JSI	Skiathos, Greece	KER	Kerman, Iran
JSR	Jessore, Bangladesh	KET	Kengtung, Myanmar
JST	Johnstown, PA	KEX	Kanabea, Papua New Guinea
JSU	Sukkertoppen, Greenland	KFA	Kiffa, Mauritania
JSY	Syros, Greece	KFG	Kalkurung, Australia
JSZ	St. Tropez, France	KFP	False Pass, AK
JTR	Thira, Greece	KGA	Kananga, Zaire
JTY	Astypalaia Is., Greece	KGB	Konge, Papua New Guinea

KGC	Kingscote, Australia	KMA	Kerema, Papua New Guinea
KGD	Kaliningrad, Russia	KMF	Kamina, Papua New Guinea
KGE	Kagau, Solomon Islands	KMG	Kunming, China
KGF	Karaganda, Kazakstan	KMI	Miyazaki, Japan
KGI	Kalgoorlie, Australia	KMJ	Kumamoto, Japan
KGL	Kigali, Rwanda	KMO	Manokotak, AK
KGO	Kirovograd, Ukraine	KMP	Keetmanshoop, Namibia
KGS	Kos, Greece	KMQ	Komatsu, Japan
KGX	Grayling, AK	KMV	Kalemyo, Myanmar
KHG	Kashi, China	KMY	Moser Bay, AK
KHH	Kaohsiung, Taiwan	KND	Kindu, Zaire
KHI	Karachi, Pakistan	KNH	Kinmen, Taiwan
KHM	Khamti, Myanmar	KNK	Kakhonak, AK
KHN	Nanchang, China	KNQ	Kone, New Caledonia
KHS	Khasab, Oman	KNS	King Is., Australia
KHV	Khabarovsk, Russia	KNW	New Stuyahok, AK
KIB	Ivanof Bay, AK	KNX	Kununurra, Australia
KID	Kristianstad, Sweden	KNZ	Kenieba, Mali
KIF	Kingfisher Lake, OT	KOA	Kona, Hawaii, HI
KIJ	Niigata, Japan	KOC	Koumac, New Caledonia
KIM	Kimberley, South Africa	KOE	Kupang, Indonesia
KIN	Kingston, Jamaica	KOI	Kirkwall, Scotland, UK
KIO	Kili Is., Marshall Islands	KOJ	Kagoshima, Japan
KIQ	Kira, Papua New Guinea	KOK	Kokkola/Pietarsaari, Finland
KIR	Kerry County, Ireland	KOP	Nakhon Phanom, Thailand
KIS	Kisumu, Kenya	KOS	Sihanoukville, Cambodia
KIT	Kithira, Greece	KOT	Kotlik, AK
KIV	Kishinev, Moldova	KOU	Koulamoutou, Gabon
KIX	Osaka/Kyoto (Kansai), Japan	KOV	Kokshetau, Kazakstan
KJA	Krasnoyarsk, Russia	KOW	Ganzhou, China
KJP	Kerama, Japan	KOY	Olga Bay, AK
KKA	Koyuk, AK	KOZ	Ouzinkie, AK
KKB	Kitoi Bay, AK	KPB	Point Baker, AK
KKC	Khon Kaen, Thailand	KPC	Port Clarence, AK
KKD	Kokoda, Papua New Guinea	KPE	Yapsiei, Papua New Guinea
KKE	Kerikeri, New Zealand	KPI	Kapit, Malaysia
KKH	Kongiganak, AK	KPK	Parks, AK
KKI	Akiachak, AK	KPN	Kipnuk, AK
KKJ	Kita Kyushu, Japan	KPO	Pohang, Korea
KKN	Kirkenes, Norway	KPR	Port Williams, AK
KKR	Kaukura Atoll, Fr. Polynesia	KPS	Kempsey, Australia
KKU	Ekuk, AK	KPV	Perryville, AK
KKX	Kikaiga Shima, Japan	KPY	Port Bailey, AK
KKZ	Koh Kong, Cambodia	KQA	Akutan, AK
KLG	Kalskag, AK	KRB	Karumba, Australia
KLL	Levelock, AK	KRF	Kramfors, Sweden
KLN	Larsen Bay, AK	KRI	Kikori, Papua New Guinea
KLO	Kalibo, Philippines	KRJ	Karawari, Papua New Guinea
KLR	Kalmar, Sweden		
KLT	Kaiserslauter, Germany	KRK	Krakow, Poland
KLU	Klagenfurt, Austria	KRL	Korla, China
KLW	Klawock, AK	KRN	Kiruna, Sweden
KLX	Kalamata, Greece	KRP	Karup, Denmark
KLZ	Kleinzee, South Africa	KRR	Krasnodar, Russia

KRS	Kristiansand, Norway	KWM	Kowanyama, Australia
KRT	Khartoum, Sudan	KWN	Quinhagak, AK
KRW	Krasnowodsk, Turkmenistan	KWO	Kawito, Papua New Guinea
KRY	Karamay, China	KWP	West Point, AK
KSA	Kosrae, Micronesia	KWT	Kwethluk, AK
KSC	Kosice, Slovakia	KWY	Kiwayu, Kenya
KSD	Karlstad, Sweden	KXA	Kasaan, AK
KSH	Kermanshah, Iran	KXF	Koro, Fiji
KSJ	Kasos Island, Greece	KYA	Konya, Turkey
KSM	St. Mary's, AK	KYK	Karluk, AK
KSN	Kostanay, Kazakstan	KYP	Kyaukpyu, Myanmar
KSO	Kastoria, Greece	KYS	Kayes, Mali
KSQ	Karshi, Uzbekistan	KYU	Koyukuk, AK
KSU	Kristiansund, Norway	KYX	Yalumet, Papua New Guinea
KSY	Kars, Turkey	KZB	Zachar Bay, AK
KTA	Karratha, Australia	KZF	Kaintiba, Papua New Guinea
KTB	Thorne Bay, AK	KZI	Kozani, Greece
KTD	Kitadaito, Japan	KZN	Kazan, Russia
KTE	Kerteh, Malaysia	KZO	Kyzl Orda, Kazakstan
KTM	Kathmandu, Nepal	KZS	Kastelorizo, Greece
KTN	Ketchikan, AK	LAB	Lablab, Papua New Guinea
KTP	Kingston (Tinson), Jamaica	LAD	Luanda, Angola
KTR	Katherine, Australia	LAE	Lae, Papua New Guinea
KTS	Brevig Mission, AK	LAF	Lafayette, IN
KTT	Kittila, Finland	LAI	Lannion, France
KTW	Katowice, Poland	LAJ	Lages, Brazil
KUA	Kuantan, Malaysia	LAM	Los Alamos, NM
KUC	Kuria, Kiribati	LAN	Lansing, MI
KUD	Kudat, Malaysia	LAO	Laoag, Philippines
KUF	Samara, Russia	LAP	La Paz, Mexico
KUH	Kushiro, Japan	LAR	Laramie, WY
KUK	Kasigluk, AK	LAS	Las Vegas, NV
KUL	Kuala Lumpur, Malaysia	LAU	Lamu, Kenya
KUM	Yakushima, Japan	LAW	Lawton, OK
KUN	Kaunas, Lithuania	LAX	Los Angeles (Intl), CA
KUO	Kuopio, Finland	LAZ	Bom Jesus Da Lapa, Brazil
KUQ	Kuri, Papua New Guinea	LBA	Leeds, England, UK
KUS	Kulusuk Is., Greenland	LBB	Lubbock, TX
KUU	Kulu, India	LBE	Latrobe, PA
KUV	Kunsan, Korea	LBF	North Platte, NE
KVA	Kavala, Greece	LBH	Sydney (Palm Beach), Australia
KVB	Skovde, Sweden		
KVC	King Cove, AK	LBL	Liberal, KS
KVD	Gyandzha, Azerbaijan	LBP	Long Banga, Malaysia
KVE	Kitava, Papua New Guinea	LBQ	Lambarene, Gabon
KVG	Kavieng, Papua New Guinea	LBS	Labasa, Fiji
KVL	Kivalina, AK	LBU	Labuan, Malaysia
KWA	Kwajalein, Marshall Islands	LBV	Libreville, Gabon
KWE	Guiyang, China	LBX	Lubang, Philippines
KWF	Waterfall, AK	LCA	Larnaca, Cyprus
KWI	Kuwait, Kuwait	LCE	La Ceiba, Honduras
KWJ	Kwangju, Korea	LCG	La Coruna, Spain
KWK	Kwigillingok, AK	LCH	Lake Charles, LA
KWL	Guilin, China	LCP	Loncopue, Argentina

LCY	London (City), England, UK	LIS	Lisbon, Portugal
LDB	Londrina, Brazil	LIT	Little Rock, AR
LDC	Lindeman Is., Australia	LIW	Loikaw, Myanmar
LDE	Lourdes/Tarbes, France	LJA	Lodja, Zaire
LDH	Lord Howe Is., Australia	LJG	Lijiang City, China
LDI	Lindi, Tanzania	LJU	Ljubljana, Slovenia
LDK	Lidkoping, Sweden	LKB	Lakeba, Fiji
LDM	Ludington, MI	LKL	Lakselv, Norway
LDN	Lamidanda, Nepal	LKN	Leknes, Norway
LDU	Lahad Datu, Malaysia	LKO	Lucknow, India
LDY	Londonderry, N. Ireland, UK	LKP	Lake Placid, NY
LEA	Learmonth, Australia	LLA	Lulea, Sweden
LED	St. Petersburg, Russia	LLI	Lalibela, Ethiopia
LEH	Le Havre, France	LLW	Lilongwe, Malawi
LEI	Almeria, Spain	LMA	Lake Minchumina, AK
LEJ	Leipzig, Germany	LMI	Lumi, Papua New Guinea
LEL	Lake Evella, Australia	LML	Lae Is., Marshall Islands
LEN	Leon, Mexico	LMM	Los Mochis, Mexico
LEQ	Lands End, England, UK	LMN	Limbang, Malaysia
LER	Leinster, Australia	LMP	Lampedusa, Italy
LET	Leticia, Colombia	LMT	Klamath Falls, OR
LEV	Bureta, Fiji	LNB	Lamen Bay, Vanuatu
LEW	Lewiston/Auburn, ME	LNE	Lonorore, Vanuatu
LEX	Lexington, KY	LNG	Lese (Lihir Island), Papua
LFT	Lafayette, LA		New Guinea
LFW	Lome, Togo	LNK	Lincoln, NE
LGA	New York (La Guardia), NY	LNO	Leonora, Australia
LGB	Long Beach, CA	LNS	Lancaster, PA
LGH	Leigh Creek, Australia	LNY	Lanai City, HI
LGI	Deadman's Cay (Long	LNZ	Linz, Austria
	Island), Bahamas	LOD	Longana, Vanuatu
LGK	Langkawi, Malaysia	LOF	Loen, Marshall Islands
LGL	Long Lellang, Malaysia	LON	London (Metro), England,
LGP	Legaspi, Philippines		UK
LGQ	Lago Agrio, Ecuador	LOS	Lagos, NIgeria
LGS	Malargue, Argentina	LOV	Monclova, Mexico
LGW	London (Gatwick), England,	LPA	Gran Canaria, Spain
	UK	LPA	Las Palmas, Canary Islands
LGZ	Leguizamo, Colombia	LPB	La Paz, Bolivia
LHE	Lahore, Pakistan	LPI	Linkoping, Sweden
LHG	Lightning Ridge, Australia	LPL	Liverpool, England, UK
LHR	London (Heathrow),	LPM	Lamap, Vanuatu
	England, UK	LPP	Lappeenranta, Finland
LHW	Lanzhou, China	LPQ	Luang Prabang, Laos
LIF	Lifou, New Caledonia	LPS	Lopez Island, WA
LIG	Limoges, France	LPT	Lampang, Thailand
LIH	Kauai Is. (Lihue), HI	LPY	Le Puy, France
LIJ	Long Island, AK	LRD	Laredo, TX
LIK	Likiep Is., Marshall Islands	LRE	Longreach, Australia
LIL	Lille, France	LRH	La Rochelle, France
LIM	Lima, Peru	LRL	Niamtougou, Togo
LIN	Milan (Linate), Italy	LRS	Leros, Greece
LIQ	Lisala, Zaire	LRT	Lorient, France
LIR	Liberia, Costa Rica	LRU	Las Cruces, NM

LSA	Losuia, Papua New Guinea
LSC	La Serena, Chile
LSE	La Crosse WI/Winona, MN
LSH	Lashio, Myanmar
LSI	Shetland Is. (Sumburgh), Scotland, UK
LSM	Long Semado, Malaysia
LSP	Las Piedras, Venezuela
LSQ	Los Angeles, Chile
LSS	Terre De Haut, Guadeloupe
LST	Launceston, Australia
LSU	Long Sukang, Malaysia
LSY	Lismore, Australia
LTK	Latakia, Syria
LTL	Lastourville, Gabon
LTN	London (Luton), England, UK
LTO	Loreto, Mexico
LTQ	Le Touquet, France
LUA	Lukla, Nepal
LUC	Laucala Island, Fiji
LUD	Luderitz, Namibia
LUG	Lugano, Switzerland
LUK	Cincinnati (Municipal), OH
LUM	Luxi, China
LUN	Lusaka, Zambia
LUO	Luena, Angola
LUP	Kalaupapa, HI
LUQ	San Luis, Argentina
LUR	Cape Lisburne, AK
LUX	Luxembourg, Luxembourg
LVB	Livramento, Brazil
LVD	Lime Village, AK
LVI	Livingstone, Zambia
LVO	Laverton, Australia
LWB	Lewisburg/Greenbrier Valley, WV
LWK	Shetland Is. (Lerwick), Scotland, UK
LWN	Gyourmi, Armenia
LWO	Lvov, Ukraine
LWS	Lewiston, ID
LWT	Lewistown, MT
LWY	Lawas, Malaysia
LXA	Lhasa, China
LXG	Luang Namtha, Laos
LXR	Luxor, Egypt
LXS	Lemnos, Greece
LYA	Luoyang, China
LYC	Lycksele, Sweden
LYG	Lianyungang, China
LYH	Lynchburg, VA
LYP	Faisalabad, Pakistan
LYR	Longyearbyen, Norway
LYS	Lyon, France
LZC	Lazaro Cardenas, Mexico
LZH	Liuzhou, China
LZO	Luzhou, China
LZR	Lizard Is., Australia
MAA	Madras/Chennai, India
MAB	Maraba, Brazil
MAD	Madrid, Spain
MAF	Midland/Odessa, TX
MAG	Madang, Papua New Guinea
MAH	Menorca, Spain
MAJ	Majuro, Marshall Islands
MAM	Matamoros, Mexico
MAN	Manchester, England, UK
MAO	Manaus, Brazil
MAQ	Mae Sot, Thailand
MAR	Maracaibo, Venezuela
MAS	Manus Is., Papua New Guinea
MAT	Matadi, Zaire
MAU	Maupiti, Fr. Polynesia
MAV	Maloelap Is., Marshall Islands
MAY	Mangrove Cay, Bahamas
MAZ	Mayaguez, PR
MBA	Mombasa, Kenya
MBD	Mmabatho, South Africa
MBE	Monbetsu, Japan
MBH	Maryborough, Australia
MBJ	Montego Bay, Jamaica
MBL	Manistee, MI
MBP	Moyobamba, Peru
MBS	Saginaw/Bay City/Midland, MI
MBS	Bay City, MI
MBU	Mbambanakira, Solomon Islands
MBW	Moorabbin, Australia
MCD	Mackinac Island, MI
MCE	Merced, CA
MCG	McGrath, AK
MCI	Kansas City (Intl), MO
MCK	McCook, NE
MCM	Monte Carlo (H/P), Monaco
MCN	Macon, GA
MCO	Orlando (Intl), FL
MCT	Muscat, Oman
MCU	Montlucon, France
MCV	MacArthur River, Australia
MCW	Mason City, IA
MCX	Makhachkala, Russia
MCY	Sunshine Coast, Australia
MCZ	Maceio, Brazil
MDC	Manado, Indonesia

MDE	Medellin (Cordova), Colombia	MIA	Miami (Intl), FL
MDG	Mudanjiang, China	MID	Merida, Mexico
MDI	Makurdi, Nigeria	MII	Marilia, Brazil
MDK	Mbandaka, Zaire	MIJ	Mili Is., Marshall Islands
MDL	Mandalay, Myanmar	MIK	Mikkeli, Finland
MDQ	Mar Del Plata, Argentina	MIL	Milan (Metro), Italy
MDS	Middle Caicos, Turks &	MIM	Merimbula, Australia
	Caicos	MIR	Monastir, Tunisia
MDT	Harrisburg (Intl), PA	MIS	Misima Is., Papua New
MDU	Mendi, Papua New Guinea		Guinea
MDW	Chicago (Midway), IL	MIU	Maiduguri, Nigeria
MDZ	Mendoza, Argentina	MJA	Manja, Madagascar
MEB	Melbourne (Essendon),	MJB	Mejit Is., Marshall Islands
	Australia	MJC	Man, Cote D'Ivoire
MED	Madinah, Saudi Arabia	MJD	Mohenjo Daro, Pakistan
MEE	Mare, New Caledonia	MJE	Majkin, Marshall Islands
MEG	Malange, Angola	MJF	Mosjoen, Norway
MEH	Mehamn, Norway	MJK	Monkey Mia, Australia
MEI	Meridian, MS	MJL	Mouila, Gabon
MEL	Melbourne (Tullamarine),	MJM	Mbuji-Mayi, Zaire
	Australia	MJN	Majunga, Madagascar
MEM	Memphis, TN	MJT	Mytilene, Greece
MES	Medan, Indonesia	MJV	Murcia, Spain
MEU	Monte Dourado, Brazil	MKC	Kansas City (Downtown),
MEX	Mexico City, Mexico		MO
MFE	McAllen/Mission, TX	MKE	Milwaukee, WI
MFF	Moanda, Gabon	MKG	Muskegon, MI
MFG	Muzaffarabad, Pakistan	MKK	Hoolehua (Molokai), HI
MFJ	Moala, Fiji	MKL	Jackson, TN
MFM	Macau, Macau	MKM	Mukah, Malaysia
MFN	Milford Sound, New Zealand	MKN	Malekolon, Papua New
MFO	Manguna, Papua New		Guinea
	Guinea	MKP	Makemo, Fr. Polynesia
MFR	Medford, OR	MKQ	Merauke, Indonesia
MFU	Mfuwe, Zambia	MKR	Meekatharra, Australia
MFZ	Mesalia, Papua New Guinea	MKS	Mekane Selam, Ethiopia
MGA	Managua, Nicaragua	MKU	Makokou, Gabon
MGB	Mount Gambier, Australia	MKY	Mackay, Australia
MGD	Magdalena, Bolivia	MKZ	Malacca, Malaysia
MGF	Maringa, Brazil	MLA	Malta, Malta
MGH	Margate, South Africa	MLB	Melbourne, FL
MGM	Montgomery, AL	MLE	Male, Maldives
MGQ	Mogadishu, Somalia	MLG	Malang, Indonesia
MGS	Mangaia, Cook Islands	MLH	Mulhouse, France/Basel,
MGT	Millingimbi, Australia		Switzerland
MGW	Morgantown, WV	MLI	Moline, IL
MGZ	Myeik, Myanmar	MLL	Marshall, AK
MHD	Mashad, Iran	MLM	Morelia, Mexico
MHG	Mannheim, Germany	MLN	Melilla, Spain
MHH	Marsh Harbour, Bahamas	MLO	Milos, Greece
MHK	Manhattan, KS	MLQ	Malalaua, Papua New
MHQ	Mariehamn, Finland		Guinea
MHT	Manchester, NH	MLS	Miles City, MT
MHX	Manihiki Is., Cook Islands	MLU	Monroe, LA

MLW	Monrovia (Sprigg Payne), Liberia
MLX	Malatya, Turkey
MLY	Manley Hot Springs, AK
MMA	Malmo (Metro), Sweden
MMB	Memanbetsu, Japan
MMD	Minami Daito, Japan
MME	Teesside, England, UK
MMG	Mount Magnet, Australia
MMJ	Matsumoto, Japan
MMK	Murmansk, Russia
MMO	Maio, Cape Verde Islands
MMX	Malmo (Sturup), Sweden
MMY	Miyako Jima, Japan
MNB	Moanda, Zaire
MNF	Mana, Fiji
MNG	Maningrida, Australia
MNI	Montserrat, Montserrat
MNJ	Mananjary, Madagascar
MNK	Maiana, Kiribati
MNL	Manila, Philippines
MNT	Minto, AK
MNU	Maulmyine, Myanmar
MNY	Mono Is., Solomon Islands
MOA	Moa, Cuba
MOB	Mobile AL/Pascagoula, MS
MOC	Montes Claros, Brazil
MOD	Modesto, CA
MOF	Maumere, Indonesia
MOG	Mong Hsat, Myanmar
MOI	Mitiaro, Cook Islands
MOL	Molde, Norway
MON	Mount Cook, New Zealand
MOQ	Morondava, Madagascar
MOT	Minot, ND
MOU	Mountain Village, AK
MOW	Moscow (Metro), Russia
MOZ	Moorea, Fr. Polynesia
MPA	Mpacha, Namibia
MPD	Mirpur Khas, Pakistan
MPH	Caticlan, Philippines
MPL	Montpellier, France
MPM	Maputo, Mozambique
MPN	Mount Pleasant, Falkland Is.
MPU	Mapua, Papua New Guinea
MPV	Montpelier/Barre, VT
MPW	Mariupol, Ukraine
MQF	Magnitogorsk, Russia
MQH	Minacu, Brazil
MQL	Mildura, Australia
MQN	Mo I Rana, Norway
MQT	Marquette, MI
MQX	Makale, Ethiopia
MRB	Martinsburg, WV

MRD	Merida, Venezuela
MRE	Mara Lodges, Kenya
MRS	Marseille, France
MRU	Mauritius, Mauritius
MRV	Mineralnye Vody, Russia
MRY	Monterey/Carmel, CA
MRZ	Moree, Australia
MSA	Muskrat Dam, OT
MSH	Masirah, Oman
MSJ	Misawa, Japan
MSK	Mastic Point, Bahamas
MSL	Muscle Shoals/Florence/ Sheffield, AL
MSL	Florence, AL
MSL	Sheffield, AL
MSN	Madison, WI
MSO	Missoula, MT
MSP	Minneapolis/St. Paul, MN
MSQ	Minsk, Belarus
MSR	Mus, Turkey
MSS	Massena, NY
MST	Maastricht, Netherlands
MSU	Maseru, Lesotho
MSY	New Orleans, LA
MSZ	Namibe, Angola
MTF	Mizan Teferi, Ethiopia
MTH	Marathon, FL
MTI	Mosteiros, Cape Verde Islands
MTJ	Montrose, CO
MTK	Makin Is., Kiribati
MTL	Maitland, Australia
MTM	Metlakatia, AK
MTO	Mattoon, IL
MTR	Monteria, Colombia
MTS	Manzini, Swaziland
MTT	Minatitlan, Mexico
MTV	Mota Lava, Vanuatu
MTY	Monterrey, Mexico
MUA	Munda, Solomon Islands
MUB	Maun, Botswana
MUC	Munich, Germany
MUE	Kamuela, HI
MUK	Mauke Is., Cook Islands
MUN	Maturin, Venezuela
MUR	Marudi, Malaysia
MUW	Mascara, Algeria
MUX	Multan, Pakistan
MUZ	Musoma, Tanzania
MVB	Franceville, Gabon
MVD	Montevideo, Uruguay
MVM	Kayenta, AZ
MVN	Mount Vernon, IL
MVR	Maroua, Cameroon

MVS	Mucuri, Brazil	NAT	Natal, Brazil
MVT	Mataiva, Fr. Polynesia	NAW	Narathiwat, Thailand
MVY	Martha's Vineyard, MA	NBC	Naberevnye Chelny, Russia
MWA	Marion, IL	NBO	Nairobi (Metro), Kenya
MWD	Mianwali, Pakistan	NCA	North Caicos, Turks & Caicos
MWF	Maewo, Vanuatu	NCE	Nice, France
MWH	Moses Lake, WA	NCI	Necocli, Colombia
MWI	Maramuni, Papua New	NCL	Newcastle, England, UK
	Guinea	NCR	San Carlos, Nicaragua
MWU	Mussau, Papua New Guinea	NCU	Nukus, Uzbekistan
MWV	Mundulkiri, Cambodia	NCY	Annecy, France
MWZ	Mwanza, Tanzania	NDB	Nouadhibou, Mauritania
MXH	Moro, Papua New Guinea	NDG	Qiqihar, China
MXL	Mexicali, Mexico	NDI	Namudi, Papua New Guinea
MXM	Morombe, Madagascar	NDJ	Ndjamena, Chad
MXP	Milan (Malpensa), Italy	NDK	Namdrik Is., Marshall
MXS	Maota, Savai'i Is., Western		Islands
	Samoa	NDM	Mendi, Ethiopia
MXT	Maintirano, Madagascar	NDU	Rundu, Namibia
MXX	Mora, Sweden	NDZ	Nordholz-Spieka, Germany
MXZ	Meixian, China	NEF	Neftekamsk, Russia
MYA	Moruya, Australia	NEG	Negril, Jamaica
MYD	Malindi, Kenya	NEJ	Nejjo, Ethiopia
MYE	Miyake Jima, Japan	NER	Neryungri, Russia
MYF	San Diego (Montgomery), CA	NEU	Sam Neua, Laos
MYG	Mayaguana, Bahamas	NEV	Nevis, Leeward Islands
MYJ	Matsuyama, Japan	NFG	Nefteyugansk, Russia
MYQ	Mysore, India	NFO	Niuafo'ou, Tonga
MYR	Myrtle Beach, SC	NGA	Young, Australia
MYT	Myitkyina, Myanmar	NGB	Ningbo, China
MYU	Mekoryuk, AK	NGD	Anegada, BVI
MYW	Mtwara, Tanzania	NGE	Ngaoundere, Cameroon
MYX	Menyamya, Papua New	NGI	Ngau Is., Fiji
	Guinea	NGO	Nagoya, Japan
MYY	Miri, Malaysia	NGS	Nagasaki, Japan
MZC	Mitzic, Gabon	NGX	Manang, Nepal
MZG	Makung, Taiwan	NHA	Nha-Trang, Viet Nam
MZI	Mopti, Mali	NHV	Nuku Hiva, Fr. Polynesia
MZK	Marakei, Kiribati	NIB	Nikolai, AK
MZL	Manizales, Colombia	NIC	Nicosia, Cyprus
MZM	Metz, France	NIG	Nikunau, Kiribati
MZO	Manzanillo, Cuba	NIM	Niamey, Niger
MZP	Motueka, New Zealand	NIX	Nioro, Mali
MZT	Mazatlan, Mexico	NJC	Nizhnevartovsk, Russia
MZV	Mulu, Malaysia	NKC	Nouakchott, Mauritania
NAA	Narrabri, Australia	NKG	Nanjing (Nanking), China
NAG	Nagpur, India	NKI	Naukiti, AK
NAK	Nakhon Ratchasima,	NKN	Nanking, Papua New Guinea
	Thailand	NKY	Nkayi, Congo
NAN	Nadi, Fiji	NLA	Ndola, Zambia
NAO	Nanchong, China	NLD	Nuevo Laredo, Mexico
NAP	Naples, Italy	NLG	Nelson Lagoon, AK
NAR	Nare, Colombia	NLK	Norfolk Is., Pacific Ocean
NAS	Nassau, Bahamas	NLP	Nelspruit, South Africa

NLV	Nikolaev, Ukraine	NYK	Nanyuki, Kenya
NMA	Namangan, Uzbekistan	NYM	Nadym, Russia
NME	Nightmute, AK	NYN	Nyngan, Australia
NMG	San Miguel, Panama	NYO	Nykoping, Sweden
NNB	Santa Ana, Solomon Islands	NYU	Nyaung-u, Myanmar
NNG	Nanning, China	OAG	Orange, Australia
NNK	Naknek, AK	OAJ	Jacksonville, NC
NNL	Nondalton, AK	OAK	Oakland, CA
NNT	Nan, Thailand	OAL	Cacoal, Brazil
NNY	Nanyang, China	OAX	Oaxaca, Mexico
NOB	Nosara Beach, Costa Rica	OBO	Obihiro, Japan
NOC	Connaught/Knock, Ireland	OBU	Kobuk, AK
NOJ	Nojabrxsk, Russia	OCH	Lufkin, TX
NON	Nonouti, Kiribati	OCJ	Ocho Rios, Jamaica
NOO	Naoro, Papua New Guinea	OCV	Ocana, Colombia
NOS	Nossi-be, Madagascar	ODE	Odense, Denmark
NOU	Noumea, New Caledonia	ODN	Long Seridan, Malaysia
NOV	Huambo, Angola	ODS	Odessa, Ukraine
NPE	Napier, New Zealand	ODW	Oak Harbor, WA
NPL	New Plymouth, New Zealand	ODY	Oudomxay, Laos
NQL	Niquelandia, Brazil	OER	Ornskoldsvik, Sweden
NQN	Neuquen, Argentina	OFK	Norfolk, NE
NQU	Nuqui, Colombia	OFU	Ofu Island, AS
NQY	Newquay, England, UK	OGG	Kahului, HI
NRA	Narrandera, Australia	OGN	Yonaguni Jima, Japan
NRK	Norrkoping, Sweden	OGS	Ogdensburg, NY
NRT	Tokyo (Narita), Japan	OGV	Ongava Game Reserve,
NSK	Norilsk, Russia		Namibia
NSN	Nelson, New Zealand	OGX	Ouargla, Algeria
NSO	Scone, Australia	OGZ	Vladikavkaz, Russia
NST	Nakhon Si Thammarat,	OHD	Ohrid, Macedonia
	Thailand	OIL	Oil City, PA
NTE	Nantes, France	OIM	Oshima, Japan
NTG	Nantong, China	OIR	Okushiri, Japan
NTL	Newcastle, Australia	OIT	Oita, Japan
NTN	Normanton, Australia	OKA	Okinawa, Japan
NTO	Santo Antao, Cape Verde	OKC	Oklahoma City, OK
	Islands	OKD	Sapporo (Okadama), Japan
NTT	Niuatoputapu, Tonga	OKE	Okino Erabu, Japan
NTY	Sun City, South Africa	OKI	Oki Island, Japan
NUB	Numbulwar, Australia	OKJ	Okayama, Japan
NUE	Nuremberg, Germany	OKN	Okondja, Gabon
NUI	Nuiqsut, AK	OKR	Yorke Is., Australia
NUL	Nulato, AK	OKU	Mokuti Lodge, Namibia
NUP	Nunapitchuk, AK	OLB	Olbia, Italy
NUS	Norsup, Vanuatu	OLF	Wolf Point, MT
NUX	Novyj Urengoj, Russia	OLH	Old Harbour, AK
NVA	Neiva, Colombia	OLJ	Olpoi, Vanuatu
NVG	Nueva Guinea, Nicaragua	OLP	Olympic Dam, Australia
NVK	Narvik, Norway	OMA	Omaha, NE
NVT	Navegantes, Brazil	OMB	Omboue, Gabon
NWI	Norwich, England, UK	OMD	Oranjemund, Namibia
NWT	Nowata, Papua New Guinea	OME	Nome, AK
NYC	New York (Metro), NY	OMH	Urmieh, Iran

OMO	Mostar, Bosnia
OMR	Oradea, Romania
OMS	Omsk, Russia
ONA	Winona, MN
ONB	Ononge, Papua New Guinea
OND	Ondangwa, Namibia
ONG	Mornington, Australia
ONT	Ontario, CA
ONX	Colon, Panama
OOK	Toksook Bay, AK
OOL	Gold Coast, Australia
OOM	Cooma, Australia
OOT	Onotoa, Kiribati
OPB	Open Bay, Papua New Guinea
OPO	Porto, Portugal
OPS	Sinop, Brazil
OPU	Balimo, Papua New Guinea
ORB	Orebro, Sweden
ORD	Chicago (O'Hare), IL
ORF	Norfolk, VA
ORG	Paramaribo (Zorg En Hoop), Suriname
ORH	Worcester, MA
ORI	Port Lions, AK
ORK	Cork, Ireland
ORL	Orlando (Herndon), FL
ORN	Oran, Algeria
ORV	Noorvik, AK
ORW	Ormara, Pakistan
ORY	Paris (Orly), France
OSA	Osaka (Metro), Japan
OSD	Ostersund, Sweden
OSH	Oshkosh, WI
OSI	Osijek, Croatia
OSK	Oskarshamn, Sweden
OSL	Oslo (Metro), Norway
OSR	Ostrava, Czech Rep.
OSS	Osh, Kyrgyzstan
OSW	Orsk, Russia
OSY	Namsos, Norway
OSZ	Koszalin, Poland
OTD	Contadora, Panama
OTH	North Bend, OR
OTM	Ottumwa, IA
OTP	Bucharest (Otopeni), Romania
OTR	Coto 47, Costa Rica
OTS	Anacortes, WA
OTU	Otu, Colombia
OTZ	Kotzebue, AK
OUA	Ouagadougou, Burkina Faso
OUD	Oujda, Morocco
OUE	Ouesso, Congo
OUL	Oulu, Finland
OUZ	Zouerate, Mauritania
OVB	Novosibirsk, Russia
OVD	Asturias, Spain
OWB	Owensboro, KY
OXB	Bissau, Guinea Bissau
OXR	Oxnard, CA
OYE	Oyem, Gabon
OZH	Zaporozhye, Ukraine
OZZ	Ouarzazate, Morocco
PAC	Panama City (Paitilla), Panama
PAD	Paderborn, Germany
PAH	Paducah, KY
PAJ	Para Chinar, Pakistan
PAP	Port Au Prince, Haiti
PAR	Paris (Metro), France
PAS	Paros, Greece
PAT	Patna, India
PAV	Paulo Afonso, Brazil
PAZ	Poza Rica, Mexico
PBC	Puebla, Mexico
PBD	Porbandar, India
PBE	Puerto Berrio, Colombia
PBH	Paro, Bhutan
PBI	West Palm Beach, FL
PBJ	Paama, Vanuatu
PBM	Paramaribo, Suriname
PBO	Paraburdoo, Australia
PBP	Punta Islita, Costa Rica
PBU	Putao, Myanmar
PBZ	Plettenberg Bay, South Africa
PCA	Portage Creek, AK
PCL	Pucallpa, Peru
PCM	Playa Del Carmen, Mexico
PCP	Principe Is., Principe Is.
PCR	Puerto Carreno, Colombia
PDA	Puerto Inirida, Colombia
PDB	Pedro Bay, AK
PDG	Padang, Indonesia
PDL	Ponta Delgada, Portugal
PDP	Punta Del Este, Uruguay
PDS	Piedras Negras, Mexico
PDT	Pendleton, OR
PDX	Portland, OR
PEA	Penneshaw, Australia
PEC	Pelican, AK
PEE	Perm, Russia
PEG	Perugia, Italy
PEI	Pereira, Colombia
PEK	Beijing (Capital), China
PEM	Puerto Maldonado, Peru
PEN	Penang, Malaysia
PER	Perth, Australia

PES	Petrozavodsk, Russia	PKY	Palangkaraya, Indonesia
PET	Pelotas, Brazil	PKZ	Pakse, Laos
PEU	Puerto Lempira, Honduras	PLB	Plattsburgh, NY
PEW	Peshawar, Pakistan	PLH	Plymouth, England, UK
PFB	Passo Fundo, Brazil	PLJ	Placencia, Belize
PFJ	Patreksfjordur, Iceland	PLM	Palembang, Indonesia
PFN	Panama City, FL	PLN	Pellston, MI
PFO	Paphos, Cyprus	PLO	Port Lincoln, Australia
PGA	Page, AZ	PLP	La Palma, Panama
PGF	Perpignan, France	PLQ	Palanga, Lithuania
PGK	Pangkalpinang, Indonesia	PLS	Providenciales, Turks &
PGL	Pascagoula, MS		Caicos
PGV	Greenville, NC	PLU	Belo Horizonte (Pampulha),
PGX	Perigueux, France		Brazil
PGZ	Ponta Grossa, Brazil	PLW	Palu, Indonesia
PHB	Parnaiba, B razil	PLX	Semipalatinsk, Kazakstan
PHC	Port Harcourt, Nigeria	PLZ	Port Elizabeth, South Africa
PHE	Port Hedland, Australia	PMA	Pemba, Tanzania
PHF	Hampton/Newport News/	PMC	Puerto Montt, Chile
	Wmsbrg, VA	PMD	Palmdale/Lancaster, CA
PHL	Philadelphia (Intl), PA	PMF	Parma, Italy
PHO	Point Hope, AK	PMG	Ponta Pora, Brazil
PHR	Pacific Harbour, Fiji	PMI	Palma Mallorca, Spain
PHS	Phitsanulok, Thailand	PML	Port Moller, AK
PHW	Phalaborwa, South Africa	PMN	Pumani, Papua New Guinea
PHX	Phoenix, AZ	PMO	Palermo, Italy
PIA	Peoria, IL	PMR	Palmerston N., New Zealand
PIB	Laurel (Hattiesburg), MS	PMV	Porlamar, Venezuela
PID	Nassau (Paradise Is.),	PMW	Palmas, Brazil
	Bahamas	PMY	Puerto Madryn, Argentina
PIE	St. Petersburg/Clearwater,	PMZ	Palmar, Costa Rica
	FL	PNA	Pamplona, Spain
PIF	Pingtung, Taiwan	PNB	Porto Nacional, Brazil
PIH	Pocatello, ID	PNC	Ponca City, OK
PIK	Glasgow (Prestwick),	PND	Punta Gorda, Belize
	Scotland, UK	PNH	Phnom Penh, Cambodia
PIP	Pilot Point, AK	PNI	Pohnpei, Micronesia
PIR	Pierre, SD	PNK	Pontianak, Indonesia
PIS	Poitiers, France	PNL	Pantelleria, Italy
PIT	Pittsburgh, PA	PNP	Popondetta, Papua New
PIU	Piura, Peru		Guinea
PIX	Pico Island, Portugal	PNQ	Poona, India
PIZ	Point Lay, AK	PNR	Pointe Noire, Congo
PJC	Pedro Juan Caballero,	PNS	Pensacola, FL
	Paraguay	PNZ	Petrolina, Brazil
PJG	Panjgur, Pakistan	POA	Porto Alegre, Brazil
PJM	Puerto Jiminez, Costa Rica	POG	Port Gentil, Gabon
PKA	Napaiskak, AK	POI	Potosi, Bolivia
PKB	Marietta/Parkersburg, WV	POJ	Patos De Minas, Brazil
PKC	Petropavlovsk-Kamchats,	POL	Pemba, Mozambique
	Russia	POM	Port Moresby, Papua New
PKE	Parkes, Australia		Guinea
PKR	Pokhara, Nepal	POP	Puerto Plata, Dominican
PKU	Pekanbaru, Indonesia		Rep.

POR	Pori, Finland	PUQ	Punta Arenas, Chile
POS	Port of Spain, Trinidad &	PUS	Pusan, Korea
	Tobago	PUT	Puttaparthi, India
POT	Port Antonio, Jamaica	PUU	Puerto Asis, Colombia
POU	Poughkeepsie, NY	PUV	Poum, New Caledonia
POY	Lovell, WY	PUW	Pullman, WA
POZ	Poznan, Poland	PUY	Pula, Croatia
PPB	Pres. Prudente, Brazil	PUZ	Puerto Cabezas, Nicaragua
PPE	Puerto Penasco, Mexico	PVA	Providencia, Colombia
PPG	Pago Pago, AS	PVC	Provincetown, MA
PPK	Petropavlovsk, Kazakstan	PVD	Providence, RI
PPL	Phaplu, Nepal	PVH	Porto Velho, Brazil
PPN	Popayan, Colombia	PVK	Preveza/Lefkas, Greece
PPP	Proserpine, Australia	PVR	Puerto Vallarta, Mexico
PPQ	Paraparaumu, New Zealand	PWK	Chicago (Pal Waukee), IL
PPS	Puerto Princesa, Philippines	PWM	Portland, ME
PPT	Papeete, Fr. Polynesia	PWQ	Pavlodar, Kazakstan
PPV	Port Protection, AK	PXM	Puerto Escondido, Mexico
PPY	Pouso Alegre, Brazil	PXO	Porto Santo, Portugal
PQI	Presque Isle, ME	PXU	Pleiku, Viet Nam
PQM	Palenque, Mexico	PYE	Penrhyn Is., Cook Islands
PQQ	Port Macquarie, Australia	PYH	Puerto Ayacucho, Venezuela
PQS	Pilot Station, AK	PZB	Pietermaritzburg, South
PRC	Prescott, AZ		Africa
PRG	Prague, Czech Rep.	PZE	Penzance, England, UK
PRH	Phrae, Thailand	PZH	Zhob, Pakistan
PRI	Praslin Is., Seychelles Is.	PZO	Puerto Ordaz, Venezuela
PRN	Pristina, Yugoslavia	PZU	Port Sudan, Sudan
PRS	Parasi, Solomon Islands	QBC	Bella Coola, BC
PSA	Pisa, Italy	QFK	Selje, Norway
PSB	Bellefonte/Philipsburg, PA	QFQ	Maloy Harbor, Norway
PSC	Pasco, WA	QNY	New York (Marine Air Term.),
PSE	Ponce, PR		NY
PSG	Petersburg, AK	QRO	Queretaro, Mexico
PSI	Pasni, Pakistan	RAB	Rabaul, Papua New Guinea
PSO	Pasto, Colombia	RAD	Tortola (Road Town), BVI
PSP	Palm Springs, CA	RAE	Arar, Saudi Arabia
PSR	Pescara, Italy	RAF	Ras An Naqb, Egypt
PSS	Posadas, Argentina	RAH	Rafha, Saudi Arabia
PSZ	Puerto Suarez, Bolivia	RAI	Praia, Cape Verde Islands
PTA	Port Alsworth, AK	RAJ	Rajkot, India
PTD	Port Alexander, AK	RAK	Marrakech, Morocco
PTF	Malololailai, Fiji	RAL	Riverside, CA
PTG	Pietersburg, South Africa	RAM	Ramingining, Australia
PTH	Port Heiden, AK	RAO	Ribeirao Preto, Brazil
PTJ	Portland, Australia	RAP	Rapid City, SD
PTP	Pointe A Pitre, Guadeloupe	RAR	Rarotonga, Cook Islands
PTU	Platinum, AK	RAS	Rasht, Iran
PTY	Panama City (Tocumen Intl),	RAW	Arawa, Papua New Guinea
	Panama	RAZ	Rawala Kot, Pakistan
PUB	Pueblo, CO	RBA	Rabat, Morocco
PUF	Pau, France	RBJ	Rebun, Japan
PUG	Port Augusta, Australia	RBP	Rabaraba, Papua New
PUJ	Punta Cana, Dominican Rep.		Guinea

RBR	Rio Branco, Brazil	RKS	Rock Springs, WY
RBV	Ramata, Solomon Islands	RKT	Ras Al Khaimah, UAE
RBY	Ruby, AK	RKU	Yule Is., Papua New Guinea
RCB	Richards Bay, South Africa	RKV	Reykjavik (Domestic),
RCE	Roche Harbor, WA		Iceland
RCH	Riohacha, Colombia	RLG	Rostock-Laage, Germany
RCL	Redcliffe, Vanuatu	RMA	Roma, Australia
RCM	Richmond, Australia	RMK	Renmark, Australia
RCU	Rio Cuarto, Argentina	RMP	Rampart, AK
RDC	Redencao, Brazil	RNB	Ronneby, Sweden
RDD	Redding, CA	RNE	Roanne, France
RDG	Reading, PA	RNI	Corn Is., Nicaragua
RDM	Bend/Redmond, OR	RNJ	Yoronjima, Japan
RDS	Rincon de los Sauces,	RNL	Rennell, Solomon Islands
	Argentina	RNN	Bornholm, Denmark
RDU	Raleigh/Durham, NC	RNO	Reno, NV
RDV	Red Devil, AK	RNS	Rennes, France
RDZ	Rodez, France	ROA	Roanoke, VA
REC	Recife, Brazil	ROB	Monrovia (Roberts Intl),
REG	Reggio Calabria, Italy		Liberia
REK	Reykjavik (Metro), Iceland	ROC	Rochester, NY
REL	Trelew, Argentina	ROK	Rockhampton, Australia
REN	Orenburg, Russia	ROM	Rome (Metro), Italy
REP	Siem Reap, Cambodia	ROO	Rondonopolis, Brazil
RES	Resistencia, Argentina	ROP	Rota, Mariana Islands
RET	Rost, Norway	ROR	Koror, Palau
REU	Reus, Spain	ROS	Rosario, Argentina
REX	Reynosa, Mexico	ROT	Rotorua, New Zealand
RFD	Rockford, IL	ROV	Rostov, Russia
RFP	Raiatea, Fr. Polynesia	ROW	Roswell, NM
RGA	Rio Grande, Argentina	RPM	Ngukurr, Australia
RGI	Rangiroa, Fr. Polynesia	RPN	Rosh Pina, Israel
RGL	Rio Gallegos, Argentina	RPR	Raipur, India
RGN	Yangon, Myanmar	RRG	Rodrigues Island, Mauritius
RHE	Reims, France	RRS	Roros, Norway
RHI	Rhinelander, WI	RSA	Santa Rosa, Argentina
RHO	Rhodes, Greece	RSD	Rock Sound, Bahamas
RIA	Santa Maria, Brazil	RSE	Sydney (Rose Bay), Australia
RIB	Riberalta, Bolivia	RSH	Russian Mission, AK
RIC	Richmond/Wmsbrg, VA	RSJ	Rosario, WA
RIG	Rio Grande, Brazil	RST	Rochester, MN
RIJ	Rioja, Peru	RSU	Yosu, Korea
RIK	Carrillo, Costa Rica	RSW	Fort Myers (Regional), FL
RIN	Ringi Cove, Solomon Islands	RTA	Rotuma, Fiji
RIO	Rio De Janeiro (Metro),	RTB	Roatan, Honduras
	Brazil	RTM	Rotterdam, Netherlands
RIS	Rishiri, Japan	RTS	Rottnest Is., Australia
RIW	Riverton, WY	RTW	Saratov, Russia
RIX	Riga, Latvia	RUH	Riyadh, Saudi Arabia
RIY	Riyan Mukalla, Yemen	RUI	Ruidoso, NM
RJH	Rajshahi, Bangladesh	RUN	Reunion Island, Indian
RKD	Rockland, ME		Ocean
RKE	Copenhagen-Roskilde,	RUR	Rurutu Is., Fr. Polynesia
	Denmark	RUS	Marau Sound, Solomon

	Islands	SDF	Louisville, KY
RUT	Rutland, VT	SDJ	Sendai, Japan
RVA	Farafangana, Madagascar	SDK	Sandakan, Malaysia
RVH	St. Petersburg (Rzhevka),	SDL	Sundsvall, Sweden
	Russia	SDM	San Diego (Brown Field), CA
RVK	Roervik, Norway	SDN	Sandane, Norway
RVN	Rovaniemi, Finland	SDP	Sand Point, AK
RWI	Rocky Mount/Wilson, NC	SDQ	Santo Domingo, Dominican
RXS	Roxas City, Philippines		Rep.
RYK	Rahim Yar Khan, Pakistan	SDR	Santander, Spain
SAB	Saba, Neth. Antilles	SDT	Saidu Sharif, Pakistan
SAF	Santa Fe, NM	SDU	Rio De Janeiro (Dumont),
SAH	Sana'a, Yemen Arab Rep.		Brazil
SAK	Saudarkrokur, Iceland	SDV	Tel Aviv/Jaffa (Sde Dov),
SAL	San Salvador, El Salvador		Israel
SAM	Salamo, Papua New Guinea	SDZ	Shetland Is., Scotland, UK
SAN	San Diego (Lindberg), CA	SEA	Seattle/Tacoma, WA
SAO	Sao Paulo (Metro), Brazil	SEL	Seoul, Korea
SAP	San Pedro Sula, Honduras	SEY	Selibaby, Mauritania
SAQ	San Andros, Bahamas	SEZ	Mahe Is., Seychelles
SAT	San Antonio, TX	SFA	Sfax, Tunisia
SAV	Savannah, GA	SFD	San Fernando De Apure,
SAX	Sambu, Panama		Venezuela
SBA	Santa Barbara, CA	SFG	St. Maarten (Esperance),
SBH	St. Barthelemy, Guadeloupe		Neth. Antilles
SBK	St. Brieuc, France	SFJ	Kangerlussuaq, Greenland
SBN	South Bend, IN	SFN	Santa Fe, Argentina
SBP	San Luis Obispo, CA	SFO	San Francisco, CA
SBS	Steamboat Springs, CO	SFQ	Sanliurfa, Turkey
SBU	Springbok, South Africa	SFT	Skelleftea, Sweden
SBW	Sibu, Malaysia	SFU	Safia, Papua New Guinea
SBY	Salisbury, MD	SGC	Surgut, Russia
SBZ	Sibiu, Romania	SGD	Sonderborg, Denmark
SCC	Prudhoe Bay/Deadhorse, AK	SGF	Springfield, MO
SCE	State College, PA	SGN	Ho Chi Minh, Viet Nam
SCJ	Smith Cove, AK	SGO	St. George, Australia
SCK	Stockton, CA	SGR	Sugarland, TX
SCL	Santiago, Chile	SGU	St. George, UT
SCM	Scammon Bay, AK	SGY	Skagway, AK
SCN	Saarbruecken, Germany	SHA	Shanghai, China
SCO	Aktau. Kazakstan	SHB	Nakashibetsu, Japan
SCQ	Santiago De Compostela,	SHC	Indaselassie, Ethiopia
	Spain	SHD	Staunton (Shenandoah
SCT	Socotra, Yemen		Valley), VA
SCU	Santiago, Cuba	SHE	Shenyang, China
SCV	Suceava, Romania	SHG	Shungnak, AK
SCX	Salina Cruz, Mexico	SHH	Shishmaref, AK
SCY	San Cristobal, Ecuador	SHJ	Sharjah, UAE
SCZ	Santa Cruz Is., Solomon	SHO	Sokcho, Korea
	Islands	SHP	Qinhuangdao, China
SDA	Baghdad (Saddam), Iraq	SHR	Sheridan, WY
SDD	Lubango, Angola	SHS	Shashi, China
SDE	Santiago Del Estero,	SHT	Shepparton, Australia
	Argentina	SHV	Shreveport, LA

SHW	Sharurah, Saudi Arabia
SHX	Shageluk, AK
SIA	Xi An (Xiguan), China
SIC	Sinop, Turkey
SID	Sal, Cape Verde Islands
SIF	Simra, Nepal
SIG	San Juan (Isla Grand), PR
SIL	Sila, Papua New Guinea
SIN	Singapore (Changi), Singapore
SIP	Simferopol, Ukraine
SIR	Sion, Switzerland
SIT	Sitka, AK
SIU	Siuna, Nicaragua
SIX	Singleton, Australia
SJB	San Joaquin, Bolivia
SJC	San Jose, CA
SJD	San Jose Cabo, Mexico
SJI	San Jose, Philippines
SJJ	Sarajevo, Bosnia
SJK	Sao Jose Dos Campos, Brazil
SJO	San Jose, Costa Rica
SJP	Sao Jose Do Rio Preto, Brazil
SJT	San Angelo, TX
SJU	San Juan (Munoz Marin), PR
SJW	Shijiazhuang, China
SJY	Seinajoki, Finland
SJZ	Sao Jorge Island, Portugal
SKB	St. Kitts, St. Kitts & Nevis
SKD	Samarkand, Uzbekistan
SKE	Skien, Norway
SKG	Thessaloniki, Greece
SKH	Surkhet, Nepal
SKK	Shaktoolik, AK
SKL	Isle of Skye, Scotland, UK
SKN	Stokmarknes, Norway
SKO	Sokoto, Nigeria
SKP	Skopje, Macedonia
SKS	Vojens, Denmark
SKU	Skiros, Greece
SKZ	Sukkur, Pakistan
SLA	Salta, Argentina
SLC	Salt Lake City, UT
SLE	Salem, OR
SLH	Sola, Vanuatu
SLK	Saranac Lake, NY
SLL	Salalah, Oman
SLM	Salamanca, Spain
SLN	Salina, KS
SLP	San Luis Potosi, Mexico
SLQ	Sleetmute, AK
SLU	St. Lucia, West Indies
SLV	Simla, India
SLW	Saltillo, Mexico
SLX	Salt Cay, Turks & Caicos
SLY	Salehard, Russia
SLZ	Sao Luiz, Brazil
SMA	Santa Maria, Portugal
SMF	Sacramento (Metro), CA
SMI	Samos, Greece
SMK	St. Michael, AK
SML	Stella Maris, Bahamas
SMM	Semporna, Malaysia
SMR	Santa Marta, Colombia
SMX	Santa Maria, CA
SNA	Orange County/Santa Ana, CA
SNB	Snake Bay, Australia
SNE	Sao Nicolau, Cape Verde Islands
SNN	Shannon, Ireland
SNO	Sakon Nakhon, Thailand
SNP	St. Paul Island, AK
SNV	Santa Elena, Venezuela
SNW	Thandwe, Myanmar
SNY	Sidney, NE
SOC	Solo City, Indonesia
SOF	Sofia, Bulgaria
SOG	Sogndal, Norway
SOI	South Molle Is., Australia
SOJ	Sorkjosen, Norway
SOM	San Tome, Venezuela
SON	Espirtu Santo, Vanuatu
SOO	Soderhamn, Sweden
SOP	Pinehurst, NC
SOQ	Sorong, Indonesia
SOU	Southampton, England, UK
SOW	Show Low, AZ
SOX	Sogamoso, Colombia
SPC	Santa Cruz La Palma, Spain
SPD	Saidpur, Bangladesh
SPI	Springfield, IL
SPK	Sapporo (Metro), Japan
SPN	Saipan, Mariana Islands
SPP	Menongue, Angola
SPR	San Pedro, Belize
SPS	Wichita Falls, TX
SPU	Split, Croatia
SPW	Spencer, IA
SQC	Southern Cross, Australia
SQH	Son La, Viet Nam
SQI	Sterling/Rock Falls, IL
SQO	Storuman, Sweden
SRA	Santa Rosa, Brazil
SRE	Sucre, Bolivia
SRG	Semarang, Indonesia
SRI	Samarinda, Indonesia
SRJ	San Borja, Bolivia

SRP	Stord, Norway
SRQ	Sarasota/Bradenton, FL
SRV	Stony River, AK
SRY	Sary, Iran
SRZ	Santa Cruz (Trompillo), Bolivia
SSA	Salvador, Brazil
SSG	Malabo, Equatorial Guinea
SSH	Sharm El Sheikh, Egypt
SSJ	Sandnessjoen, Norway
SSM	Sault Ste. Marie (Metro), MI
SSR	Sara, Vanuatu
SSX	Samsun, Turkey
SSY	M'banza Congo, Angola
STC	St. Cloud, MN
STE	Stevens Point, WI
STG	St. George Island, AK
STI	Santiago, Dominican Rep.
STL	St. Louis (Lambert), MO
STM	Santarem, Brazil
STN	London (Stansted), England, UK
STO	Stockholm (Metro), Sweden
STR	Stuttgart, Germany
STS	Santa Rosa, CA
STT	St. Thomas, VI
STV	Surat, India
STW	Stavropol, Russia
STX	St. Croix, VI
STZ	Santa Terezinha, Brazil
SUB	Surabaya, Indonesia
SUF	Lamezia/Terme, Italy
SUH	Sur, Oman
SUJ	Satu Mare, Romania
SUL	Sui, Pakistan
SUN	Sun Valley, ID
SUR	Summer Beaver, OT
SUV	Suva, Fiji
SUW	Superior, WI
SUX	Sioux City, IA
SVA	Savoonga, AK
SVB	Sambava, Madagascar
SVC	Silver City, NM
SVD	St. Vincent, Windward Islands
SVG	Stavanger, Norway
SVI	San Vincente Del Caguan, Colombia
SVJ	Svolvaer, Norway
SVL	Savonlinna, Finland
SVO	Moscow (Sheremetyevo), Russia
SVP	Kuito, Angola
SVQ	Seville, Spain

SVS	Stevens Village, AK
SVU	Savusavu, Fiji
SVX	Ekaterinburg, Russia
SVZ	San Antonio, Venezuela
SWA	Shantou, China
SWD	Seward, AK
SWF	Newburgh (Stewart), NY
SWG	Satwag, Papua New Guinea
SWJ	South West Bay, Vanuatu
SWP	Swakopmund, Namibia
SWR	Silur, Papua New Guinea
SWT	Strzhewoi, Russia
SXB	Strasbourg, France
SXE	Sale, Australia
SXF	Berlin (Schoenefeld), Germany
SXH	Sehulea, Papua New Guinea
SXL	Sligo, Ireland
SXM	St. Maarten, Neth. Antilles
SXO	Sao Felix Do Araguaia, Brazil
SXP	Sheldon Point, AK
SXR	Srinagar, India
SXW	Sauren, Papua New Guines
SXX	Sao Felix Do Xingu, Brazil
SXZ	Siirit, Turkey
SYB	Seal Bay, AK
SYD	Sydney, Australia
SYE	Sadah, Yemen Arab Rep.
SYM	Simao, China
SYO	Shonai, Japan
SYP	Santiago, Panama
SYR	Syracuse, NY
SYW	Sehwen Sharif, Pakistan
SYX	Sanya, China
SYY	Stornoway, Scotland, UK
SYZ	Shiraz, Iran
SZA	Soyo, Angola
SZG	Salzburg, Austria
SZK	Skukuza, South Africa
SZX	Shenzhen, China
SZZ	Szczecin, Poland
TAB	Tobago, Trinidad & Tobago
TAC	Tacloban, Philippines
TAE	Taegu, Korea
TAH	Tanna, Vanuatu
TAI	Taiz, Yemen
TAK	Takamatsu, Japan
TAL	Tanana, AK
TAM	Tampico, Mexico
TAO	Qingdao, China
TAP	Tapachula, Mexico
TAS	Tashkent, Uzbekistan
TAT	Tatry/Poprad, Slovakia
TAV	Tau, AS

TBB	Tuy Hoa, Vietnam
TBE	Timbunke, Papua New Guinea
TBF	Tabiteuea North, Kiribati
TBG	Tabubil, Papua New Guinea
TBI	The Bight, Bahamas
TBJ	Tabarka, Tunisia
TBO	Tabora, Tanzania
TBP	Tumbes, Peru
TBS	Tbilisi, Georgia
TBT	Tabatinga, Brazil
TBU	Tongatapu, Tonga
TBZ	Tabriz, Iran
TCA	Tennant Creek, Australia
TCB	Treasure Cay, Bahamas
TCG	Tacheng, China
TCH	Tchibanga, Gabon
TCI	Tenerife (Metro), Spain
TCL	Tuscaloosa, AL
TCO	Tumaco, Colombia
TCP	Taba, Egypt
TCQ	Tacna, Peru
TCR	Tuticorin, India
TCT	Takotna, AK
TDB	Tetabedi, Papua New Guinea
TDD	Trinidad, Bolivia
TED	Thisted, Denmark
TEE	Tbessa, Algeria
TEH	Tetlin, AK
TEO	Terapo, Papua New Guinea
TEP	Teptep, Papua New Guinea
TER	Terceira Is., Portugal
TET	Tete, Mozambique
TEU	Te Anau, New Zealand
TEX	Telluride, CO
TEZ	Tezpur, India
TFF	Tefe, Brazil
TFI	Tufi, Papua New Guinea
TFM	Telefomin, Papua New Guinea
TFN	Tenerife (N. Los Rodeo), Spain
TFS	Tenerife (Reina Sofia), Spain
TGD	Podgorica, Yugoslavia
TGG	Kuala Terengganu, Malaysia
TGH	Tongoa, Vanuatu
TGI	Tingo Maria, Peru
TGJ	Tiga, New Caledonia
TGM	Tirgu Mures, Romania
TGN	Traralgon, Australia
TGR	Touggourt, Algeria
TGU	Tegucigalpa, Honduras
TGZ	Tuxtla Gutierrez, Mexico
THE	Teresina, Brazil
THF	Berlin (Tempelhof), Germany
THG	Thangool, Australia
THL	Tachilek, Myanmar
THN	Trollhattan, Sweden
THR	Tehran, Iran
THS	Sukhothai, Thailand
THU	Pituffik, Greenland
THV	York, PA
TIA	Tirana, Albania
TIC	Tinak Is., Marshall Islands
TID	Tiaret, Algeria
TIE	Tippi, Ethiopia
TIF	Taif, Saudi Arabia
TIH	Tikehau Atoll, Fr. Polynesia
TIJ	Tijuana, Mexico
TIM	Tembagapura, Indonesia
TIN	Tindouf, Algeria
TIP	Tripoli, Libya
TIQ	Tinian, Mariana Islands
TIR	Tirupati, India
TIS	Thursday Is., Australia
TIU	Timaru, New Zealand
TIV	Tivat, Yugoslavia
TIY	Tidjikja, Mauritania
TIZ	Tari, Papua New Guinea
TJA	Tarija, Bolivia
TJH	Toyooka, Japan
TJI	Trujillo, Honduras
TJK	Tokat, Turkey
TJM	Tyumen, Russia
TKB	Tekadu, Papua New Guinea
TKE	Tenakee Springs, AK
TKG	Bandar Lampung, Indonesia
TKJ	Tok, AK
TKK	Truk, Micronesia
TKN	Tokunoshima, Japan
TKP	Takapoto, Fr. Polynesia
TKQ	Kigoma, Tanzania
TKS	Tokushima, Japan
TKU	Turku, Finland
TKX	Takaroa, Fr. Polynesia
TLA	Teller, AK
TLE	Tulear, Madagascar
TLH	Tallahassee, FL
TLJ	Tatalina, AK
TLL	Tallinn, Estonia
TLM	Tlemsen, Algeria
TLN	Toulon, France
TLS	Toulouse, France
TLT	Tuluksak, AK
TLV	Tel Aviv (Jaffa), Israel
TME	Tame, Colombia
TMG	Tomanggong, Malaysia
TMI	Tumling Tar, Nepal

TMJ	Termez, Uzbekistan
TMM	Tamatave, Madagascar
TMN	Tamana Island, Kiribati
TMP	Tampere, Finland
TMR	Tamanrasset, Algeria
TMS	Sao Tome Island
TMT	Trombetas, Brazil
TMU	Tambor, Costa Rica
TMW	Tamworth, Australia
TMX	Timimoun, Algeria
TNA	Jinan, China
TNC	Tin City, AK
TNE	Tanegashima, Japan
TNG	Tangier, Morocco
TNK	Tununak, AK
TNN	Tainan, Taiwan
TNO	Tamarindo, Costa Rica
TNR	Antananarivo, Madagascar
TNX	Stung Treng, Cambodia
TOD	Tioman, Malaysia
TOE	Tozeur, Tunisia
TOF	Tomsk, Russia
TOG	Togiak, AK
TOH	Torres, Vanuatu
TOL	Toledo, OH
TOM	Timbuktu (Tombouctou), Mali
TOP	Topeka, KS
TOS	Tromso, Norway
TOU	Touho, New Caledonia
TOV	Tortola (Westend), BVI
TOW	Toledo, Brazil
TOY	Toyama, Japan
TPA	Tampa/St. Pete., FL
TPE	Taipei (Chiang Kai Shek), Taiwan
TPI	Tapini, Papua New Guinea
TPJ	Taplejung, Nepal
TPP	Tarapoto, Peru
TPQ	Tepic, Mexico
TPS	Trapani, Italy
TRA	Taramajima, Japan
TRB	Turbo, Colombia
TRC	Torreon, Mexico
TRD	Trondheim, Norway
TRE	Tiree, Scotland, UK
TRF	Sandefjord, Norway
TRG	Tauranga, New Zealand
TRI	Tri-City Airport (Bristol/ Johnson City/Kingsport), TN
TRK	Tarakan, Indonesia
TRN	Turin, Italy
TRO	Taree, Australia
TRS	Trieste, Italy

TRU	Trujillo, Peru
TRV	Trivandrum, India
TRW	Tarawa, Kiribati
TRZ	Tiruchirapally, India
TSA	Taipei (Sung Shan), Taiwan
TSB	Tsumeb, Namibia
TSE	Akmola, Kazakstan
TSH	Tshikapa, Zaire
TSJ	Tsushima, Japan
TSN	Tianjin, China
TSO	Isles of Scilly (Tresco), UK
TSR	Timisoara, Romania
TSS	New York (E34th St. H/P), NY
TST	Trang, Thailand
TSU	Tabiteuea South, Kiribati
TSV	Townsville, Australia
TTA	Tan Tan, Morocco
TTE	Ternate, Indonesia
TTJ	Tottori, Japan
TTN	Trenton, NJ
TTQ	Tortuquero, Costa Rica
TTR	Tanjung Pandan, Indonesia
TTS	Tsaratanana, Madagascar
TTT	Taitung, Taiwan
TTU	Tetuan, Morocco
TUB	Tubuai, Fr. Polynesia
TUC	Tucuman, Argentina
TUF	Tours, France
TUG	Tuguegarao, Philippines
TUI	Turaif, Saudi Arabia
TUJ	Tum, Ethiopia
TUK	Turbat, Pakistan
TUL	Tulsa, OK
TUN	Tunis, Tunisia
TUO	Taupo, New Zealand
TUP	Tupelo, MS
TUR	Tucurui, Brazil
TUS	Tucson, AZ
TUU	Tabuk, Saudi Arabia
TUZ	Tucuma, Brazil
TVA	Morafenobe, Madagascar
TVC	Traverse City, MI
TVF	Thief River Falls, MN
TVL	Lake Tahoe, CA
TVU	Taveuni, Fiji
TVY	Dawe, Myanmar
TWA	Twin Hills, AK
TWB	Toowoomba, Australia
TWF	Twin Falls, ID
TWU	Tawau, Malaysia
TXG	Taichung, Taiwan
TXK	Texarkana, AR
TXL	Berlin (Tegel), Germany

TXN	Tunxi, China	UNG	Kiunga, Papua New Guinea
TYF	Torsby, Sweden	UNI	Union Island, St. Vincent
TYL	Talara, Peru	UNK	Unalakleet, AK
TYN	Taiyuan, China	UNN	Ranong, Thailand
TYO	Tokyo (Metro), Japan	UNT	Unst, Shetland Is., Scotland,
TYR	Tyler, TX		UK
TYS	Knoxville, TN	UPG	Ujung Pandang, Indonesia
TZA	Belize City (Municipal),	UPN	Uruapan, Mexico
	Belize	URA	Uralsk, Kazakstan
TZN	South Andros, Bahamas	URC	Urumqi, China
TZX	Trabzon, Turkey	URG	Uruguaiana, Brazil
UAK	Narsarsuaq, Greenland	URJ	Uraj, Russia
UAQ	San Juan, Argentina	URO	Rouen, France
UAS	Samburu, Kenya	URR	Urrao, Colombia
UBA	Uberaba, Brazil	URT	Surat Thani, Thailand
UBI	Buin, Papua New Guinea	URY	Gurayat, Saudi Arabia
UBJ	Ube, Japan	USH	Ushuaia, Argentina
UBP	Ubon Ratchathani, Thailand	USL	Useless Loop, Australia
UBS	Columbus, MS	USM	Koh Samui, Thailand
UCA	Utica, New York	USN	Ulsan, Korea
UCT	Ukhta, Russia	USU	Busuanga, Philippines
UDI	Uberlandia, Brazil	UTH	Udon Thani, Thailand
UDR	Udaipur, India	UTK	Utirik Is., Marshall Islands
UEE	Queenstown, Australia	UTN	Upington, South Africa
UEL	Quelimane, Mozambique	UTO	Utopia Creek, AK
UEO	Kumejima, Japan	UTP	Utapao, Thailand
UET	Quetta, Pakistan	UTT	Umtata, South Africa
UFA	Ufa, Russia	UUD	Ulan-Ude, Russia
UGB	Pilot Point (Ugashik), AK	UUS	Yuzhno-Sakhalinsk, Russia
UGC	Urgench, Uzbekistan	UVE	Ouvea, New Caledonia
UGI	Uganik, AK	UVF	St. Lucia (Hewanorra), West
UGO	Uige, Angola		Indies
UIB	Quibdo, Colombia	UVL	New Valley, Egypt
UIH	Qui Nhon, Viet Nam	UVO	Uvol, Papua New Guinea
UII	Utila, Honduras	UYN	Yulin, China
UIK	Ust-Ilimsk, Russia	VAA	Vaasa, Finland
UIN	Quincy, IL	VAG	Varginha, Brazil
UIO	Quito, Ecuador	VAI	Vanimo, Papua New Guinea
UIP	Quimper, France	VAK	Chevak, AK
UIQ	Quine Hill, Vanuatu	VAN	Van, Turkey
UIT	Jaluit Is., Marshall Islands	VAO	Suavanao, Solomon Islands
UJE	Ujae Is., Marshall Islands	VAR	Varna, Bulgaria
UKK	Ust-Kamenogorsk,	VAS	Sivas, Turkey
	Kazakstan	VAV	Vava'u, Tonga
UKU	Nuku, Papua New Guinea	VAW	Vardoe, Norway
ULB	Ulei, Vanuatu	VBV	Vanuabalavu, Fiji
ULD	Ulundi, South Africa	VBY	Visby, Sweden
ULE	Sule, Papua New Guinea	VCD	Victoria R. Downs, Australia
ULG	Ulgit, Mongolia	VCE	Venice, Italy
ULN	Ulan Bator, Mongolia	VCP	Sao Paolo (Viracopas), Brazil
ULP	Quilpie, Australia	VCT	Victoria, TX
UMD	Uummannaq, Greenland	VDA	Ovda, Israel
UME	Umea, Sweden	VDB	Fagernes, Norway
UMR	Woomera, Australia	VDC	Vitoria Da Conquista, Brazil

VDE	Valverde, Spain	VUP	Valledupar, Colombia
VDM	Viedma, Argentina	VVC	Villavicencio, Colombia
VDS	Vadso, Norway	VVI	Santa Cruz (Viru Viru),
VDZ	Valdez, AK		Bolivia
VEE	Venetie, AK	VVO	Vladivostok, Russia
VEL	Vernal, UT	VVZ	Illizi, Algeria
VER	Veracruz, Mexico	VXC	Lichinga, Mozambique
VEV	Barakoma, Solomon Islands	VXE	Sao Vicente, Cape Verde
VEY	Vestmannaeyjar, Iceland		Islands
VFA	Victoria Falls, Zimbabwe	VXO	Vaxjo, Sweden
VGD	Vologda, Russia	WAA	Wales, AK
VGO	Vigo, Spain	WAE	Wadi-Ad-Dawasir, Saudi
VGT	Las Vegas (N. Terminal), NV		Arabia
VHC	Saurimo, Angola	WAG	Wanganui, New Zealand
VHM	Vilhelmina, Sweden	WAI	Antosohihy, Madagascar
VIA	Videira, Brazil	WAM	Ambatondrazaka,
VIE	Vienna, Austria		Madagascar
VII	Vinh City, Vietnam	WAQ	Antsalova, Madagascar
VIJ	Virgin Gorda, BVI	WAS	Washington (Metro), DC
VIL	Dakhla, Morocco	WAT	Waterford, Ireland
VIS	Visalia, CA	WAW	Warsaw, Poland
VIT	Vitoria, Spain	WBB	Stebbins, AK
VIU	Viru, Solomon Islands	WBM	Wapenamanda, Papua New
VIV	Vivigani, Papua New Guinea		Guinea
VKO	Moscow (Vnukovo), Russia	WBQ	Beaver, AK
VKS	Vicksburg, MS	WDG	Enid, OK
VLC	Valencia, Spain	WDH	Windhoek (Intl), Namibia
VLD	Valdosta, GA	WED	Wedau, Papua New Guinea
VLG	Villa Gesell, Argentina	WEF	Weifang, China
VLI	Port Vila, Vanuatu	WEH	Weihai, China
VLL	Valladolid, Spain	WEI	Weipa, Australia
VLN	Valencia, Venezuela	WFI	Fianarantsoa, Madagascar
VLP	Vila Rica, Brazil	WFK	Frenchville, ME
VLS	Valesdir, Vanuatu	WGA	Wagga Wagga, Australia
VME	Villa Mercedes, Argentina	WGE	Walgett, Australia
VMU	Baimuru, Papua New Guinea	WGP	Waingapu, Indonesia
VNA	Saravane, Laos	WHD	Hyder, AK
VNO	Vilnius, Lithuania	WHK	Whakatane, New Zealand
VNS	Varanasi, India	WHR	Vail (Stolport), CO
VNY	Los Angeles (Van Nuys), CA	WIC	Wick, Scotland, UK
VOG	Volgograd, Russia	WIL	Nairobi (Wilson), Kenya
VOH	Vohemar, Madagascar	WIN	Winton, Australia
VOZ	Voronezh, Russia	WIR	Wairoa, New Zealand
VQS	Vieques, PR	WIU	Witu, Papua New Guinea
VRA	Varadero, Cuba	WJA	Woja, Marshall Islands
VRC	Virac, Philippines	WKA	Wanaka, New Zealand
VRK	Varkaus, Finland	WKJ	Wakkanai, Japan
VRN	Verona, Italy	WKK	Aleknagik, AK
VRY	Vaeroy, Norway	WKR	Walker's Cay, Bahamas
VSA	Villahermosa, Mexico	WLG	Wellington, New Zealand
VST	Vasteras, Sweden	WLH	Walaha, Vanuatu
VTE	Vientiane, Laos	WLK	Selawik, AK
VTU	Las Tunas, Cuba	WLL	Wollogorang, Australia
VTZ	Vishakhapatnam, India	WLS	Wallis Is., Wallis & Futuna

	Islands		
		XBN	Biniguni, Papua New Guinea
WMA	Mandritsara, Madagascar	XCH	Christmas Is., Indian Ocean
WME	Mount Keith, Australia	XFN	Xiangfan, China
WMH	Mountain Home, AR	XIC	Xichang, China
WMK	Meyers Chuck, AK	XIY	Xi An (Xianyang), China
WMN	Maroantsetra, Madagascar	XKH	Xieng Khouang, Laos
WMO	White Mountain, AK	XKS	Kasabonika, OT
WMR	Mananara, Madagascar	XLB	Lac Brochet, MB
WNA	Napakiak, AK	XMG	Mahendranagar, Nepal
WNN	Wunnummin Lake, OT	XMH	Manihi, Fr. Polynesia
WNP	Naga, Philippines	XMN	Xiamen, China
WNR	Windorah, Australia	XNN	Xining, China
WNS	Nawabshah, Pakistan	XPK	Pukatawagan, MB
WNZ	Wenzhou, China	XQP	Quepos, Costa Rica
WRE	Whangarei, New Zealand	XQU	Qualicum, BC
WRG	Wrangell, AK	XRY	Jerez de la Frontera, Spain
WRL	Worland, WY	XSC	South Caicos, Turks & Caicos
WRO	Wroclaw, Poland	XSI	South Indian Lake, MB
WRY	Westray, Scotland, UK	XTG	Thargomindah, Australia
WSN	South Naknek, AK	XYA	Yandina, Solomon Islands
WSP	Waspam, Nicaragua	YAA	Anahim Lake, BC
WST	Westerly, RI	YAB	Arctic Bay, NT
WSU	Wasu, Papua New Guinea	YAC	Cat Lake, OT
WSX	Westsound, WA	YAG	Fort Francis, OT
WSZ	Westport, New Zealand	YAK	Yakutat, AK
WTD	West End, Bahamas	YAM	Sault Ste. Marie, OT
WTE	Wotje Is., Marshall Islands	YAO	Yaounde, Cameroon
WTK	Noatak, AK	YAP	Yap, Micronesia
WTL	Tuntutuliak, AK	YAT	Attawapiskat, OT
WTO	Wotho, Marshall Islands	YAX	Angling Lake, OT
WTP	Woitape Is., Papua New	YAY	St. Anthony, NF
	Guinea	YAZ	Tofino, BC
WTS	Tsiroanomandidy,	YBA	Banff, AB
	Madagascar	YBC	Baie Comeau, QU
WUD	Wudinna, Australia	YBE	Uranium City, SA
WUG	Wau, Papua New Guinea	YBG	Bagotville, QU
WUH	Wuhan, China	YBI	Black Tickle, NF
WUN	Wiluna, Australia	YBK	Baker Lake, NT
WUS	Wuyishan, China	YBL	Campbell River, BC
WUZ	Wuzhou, China	YBP	Yibin, China
WVB	Walvis Bay, Namibia	YBR	Brandon, MB
WVK	Manakara, Madagascar	YBS	Opapamiska Lake, OT
WVN	Wilhelmshaven, Germany	YBT	Brochet, MB
WWK	Wewak, Papua New Guinea	YBV	Berens River, MB
WWP	Whale Pass, AK	YBW	Bedwell Harbour, BC
WWT	Newtok, AK	YBX	Blanc Sablon, QU
WWY	West Wyalong, Australia	YCB	Cambridge Bay, NT
WXN	Wanxian, China	YCD	Nanaimo, BC
WYA	Whyalla, Australia	YCG	Castlegar, BC
WYN	Wyndham, Australia	YCH	Chatham, NB
WZY	Nassau (SPB), Bahamas	YCK	Colville Lake, NT
XAP	Chapeco, Brazil	YCL	Charlo, NB
XAY	Xayabury, Laos	YCN	Cochrane, OT
XBE	Bearskin Lake, OT	YCR	Cross Lake, MB

YCS	Chesterfield Inlet, NT	YIB	Atikokan, OT
YCY	Clyde River, NT	YIF	Pakuashipi, QU
YDA	Dawson City, YT	YIH	Yichang, China
YDF	Deer Lake, NF	YIK	Ivujivik, QU
YDI	Davis Inlet, NF	YIN	Yining, China
YDL	Dease Lake, BC	YIO	Pond Inlet, NT
YDN	Dauphin, MB	YIV	Island Lake, MB
YDP	Nain, NF	YIW	Yiwu, China
YDQ	Dawson Creek, BC	YJT	Stephenville, NF
YDS	Desolation Sound, BC	YKA	Kamloops, BC
YEA	Edmonton (Metro), AB	YKG	Kangirsuk, QU
YEC	Yechon, Korea	YKL	Schefferville, QU
YED	Edmonton (Namao), AB	YKM	Yakima, WA
YEG	Edmonton (Intl), AB	YKN	Yankton, SD
YEK	Arviat, NT	YKQ	Waskaganish, QU
YEL	Elliot Lake, OT	YKS	Yakutsk, Russia
YER	Fort Severn, OT	YKU	Chisasibi, QU
YEV	Inuvik, NT	YKX	Kirkland Lake, OT
YFA	Fort Albany, OT	YLC	Kimmirut/Lake Harbour, NT
YFB	Iqaluit, NT	YLD	Chapleau, OT
YFC	Fredericton, NB	YLH	Lansdowne House, OT
YFH	Fort Hope, OT	YLL	Lloydminster, AB
YFO	Flin Flon, MB	YLR	Leaf Rapids, MB
YFR	Fort Resolution, NT	YLS	Lebel-Sur-Quevillion, QU
YFS	Fort Simpson, NT	YLW	Kelowna, BC
YFX	Fox Harbour, NF	YMH	Mary's Harbour, NF
YGB	Gillies Bay, BC	YMM	Fort McMurray, AB
YGG	Ganges Harbor, BC	YMN	Makkovik, NF
YGH	Fort Good Hope, NT	YMO	Moosonee, OT
YGJ	Yonago, Japan	YMQ	Montreal (Metro), QU
YGK	Kingston, OT	YMS	Yurimaguas, Peru
YGL	La Grande, QU	YMT	Chibougamau, QU
YGO	Gods Narrows, MB	YMX	Montreal (Mirabel), QU
YGP	Gaspe, QU	YNA	Natashquan, QU
YGQ	Geraldton, OT	YNB	Yanbo, Saudi Arabia
YGR	Iles de la Madeleine, QU	YNC	Wemindji, QU
YGT	Igloolik, NT	YND	Gatineau/Hull, QU
YGV	Havre St. Pierre, QU	YNE	Norway House, MB
YGW	Kuujjuarapik, QU	YNG	Youngstown, OH
YGX	Gillam, MB	YNJ	Yanji, China
YGZ	Grise Fiord, NT	YNL	Points North Landing, SA
YHA	Port Hope Simpson, NF	YNO	North Spirit Lake, OT
YHD	Dryden, OT	YNS	Nemiscau, QU
YHF	Hearst, OT	YNT	Yantai, China
YHG	Charlottetown, NF	YOC	Old Crow, YT
YHI	Holman Island, NT	YOH	Oxford House, MB
YHK	Gjoa Haven, NT	YOJ	High Level, AB
YHM	Hamilton, OT	YOL	Yola, Nigeria
YHN	Hornepayne, OT	YOP	Rainbow Lake, AB
YHO	Hopedale, NF	YOW	Ottawa (Intl), OT
YHR	Chevery, QU	YPA	Prince Albert, SA
YHS	Sechelt, BC	YPB	Port Alberni, BC
YHY	Hay River, NT	YPC	Paulatuk, NT
YHZ	Halifax (Intl), NS	YPE	Peace River, AB

YPH	Inukjuak, QU		YTO	Toronto (Metro), OT
YPJ	Aupaluk, QU		YTQ	Tasiujuaq, QU
YPL	Pickle Lake, OT		YTS	Timmins, OT
YPM	Pikangikum, OT		YTZ	Toronto (Toronto Is.), OT
YPN	Port Menier, QU		YUB	Tuktoyaktuk, NT
YPO	Peawanuk, OT		YUD	Umiujaq, QU
YPR	Prince Rupert, BC		YUF	Pelly Bay, NT
YPT	Pender Harbor, BC		YUL	Montreal (Dorval), QU
YPW	Powell River, BC		YUM	Yuma, AZ
YPY	Fort Chipewyan, AB		YUT	Repluse Bay, NT
YQB	Quebec, QU		YUX	Hall Beach, NT
YQC	Quaqtaq, QU		YUY	Rouyn, QU
YQD	The Pas, MB		YVA	Moroni, Comoros
YQG	Windsor, OT		YVC	La Ronge, SA
YQH	Watson Lake, YT		YVM	Broughton Island, NT
YQI	Yarmouth, NS		YVO	Val D'Or, QU
YQK	Kenora, OT		YVP	Kuujjuaq, QU
YQL	Lethbridge, AB		YVQ	Norman Wells, NT
YQM	Moncton, NB		YVR	Vancouver (Intl), BC
YQQ	Comox, BC		YVZ	Deer Lake, OT
YQR	Regina, SA		YWB	Kangiqsujuaq, QU
YQT	Thunder Bay, OT		YWG	Winnipeg, MB
YQU	Grande Prairie, AB		YWH	Victoria (Inner Harbour), BC
YQX	Gander, NF		YWJ	Deline, NT
YQY	Sydney, NS		YWK	Wabush, NF
YQZ	Quesnel, BC		YWL	Williams Lake, BC
YRA	Rae Lakes, NT		YWP	Webequie, OT
YRB	Resolute, NT		YXC	Cranbrook, BC
YRD	Dean River, BC		YXD	Edmonton (Muni), AB
YRF	Cartwright, NF		YXE	Saskatoon, SA
YRG	Rigolet, NF		YXH	Medicine Hat, AB
YRJ	Roberval, QU		YXJ	Fort St. John, BC
YRL	Red Lake, OT		YXK	Rimouski, QU
YRO	Ottawa (Rockcliffe), OT		YXL	Sioux Lookout, OT
YRR	Stuart Island, BC		YXN	Whale Cove, NT
YRS	Red Sucker Lake, MB		YXP	Pangnirtung, NT
YRT	Rankin Inlet, NT		YXR	Earlton, OT
YSB	Sudbury, OT		YXS	Prince George, BC
YSE	Swan River, MB		YXT	Terrace, BC
YSF	Stony Rapids, SA		YXU	London, OT
YSJ	St. John, NB		YXY	Whitehorse, YT
YSK	Sankiluaq, NT		YXZ	Wawa, OT
YSL	St. Leonard, NB		YYB	North Bay, OT
YSM	Fort Smith, NT		YYC	Calgary (Intl), AB
YSN	Salmon Arm, BC		YYD	Smithers, BC
YSO	Postville, NF		YYE	Fort Nelson, BC
YSR	Nanisivik, NT		YYF	Penticton, BC
YST	Ste. Therese Point, MB		YYG	Charlottetown, PE
YSY	Sachs Harbour, NT		YYH	Taloyoak, NT
YTA	Pembroke, OT		YYJ	Victoria (Intl), BC
YTE	Cape Dorset, NT		YYL	Lynn Lake, MB
YTF	Alma, QU		YYQ	Churchill, MB
YTH	Thompson, MB		YYR	Goose Bay, NF
YTL	Big Trout Lake, OT		YYT	St. Johns, NF

YYU	Kapuskasing, OT		ZHA	Zhambyl, Kazakstan
YYY	Mont Joli, QU		ZIG	Ziguinchor, Senegal
YYZ	Toronto (Pearson), OT		ZIH	Ixtapa/Zihautenejo, Mexico
YZE	Gore Bay, OT		ZKE	Kaschechewan, OT
YZF	Yellowknife, NT		ZKG	Kegaska, QU
YZG	Salluit, QU		ZLO	Manzanillo, Mexico
YZP	Sandspit, BC		ZLT	La Tabatiere, QU
YZS	Coral Harbour, NT		ZNA	Nanaimo (Harbour), BC
YZT	Port Hardy, BC		ZNE	Newman, Australia
YZV	Sept-Iles, QU		ZNZ	Zanzibar, Tanzania
ZAD	Zadar, Croatia		ZOS	Osorno, Chile
ZAG	Zagreb, Croatia		ZPB	Sachigo Lake, OT
ZAH	Zahedan, Iran		ZQN	Queenstown, New Zealand
ZAL	Valdivia, Chile		ZRH	Zurich, Switzerland
ZAM	Zamboanga, Philippines		ZRJ	Round Lake, OT
ZAT	Zhaotong, China		ZSA	San Salvador, Bahamas
ZAZ	Zaragoza, Spain		ZSJ	Sandy Lake, OT
ZBF	Bathurst, NB		ZSW	Prince Rupert (Seal Cove), BC
ZBR	Chah-Bahar, Iran			
ZBX	Branson, MO		ZTH	Zakinthos Is., Greece
ZBY	Sayaboury, Laos		ZTM	Shamattawa, MB
ZCL	Zacatecas, Mexico		ZUH	Zhuhai, China
ZCO	Temuco, Chile		ZUM	Churchill Falls, NF
ZEL	Bella Bella, BC		ZVA	Miandrivazo, Madagascar
ZEM	East Main, QU		ZVK	Savannakhet, Laos
ZFD	Fond du Lac, SA		ZWL	Wollaston Lake, SA
ZGI	Gods River, MB		ZWS	Stuttgart (Main RR), Germany
ZGS	Gethsemani, QU			
ZGU	Gaua, Vanuatu		ZYL	Sylhet, Bangladesh
ZHA	Zhanjiang, China		ZZU	Mzuzu, Malawi

Airlines

AB Airlines	7L	AZX	Air Chathams	CV	
Aces (Colombia)	VX	AES	Air China Int'l	CA	CCA
Action Airlines	XQ	AXQ	Air Company Elf-Air	E6	EFR
Acvila Airlines	WZ	RRM	Air Creebec	YN	CRQ
Ada Air	ZY	ADE	Air Dolomiti	EN	DLA
Adria Airways	JP	ADR	Air East	A5	AEG
Aer Lingus	EI	EIN	Air Engiadina	RQ	RQX
Aero Asia Int'l	E4		Air Europa	UX	AEA
Aero California	JR		Air Exel NL	XT	
Aero Continente	N6	ACQ	Air Express	XV	
Aero Costa Rica	ML		Air Facilities	FZ	
Aero Lineas Sosa	P4		Air Fiji	PC	FAJ
Aero Lloyd	YP	AEF	Air France	AF	AFR
Aero Zambia	Z9		Air Gabon	GN	AGN
Aero-Service (Congo)	5R		Air Georgia	DA	GEO
Aerocaribe	QA		Air Glaciers	GB	AGV
Aeroejecutivo	SX	AJO	Air Greece	JG	AGJ
Aeroflot	SU	AFL	Air Guadeloupe	TX	
Aerolineas Argentinas	AR	ARG	Air Iceland	NY	FNA
Aerolineas Dominicanas			Air India	AI	AIC
(Dominair)	YU	ADM	Air Inter Europe	IT	ITF
Aeromexico	AM	AMX	Air Inuit	3H	AIE
Aeroperlas	WL		Air Ivoire	VU	VUN
Aeroperu	PL	PLI	Air Jamaica	JM	AJM
Aerosanta Airlines	UJ	ASP	Air Jamaica Express	JQ	JMX
AeroSur (Bolivia)	5L		Air Jet	BC	AIJ
Aerosweet (Ukraine)	VV	AEW	Air Kazakstan	2Y	
African Intercontinental			Air Koryo	JS	KOR
(Gambia)	OY	AIN	Air Liberte	VD	LIB
Air 2000	DP	AMM	Air Lines of Kuban	GW	KIL
Air Affaires Afrique	6R		Air Link Pty.	DR	
Air Afrique	RK	RKA	Air Lithuania	TT	KLA
Air Algerie	AH	DAH	Air Littoral	FU	LIT
Air Alliance	3J	AAQ	Air Macau	NX	
Air Aruba	FQ	ARU	Air Madagascar	MD	MDG
Air Atlantic	9A	ATL	Air Malawi	QM	AML
Air Austral	UU	REU	Air Maldives	L6	AMI
Air Baltic	BT		Air Mali	L9	MLI
Air Belgium Int'l	AJ	ABB	Air Malta	KM	AMC
Air Bosna	JA		Air Mandalay	6T	
Air Botswana	BP	BOT	Air Manitoba	7N	NAM
Air Burundi	PB	PBU	Air Marshall Islands	CW	MRS
Air Caledonie	TY	TPC	Air Martinique	PN	
Air Caledonie Int'l	SB	ACI	Air Mauritanie	MR	MRT
Air Canada	AC	ACA	Air Mauritius	MK	MAU
Air Caraibes Exploi-			Air Midwest	ZV	AMW
tations	WS	ISB	Air Moldova	9U	MLD
Air Caribbean Ltd.	C2	CBB	Air Moldova Int'l	3R	MLV

Air Namibia	SW	NMB	Airways International	HO	AWB
Air Nauru	ON	RON	Aklak Inc.	6L	AKK
Air Nevada	LW	ANV	Alas De Venezuela	VH	
Air New Zealand	NZ	ANZ	Alaska Airlines	AS	ASA
Air Nippon	EL	ANK	Alaska Island Air	8Z	
Air Niugini	PX	ANG	Albanian Airlines	LV	LBC
Air Normandie	ID	RNO	Alitalia	AZ	AZA
Air North (Yukon Terr.)	4N		Alitalia Team	RD	NOV
Air Nostrum	YW	ANS	All Nippon Airways	NH	ANA
Air Nova	QK	ARN	Alliance Air (India)	CD	
Air Nunavit	YH		Alliance Airlines (US)	3A	AFJ
Air One	AP		Alliance (Uganda)	Y2	
Air Ontario	GX	ONT	ALM (Antillean Airlines)	LM	ALM
Air Ostrava	8K	VTR	Aloha Airlines	AQ	AAH
Air Pacific Ltd.	FJ	FJI	Aloha Islandair	WP	PRI
Air Philippines	3G	APQ	ALPI Eagles	E8	ELG
Air Rarotonga	GZ		Alpine Aviation	5A	AIP
Air Rwanda	RY	RWD	America West Airlines	HP	AWE
Air Sask Aviation	7W	ASK	American Airlines	AA	AAL
Air Senegal	DS	DSB	American Trans Air	TZ	AMT
Air Seychelles	HM	SEY	Americana de Aviacion	8A	ANE
Air Sicilia	BM		Andesmar Lineas Aereas	CK	NDR
Air Sinai	4D	ASD	Ansett Australia	AN	AAA
Air Slovakia	GM	SVK	Ansett New Zealand	ZQ	
Air South	WV	KKB	AOM French Airlines	IW	AOM
Air St. Barthelemy	OJ		APA Int'l Air	7P	APY
Air St. Martin	S6		Apollo Airlines	K6	
Air St. Pierre	PJ		Arax Airways	Y5	RXR
Air St. Thomas	ZP		Archana Airways	F5	
Air Stord	GO		Arctic Circle Air Service	5F	CIR
Air Straubing	IU	ASN	Arcus Air Logistic	ZE	AZE
Air Sunshine	YI	RSI	Ariana Afghan Airlines	FG	AFG
Air Tahiti	VT	VTA	Arkia-Israeli Airlines	IZ	AIZ
Air Tanzania	TC	ATC	Armenian Airlines	R3	
Air Tindi	8T		ARPA Aerolineas		
Air Toulouse	SH	TLE	Paraguayas	A8	
Air Transport Pyrenees	TF	TPR	Aserca (Venezuela)	R7	OCA
Air Truck	ZH	TRK	Asia Pacific Airlines	A6	MLP
Air Tungaru	VK	TUN	Asiana Airlines	OZ	AAR
Air UK	UK	UKA	Aspiring Air	OI	
Air Ukraine	6U	UKR	Associated Airlines	V2	
Air Urga	3N	URG	Athabaska Airways	9T	ABS
Air Vanuatu	NF	AVN	Atlantic Airways		
Air Vegas	6V		(Faroe Is.)	RC	FLI
Air Wisconsin	ZW	AWI	Augsburg-Airways	IQ	AUB
Air Zimbabwe	UM	AZW	Augusta Airways	HB	
Airasia	AK		Aurigny Air Services	GR	AUR
Airborne of Sweden	ZF	MIW	Aus-Air	NO	
Airkenya Aviation	QP		Austral Lineas Aereas	AU	AUT
Airlanka	UL	ALK	Austrian Airlines	OS	AUA
Airlines of Carriacou	C4		Austrian Airtransport	OG	AAT
Airlines of Tasmania	IP	ATM	Avant Airlines	OT	
Airnorth Regional	TL	ANO	Avensa (Aerovias		
AirTran	FL		Venezolanas)	VE	AVE

Aviacion Del Noreste	OC	ANW	Cape York Air Services	NS	
Aviaco (Spain)	AO	AYC	Cardinal Airlines	NN	
Aviacompany Turk-			CaribAir	B9	
menistan	T5	TUA	Caribbean Air	9G	CRB
Aviacsa	6A	CHP	Carnival Air Lines	KW	CAA
Aviaenergo	7U		Casino Express	XP	
Avianca	AV	AVA	Cathay Pacific Airways	CX	CPA
AVIATECA (Guatemala)	GU	GUG	Cayman Airways	KX	CAY
Aviation Commercial			CCAir	ED	CDL
Aviation	BJ		CEBU Pacific Air	5J	
Aviosarda SRL	DF	ADZ	Centennial Airlines	BE	CNA
Azerbaijan Hava Yollary	J2	AHY	Central Mountain Air	9M	GLR
Azzurra Air	ZS		Chalair	M6	
Bahamasair	UP	BHS	Changan Airlines	2Z	CGN
Baker Aviation	8Q	BAJ	Chautauqua Airlines	US*	CHQ
Balkan-Bulgarian			Chicago Express	C8	WDY
Airlines	LZ	LAZ	China Airlines	CI	CAL
Bangkok Airways	PG	BKP	China Eastern Airlines	MU	CES
Base Airlines	5E		China Northern Airlines	CJ	CBF
Bashkir Airlines (BAL)	V9	BTC	China Northwest Airlines	WH	CNW
Baxter Aviation	6B		China Southern Airlines	CZ	CSN
Bearskin Airlines	JV	BLS	China Southwest	SZ	CXN
Belavia	B2	BRU	China Yunnan Airlines	3Q	CYH
Bellair	7G		Chitaavia	X7	CHF
Bellview Airlines	B3	BLV	Cimber Air	QI	CIM
Bemidji Airlines	CH	BMJ	City Bird	H2	
Bering Air	8E	BRG	Cityflyer Express	FD	CFE
Berjaya Air	J8		Cityjet	WX	BCY
Bhoja Airlines	B4		Coast Air K.S.	BX	CST
Big Sky Airlines	GQ	BSY	Coastal Air Transport	DQ	CXT
Biman Bangladesh	BG	BBC	Colgan Air	9L	
Binter Canarias	NT	IBB	Columbia Pacific Airlines	7C	
Bonaire Airways	C7	BNR	Comair	OH	COM
Braathens SAFE	BU	BRA	Commercial Airways	MN	CAW
Brasil Central	JJ	BLC	Compagnie Africaine		
Bright Air	C6	BHT	d'Aviation (CAA)	E9	
Brit Air	DB	BZH	Condor Flugdienst	DE	CFG
British Airways	BA	BAW	Conquest Airlines	5C	CAC
British International	BS	BIH	Contact Air	V8	
British Mediterranean			Continental Airlines	CO	COA
Airways	KJ	LAJ	Continental Micronesia	CS	CMI
British Midland	BD	BMA	COPA Airlines (Panama)	CM	CMP
Buffalo Airways	J4	BFL	Coral Int'l Airlines	KN	
Business Air Ltd.	II	GNT	Coral Pacific Airlines	CC	
Business Express	HQ	GAA	Corporate Express		
BWIA	BW	BWA	Airlines	3C	
CACM (Corsica)	XK		Country Connection	XL	NSW
Calm Air	MO	CAV	Crimea Air	OR	CRF
Camai Air	R9		Croatia Airlines	OU	CTN
Cameroon Airlines	UY	UYC	Crossair	LX	CRX
Canadian Airlines			Cubana Airlines	CU	CUB
Int'l (CAI)	CP	CDN	Cypress Airlines	R6	
Cape Air	9K	KAP	Cyprus Airways	CY	CYP
Cape Smythe Air Service	6C	CMY	Czech Airlines (CSA)	OK	CSA

Daallo Airlines	D3	
DAC Air	6P	GCP
Danish Air Transport	DX	DTR
Debonair Airways	2G	
Delta Air Lines	DL	DAL
Deutsche BA	DI	BAG
Diamond Sakha Airlines	D8	DSL
Dinar Lineas Aereas	D7	RDN
Djibouti Airlines	MG	DJB
Dneproavia	Z6	UDN
Domodedovo Airlines	E3	DMO
Donavia	D9	DNV
Downeast Express	E7	
Druk Air	KB	DRK
Eagle Airlines (Austria)	ZN	EAV
Eagle Aviation (Kenya)	Y4	EQA
Eagle Canyon Airlines	FE	
East Line Air	P7	ESL
East West Airlines	4S	
Eastland Air	DK	ELA
Eastwind Airlines	W9	
Easyjet Airline	U2	EZY
Ecuatoriana	EU	EEA
Egyptair	MS	MSR
El Al Israel Airlines	LY	ELY
Emerald Airways	G3	JEM
Emirates	EK	UAE
Era Aviation	7H	ERH
Estonian Air	OV	ELL
Estonian Aviation (ELK)	S8	
Ethiopian Airlines	ET	ETH
Euro City Line	LP	
Europe Elite	Y6	
European Airways	L8	EAW
Eurowings	EW	EWG
EVA Airways	BR	EVA
Everest Air	E2	
Executive Airlines	NA	
Executive Express/ Interline	5W	
Express Airlines I	9E	FLG
Expresso Aereo	N8	
F.S. Air Service	Y7	
F'Airlines	4X	FLS
Fairlines	LK	
Falcon Aviation	IH	FCN
Far Eastern Air Transport	EF	FEA
Faucett Peruvian Airline	CF	CFP
Finnair	AY	FIN
Finnaviation	FA	FAV
First Air	7F	FAB
Flamenco Airways	FK	WAF
Flandre Air	IX	FRS
Flight West Airlines	YC	FWQ
Flightline Ltd.	W2	
Flying Enterprise	F3	
Formosa Airlines	VY	FOS
Forty-Mile Air	Q5	MLA
Freedom Air	ZU	FRE
Frontier Airlines	F9	
Fujian Airlines	IV	CFJ
Garuda Indonesia	GA	GIA
GB Airways	GT	GBL
Ghana Airways	GH	GHA
Gill Aviation	9C	GIL
Go One Airways	GK	
Golden Air Flyg	DC	GAO
Gomelavia	YD	
Gorda Aero Service	DV	
Grand Int'l Airways	8L	GDI
Grant Aviation	GS	
Great American Airways	MV	GRA
Great China Airlines	IF	GCA
Great Lakes Aviation	ZK	GLA
Greenlandair	GL	GRL
Guinee Airlines	G7	GIF
Gujarat Airways	G8	GUJ
Gulf Air	GF	GFA
Gulfstream Int'l Airlines	3M	
Guyana Airways	GY	GYA
Hageland Aviation	H6	
Hainan Airlines	H4	
Haines Airways	7A	
Halisa Air	WD	HBC
Hamburg Airlines	HX	HAS
Hapag Lloyd	HF	HLF
Harbor Airlines	HG	HAR
Harbour Air	H3	
Hawaiian Airlines	HA	HAL
Hazelton Airlines	ZL	HZL
Helenair	2Y	HCL
Helgoland Airlines	LE	
Heli Air Monaco	YO	MCM
Heli Inter Riviera	EC	HIN
Helicopteros Del Cusco	ES	
Helijet Airways	JB	JBA
Helikopterservice AB	YQ	SCO
Hemus Air	DU	
Hex'Air	UD	HER
Highland Air	HS	HIL
Holmstroem Air	HJ	SWE
Hong Kong Dragon	KA	HDA
Horizon Air	QX	QXE
Iakutaviatrans Aviation	K7	IKT
Iberia	IB	IBE
Icelandair	FI	ICE
Iliamna Air Taxi	LS	IAR

Airline	Code 1	Code 2
IMAIR Airline	IK	ITX
Impulse Airlines	VQ	OAA
Indian Airlines	IC	IAC
Inter-Air	D6	INL
Interbrasil Star	Q9	
Interimpex-Avioimpex	M4	AXX
Int'l Business Air	U5	IBZ
Int'l Flying Services	F4	IFS
Intersomal (UK)	A2	
Intourtrans	9B	
Iran Air	IR	IRA
Iraqi Airways	IA	IAW
Ireland Airways	2E	EIX
Island Airlines	IS	
Island Express	2S	
Islands Nationair	CN	
Islena Airlines	WC	ISV
Isles of Scilly Skybus	5Y	IOS
Istanbul Airlines	IL	IST
Japan Air Commuter	3X	JAC
Japan Air System	JD	JAS
Japan Airlines	JL	JAL
Japan Asia Airways	EG	JAA
Japan Transocean	NU	JTA
Jaro Int'l	JT	MDJ
JAT (Yugoslavia)	JU	JAT
Jersey European Airways	JY	JEA
Jet Airways (India)	9W	
JetTrain	LF	
K.D. Air	XC	KDC
Kaliningrad Air	K8	KLN
Karair	KR	KAR
Kazakhstan Airlines	K4	KZA
Kendell Airlines	KD	KDA
Kenmore Air	M5	
Kenn Borek Air	4K	KBA
Kenya Airways	KQ	KQA
Ketchikan Air Service	K3	
Keystone Air Service	BZ	
Khabarovsk Aviation Gp.	H8	KHB
Khors Aircompany	X6	KHO
Kiwi Int'l	KP	
Kiwi Travel Int'l (NZ)	KC	KIC
KLM Cityhopper	HN	
KLM Royal Dutch Airlines	KL	KLM
Korean Air Lines (KAL)	KE	KAL
Korsar	6K	
Krasair	7B	KJC
Kuwait Airways	KU	KAC
Kyrghyzstan Airlines	K2	KGA
Kyrnair	KH	
L.A.B. Flying Service	JF	LAB
La Costena	W8	
Labrador Airways	WJ	LAL
LACSA (Costa Rica)	LR	LRC
Ladeco Airlines	UC	LCO
Laker Airways	6F	
LAM (Mozambique)	TM	LAM
Lan Chile	LA	LAN
Lao Aviation	QV	LAO
LAPA (Argentina)	MJ	LPR
LAPSA (Paraguay)	PZ	LAP
Larry's Flying Service	J6	
Las Vegas Airlines	6G	
LASER (Venezuela)	KZ	LER
LATPASS Airlines	QJ	LTP
Lauda Air	NG	LDA
Lesotho Airways	QL	LAI
LGW (Germany)	HE	
LIAT (Antigua)	LI	LIA
Lincoln Airlines	RT	LRT
Linea Aerea IAACA	KG	
Lineas Aereas Allegro	LL	GRO
Lithuanian Airlines	TE	LIL
Lloyd Aereo Boliviano (LAB)	LB	LLB
Loganair	LC	LOG
Lone Star Airlines (Exec Express)	AD	
LOT Polish Airlines	LO	LOT
Love Air	4J	LOV
LTU (Germany)	LT	LTU
Lufthansa	LH	DLH
Lufthansa CityLine	CL	CLH
Luxair	LG	LGL
Lviv Airlines	L7	UKW
Macedonian Airlines	IN	
Maersk Air (Denmark)	DM	DAN
Maersk Air (UK)	VB	
Magadan Airlines	H5	
Mahalo Air	8M	
Mahfooz Aviation	M2	
Malaysian Airline System	MH	MAS
Malev Hungarian Airlines	MA	MAH
Malmo Aviation	6E	SCW
Mandarin Airlines	AE	MDA
Manx Airlines	JE	MNX
Martinair Holland	MP	MPH
Master Aviation	T9	
Maverick Airways	6M	MVR
Maya Airways	MW	MAY
MBA Pty.	CG	
Meridiana	IG	ISS
Mesa Airlines	YV	ASH

Mesaba Aviation	XJ	MES
Mexicana	MX	MXA
MIAT-Mongolian Airlines	OM	MGL
Middle East Airlines		
(AirLiban)	ME	MEA
Midway Airlines	JI	
Midwest Express Airlines	YX	MEP
Minerva Airlines	Q2	MTC
Missionary Aviation	FS	
Modi Luft	M9	
Moldavian Airlines	2M	MDV
Monarch Airlines	ZB	MON
Muk Air	ZR	MUK
Mustique Airways	Q4	MAW
Myanmar Airways	UB	UBA
Nashville Eagle	8N	
Naske Air	HC	
National Airlines		
(South Africa)	YJ	
National Jet Systems	NC	NJS
Nationwide Air	CE	NTW
Necon Air	3Z	
Nepal Airways	7E	
NEPC Airlines	D5	
New England Airlines	EJ	NEA
New York Helicopter	HD	NYH
Newair	WA	NAW
Nicaraguenses de		
Aviacion	6Y	
Nigeria Airways	WT	NGA
Nordeste-LAR	JH	NES
Nordic European Airlines	DJ	NOD
Norontair	NR	NOA
North Coast Aviation Pty.	N9	
North Flying A/S	6Z	NFA
North Vancouver Air	VL	
North-Wright Air	HW	
Northern Australia		
Airlines	FB	
Northwest Airlines	NW	NWA
NTW Air	NV	NWT
O'Connor-Mt. Gambler's		
Airlines	UQ	OCM
Odessa Airlines	5K	ODS
Olson Air Service	4B	
OLT (Germany)	OL	OLT
Olympic Airways	OA	OAL
Oman Aviation (SAOG)	WY	OAS
Orbi Georgian Airways	NQ	DVU
Orenberg Express		
Airlines	R2	ORB
Orient Express Air	OX	
Orient-Avia Airlines	V6	ORT
OY Air Botnia	KF	KFB

Pacific Airlines	BL	PIC
Pacific Airways	GX	
Pacific Coastal Airlines	8P	PCO
Pacific Eagle Airlines	JW	
Pacific Island Aviation	9J	
Pacific Midland	2W	
Pakistan Int'l Airlines		
(PIA)	PK	PIA
Pan Am Air Bridge	OP	CHK
Pan American	PA	
Pantanal	P8	PTN
Papillon Airways	HI	
Paradise Island Airlines	BK	
Passadero Transportes		
Aereos	Y8	PTB
Pelangi Air	9P	PEG
Penair	KS	PEN
Perimeter Aviation	UW	PAG
Philippine Airlines	PR	PAL
Pine State Airlines	PW	
PLUNA (Uruguay)	PU	PUA
Polynesian Ltd.	PH	PAO
Portugalia	NI	PGA
Prima Air/Flyair	QG	
Promech	Z3	
Proteus Airlines	YS	
Provincial Airlines	AG	
PT Bouraq Indonesia		
Airlines	BO	BOU
PT Mandala Airlines	RI	MDL
PT Merpati Nusantara	MZ	MNA
PT Sempati Air	SG	SSR
Ptarmigan Airways	5P	PTA
Qantas Airways	QF	QFA
Qatar Airways	Q7	QTR
Redwing Airways	RX	RWG
Reeve Aleutian Airways	RV	RVV
Regional Airlines		
(France)	VM	RGI
Regional Airlines		
(Morocco)	FN	
Regional Lineas Aereas	XG	RGN
Reguljair	R8	
Reno Air	QQ	
Rheinland Air Service	RW	RLD
Rheintalflug	WE	RTL
Rich Int'l Airways	JN	RIA
Riga Airlines	GV	RIG
Rio-Sul	SL	RSL
Rock Air	8R	RLB
Rottnest Airlines	DW	
Royal Air Cambodge	VJ	
Royal Air Maroc	AT	RAM
Royal Brunei Airlines	BI	RBA

Royal Jordanian	RJ	RJA	Solomon Airlines	IE	SOL
Royal Nepal Airlines	RA	RNA	South African Airlink	4Z	
Royal Swazi Nat'l			South African Airways		
Airways	ZC	RSN	(SAA)	SA	SAA
Royal Tongan Airlines	WR	HRH	South African Express		
Russia	R4	SDM	Airways	YB	
Ryanair Ltd.	FR	RYR	South Central Air	XE	SCA
S.A.R. Avions Taxis	QT		Southern Independent		
Sabena	SN	SAB	Air	F2	
SAETA (Ecuador)	EH	SET	Southern Winds	A4	
Sahara India Airlines	S2		Southwest Airlines	WN	SWA
Samara Airlines	E5	BRZ	Spanair	JK	SPP
Samoa Aviation	TS		Spirit Airlines	NK	
SAN (Ecuador)	WB	SAN	Suckling Airways	CB	SAY
SANSA (Costa Rica)	RZ	LRS	Sudan Airways	SD	SUD
Sardairline	N5		Sun Air	BV	
SATA Air Acores	SP	SAT	Sun Country Airlines	SY	SCX
Saudi Arabian Airlines	SV	SVA	Sunflower Airlines	PI	SUF
Scandinavian Airlines			Sunworld Int'l	SM	
System (SAS)	SK	SAS	Surinam Airways	PY	SLM
Scenic Airlines	YR	YRR	Swan Airlines	HK	
Seaborne Aviation	BB		Swiftair	W3	SWT
Selcon Airlines	U9	SEO	Swissair	SR	SWR
Servivensa	VC		Syrian Arab Airlines	RB	SYR
Shabair	SS		T.A.T. European Airlines	IJ	TAT
Shaheen Air Int'l	NL	SAI	TAAG-Angola	DT	DTA
Shandong Airlines	SC	CDG	Taca Int'l Airlines	TA	TAI
Shanghai Airlines	SF		TACV-Cabo Verde		
Shanxi Airlines	8C		Airlines	VR	TCV
Shenzhen Airlines	4G		TAESA (Mexico)	GD	
Shepparton Airlines	OB		TAL Thuringia	FC	
Shorouk Air	7Q	SHK	TAM (Brazil)	KK	TAM
Shuswap Air	3S	SFC	Tamair	GG	
SIAT	5M		TAME (Ecuador)	EQ	TAE
Siberia Airlines	S7	SBI	Tanana Air Service	4E	TNR
Sichuan Airlines	3U	CSC	TANE (Argentina)	T8	NQN
Sierra National Airlines	LJ	SLA	TAP Air Portugal	TP	TAP
SilkAir	MI	SLK	Taquan Air Service	H7	
Simmons Airlines	MQ		TAROM Romanian Air	RO	ROT
Singapore Airlines	SQ	SIA	Tasawi Air Services	9X	TWI
SK Air	PD		Tatonduk Flying Service	3K	
Skagway Air Service	7J		Tatra Air	QS	TTR
Skargardsflyg AB	5Q		Tavrey Aircompany	T6	TVR
Skippers Aviation	PQ		TCI Skyking	RU	
Sky Trans	NP		Teddy Air	ZJ	TED
Sky West Airlines	OO	SKW	Thai Airways	TG	THA
Skybus	JX		The Mt. Cook Group	NM	NZM
Skyline NEPC	D2		Top Air	B6	TOP
Skyward Aviation	K9	SGK	Tower Air	FF	TOW
Skyways AB	JZ		Trans Air	P6	
Skywest Airlines	YT		Trans Air Congo (TAC)	Y9	
Sochi Airlines	J5	PRL	Trans Cote	7T	
Sociedad Aeronautica de			Trans Pacific Airlines	DN	
Medellin	MM	SAM	Trans State Airlines	9N	

Trans Travel Airlines (TTA)	6N	
Transaero Airlines	UN	TSO
Transasia Airways	GE	
Transavia Airlines	HV	TRA
Transbrasil	TR	TBA
Transcaraibes Air Int'l	DZ	NOE
Transeast Airlines	T4	TRL
Transeuropean Airlines	UE	TEP
Transportes Aereos Da Guine-Bissau	YZ	GBU
Transportes Aeromar (Mexico)	VW	TAO
Transwede Airways	TQ	TOA
Travelair	U3	
Tropic Air	PM	
Tropical Airlines	VF	
TTA (Madagascar)	OF	
Tuninter	UG	TUI
Tunis Air	TU	TAR
Turan Air	3T	URN
Turkestan Airlines	UF	URK
Turkish Airlines	TK	THY
Turks & Caicos Airways	QW	
TWA (Trans World Airlines)	TW	TWA
Tyrolean Airways	VO	TYR
Tyumen Airlines	7M	TYM
U-Land Airlines	UI	
Uganda Airlines	QU	UGA
Ukraine Int'l Airlines	PS	AUI
UNI Airways	B7	UIA
United Airlines	UA	UAL
United Aviation	U7	UAV
United Express	DH	BLR
UP Airways	UZ	
Ural Airlines	U6	SVR
US Airways	US	USA
USAir Shuttle	TB	
Uzbekistan Airways	HY	UZB
ValuJet Airlines	J7	VJA
Vanair	V3	
Vanguard Airlines	NJ	VGD
Varig	RG	VRG
VASP (Brazil)	VP	VSP
VIASA	VA	VIA
Vieques Air Link	VI	VES
Vietnam Airlines	VN	HVN
Virgin Atlantic	VS	VIR
Virgin Express	BQ	EBA
Vladivostok Air	XF	VLK
VLM (Belgium)	VG	VLM
Vnukovo Airlines	V5	VKO
Volga Airlines	G6	VLA
Voyageur Airways	4V	VAL
Warbelow's Air Ventures	4W	VNA
Wasaya Airways	WG	WSG
West Air Sweden	PT	
West Coast Air	8O	
West Isle Air	7Y	
Westair Commuter Airlines	OE	
Western Airlines	EM	
Western Pacific	W7	
Westjet Airlines	M3	
Whyalla Airlines Pty.	WW	WWL
Wideroe's Flyveselskap	WF	WIF
Wilderness Airlines	6W	WLD
Windward Islands Airways	WM	WIA
Wings of Alaska	K5	
Wings West Airlines	RM	
World Airways	WO	WOA
Wright Air Service	8V	
Wuhan Airlines	WU	CWU
Xiamen Airlines	MF	CXA
Xinjiang Airlines	XO	CXJ
Yanda Airlines	ST	
Yemenia Yemen Airways	IY	IYE
Yute Air Alaska	4Y	
Zaire Airlines	EO	EZR
Zambian Express Airlines	OQ	SZX
Zimbabwe Express Airlines	Z7	
Zuliana	OD	

Airline Codes

2E	Ireland Airways	5Y	Isles of Scilly Skybus
2G	Debonair Airways	6A	Aviacsa
2M	Moldavian Airlines	6B	Baxter Aviation
2S	Island Express	6C	Cape Smythe Air Service
2W	Pacific Midland	6E	Malmo Aviation
2Y	Air Kazakstan	6F	Laker Airways
2Y	Helenair	6G	Las Vegas Airlines
2Z	Changan Airlines	6K	Korsar
3A	Alliance Airlines (US)	6L	Aklak Inc.
3C	Corporate Express Airlines	6M	Maverick Airways
3G	Air Philippines	6N	Trans Travel Airlines (TTA)
3H	Air Inuit	6P	DAC Air
3J	Air Alliance	6R	Air Affaires Afrique
3K	Tatonduk Flying Service	6T	Air Mandalay
3M	Gulfstream Int'l Airlines	6U	Air Ukraine
3N	Air Urga	6V	Air Vegas
3Q	China Yunnan Airlines	6W	Wilderness Airlines
3R	Air Moldova Int'l	6Y	Nicaraguenses de Aviacion
3S	Shuswap Air	6Z	North Flying A/S
3T	Turan Air	7A	Haines Airways
3U	Sichuan Airlines	7B	Krasair
3X	Japan Air Commuter	7C	Columbia Pacific Airlines
3Z	Necon Air	7E	Nepal Airways
4B	Olson Air Service	7F	First Air
4D	Air Sinai	7G	Bellair
4E	Tanana Air Service	7H	Era Aviation
4G	Shenzhen Airlines	7J	Skagway Air Service
4J	Love Air	7L	AB Airlines
4K	Kenn Borek Air	7M	Tyumen Airlines
4N	Air North (Yukon Terr.)	7N	Air Manitoba
4S	East West Airlines	7P	APA Int'l Air
4V	Voyageur Airways	7Q	Shorouk Air
4W	Warbelow's Air Ventures	7T	Trans Cote
4X	F'Airlines	7U	Aviaenergo
4Y	Yute Air Alaska	7W	Air Sask Aviation
4Z	South African Airlink	7Y	West Isle Air
5A	Alpine Aviation	8A	Americana de Aviacion
5C	Conquest Airlines	8C	Shanxi Airlines
5E	Base Airlines	8E	Bering Air
5F	Arctic Circle Air Service	8K	Air Ostrava
5J	CEBU Pacific Air	8L	Grand Int'l Airways
5K	Odessa Airlines	8M	Mahalo Air
5L	AeroSur (Bolivia)	8N	Nashville Eagle
5M	SIAT	8O	West Coast Air
5P	Ptarmigan Airways	8P	Pacific Coastal Airlines
5Q	Skargardsflyg AB	8Q	Baker Aviation
5R	Aero-Service (Congo)	8R	Rock Air
5W	Executive Express/Interline	8T	Air Tindi

8V	Wright Air Service	AGJ	Air Greece
8Z	Alaska Island Air	AGN	Air Gabon
9A	Air Atlantic	AGV	Air Glaciers
9B	Intourtrans	AH	Air Algerie
9C	Gill Aviation	AHY	Azerbaijan Hava Yollary
9E	Express Airlines I	AI	Air India
9G	Caribbean Air	AIC	Air India
9J	Pacific Island Aviation	AIE	Air Inuit
9K	Cape Air	AIJ	Air Jet
9L	Colgan Air	AIN	African Intercontinental
9M	Central Mountain Air		(Gambia)
9N	Trans State Airlines	AIP	Alpine Aviation
9P	Pelangi Air	AIZ	Arkia-Israeli Airlines
9T	Athabaska Airways	AJ	Air Belgium Int'l
9U	Air Moldova	AJM	Air Jamaica
9W	Jet Airways (India)	AJO	Aeroejecutivo
9X	Tasawi Air Services	AK	Airasia
A2	Intersomal (UK)	AKK	Aklak Inc.
A4	Southern Winds	ALK	Airlanka
A5	Air East	ALM	ALM (Antillean Airlines)
A6	Asia Pacific Airlines	AM	Aeromexico
A8	ARPA Aerolineas Paraguayas	AMC	Air Malta
AA	American Airlines	AMI	Air Maldives
AAA	Ansett Australia	AML	Air Malawi
AAH	Aloha Airlines	AMM	Air 2000
AAL	American Airlines	AMT	American Trans Air
AAQ	Air Alliance	AMW	Air Midwest
AAR	Asiana Airlines	AMX	Aeromexico
AAT	Austrian Airtransport	AN	Ansett Australia
ABB	Air Belgium Int'l	ANA	All Nippon Airways
ABS	Athabaska Airways	ANE	Americana de Aviacion
AC	Air Canada	ANG	Air Niugini
ACA	Air Canada	ANK	Air Nippon
ACI	Air Caledonie Int'l	ANO	Airnorth Regional
ACQ	Aero Continente	ANS	Air Nostrum
AD	Lone Star Airlines (Exec	ANV	Air Nevada
	Express)	ANW	Aviacion Del Noreste
ADE	Ada Air	ANZ	Air New Zealand
ADM	Aerolineas Dominicanas	AO	Aviaco (Spain)
	(Dominair)	AOM	AOM French Airlines
ADR	Adria Airways	AP	Air One
ADZ	Aviosarda SRL	APQ	Air Philippines
AE	Mandarin Airlines	APY	APA Int'l Air
AEA	Air Europa	AQ	Aloha Airlines
AEF	Aero Lloyd	AR	Aerolineas Argentinas
AEG	Air East	ARG	Aerolineas Argentinas
AES	Aces (Colombia)	ARN	Air Nova
AEW	Aerosweet (Ukraine)	ARU	Air Aruba
AF	Air France	AS	Alaska Airlines
AFG	Ariana Afghan Airlines	ASA	Alaska Airlines
AFJ	Alliance Airlines (US)	ASD	Air Sinai
AFL	Aeroflot	ASH	Mesa Airlines
AFR	Air France	ASK	Air Sask Aviation
AG	Provincial Airlines	ASN	Air Straubing

ASP	Aerosanta Airlines	BL	Pacific Airlines
AT	Royal Air Maroc	BLC	Brasil Central
ATC	Air Tanzania	BLR	United Express
ATL	Air Atlantic	BLS	Bearskin Airlines
ATM	Airlines of Tasmania	BLV	Bellview Airlines
AU	Austral Lineas Aereas	BM	Air Sicilia
AUA	Austrian Airlines	BMA	British Midland
AUB	Augsburg-Airways	BMJ	Bemidji Airlines
AUI	Ukraine Int'l Airlines	BNR	Bonaire Airways
AUR	Aurigny Air Services	BO	PT Bouraq Indonesia Airlines
AUT	Austral Lineas Aereas	BOT	Air Botswana
AV	Avianca	BOU	PT Bouraq Indonesia Airlines
AVA	Avianca	BP	Air Botswana
AVE	Avensa (Aerovias	BQ	Virgin Express
	Venezolanas)	BR	EVA Airways
AVN	Air Vanuatu	BRA	Braathens SAFE
AWB	Airways International	BRG	Bering Air
AWE	America West Airlines	BRU	Belavia
AWI	Air Wisconsin	BRZ	Samara Airlines
AXQ	Action Airlines	BS	British International
AXX	Interimpex-Avioimpex	BSY	Big Sky Airlines
AY	Finnair	BT	Air Baltic
AYC	Aviaco (Spain)	BTC	Bashkir Airlines (BAL)
AZ	Alitalia	BU	Braathens SAFE
AZA	Alitalia	BV	Sun Air
AZE	Arcus Air Logistic	BW	BWIA
AZW	Air Zimbabwe	BWA	BWIA
AZX	AB Airlines	BX	Coast Air K.S.
B2	Belavia	BZ	Keystone Air Service
B3	Bellview Airlines	BZH	Brit Air
B4	Bhoja Airlines	C2	Air Caribbean Ltd.
B6	Top Air	C4	Airlines of Carriacou
B7	UNI Airways	C6	Bright Air
B9	CaribAir	C7	Bonaire Airways
BA	British Airways	C8	Chicago Express
BAG	Deutsche BA	CA	Air China Int'l
BAJ	Baker Aviation	CAA	Carnival Air Lines
BAW	British Airways	CAC	Conquest Airlines
BB	Seaborne Aviation	CAL	China Airlines
BBC	Biman Bangladesh	CAV	Calm Air
BC	Air Jet	CAW	Commercial Airways
BCY	Cityjet	CAY	Cayman Airways
BD	British Midland	CB	Suckling Airways
BE	Centennial Airlines	CBB	Air Caribbean Ltd.
BFL	Buffalo Airways	CBF	China Northern Airlines
BG	Biman Bangladesh	CC	Coral Pacific Airlines
BHS	Bahamasair	CCA	Air China Int'l
BHT	Bright Air	CD	Alliance Air (India)
BI	Royal Brunei Airlines	CDG	Shandong Airlines
BIH	British International	CDL	CCAir
BJ	Aviation Commercial	CDN	Canadian Airlines
	Aviation		International (CAI)
BK	Paradise Island Airlines	CE	Nationwide Air
BKP	Bangkok Airways	CES	China Eastern Airlines

CF	Faucett Peruvian Airline	CYP	Cyprus Airways
CFE	Cityflyer Express	CZ	China Southern Airlines
CFG	Condor Flugdienst	D2	Skyline NEPC
CFJ	Fujian Airlines	D3	Daallo Airlines
CFP	Faucett Peruvian Airline	D5	NEPC Airlines
CG	MBA Pty.	D6	Inter-Air
CGN	Changan Airlines	D7	Dinar Lineas Aereas
CH	Bemidji Airlines	D8	Diamond Sakha Airlines
CHF	Chitaavia	D9	Donavia
CHK	Pan Am Air Bridge	DA	Air Georgia
CHP	Aviacsa	DAH	Air Algerie
CHQ	Chautauqua Airlines	DAL	Delta Air Lines
CI	China Airlines	DAN	Maersk Air (Denmark)
CIM	Cimber Air	DB	Brit Air
CIR	Arctic Circle Air Service	DC	Golden Air Flyg
CJ	China Northern Airlines	DE	Condor Flugdienst
CK	Andesmar Lineas Aereas	DF	Aviosarda SRL
CL	Lufthansa CityLine	DH	United Express
CLH	Lufthansa CityLine	DI	Deutsche BA
CM	COPA Airlines (Panama)	DJ	Nordic European Airlines
CMI	Continental Micronesia	DJB	Djibouti Airlines
CMP	COPA Airlines (Panama)	DK	Eastland Air
CMY	Cape Smythe Air Service	DL	Delta Air Lines
CN	Islands Nationair	DLA	Air Dolomiti
CNA	Centennial Airlines	DLH	Lufthansa
CNW	China Northwest Airlines	DM	Maersk Air (Denmark)
CO	Continental Airlines	DMO	Domodedovo Airlines
COA	Continental Airlines	DN	Trans Pacific Airlines
COM	Comair	DNV	Donavia
CP	Canadian Airlines	DP	Air 2000
	International (CAI)	DQ	Coastal Air Transport
CPA	Cathay Pacific Airways	DR	Air Link Pty.
CRB	Caribbean Air	DRK	Druk Air
CRF	Crimea Air	DS	Air Senegal
CRQ	Air Creebec	DSB	Air Senegal
CRX	Crossair	DSL	Diamond Sakha Airlines
CS	Continental Micronesia	DT	TAAG-Angola
CSA	Czech Airlines (CSA)	DTA	TAAG-Angola
CSC	Sichuan Airlines	DTR	Danish Air Transport
CSN	China Southern Airlines	DU	Hemus Air
CST	Coast Air K.S.	DV	Gorda Aero Service
CTN	Croatia Airlines	DVU	Orbi Georgian Airways
CU	Cubana Airlines	DW	Rottnest Airlines
CUB	Cubana Airlines	DX	Danish Air Transport
CV	Air Chathams	DZ	Transcaraibes Air Int'l
CW	Air Marshall Islands	E2	Everest Air
CWU	Wuhan Airlines	E3	Domodedovo Airlines
CX	Cathay Pacific Airways	E4	Aero Asia Int'l
CXA	Xiamen Airlines	E5	Samara Airlines
CXJ	Xinjiang Airlines	E6	Air Company Elf-Air
CXN	China Southwest	E7	Downeast Express
CXT	Coastal Air Transport	E8	ALPI Eagles
CY	Cyprus Airways	E9	Compagnie Africaine
CYH	China Yunnan Airlines		d'Aviation (CAA)

EAV	Eagle Airlines (Austria)
EAW	European Airways
EBA	Virgin Express
EC	Heli Inter Riviera
ED	CCAir
EEA	Ecuatoriana
EF	Far Eastern Air Transport
EFR	Air Company Elf-Air
EG	Japan Asia Airways
EH	SAETA (Ecuador)
EI	Aer Lingus
EIN	Aer Lingus
EIX	Ireland Airways
EJ	New England Airlines
EK	Emirates
EL	Air Nippon
ELA	Eastland Air
ELG	ALPI Eagles
ELL	Estonian Air
ELY	El Al Israel Airlines
EM	Western Airlines
EN	Air Dolomiti
EO	Zaire Airlines
EQ	TAME (Ecuador)
EQA	Eagle Aviation (Kenya)
ERH	Era Aviation
ES	Helicopteros Del Cusco
ESL	East Line Air
ET	Ethiopian Airlines
ETH	Ethiopian Airlines
EU	Ecuatoriana
EVA	EVA Airways
EW	Eurowings
EWG	Eurowings
EZR	Zaire Airlines
EZY	Easyjet Airline
F2	Southern Independent Air
F3	Flying Enterprise
F4	Int'l Flying Services
F5	Archana Airways
F9	Frontier Airlines
FA	Finnaviation
FAB	First Air
FAJ	Air Fiji
FAV	Finnaviation
FB	Northern Australia Airlines
FC	TAL Thuringia
FCN	Falcon Aviation
FD	Cityflyer Express
FE	Eagle Canyon Airlines
FEA	Far Eastern Air Transport
FF	Tower Air
FG	Ariana Afghan Airlines
FI	Icelandair

FIN	Finnair
FJ	Air Pacific Ltd.
FJI	Air Pacific Ltd.
FK	Flamenco Airways
FL	AirTran
FLG	Express Airlines I
FLI	Atlantic Airways (Faroe Is.)
FLS	F'Airlines
FN	Regional Airlines (Morocco)
FNA	Air Iceland
FOS	Formosa Airlines
FQ	Air Aruba
FR	Ryanair Ltd.
FRE	Freedom Air
FRS	Flandre Air
FS	Missionary Aviation
FU	Air Littoral
FWQ	Flight West Airlines
FZ	Air Facilities
G3	Emerald Airways
G6	Volga Airlines
G7	Guinee Airlines
G8	Gujarat Airways
GA	Garuda Indonesia
GAA	Business Express
GAO	Golden Air Flyg
GB	Air Glaciers
GBL	GB Airways
GBU	Transportes Aereos Da Guine-Bissau
GCA	Great China Airlines
GCP	DAC Air
GD	TAESA (Mexico)
GDI	Grand Int'l Airways
GE	Transasia Airways
GEO	Air Georgia
GF	Gulf Air
GFA	Gulf Air
GG	Tamair
GH	Ghana Airways
GHA	Ghana Airways
GIA	Garuda Indonesia
GIF	Guinee Airlines
GIL	Gill Aviation
GK	Go One Airways
GL	Greenlandair
GLA	Great Lakes Aviation
GLR	Central Mountain Air
GM	Air Slovakia
GN	Air Gabon
GNT	Business Air Ltd.
GO	Air Stord
GQ	Big Sky Airlines
GR	Aurigny Air Services

108   *THE INTREPID TRAVELER'S COMPLETE DESK REFERENCE*

GRA	Great American Airways	HZL	Hazelton Airlines
GRL	Greenlandair	IA	Iraqi Airways
GRO	Lineas Aereas Allegro	IAC	Indian Airlines
GS	Grant Aviation	IAR	Iliamna Air Taxi
GT	GB Airways	IAW	Iraqi Airways
GU	AVIATECA (Guatemala)	IB	Iberia
GUG	AVIATECA (Guatemala)	IBB	Binter Canarias
GUJ	Gujarat Airways	IBE	Iberia
GV	Riga Airlines	IBZ	Int'l Business Air
GW	Air Lines of Kuban	IC	Indian Airlines
GX	Air Ontario	ICE	Icelandair
GX	Pacific Airways	ID	Air Normandie
GY	Guyana Airways	IE	Solomon Airlines
GYA	Guyana Airways	IF	Great China Airlines
GZ	Air Rarotonga	IFS	Int'l Flying Services
H2	City Bird	IG	Meridiana
H3	Harbour Air	IH	Falcon Aviation
H4	Hainan Airlines	II	Business Air Ltd.
H5	Magadan Airlines	IJ	T.A.T. European Airlines
H6	Hageland Aviation	IK	IMAIR Airline
H7	Taquan Air Service	IKT	Iakutaviatrans Aviation
H8	Khabarovsk Aviation Gp.	IL	Istanbul Airlines
HA	Hawaiian Airlines	IN	Macedonian Airlines
HAL	Hawaiian Airlines	INL	Inter-Air
HAR	Harbor Airlines	IOS	Isles of Scilly Skybus
HAS	Hamburg Airlines	IP	Airlines of Tasmania
HB	Augusta Airways	IQ	Augsburg-Airways
HBC	Halisa Air	IR	Iran Air
HC	Naske Air	IRA	Iran Air
HCL	Helenair	IS	Island Airlines
HD	New York Helicopter	ISB	Air Caraibes Exploitations
HDA	Hong Kong Dragon	ISS	Meridiana
HE	LGW (Germany)	IST	Istanbul Airlines
HER	Hex'Air	ISV	Islena Airlines
HF	Hapag Lloyd	IT	Air Inter Europe
HG	Harbor Airlines	ITF	Air Inter Europe
HI	Papillon Airways	ITX	IMAIR Airline
HIL	Highland Air	IU	Air Straubing
HIN	Heli Inter Riviera	IV	Fujian Airlines
HJ	Holmstroem Air	IW	AOM French Airlines
HK	Swan Airlines	IX	Flandre Air
HLF	Hapag Lloyd	IY	Yemenia Yemen Airways
HM	Air Seychelles	IYE	Yemenia Yemen Airways
HN	KLM Cityhopper	IZ	Arkia-Israeli Airlines
HO	Airways International	J2	Azerbaijan Hava Yollary
HP	America West Airlines	J4	Buffalo Airways
HQ	Business Express	J5	Sochi Airlines
HRH	Royal Tongan Airlines	J6	Larry's Flying Service
HS	Highland Air	J7	ValuJet Airlines
HV	Transavia Airlines	J8	Berjaya Air
HVN	Vietnam Airlines	JA	Air Bosna
HW	North-Wright Air	JAA	Japan Asia Airways
HX	Hamburg Airlines	JAC	Japan Air Commuter
HY	Uzbekistan Airways	JAL	Japan Airlines

JAS	Japan Air System	KH	Kyrnair
JAT	JAT (Yugoslavia)	KHB	Khabarovsk Aviation Gp.
JB	Helijet Airways	KHO	Khors Aircompany
JBA	Helijet Airways	KIC	Kiwi Travel Int'l (NZ)
JD	Japan Air System	KIL	Air Lines of Kuban
JE	Manx Airlines	KJ	British Mediterranean
JEA	Jersey European Airways		Airways
JEM	Emerald Airways	KJC	Krasair
JF	L.A.B. Flying Service	KK	TAM (Brazil)
JG	Air Greece	KKB	Air South
JH	Nordeste-LAR	KL	KLM Royal Dutch Airlines
JI	Midway Airlines	KLA	Air Lithuania
JJ	Brasil Central	KLM	KLM Royal Dutch Airlines
JK	Spanair	KLN	Kaliningrad Air
JL	Japan Airlines	KM	Air Malta
JM	Air Jamaica	KN	Coral Int'l Airlines
JMX	Air Jamaica Express	KOR	Air Koryo
JN	Rich Int'l Airways	KP	Kiwi Int'l
JP	Adria Airways	KQ	Kenya Airways
JQ	Air Jamaica Express	KQA	Kenya Airways
JR	Aero California	KR	Karair
JS	Air Koryo	KS	Penair
JT	Jaro Int'l	KU	Kuwait Airways
JTA	Japan Transocean	KW	Carnival Air Lines
JU	JAT (Yugoslavia)	KX	Cayman Airways
JV	Bearskin Airlines	KZ	LASER (Venezuela)
JW	Pacific Eagle Airlines	KZA	Kazakhstan Airlines
JX	Skybus	L6	Air Maldives
JY	Jersey European Airways	L7	Lviv Airlines
JZ	Skyways AB	L8	European Airways
K2	Kyrghyzstan Airlines	L9	Air Mali
K3	Ketchikan Air Service	LA	Lan Chile
K4	Kazakhstan Airlines	LAB	L.A.B. Flying Service
K5	Wings of Alaska	LAI	Lesotho Airways
K6	Apollo Airlines	LAJ	British Mediterranean
K7	Iakutaviatrans Aviation		Airways
K8	Kaliningrad Air	LAL	Labrador Airways
K9	Skyward Aviation	LAM	LAM (Mozambique)
KA	Hong Kong Dragon	LAN	Lan Chile
KAC	Kuwait Airways	LAO	Lao Aviation
KAL	Korean Air Lines (KAL)	LAP	LAPSA (Paraguay)
KAP	Cape Air	LAZ	Balkan-Bulgarian Airlines
KAR	Karair	LB	Lloyd Aereo Boliviano (LAB)
KB	Druk Air	LBC	Albanian Airlines
KBA	Kenn Borek Air	LC	Loganair
KC	Kiwi Travel Int'l (NZ)	LCO	Ladeco Airlines
KD	Kendell Airlines	LDA	Lauda Air
KDA	Kendell Airlines	LE	Helgoland Airlines
KDC	K.D. Air	LER	LASER (Venezuela)
KE	Korean Air Lines (KAL)	LF	JetTrain
KF	OY Air Botnia	LG	Luxair
KFB	OY Air Botnia	LGL	Luxair
KG	Linea Aerea IAACA	LH	Lufthansa
KGA	Kyrghyzstan Airlines	LI	LIAT (Antigua)

LIA	LIAT (Antigua)	MG	Djibouti Airlines
LIB	Air Liberte	MGL	MIAT-Mongolian Airlines
LIL	Lithuanian Airlines	MH	Malaysian Airline System
LIT	Air Littoral	MI	SilkAir
LJ	Sierra National Airlines	MIW	Airborne of Sweden
LK	Fairlines	MJ	LAPA (Argentina)
LL	Lineas Aereas Allegro	MK	Air Mauritius
LLB	Lloyd Aereo Boliviano (LAB)	ML	Aero Costa Rica
LM	ALM (Antillean Airlines)	MLA	Forty-Mile Air
LO	LOT Polish Airlines	MLD	Air Moldova
LOG	Loganair	MLI	Air Mali
LOT	LOT Polish Airlines	MLP	Asia Pacific Airlines
LOV	Love Air	MLV	Air Moldova Int'l
LP	Euro City Line	MM	Sociedad Aeronautica de
LPR	LAPA (Argentina)		Medellin
LR	LACSA (Costa Rica)	MN	Commercial Airways
LRC	LACSA (Costa Rica)	MNA	PT Merpati Nusantara
LRS	SANSA (Costa Rica)	MNX	Manx Airlines
LRT	Lincoln Airlines	MO	Calm Air
LS	Iliamna Air Taxi	MON	Monarch Airlines
LT	LTU (Germany)	MP	Martinair Holland
LTP	LATPASS Airlines	MPH	Martinair Holland
LTU	LTU (Germany)	MQ	Simmons Airlines
LV	Albanian Airlines	MR	Air Mauritanie
LW	Air Nevada	MRS	Air Marshall Islands
LX	Crossair	MRT	Air Mauritanie
LY	El Al Israel Airlines	MS	Egyptair
LZ	Balkan-Bulgarian Airlines	MSR	Egyptair
M2	Mahfooz Aviation	MTC	Minerva Airlines
M3	Westjet Airlines	MU	China Eastern Airlines
M4	Interimpex-Avioimpex	MUK	Muk Air
M5	Kenmore Air	MV	Great American Airways
M6	Chalair	MVR	Maverick Airways
M9	Modi Luft	MW	Maya Airways
MA	Malev Hungarian Airlines	MX	Mexicana
MAH	Malev Hungarian Airlines	MXA	Mexicana
MAS	Malaysian Airline System	MZ	PT Merpati Nusantara
MAU	Air Mauritius	N5	Sardairline
MAW	Mustique Airways	N6	Aero Continente
MAY	Maya Airways	N8	Expresso Aereo
MCM	Heli Air Monaco	N9	North Coast Aviation Pty.
MD	Air Madagascar	NA	Executive Airlines
MDA	Mandarin Airlines	NAM	Air Manitoba
MDG	Air Madagascar	NAW	Newair
MDJ	Jaro Int'l	NC	National Jet Systems
MDL	PT Mandala Airlines	NDR	Andesmar Lineas Aereas
MDV	Moldavian Airlines	NEA	New England Airlines
ME	Middle East Airlines (AirLiban)	NES	Nordeste-LAR
		NF	Air Vanuatu
MEA	Middle East Airlines (AirLiban)	NFA	North Flying A/S
		NG	Lauda Air
MEP	Midwest Express Airlines	NGA	Nigeria Airways
MES	Mesaba Aviation	NH	All Nippon Airways
MF	Xiamen Airlines	NI	Portugalia

NJ	Vanguard Airlines	OP	Pan Am Air Bridge
NJS	National Jet Systems	OQ	Zambian Express Airlines
NK	Spirit Airlines	OR	Crimea Air
NL	Shaheen Air Int'l	ORB	Orenberg Express Airlines
NM	The Mt. Cook Group	ORT	Orient-Avia Airlines
NMB	Air Namibia	OS	Austrian Airlines
NN	Cardinal Airlines	OT	Avant Airlines
NO	Aus-Air	OU	Croatia Airlines
NOA	Norontair	OV	Estonian Air
NOD	Nordic European Airlines	OX	Orient Express Air
NOE	Transcaraibes Air Int'l	OY	African Intercontinental
NOV	Alitalia Team		(Gambia)
NP	Sky Trans	OZ	Asiana Airlines
NQ	Orbi Georgian Airways	P4	Aero Lineas Sosa
NQN	TANE (Argentina)	P6	Trans Air
NR	Norontair	P7	East Line Air
NS	Cape York Air Services	P8	Pantanal
NSW	Country Connection	PA	Pan American
NT	Binter Canarias	PAG	Perimeter Aviation
NTW	Nationwide Air	PAL	Philippine Airlines
NU	Japan Transocean	PAO	Polynesian Ltd.
NV	NTW Air	PB	Air Burundi
NW	Northwest Airlines	PBU	Air Burundi
NWA	Northwest Airlines	PC	Air Fiji
NWT	NTW Air	PCO	Pacific Coastal Airlines
NX	Air Macau	PD	SK Air
NY	Air Iceland	PEG	Pelangi Air
NYH	New York Helicopter	PEN	Penair
NZ	Air New Zealand	PG	Bangkok Airways
NZM	The Mt. Cook Group	PGA	Portugalia
OA	Olympic Airways	PH	Polynesian Ltd.
OAA	Impulse Airlines	PI	Sunflower Airlines
OAL	Olympic Airways	PIA	Pakistan Int'l Airlines (PIA)
OAS	Oman Aviation (SAOG)	PIC	Pacific Airlines
OB	Shepparton Airlines	PJ	Air St. Pierre
OC	Aviacion Del Noreste	PK	Pakistan Int'l Airlines (PIA)
OCA	Aserca (Venezuela)	PL	Aeroperu
OCM	O'Connor-Mt. Gambler's	PLI	Aeroperu
	Airlines	PM	Tropic Air
OD	Zuliana	PN	Air Martinique
ODS	Odessa Airlines	PQ	Skippers Aviation
OE	Westair Commuter Airlines	PR	Philippine Airlines
OF	TTA (Madagascar)	PRI	Aloha Islandair
OG	Austrian Airtransport	PRL	Sochi Airlines
OH	Comair	PS	Ukraine Int'l Airlines
OI	Aspiring Air	PT	West Air Sweden
OJ	Air St. Barthelemy	PTA	Ptarmigan Airways
OK	Czech Airlines (CSA)	PTB	Passadero Transportes
OL	OLT (Germany)		Aereos
OLT	OLT (Germany)	PTN	Pantanal
OM	MIAT-Mongolian Airlines	PU	PLUNA (Uruguay)
ON	Air Nauru	PUA	PLUNA (Uruguay)
ONT	Air Ontario	PW	Pine State Airlines
OO	Sky West Airlines	PX	Air Niugini

PY	Surinam Airways	RNA	Royal Nepal Airlines
PZ	LAPSA (Paraguay)	RNO	Air Normandie
Q2	Minerva Airlines	RO	TAROM Romanian Air
Q4	Mustique Airways	RON	Air Nauru
Q5	Forty-Mile Air	ROT	TAROM Romanian Air
Q7	Qatar Airways	RQ	Air Engiadina
Q9	Interbrasil Star	RQX	Air Engiadina
QA	Aerocaribe	RRM	Acvila Airlines
QF	Qantas Airways	RSI	Air Sunshine
QFA	Qantas Airways	RSL	Rio-Sul
QG	Prima Air/Flyair	RSN	Royal Swazi Nat'l Airways
QI	Cimber Air	RT	Lincoln Airlines
QJ	LATPASS Airlines	RTL	Rheintalflug
QK	Air Nova	RU	TCI Skyking
QL	Lesotho Airways	RV	Reeve Aleutian Airways
QM	Air Malawi	RVV	Reeve Aleutian Airways
QP	Airkenya Aviation	RW	Rheinland Air Service
QQ	Reno Air	RWD	Air Rwanda
QS	Tatra Air	RWG	Redwing Airways
QT	S.A.R. Avions Taxis	RX	Redwing Airways
QTR	Qatar Airways	RXR	Arax Airways
QU	Uganda Airlines	RY	Air Rwanda
QV	Lao Aviation	RYR	Ryanair Ltd.
QW	Turks & Caicos Airways	RZ	SANSA (Costa Rica)
QX	Horizon Air	S2	Sahara India Airlines
QXE	Horizon Air	S6	Air St. Martin
R2	Orenberg Express Airlines	S7	Siberia Airlines
R3	Armenian Airlines	S8	Estonian Aviation (ELK)
R4	Russia	SA	South African Airways (SAA)
R6	Cypress Airlines	SAA	South African Airways (SAA)
R7	Aserca (Venezuela)	SAB	Sabena
R8	Reguljair	SAI	Shaheen Air Int'l
R9	Camai Air	SAM	Sociedad Aeronautica de
RA	Royal Nepal Airlines		Medellin
RAM	Royal Air Maroc	SAN	SAN (Ecuador)
RB	Syrian Arab Airlines	SAS	Scandinavian Airlines
RBA	Royal Brunei Airlines		System (SAS)
RC	Atlantic Airways (Faroe Is.)	SAT	SATA Air Acores
RD	Alitalia Team	SAY	Suckling Airways
RDN	Dinar Lineas Aereas	SB	Air Caledonie Int'l
REU	Air Austral	SBI	Siberia Airlines
RG	Varig	SC	Shandong Airlines
RGI	Regional Airlines (France)	SCA	South Central Air
RGN	Regional Lineas Aereas	SCO	Helikopterservice AB
RI	PT Mandala Airlines	SCW	Malmo Aviation
RIA	Rich Int'l Airways	SCX	Sun Country Airlines
RIG	Riga Airlines	SD	Sudan Airways
RJ	Royal Jordanian	SDM	Russia
RJA	Royal Jordanian	SEO	Selcon Airlines
RK	Air Afrique	SET	SAETA (Ecuador)
RKA	Air Afrique	SEY	Air Seychelles
RLB	Rock Air	SF	Shanghai Airlines
RLD	Rheinland Air Service	SFC	Shuswap Air
RM	Wings West Airlines	SG	PT Sempati Air

SGK	Skyward Aviation	TC	Air Tanzania
SH	Air Toulouse	TCV	TACV-Cabo Verde Airlines
SHK	Shorouk Air	TE	Lithuanian Airlines
SIA	Singapore Airlines	TED	Teddy Air
SK	Scandinavian Airlines	TEP	Transeuropean Airlines
	System (SAS)	TF	Air Transport Pyrenees
SKW	Sky West Airlines	TG	Thai Airways
SL	Rio-Sul	THA	Thai Airways
SLA	Sierra National Airlines	THY	Turkish Airlines
SLK	SilkAir	TK	Turkish Airlines
SLM	Surinam Airways	TL	Airnorth Regional
SM	Sunworld Int'l	TLE	Air Toulouse
SN	Sabena	TM	LAM (Mozambique)
SOL	Solomon Airlines	TNR	Tanana Air Service
SP	SATA Air Acores	TOA	Transwede Airways
SPP	Spanair	TOP	Top Air
SQ	Singapore Airlines	TOW	Tower Air
SR	Swissair	TP	TAP Air Portugal
SS	Shabair	TPC	Air Caledonie
SSR	PT Sempati Air	TPR	Air Transport Pyrenees
ST	Yanda Airlines	TQ	Transwede Airways
SU	Aeroflot	TR	Transbrasil
SUD	Sudan Airways	TRA	Transavia Airlines
SUF	Sunflower Airlines	TRK	Air Truck
SV	Saudi Arabian Airlines	TRL	Transeast Airlines
SVA	Saudi Arabian Airlines	TS	Samoa Aviation
SVK	Air Slovakia	TSO	Transaero Airlines
SVR	Ural Airlines	TT	Air Lithuania
SW	Air Namibia	TTR	Tatra Air
SWA	Southwest Airlines	TU	Tunis Air
SWE	Holmstroem Air	TUA	Aviacompany Turkmenistan
SWR	Swissair	TUI	Tuninter
SWT	Swiftair	TUN	Air Tungaru
SX	Aeroejecutivo	TVR	Tavrey Aircompany
SY	Sun Country Airlines	TW	TWA (Trans World Airlines)
SYR	Syrian Arab Airlines	TWA	TWA (Trans World Airlines)
SZ	China Southwest	TWI	Tasawi Air Services
SZX	Zambian Express Airlines	TX	Air Guadeloupe
T4	Transeast Airlines	TY	Air Caledonie
T5	Aviacompany Turkmenistan	TYM	Tyumen Airlines
T6	Tavrey Aircompany	TYR	Tyrolean Airways
T8	TANE (Argentina)	TZ	American Trans Air
T9	Master Aviation	U2	Easyjet Airline
TA	Taca Int'l Airlines	U3	Travelair
TAE	TAME (Ecuador)	U5	Int'l Business Air
TAI	Taca Int'l Airlines	U6	Ural Airlines
TAM	TAM (Brazil)	U7	United Aviation
TAO	Transportes Aeromar	U9	Selcon Airlines
	(Mexico)	UA	United Airlines
TAP	TAP Air Portugal	UAE	Emirates
TAR	Tunis Air	UAL	United Airlines
TAT	T.A.T. European Airlines	UAV	United Aviation
TB	USAir Shuttle	UB	Myanmar Airways
TBA	Transbrasil	UBA	Myanmar Airways

UC	Ladeco Airlines
UD	Hex'Air
UDN	Dneproavia
UE	Transeuropean Airlines
UF	Turkestan Airlines
UG	Tuninter
UGA	Uganda Airlines
UI	U-Land Airlines
UIA	UNI Airways
UJ	Aerosanta Airlines
UK	Air UK
UKA	Air UK
UKR	Air Ukraine
UKW	Lviv Airlines
UL	Airlanka
UM	Air Zimbabwe
UN	Transaero Airlines
UP	Bahamasair
UQ	O'Connor-Mt. Gambler's Airlines
URG	Air Urga
URK	Turkestan Airlines
URN	Turan Air
US	US Airways
US*	Chautauqua Airlines
USA	US Airways
UU	Air Austral
UW	Perimeter Aviation
UX	Air Europa
UY	Cameroon Airlines
UYC	Cameroon Airlines
UZ	UP Airways
UZB	Uzbekistan Airways
V2	Associated Airlines
V3	Vanair
V5	Vnukovo Airlines
V6	Orient-Avia Airlines
V8	Contact Air
V9	Bashkir Airlines (BAL)
VA	VIASA
VAL	Voyageur Airlines
VB	Maersk Air (UK)
VC	Servivensa
VD	Air Liberte
VE	Avensa (Aerovias Venezolanas)
VES	Vieques Air Link
VF	Tropical Airlines
VG	VLM (Belgium)
VGD	Vanguard Airlines
VH	Alas De Venezuela
VI	Vieques Air Link
VIA	VIASA
VIR	Virgin Atlantic
VJ	Royal Air Cambodge
VJA	ValuJet Airlines
VK	Air Tungaru
VKO	Vnukovo Airlines
VL	North Vancouver Air
VLA	Volga Airlines
VLK	Vladivostok Air
VLM	VLM (Belgium)
VM	Regional Airlines (France)
VN	Vietnam Airlines
VNA	Warbelow's Air Ventures
VO	Tyrolean Airways
VP	VASP (Brazil)
VQ	Impulse Airlines
VR	TACV-Cabo Verde Airlines
VRG	Varig
VS	Virgin Atlantic
VSP	VASP (Brazil)
VT	Air Tahiti
VTA	Air Tahiti
VTR	Air Ostrava
VU	Air Ivoire
VUN	Air Ivoire
VV	Aerosweet (Ukraine)
VW	Transportes Aeromar (Mexico)
VX	Aces (Colombia)
VY	Formosa Airlines
W2	Flightline Ltd.
W3	Swiftair
W7	Western Pacific
W8	La Costena
W9	Eastwind Airlines
WA	Newair
WAF	Flamenco Airways
WB	SAN (Ecuador)
WC	Islena Airlines
WD	Halisa Air
WDY	Chicago Express
WE	Rheintalflug
WF	Wideroe's Flyveselskap
WG	Wasaya Airways
WH	China Northwest Airlines
WIA	Windward Islands Airways
WIF	Wideroe's Flyveselskap
WJ	Labrador Airways
WL	Aeroperlas
WLD	Wilderness Airlines
WM	Windward Islands Airways
WN	Southwest Airlines
WO	World Airways
WOA	World Airways
WP	Aloha Islandair
WR	Royal Tongan Airlines

WS	Air Caraibes Exploitations	YJ	National Airlines (South Africa)
WSG	Wasaya Airways		
WT	Nigeria Airways	YN	Air Creebec
WU	Wuhan Airlines	YO	Heli Air Monaco
WV	Air South	YP	Aero Lloyd
WW	Whyalla Airlines Pty.	YQ	Helikopterservice AB
WWL	Whyalla Airlines Pty.	YR	Scenic Airlines
WX	Cityjet	YRR	Scenic Airlines
WY	Oman Aviation (SAOG)	YS	Proteus Airlines
WZ	Acvila Airlines	YT	Skywest Airlines
X6	Khors Aircompany	YU	Aerolineas Dominicanas (Dominair)
X7	Chitaavia		
XC	K.D. Air	YV	Mesa Airlines
XE	South Central Air	YW	Air Nostrum
XF	Vladivostok Air	YX	Midwest Express Airlines
XG	Regional Lineas Aereas	YZ	Transportes Aereos Da Guine-Bissau
XJ	Mesaba Aviation		
XK	CACM (Corsica)	Z3	Promech
XL	Country Connection	Z6	Dneproavia
XO	Xinjiang Airlines	Z7	Zimbabwe Express Airlines
XP	Casino Express	Z9	Aero Zambia
XQ	Action Airlines	ZB	Monarch Airlines
XT	Air Exel NL	ZC	Royal Swazi Nat'l Airways
XV	Air Express	ZE	Arcus Air Logistic
Y2	Alliance (Uganda)	ZF	Airborne of Sweden
Y4	Eagle Aviation (Kenya)	ZH	Air Truck
Y5	Arax Airways	ZJ	Teddy Air
Y6	Europe Elite	ZK	Great Lakes Aviation
Y7	F.S. Air Service	ZL	Hazelton Airlines
Y8	Passadero Transportes Aereos	ZN	Eagle Airlines (Austria)
		ZP	Air St. Thomas
Y9	Trans Air Congo (TAC)	ZQ	Ansett New Zealand
YB	South African Express Airways	ZR	Muk Air
		ZS	Azzurra Air
YC	Flight West Airlines	ZU	Freedom Air
YD	Gomelavia	ZV	Air Midwest
YH	Air Nunavit	ZW	Air Wisconsin
YI	Air Sunshine	ZY	Ada Air

Hotels & Rental Cars

Hotel Companies

Adams Mark Hotels	AM	Doubletree Hotels	DT
Airco Servicestal	AZ	E R S	ER
All Suites	AS	Econolodge	EO
Ambassador Services	AV	El San Juan Hotels	EJ
Amerisuites	AJ	Embassy Suites	ES
AMR Info Service	AR	Expotel Room Center	RN
ANA Hotels Int'l	AN	Fairfield Inn	FN
Anasazi Service Corp.	AX	Fairmont Hotels	FA
Aston Hotels & Resorts	AH	Fiesta Americana	FH
Astra Worldwide Hotel	AW	Fimotel	FL
Astron Hotels	AP	Forte Hotels	FE
Bachelor Quarters	BQ	Four Seasons Hotels	FS
Bartell Hotels	BB	Friendship Inns	FZ
Bed & Breakfast Direct	BD	Garden Plaza Hotels	GP
Best Western Int'l	BW	Global Home Network	HN
Biltmore Hotels	BM	Global Reservations	GR
Bravo Communication	GB	Golden Tulip Hotels	GT
BTH Hotels	BT	Grand Heritage	GH
Canadian Pacific Hotels	CP	Grand Traditions Hotels	GD
Caribbean Information	CB	Grande Collection of Hotels	GC
Carlyle Hotel	CH	Grande Devere Hotel	FT
CDL Millennium	MU	Grupo Sol	ME
Clarion Collection	CC	Guesthouse International	GA
Classic International Hotels	IH	Hampton Inns	HX
Coast Westcoast Hotel	WX	Harrahs Hotels	HR
Colony Resorts	CS	Harvey Hotels	HV
Comfort Inns	CI	Hawaiian Pacific Resorts	HP
Concorde Hotels	CD	Hawthorne Suites	BH
Consort Hotels	CN	Helmsley Harley Hotel	HE
Copthorne Hotels	BC	Hilton Hotels	HH
Corporate Resorts	CZ	Hilton International	HL
Country Comfort	TH	Holiday Inn Worldwide	HI
Country Inn By Carlson	CX	Homewood Suites	HG
Courtyard	CY	Hotel Connect Services	AC
Courtyard Inns Canada	XS	Hotel Des Gouveneurs	HQ
Crescent Hotels	CQ	Hotel Link	HU
Crown Sterling	OO	Hotel Okura	OC
Datalead Communications	DC	Hotels Camino Real	XC
Days Inns	DI	Howard Johnson	HJ
Delta Hotels	DE	Hyatt Hotels	HY
Design Hotels	DS	Ian Schrager	MR
Disneyland Paris Hotels	ED	Innlink	SM
Doral Hotels	DA	Insignia Resorts	IG
Dorint Hotels	DO	Int'l Travel & Resorts	IT

Int'l Travel Svcs, Broward	TS	Radisson Hotels	RD
Inter Europe Hotels	IE	Ramada Hotels	NR
Inter-Continental Hotels	IC	Ramada Inns	RA
Intourist	IS	Reconline	ON
Intourtrans	IN	Red Lion Hotels	RL
Jack Tar Villages	JV	Red Roof Inns	RV
Japan Travel Bureau, Inc.	JJ	Regal Hotels Int'l	RQ
Jarvinen Worldwide Hotels	JA	Regent Int'l Hotels	RE
Jolly Hotels	JH	Registry Hotels	RH
Jumer Hotels	JU	Renaissance Hotels	BR
Kempinski Hotels	KI	Residence Inn	RC
Key System	KK	Resinter	RT
Keytel Hotels	KY	Righa Royal Hotels	RR
Kimton Hotel Group	KC	Ritz-Carlton Hotels	RZ
La Quinta Motor Inns	LQ	Robert F. Warner	RW
Lanyon Ltd.	LL	Rodeway Inns	RI
Las Vegas Travel	NV	Romantik Hotels	RM
Leading Hotels	LW	Royce Hotels	RY
Lexington Management	LM	Ruby Foo	RF
Little America Hotels	LA	Sarova Hotels	SV
Loews Hotels	LZ	Sceptre Hospitality	SC
LRI	LH	Select Marketing Hotels	SQ
Mandarin Oriental	MO	Shangri-La Hotels	SG
Manhattan East Suites	NY	Sheraton Hotels	SI
Marco Polo Hotels	MH	Shiloh Inns	BP
Maritime Hotels	MM	Signature Inns	SJ
Marriott Hotels	MC	Sleep Inns	SZ
MGM Grand Hotel	MG	Small Luxury Hotels	LX
Mirvac Hotels	MV	Sonesta Hotels	SO
Monte Carlo Resorts	MN	Southern Pacific Hotels	SP
Movenpick Hotels	MK	SRS Hotels	SR
Ms Minto Pl Suites	MS	Stakis Hotel Group	SK
My Favorite Sunset	CU	Stations Casinos Hotels	LV
Navy Lodging	NL	Sterling International	WR
Nendels Corporation	NE	Summerfield Suites	SS
New Otani Hotels	NO	Summit Int'l Hotels	XL
Nikko Hotels Int'l	NK	Supranational Hotels	SX
Nordic Team Hotels	NT	Susse Chalet	CE
NTA Hotel Ryokan	NH	Swallow Hotels	UK
Oberoi Hotels	OB	Swissotel	SL
Omni Hotels	OM	The Small Hotel Co.	SB
Outrigger Hotels	OR	Thistle Hotels	TI
Pan Pacific Hotels	PF	Thomas Hotels	HB
Park Inn Int'l	PA	Top International Hotels	TP
Park Lane Hotels	PL	Tranquility Base	BZ
Park Plaza Hotels	PK	Travamerica	TA
Pointe Resorts	PO	Travelodge	TL
Preferred Hotels	PH	Treff Hotels	TX
Premier World Marketing	PE	Trust International	TR
Prima Hotels	PW	Ultimate Resorts	UR
Princess Hotels	PI	Unihotel	UL
Quality Hotel Reservations	QR	Utell Hotels	UI
Quality Inns	QI	Vacation Break	VB
Queens Moat Houses	QL	Vacation Network	VN

Vagabond Inns	VA	Wellesley Inns	WL
Venture Inns	VI	Westin Hotels	WI
Vidafel Resorts	VV	Westmark Hotels	WM
Village Resorts	VR	Wingate Inns	WG
Villas By Marriott	MB	World Class Hotels	WC
VIP Reservations	VP	World Hotels & Resorts	WW
Walt Disney Hotels	DW	Wyndham Hotels	WY
Warwick Hotels	WK		

Rental Car Companies

Able	ZB	Intercontinental	IC
ACE	FA	ITS	SL
Advantage	AD	Kemwel	KG
Alamo	AL	Kenning	KN
All American	AB	Ladki Int'l	RL
Allstate	LV	Major	MJ
Americar	AF	Midway	MW
ANSA	AN	Montgomery Ward	ZW
Auto Europe	ZU	National	ZL
Avis	ZI	Payless	ZA
Budget	ZD	Pinellas Rent A Car	PI
Charlie Car Rental	CH	Practical Rental	AS
Discount Rentals	DS	Red and Blue	BL
Dollar	ZR	Rent Rite	RR
Enterprise	ET	Resort	RS
Eurodollar	ED	Save Auto Rental	SV
Europcar	EP	Savmor Rentacar	PS
European	EC	Sears	ZS
Exchange	XR	Test Car	JL
General	ZN	Thrifty	ZT
Hayat Car	HT	Tilden	TS
Hertz	ZE	Town and Country	CC
Holiday Autos	HA	Triangle	TR
Holiday House	HH	US Rent A Car	EX
Holiday Rent	HO	Value	GO
InterAmerican	IA	Vanwijk European	VW

Hotel & Rental Car Codes

Hotel Codes

AC	Hotel Connect Services	DT	Doubletree Hotels
AH	Aston Hotels & Resorts	DW	Walt Disney Hotels
AJ	Amerisuites	ED	Disneyland Paris Hotels
AM	Adams Mark Hotels	EJ	El San Juan Hotels
AN	ANA Hotels Int'l	EO	Econolodge
AP	Astron Hotels	ER	E R S
AR	AMR Info Service	ES	Embassy Suites
AS	All Suites	FA	Fairmont Hotels
AV	Ambassador Services	FE	Forte Hotels
AW	Astra Worldwide Hotel	FH	Fiesta Americana
AX	Anasazi Service Corp.	FL	Fimotel
AZ	Airco Servicestal	FN	Fairfield Inn
BB	Bartell Hotels	FS	Four Seasons Hotels
BC	Copthorne Hotels	FT	Grande Devere Hotel
BD	Bed & Breakfast Direct	FZ	Friendship Inns
BH	Hawthorne Suites	GA	Guesthouse International
BM	Biltmore Hotels	GB	Bravo Communication
BP	Shiloh Inns	GC	Grande Collection of Hotels
BQ	Bachelor Quarters	GD	Grand Traditions Hotels
BR	Renaissance Hotels	GH	Grand Heritage
BT	BTH Hotels	GP	Garden Plaza Hotels
BW	Best Western Int'l	GR	Global Reservations
BZ	Tranquility Base	GT	Golden Tulip Hotels
CB	Caribbean Information	HB	Thomas Hotels
CC	Clarion Collection	HE	Helmsley Harley Hotel
CD	Concorde Hotels	HG	Homewood Suites
CE	Susse Chalet	HH	Hilton Hotels
CH	Carlyle Hotel	HI	Holiday Inn Worldwide
CI	Comfort Inns	HJ	Howard Johnson
CN	Consort Hotels	HL	Hilton International
CP	Canadian Pacific Hotels	HN	Global Home Network
CQ	Crescent Hotels	HP	Hawaiian Pacific Resorts
CS	Colony Resorts	HQ	Hotel Des Gouveneurs
CU	My Favorite Sunset	HR	Harrahs Hotels
CX	Country Inn By Carlson	HU	Hotel Link
CY	Courtyard	HV	Harvey Hotels
CZ	Corporate Resorts	HX	Hampton Inns
DA	Doral Hotels	HY	Hyatt Hotels
DC	Datalead Communications	IC	Inter-Continental Hotels
DE	Delta Hotels	IE	Inter Europe Hotels
DI	Days Inns	IG	Insignia Resorts
DO	Dorint Hotels	IH	Classic International Hotels
DS	Design Hotels	IN	Intourtrans

IS	Intourist	PL	Park Lane Hotels
IT	Int'l Travel & Resorts	PO	Pointe Resorts
JA	Jarvinen Worldwide Hotels	PW	Prima Hotels
JH	Jolly Hotels	QI	Quality Inns
JJ	Japan Travel Bureau, Inc.	QL	Queens Moat Houses
JU	Jumer Hotels	QR	Quality Hotel Reservations
JV	Jack Tar Villages	RA	Ramada Inns
KC	Kimton Hotel Group	RC	Residence Inn
KI	Kempinski Hotels	RD	Radisson Hotels
KK	Key System	RE	Regent Int'l Hotels
KY	Keytel Hotels	RF	Ruby Foo
LA	Little America Hotels	RH	Registry Hotels
LH	LRI	RI	Rodeway Inns
LL	Lanyon Ltd.	RL	Red Lion Hotels
LM	Lexington Management	RM	Romantik Hotels
LQ	La Quinta Motor Inns	RN	Expotel Room Center
LV	Stations Casinos Hotels	RQ	Regal Hotels Int'l
LW	Leading Hotels	RR	Righa Royal Hotels
LX	Small Luxury Hotels	RT	Resinter
LZ	Loews Hotels	RV	Red Roof Inns
MB	Villas By Marriott	RW	Robert F. Warner
MC	Marriott Hotels	RY	Royce Hotels
ME	Grupo Sol	RZ	Ritz-Carlton Hotels
MG	MGM Grand Hotel	SB	The Small Hotel Co.
MH	Marco Polo Hotels	SC	Sceptre Hospitality
MK	Movenpick Hotels	SG	Shangri-La Hotels
MM	Maritime Hotels	SI	Sheraton Hotels
MN	Monte Carlo Resorts	SJ	Signature Inns
MO	Mandarin Oriental	SK	Stakis Hotel Group
MR	Ian Schrager	SL	Swissotel
MS	Ms Minto Pl Suites	SM	Innlink
MU	CDL Millennium	SO	Sonesta Hotels
MV	Mirvac Hotels	SP	Southern Pacific Hotels
NE	Nendels Corporation	SQ	Select Marketing Hotels
NH	NTA Hotel Ryokan	SR	SRS Hotels
NK	Nikko Hotels Int'l	SS	Summerfield Suites
NL	Navy Lodging	SV	Sarova Hotels
NO	New Otani Hotels	SX	Supranational Hotels
NR	Ramada Hotels	SZ	Sleep Inns
NT	Nordic Team Hotels	TA	Travamerica
NV	Las Vegas Travel	TH	Country Comfort
NY	Manhattan East Suites	TI	Thistle Hotels
OB	Oberoi Hotels	TL	Travelodge
OC	Hotel Okura	TP	Top International Hotels
OM	Omni Hotels	TR	Trust International
ON	Reconline	TS	Int'l Travel Svcs, Broward
OO	Crown Sterling	TX	Treff Hotels
OR	Outrigger Hotels	UI	Utell Hotels
PA	Park Inn Int'l	UK	Swallow Hotels
PE	Premier World Marketing	UL	Unihotel
PF	Pan Pacific Hotels	UR	Ultimate Resorts
PH	Preferred Hotels	VA	Vagabond Inns
PI	Princess Hotels	VB	Vacation Break
PK	Park Plaza Hotels	VI	Venture Inns

VN	Vacation Network	WM	Westmark Hotels
VP	VIP Reservations	WR	Sterling International
VR	Village Resorts	WW	World Hotels & Resorts
VV	Vidafel Resorts	WX	Coast Westcoast Hotel
WC	World Class Hotels	WY	Wyndham Hotels
WG	Wingate Inns	XC	Hotels Camino Real
WI	Westin Hotels	XL	Summit Int'l Hotels
WK	Warwick Hotels	XS	Courtyard Inns Canada
WL	Wellesley Inns		

Rental Car Codes

AB	All American		LV	Allstate
AD	Advantage		MJ	Major
AF	Americar		MW	Midway
AL	Alamo		PI	Pinellas Rent A Car
AN	ANSA		PS	Savmor Rentacar
AS	Practical Rental		RL	Ladki Int'l
BL	Red and Blue		RR	Rent Rite
CC	Town and Country		RS	Resort
CH	Charlie Car Rental		SL	ITS
DS	Discount Rentals		SV	Save Auto Rental
EC	European		TR	Triangle
ED	Eurodollar		TS	Tilden
EP	Europcar		VW	Vanwijk European
ET	Enterprise		XR	Exchange
EX	US Rent A Car		ZA	Payless
FA	ACE		ZB	Able
GO	Value		ZD	Budget
HA	Holiday Autos		ZE	Hertz
HH	Holiday House		ZI	Avis
HO	Holiday Rent		ZL	National
HT	Hayat Car		ZN	General
IA	InterAmerican		ZR	Dollar
IC	Intercontinental		ZS	Sears
JL	Test Car		ZT	Thrifty
KG	Kemwel		ZU	Auto Europe
KN	Kenning		ZW	Montgomery Ward

Countries & Currencies

Note: The layout of this section differs from that of other sections in *Part I*. Whereas other sections are laid out two columns per page, this section contains only one column, with each entry containing four items of information. The information in each line is meant to be read straight across the page, as follows: first the country name, then the two-digit code for that country, then the unit of currency for that country, and, finally, the three-digit code for that currency.

Afghanistan	AF	Afghani	AFA
Albania	AL	Lek	ALL
Algeria	DZ	Algerian Dinar	DZD
American Samoa	AS	US Dollar	USD
Andorra	AD	Andorran Peseta	ADP
Angola	AO	Kwanza Readjustado	AOR
Anguilla	AI	East Caribbean Dollar	XCD
Antarctica	AQ		
Antigua & Barbuda	AG	East Caribbean Dollar	XCD
Argentina	AR	Argentine Peso	ARS
Armenia	AM	Dram	AMD
Aruba	AW	Aruban Guilder	AWG
Australia	AU	Australian Dollar	AUD
Austria	AT	Schilling	ATS
Azerbaijan	AZ	Manat	AZM
Bahamas	BS	Bahamian Dollar	BSD
Bahrain	BH	Bahrani Dinar	BHD
Bangladesh	BD	Taka	BDT
Barbados	BB	Barbados Dollar	BBD
Belarus	BY	Belorussian Ruble	BYB
Belgium	BE	Belgian Franc	BEF
Belize	BZ	Belize Dollar	BZD
Benin	BJ	CFA Franc BCEAO	XOF
Bermuda	BM	Bermudian Dollar	BMD
Bhutan	BT	Ngultrum	BTN
Bolivia	BO	Boliviano	BOB
Bosnia Hercegovina	BA	Bosnian Dinar	BAD
Botswana	BW	Pula	BWP
Bouvet Island	BV	Norwegian Krona	NOK
Brazil	BR	Real	BRL
British Indian Ocean	IO	U.S. Dollar	USD
Britsh Virgin Islands	VG	U.S. Dollar	USD
Brunei Darussalam	BN	Brunei Dollar	BND

Bulgaria	BG	Lev	BGL
Burkina Faso	BF	CFA Franc BCEAO	XOF
Burundi	BI	Burundi Franc	BIF
Cambodia	KH	Riel	KHR
Cameroon	CM	CFA Franc BEAC	XAF
Canada	CA	Canadian Dollar	CAD
Cape Verde	CV	Escudo	CVE
Cayman Islands	KY	Cayman Islands Dollar	KYD
Central African Republic	CF	CFA Franc BEAC	XAF
Chad	TD	CFA Franc BEAC	XAF
Chile	CL	Chilean Peso	CLP
China	CN	Yuan Renminbi	CNY
Christmas Islands	CX	Australian Dollar	AUD
Cocos (Keeling) Islands	CC	Australian Dollar	AUD
Colombia	CO	Colombian Peso	COP
Comoros	KM	Comoro Franc	KMF
Congo	CG	CFA Franc BEAC	XAF
Cook Islands	CK	New Zealand Dollar	NZD
Costa Rica	CR	Costa Rican Colon	CRC
Cote d'Ivoire	CI	CFA Franc BCEAO	XOF
Croatia	HR	Kuna	HRK
Cuba	CU	Cuban Peso	CUP
Cyprus	CY	Cyprus Pound	CYP
Czech Republic	CZ	Koruna	CZK
Denmark	DK	Danish Krone	DKK
Djibouti	DJ	Djibouti Franc	DJF
Dominica	DM	East Caribbean Dollar	XCD
Dominican Republic	DO	Dominican Peso	DOP
East Timor	TP	Timor Escudo	TPE
Ecuador	EC	Sucre	ECS
Egypt	EG	Egyptian Pound	EGP
El Salvador	SV	El Salvador Colon	SVC
Equatorial Guinea	GQ	CFA Franc BEAC	XAF
Eritrea	ER	Ethiopian Birr	ETB
Estonia	EE	Kroon	EEK
Ethiopia	ET	Ethiopian Birr	ETB
European Community		European Currency ('Euro')	XEU
Faeroe Islands	FO	Danish Krone	DKK
Falkland Islands	FK	Falkland Island Pound	FKP
Fiji	FJ	Fiji Dollar	FJD
Finland	FI	Markka	FIM
France	FR	French Franc	FRF
French Guiana	GF	French Franc	FRF
French Polynesia	PF	CFP Franc	XPF
French Southern Territories	TF	French Franc	FRF
Gabon	GA	CFA Franc BEAC	XAF
Gambia	GM	Dalasi	GMD
Georgia	GE	Lari	GEL
Germany	DE	Deutsche Mark	DEM
Ghana	GH	Cedi	GHC
Gibraltar	GI	Gibraltar Pound	GIP
Greece	GR	Drachma	GRD
Greenland	GL	Danish Krone	DKK
Grenada	GD	East Caribbean Dollar	XCD

Guadeloupe	GP	French Franc	FRF
Guam	GU	US Dollar	USD
Guatemala	GT	Quetzal	GTQ
Guinea	GN	Guinea Franc	GNF
Guinea-Bissau	GW	Guinea-Bissau Peso	GWP
Guyana	GY	Guyana Dollar	GYD
Haiti	HT	Gourde	HTG
Heard & McDonald Isl.	HM	Australian Dollar	AUD
Honduras	HN	Lempira	HNL
Hong Kong	HK	Hong Kong Dollar	HKD
Hungary	HU	Forint	HUF
Iceland	IS	Iceland Krona	ISK
India	IN	Indian Rupee	INR
Indonesia	ID	Indonesian Rupiah	IDR
Iran	IR	Iranian Rial	IRR
Iraq	IQ	Iraqi Dinar	IQD
Ireland	IE	Irish Pound	IEP
Israel	IL	Shekel	ILS
Italy	IT	Italian Lira	ITL
Jamaica	JM	Jamaican Dollar	JMD
Japan	JP	Yen	JPY
Jordan	JO	Jordanian Dinar	JOD
Kazakhstan	KZ	Tenge	KZT
Kenya	KE	Kenyan Shilling	KES
Kiribati	KI	Australian Dollar	AUD
Korea, North	KP	North Korean Won	KPW
Korea, South	KR	Korean Won	KRW
Kuwait	KW	Kuwaiti Dinar	KWD
Kyrgyzstan	KG	Som	KGS
Laos	LA	Kip	LAK
Latvia	LV	Latvian Lats	LVL
Lebanon	LB	Lebanese Pound	LBP
Lesotho	LS	Loti	LSL
Liberia	LR	Liberian Dollar	LRD
Libya	LY	Libyan Dinar	LYD
Liechtenstein	LI	Swiss Franc	CHF
Lithuania	LT	Litas	LTL
Luxembourg	LU	Luxembourg Franc	LUF
Macau	MO	Pataca	MOP
Macedonia	MK	Denar	MKD
Madagascar	MG	Malagasy Franc	MGF
Malawi	MW	Kwacha	MWK
Malaysia	MY	Malaysian Ringgit	MYR
Maldives	MV	Rufiyaa	MVR
Mali	ML	CFA Franc BCEAO	XOF
Malta	MT	Maltese Lira	MTL
Marshall Islands	MH	US Dollar	USD
Martinique	MQ	French Franc	FRF
Mauritania	MR	Ouguiya	MRO
Mauritius	MU	Mauritius Rupee	MUR
Mayotte	YT	French Franc	FRF
Mexico	MX	Mexican Peso	MXN
Micronesia	FM	US Dollar	USD
Moldova	MD	Moldovan Leu	MDL

Monaco	MC	French Franc	FRF
Mongolia	MN	Tugrik	MNT
Montserrat	MS	East Caribbean Dollar	XCD
Morocco	MA	Moroccan Dirham	MAD
Mozambique	MZ	Metical	MZM
Myanmar	MM	Kyat	MMK
Namibia	NA	Namibian Dollar	NAD
Nauru	NR	Australian Dollar	AUD
Nepal	NP	Nepalese Rupee	NPR
Netherlands	NL	Netherlands Guilder	NLG
Netherlands Antilles	AN	Netherlands Antillian Guilder	ANG
New Caledonia	NC	CFP Franc	XPF
New Zealand	NZ	New Zealand Dollar	NZD
Nicaragua	NI	Cordoba Oro	NIO
Niger	NE	CFA Franc BCEAO	XOF
Nigeria	NG	Naira	NGN
Niue	NU	New Zealand Dollar	NZD
Norfolk Island	NF	Australian Dollar	AUD
Northern Mariana Islands	MP	US Dollar	USD
Norway	NO	Norwegian Krone	NOK
Oman	OM	Rial Omani	OMR
Pakistan	PK	Pakistani Rupee	PKR
Palau	PW	US Dollar	USD
Panama	PA	Balboa	PAB
Papua New Guinea	PG	Kina	PGK
Paraguay	PY	Guarani	PYG
Peru	PE	Nuevo Sol	PES
Philippines	PH	Philippine Peso	PHP
Pitcairn Island	PN	New Zealand Dollar	NZD
Poland	PL	Zloty	PLZ
Portugal	PT	Portuguese Escudo	PTE
Puerto Rico	PR	US Dollar	USD
Qatar	QA	Qatari Rial	QAR
Reunion	RE	French Franc	FRF
Romania	RO	Romanian Leu	ROL
Russian Federation	RU	Russian Ruble	RUR
Rwanda	RW	Rwanda Franc	RWF
Saint Helena	SH	St. Helena Pound	SHP
Saint Kitts & Nevis	KN	East Caribbean Dollar	XCD
Saint Lucia	LC	East Caribbean Dollar	XCD
Saint Pierre & Miquelon	PM	French Franc	FRF
Saint Vincent & Grenadines	VC	East Caribbean Dollar	XCD
Samoa, Western	WS	Samoan Tala	WST
San Marino	SM	Italian Lira	ITL
Sao Tome & Principe	ST	Dobra	STD
Saudi Arabia	SA	Saudi Riyal	SAR
Senegal	SN	CFA Franc BCEAO	XOF
Seychelles	SC	Seychelles Rupee	SCR
Sierra Leone	SL	Leone	SLL
Singapore	SG	Singapore Dollar	SGD
Slovakia	SK	Koruna	SKK
Slovenia	SI	Tolar	SIT
Solomon Islands	SB	Solomon Islands Dollar	SBD
Somalia	SO	Somali Shilling	SOS

South Africa	ZA	South African Rand	ZAR
Spain	ES	Spanish Peseta	ESP
Sri Lanka	LK	Sri Lanka Rupee	LKR
Sudan	SD	Sudanese Dinar	SDD
Suriname	SR	Suriname Guilder	SRG
Svalbard & Jan Mayen Isl.	SJ	Norwegian Krone	NOK
Swaziland	SZ	Lilangeni	SZL
Sweden	SE	Swedish Krona	SEK
Switzerland	CH	Swiss Franc	CHF
Syria	SY	Syrian Pound	SYP
Taiwan (China)	TW	New Taiwan Dollar	TWD
Tajikistan	TJ	Tajik Ruble	TJR
Tanzania	TZ	Tanzanian Shilling	TZS
Thailand	TH	Thai Baht	THB
Togo	TG	CFA Franc BCEAO	XOF
Tokelau	TK	New Zealand Dollar	NZD
Tonga	TO	Pa'anga	TOP
Trinidad & Tobago	TT	Trinidad Dollar	TTD
Tunisia	TN	Tunisian Dinar	TND
Turkey	TR	Turkish Lira	TRL
Turkmenistan	TM	Manat	TMM
Turks & Caicos Is.	TC	US Dollar	USD
Tuvalu	TV	Australian Dollar	AUD
Uganda	UG	Uganda Shilling	UGX
Ukraine	UA	Karbovanet	UAK
United Arab Emirates	AE	UAE Dirham	AED
United Kingdom (England)	GB	Pound Sterling	GBP
United States	US	US Dollar	USD
United States (minor outlying islands)	UM	US Dollar	USD
Uruguay	UY	Peso Uruguayo	UYU
Uzbekistan	UZ	Sum	UZS
Vanuatu	VU	Vatu	VUV
Vatican City	VA	Italian Lira	ITL
Venezuela	VE	Bolivar	VEB
Vietnam	VN	Dong	VND
Virgin Islands (British)	VG	US Dollar	USD
Virgin Islands (US)	VI	US Dollar	USD
Wallis & Futuna Islands	WF	CFP Franc	XPF
Western Sahara	EH	Moroccan Dirham	MAD
Yemen	YE	Yemeni Rial	YER
Yugoslavia	YU	New Yugoslavian Dinar	YUN
Zaire	ZR	New Zaire	ZRN
Zambia	ZM	Kwacha	ZMK
Zimbabwe	ZW	Zimbabwe Dollar	ZWD

Country & Currency Codes

AD	Andorra	BMD	Bermudian Dollar
ADP	Andorran Peseta	BN	Brunei Darussalam
AE	United Arab Emirates	BND	Brunei Dollar
AED	UAE Dirham	BO	Bolivia
AF	Afghanistan	BOB	Boliviano
AFA	Afghani	BR	Brazil
AG	Antigua & Barbuda	BRL	Real
AI	Anguilla	BS	Bahamas
AL	Albania	BSD	Bahamian Dollar
ALL	Lek	BT	Bhutan
AM	Armenia	BTN	Ngultrum
AMD	Dram	BV	Bouvet Island
AN	Netherlands Antilles	BW	Botswana
ANG	Netherlands Antillian Guilder	BWP	Pula
		BY	Belarus
AO	Angola	BYB	Belorussian Ruble
AOR	Kwanza Readjustado	BZ	Belize
AQ	Antarctica	BZD	Belize Dollar
AR	Argentina	CA	Canada
ARS	Argentine Peso	CAD	Canadian Dollar
AS	American Samoa	CC	Cocos (Keeling) Islands
AT	Austria	CF	Central African Republic
ATS	Schilling	CG	Congo
AU	Australia	CH	Switzerland
AUD	Australian Dollar	CHF	Swiss Franc
AW	Aruba	CI	Cote d'Ivoire
AWG	Aruban Guilder	CK	Cook Islands
AZ	Azerbaijan	CL	Chile
AZM	Manat	CLP	Chilean Peso
BA	Bosnia Hercegovina	CM	Cameroon
BAD	Bosnian Dinar	CN	China
BB	Barbados	CNY	Yuan Renminbi
BBD	Barbados Dollar	CO	Colombia
BD	Bangladesh	COP	Colombian Peso
BDT	Taka	CR	Costa Rica
BE	Belgium	CRC	Costa Rican Colon
BEF	Belgian Franc	CU	Cuba
BF	Burkina Faso	CUP	Cuban Peso
BG	Bulgaria	CV	Cape Verde
BGL	Lev	CVE	Escudo
BH	Bahrain	CX	Christmas Islands
BHD	Bahrani Dinar	CY	Cyprus
BI	Burundi	CYP	Cyprus Pound
BIF	Burundi Franc	CZ	Czech Republic
BJ	Benin	CZK	Koruna
BM	Bermuda	DE	Germany

DEM	Deutsche Mark		GU	Guam
DJ	Djibouti		GW	Guinea-Bissau
DJF	Djibouti Franc		GWP	Guinea-Bissau Peso
DK	Denmark		GY	Guyana
DKK	Danish Krone		GYD	Guyana Dollar
DM	Dominica		HK	Hong Kong
DO	Dominican Republic		HKD	Hong Kong Dollar
DOP	Dominican Peso		HM	Heard & McDonald Isl.
DZ	Algeria		HN	Honduras
DZD	Algerian Dinar		HNL	Lempira
EC	Ecuador		HR	Croatia
ECS	Sucre		HRK	Kuna
EE	Estonia		HT	Haiti
EEK	Kroon		HTG	Gourde
EG	Egypt		HU	Hungary
EGP	Egyptian Pound		HUF	Forint
EH	Western Sahara		ID	Indonesia
ER	Eritrea		IDR	Indonesian Rupiah
ES	Spain		IE	Ireland
ESP	Spanish Peseta		IEP	Irish Pound
ET	Ethiopia		IL	Israel
ETB	Ethiopian Birr		ILS	Shekel
FI	Finland		IN	India
FIM	Markka		INR	Indian Rupee
FJ	Fiji		IO	British Indian Ocean
FJD	Fiji Dollar		IQ	Iraq
FK	Falkland Islands		IQD	Iraqi Dinar
FKP	Falkland Island Pound		IR	Iran
FM	Micronesia		IRR	Iranian Rial
FO	Faeroe Islands		IS	Iceland
FR	France		ISK	Iceland Krona
FRF	French Franc		IT	Italy
GA	Gabon		ITL	Italian Lira
GB	United Kingdom (England)		JM	Jamaica
GBP	Pound Sterling		JMD	Jamaican Dollar
GD	Grenada		JO	Jordan
GE	Georgia		JOD	Jordanian Dinar
GEL	Lari		JP	Japan
GF	French Guiana		JPY	Yen
GH	Ghana		KE	Kenya
GHC	Cedi		KES	Kenyan Shilling
GI	Gibraltar		KG	Kyrgyzstan
GIP	Gibraltar Pound		KGS	Som
GL	Greenland		KH	Cambodia
GM	Gambia		KHR	Riel
GMD	Dalasi		KI	Kiribati
GN	Guinea		KM	Comoros
GNF	Guinea Franc		KMF	Comoro Franc
GP	Guadeloupe		KN	Saint Kitts & Nevis
GQ	Equatorial Guinea		KP	Korea, North
GR	Greece		KPW	North Korean Won
GRD	Drachma		KR	Korea, South
GT	Guatemala		KRW	Korean Won
GTQ	Quetzal		KW	Kuwait

KWD	Kuwaiti Dinar	MWK	Kwacha
KY	Cayman Islands	MX	Mexico
KYD	Cayman Islands Dollar	MXN	Mexican Peso
KZ	Kazakhstan	MY	Malaysia
KZT	Tenge	MYR	Malaysian Ringgit
LA	Laos	MZ	Mozambique
LAK	Kip	MZM	Metical
LB	Lebanon	NA	Namibia
LBP	Lebanese Pound	NAD	Namibian Dollar
LC	Saint Lucia	NC	New Caledonia
LI	Liechtenstein	NE	Niger
LK	Sri Lanka	NF	Norfolk Island
LKR	Sri Lanka Rupee	NG	Nigeria
LR	Liberia	NGN	Naira
LRD	Liberian Dollar	NI	Nicaragua
LS	Lesotho	NIO	Cordoba Oro
LSL	Loti	NL	Netherlands
LT	Lithuania	NLG	Netherlands Guilder
LTL	Litas	NO	Norway
LU	Luxembourg	NOK	Norwegian Krona
LUF	Luxembourg Franc	NP	Nepal
LV	Latvia	NPR	Nepalese Rupee
LVL	Latvian Lats	NR	Nauru
LY	Libya	NU	Niue
LYD	Libyan Dinar	NZ	New Zealand
MA	Morocco	NZD	New Zealand Dollar
MAD	Moroccan Dirham	OM	Oman
MC	Monaco	OMR	Rial Omani
MD	Moldova	PA	Panama
MDL	Moldovan Leu	PAB	Balboa
MG	Madagascar	PE	Peru
MGF	Malagasy Franc	PES	Nuevo Sol
MH	Marshall Islands	PF	French Polynesia
MK	Macedonia	PG	Papua New Guinea
MKD	Denar	PGK	Kina
ML	Mali	PH	Philippines
MM	Myanmar	PHP	Philippine Peso
MMK	Kyat	PK	Pakistan
MN	Mongolia	PKR	Pakistani Rupee
MNT	Tugrik	PL	Poland
MO	Macau	PLZ	Zloty
MOP	Pataca	PM	Saint Pierre & Miquelon
MP	Northern Mariana Islands	PN	Pitcairn Island
MQ	Martinique	PR	Puerto Rico
MR	Mauritania	PT	Portugal
MRO	Ouguiya	PTE	Portuguese Escudo
MS	Montserrat	PW	Palau
MT	Malta	PY	Paraguay
MTL	Maltese Lira	PYG	Guarani
MU	Mauritius	QA	Qatar
MUR	Mauritius Rupee	QAR	Qatari Rial
MV	Maldives	RE	Reunion
MVR	Rufiyaa	RO	Romania
MW	Malawi	ROL	Romanian Leu

RU	Russian Federation	TP	East Timor
RUR	Russian Ruble	TPE	Timor Escudo
RW	Rwanda	TR	Turkey
RWF	Rwanda Franc	TRL	Turkish Lira
SA	Saudi Arabia	TT	Trinidad & Tobago
SAR	Saudi Riyal	TTD	Trinidad Dollar
SB	Solomon Islands	TV	Tuvalu
SBD	Solomon Islands Dollar	TW	Taiwan (China)
SC	Seychelles	TWD	New Taiwan Dollar
SCR	Seychelles Rupee	TZ	Tanzania
SD	Sudan	TZS	Tanzanian Shilling
SDD	Sudanese Dinar	UA	Ukraine
SE	Sweden	UAK	Karbovanet
SEK	Swedish Krona	UG	Uganda
SG	Singapore	UGX	Uganda Shilling
SGD	Singapore Dollar	UM	United States (minor islands)
SH	Saint Helena	US	United States
SHP	St. Helena Pound	USD	U.S. Dollar
SI	Slovenia	UY	Uruguay
SIT	Tolar	UYU	Peso Uruguayo
SJ	Svalbard & Jan Mayen Isl.	UZ	Uzbekistan
SK	Slovakia	UZS	Sum
SKK	Koruna	VA	Vatican City
SL	Sierra Leone	VC	Saint Vincent & Grenadines
SLL	Leone	VE	Venezuela
SM	San Marino	VEB	Bolivar
SN	Senegal	VG	Britsh Virgin Islands
SO	Somalia	VG	Virgin Islands (British)
SOS	Somali Shilling	VI	Virgin islands (US)
SR	Suriname	VN	Vietnam
SRG	Suriname Guilder	VND	Dong
ST	Sao Tome & Principe	VU	Vanuatu
STD	Dobra	VUV	Vatu
SV	El Salvador	WF	Wallis & Futuna Islands
SVC	El Salvador Colon	WS	Samoa, Western
SY	Syria	WST	Samoan Tala
SYP	Syrian Pound	XAF	CFA Franc BEAC
SZ	Swaziland	XCD	East Caribbean Dollar
SZL	Lilangeni	XEU	European Currency ('Euro')
TC	Turks & Caicos Is.	XOF	CFA Franc BCEAO
TD	Chad	XPF	CFP Franc
TF	French Southern Territories	YE	Yemen
TG	Togo	YER	Yemeni Rial
TH	Thailand	YT	Mayotte
THB	Thai Baht	YU	Yugoslavia
TJ	Tajikistan	YUN	New Yugoslavian Dinar
TJR	Tajik Ruble	ZA	South Africa
TK	Tokelau	ZAR	South African Rand
TM	Turkmenistan	ZM	Zambia
TMM	Manat	ZMK	Kwacha
TN	Tunisia	ZR	Zaire
TND	Tunisian Dinar	ZRN	New Zaire
TO	Tonga	ZW	Zimbabwe
TOP	Pa'anga	ZWD	Zimbabwe Dollar

Part Two:

Industry Contacts & Information Sources

Supplier Contact Numbers

This section contains telephone numbers — usually toll-free — for suppliers of the major travel products: airlines, hotels, rental cars, tours, and cruises.

We have attempted to be more rather than less inclusive, but we have made no attempt to be encyclopedic. In other words, there are companies in each category that are not listed, either intentionally or unintentionally.

This is especially true in the tour operators category. There are thousands of tour operators and any attempt to list them all would be quixotic. Consequently, we limited the listing to operators that have toll-free numbers, on the theory that those are the ones you will be most likely to call. There are many excellent tour operators who, for one reason or another, have opted not to have toll-free numbers. That fact alone should not disqualify them from your consideration.

We have also included the phone numbers of some non-scheduled charter airlines which are not carried on CRSs and consequently were not listed in the previous section on airline codes.

The listings in this section are not intended to be a substitute for specialized directories such as *The Official Hotel Guide*, *The Official Tour Directory* or any of the other excellent guides which provide in-depth information and exhaustive listings of the travel industry segments they cover. Rather, this section is intended as a sort of shorthand phone book to be used when you need to contact a specific supplier but don't remember the number. We have also left space for you to jot down the numbers of additional suppliers with which you may be doing business. That way, this book will become an on-going resource.

Airlines

Aces	800-846-2237	Venezolanos)	800-428-3672
Aer Lingus	800-223-6537	Avianca	800-284-2622
Aero California	800-237-6225	AVIATECA	800-327-9832
Aeroflot	800-995-5555	Bahamasair	800-222-4262
Aerolineas Argentinas	800-333-0276	Balair/CTA	800-322-5247
Aeromexico	800-237-6639	Balkan-Bulgarian	
Aeroperu	800-777-7717	Airlines	800-822-1106
Air Afrique	800-456-9192	Bemidji Airlines	800-332-7133
Air Aruba	800-882-7822	Big Sky Airways	800-237-7778
Air Caledonie	800-677-4277	British Airways	800-247-9297
Air Canada	800-869-9000	British Midland	800-788-0555
Air China	800-982-8802	Business Express	800-221-1212
Air Europa	888-238-7672	BWIA	800-538-2942
Air Fiji	800-677-4277	Cameroon Airlines	800-677-4277
Air France	800-237-2747	Canadian Airlines	
Air Gabon	800-237-2747	International (CAI)	800-426-7000
Air India	800-223-7776	Cape Air	800-352-0714
Air Inter Europe	800-237-2747	Cape Smythe Air Service	907-852-8333
Air Jamaica	800-523-5585	Carnival Air Lines	800-824-7386
Air Lanka	800-247-5265	Cathay Pacific Airways	800-233-2742
Air Mauritius	800-537-1182	Cayman Airways	800-422-9626
Air Nauru	800-677-4277	CCAir	800-868-2515
Air Nevada	800-634-6377	Chautauqua Airlines	800-428-4322
Air New Zealand	800-262-2468	Chicago Express	800-264-3929
Air Niugini	714-752-5440	China Airlines	800-227-5118
Air St. Thomas	800-522-3084	China Eastern Airlines	800-200-5118
Air Seychelles	800-677-4277	City Bird	888-248-9243
Air South	800-247-7688	Comair	800-543-7308
Air Sunshine	800-327-8900	Condor Flugdienst	800-524-6975
Air Tanzania	212-688-1927	Conquest Airlines	800-722-0860
Air Tran	800-247-8726	Continental Airlines	800-525-0280
Air Ukraine	800-857-2463	COPA Airlines	800-892-2672
Air Vanuatu	800-677-4277	Corsair French	
Air Wisconsin	800-241-6522	Airlines	800-677-0720
Air Zimbabwe	800-742-3006	Croatia Airlines	800-247-5353
Alaska Airlines	800-426-0333	Czech Airlines (CSA)	800-223-2365
Alitalia	800-223-5730	Cyprus Airways	800-333-2977
All Nippon Airways	800-235-9262	Debonair	888-332-6688
Allegheny Airlines	717-948-5400	Delta Air Lines	800-221-1212
ALM (Antillean Airlines)	800-327-7230	Egyptair	800-334-6787
Aloha Airlines	800-367-5250	El Al Israel Airlines	800-223-6700
America West Airlines	800-235-9292	Emirates Airlines	800-777-3999
American Airlines	800-433-7300	Ethiopian Airlines	800-445-2733
American Trans Air	800-225-2995	Evergreen International	800-382-2746
Ansett Australia	800-366-1300	Executive Airlines	800-645-9572
Ansett New Zealand	800-366-1300	Faucett Peruvian Airline	800-334-3356
Arkia-Israeli	800-888-5127	Finnair	800-950-5000
Asiana Airlines	800-227-4262	Frontier Airlines	800-432-1359
Austrian Airlines	800-843-0002	Garuda Indonesia	800-342-7832
Avensa (Aerovias		Ghana Airways	212-371-2810

Grand Canyon Airlines	800-528-2413	Qantas Airways	800-227-4500
Gulf Air	800-359-4853	Reeve Aleutian Airways	800-544-2248
Guyana Airways	800-242-4210	Reno Air	800-736-6247
Hawaiian Airlines	800-367-5320	Rich Int'l Airways	305-871-5113
Horizon Airlines	800-547-9308	Royal Air Maroc	800-344-6726
Iberia	800-772-4642	Royal Jordanian	800-755-6732
Icelandair	800-223-5500	Royal Nepal	800-266-3725
Islandair	800-367-5250	Sabena	800-955-2000
Japan Airlines	800-525-3663	SAETA (Ecuador)	212-827-2382
Kendell Airlines	800-441-6880	Saudi Arabian Airlines	800-472-8342
Kenmore Air	800-543-9595	Scandinavian Airlines	
Kenya Airways	800-343-2506	System (SAS)	800-221-2350
Kiwi Int'l	800-538-5494	Scenic Airlines	800-638-3200
KLM Royal Dutch		Simmons Airlines	800-433-7300
Airlines	800-374-7747	Singapore Airlines	800-742-3333
Korean Air Lines (KAL)	800-438-5000	Sky West Airlines	800-453-9417
Kuwait Airways	800-458-9248	Solomon Airlines	800-677-4277
LACSA	800-225-2272	South African Airways	
Ladeco Airlines	800-825-2332	(SAA)	800-722-9675
Lan Chile	800-735-5526	Southcentral Air	907-283-7676
Lithuanian Airlines	800-711-3958	Southwest Airlines	800-531-5600
Lloyd Aero Bolivano		Spanair	212-695-8660
(LAB)	800-327-7407	Sun Country Airlines	800-752-1218
Lone Star Airlines	800-877-3932	Surinam Airways	800-327-6864
LOT Polish Airlines	800-528-7208	Swissair	800-221-4750
LTU International	800-888-0200	Taca Int'l Airlines	800-535-8780
Lufthansa	800-645-3880	TAESA	800-328-2372
Malaysia Airlines	800-552-9264	TAP Air Portugal	800-221-7370
Malev Hungarian		TAROM Romanian Air	212-687-6013
Airlines	800-223-6884	Thai Airways	800-426-5204
Martinair Holland	800-627-8462	Tower Air	800-348-6937
Mesa Airlines	800-637-2247	Transbrasil Int'l	888-872-3153
Mexicana	800-531-7923	Turkish Airlines	800-874-8875
Middle East Airlines		TWA (Trans World	
(AirLiban)	212-664-7310	Airlines)	800-221-2000
Midway	800-446-4392	United Airlines	800-241-6522
Midwest Express Airlines	800-452-2022	USAirways	800-428-4322
Nantucket Airlines	800-635-8787	US Air Express	800-428-4322
New England Airlines	800-243-2460	ValuJet Airlines	800-825-8538
New York Helicopter	800-645-3494	Vanair	800-677-4277
Nica Airlines	800-831-6422	Vanguard	800-826-4827
Nigeria Airways	212-935-2703	Varig	800-468-2744
North American Airlines	718-656-2650	VIASA	800-468-4272
Northwest Airlines	800-225-2525	Virgin Atlantic	800-862-8621
Olympic Airways	800-223-1226	Western Pacific	800-930-3030
Pakistan Int'l Airways		Wings of Alaska	907-789-0790
(PIA)	800-221-2552	Wings of the World	800-634-9464
Pan American	800-359-7262	Wings West	800-433-7300
Paradise Island Airlines	800-428-4322	World Airways	800-967-5350
Philippine Airlines	800-435-9725	Yemen Airways	800-257-1133
Pine State Airlines	800-353-6334	Zambia Airways	212-319-4029
Polynesian Airlines	800-677-4277		

Additional Airline Contacts

Hotels

Adams Mark Hotels	800-444-2326	Hotels	800-876-5278
ANA Hotels Int'l	800-262-4683	Jolly Hotels	800-221-2626
Ashford Dromoland		Keith Prowse	800-669-8687
Castles	800-346-7007	Kempinski Hotels	800-426-3135
Aston Hotels & Resorts	800-922-7866	Knights Inns	800-854-5644
Barclay International	800-845-6636	La Quinta Motor Inns	800-531-5900
Best Western Int'l	800-528-1234	Las Vegas Reservations	
BTH Hotels	800-221-1074	Systems	800-233-5594
Budgetel	800-428-3438	Leading Hotels	800-223-6800
Canadian Pacific Hotels	800-441-1414	Loews Hotels	800-235-6397
Choice Hotels	800-221-2222	Mandarin Oriental	800-526-6566
Clarion Inns	800-252-7466	Manhattan East Suites	800-637-8483
Club Med	800-258-2633	Marriott Hotels	800-831-1000
Colony Resorts	800-777-1700	Meridien Hotels	800-543-4300
Comfort Inns	800-228-5150	Motel 6	800-440-6000
Concorde Hotels	800-888-4747	Nendels Corporation	800-547-0106
Condo & Villa Authority	800-831-5512	New Otani Hotels	800-421-8795
Conrad Int'l	800-932-3322	Nikko Hotels Int'l	800-645-5687
Courtyard	800-321-2211	Novotel	800-668-6835
Days Inns	800-633-1414	Oberoi Hotels	800-562-3764
Delta Hotels	800-268-1133	Omni Hotels	800-843-6664
Disneyland Resorts	800-542-5391	Orient Express Hotels	800-237-1236
Doral Hotels	800-223-6725	Outrigger Hotels	800-822-4282
Doubletree Hotels	800-222-8733	Pan Pacific Hotels	800-327-8585
Econolodge	800-553-2666	Park Inn Int'l	800-437-7275
Embassy Suites	800-362-2779	Park Lane Hotels	800-338-1338
Fairfield Inn	800-228-2800	Park Plaza Int'l	800-670-7275
Fairmont Hotels	800-527-4727	Passport Inns	800-251-1962
Forte Hotels	800-225-5843	Pointe Resorts	800-876-4683
Four Seasons Hotels	800-332-3422	Preferred Hotels	800-323-7500
Golden Tulip Hotels	800-344-1212	Premier World Mktg.	800-877-3643
Grand Heritage	800-437-4824	Prima Hotels	800-447-7462
Grande Hotels	800-468-3750	Prince Hotels	800-542-8686
Hampton Inns	800-426-7866	Princess Hotels	800-223-1818
Harley Hotels	800-321-2323	Quality Inns	800-228-5151
Harrah's Hotels	800-427-7247	Radisson Hotels	800-333-3333
Hawaiian Pacific Resorts	800-367-5004	Ramada	800-228-3838
Helmsley Hotels	800-221-4982	Ramada Int'l	800-854-7854
Hilton Hotels	800-445-8677	Red Carpet	800-251-1962
Historic Hotels	800-678-8946	Red Lion Hotels	800-541-1111
Holiday Inn Worldwide	800-465-4329	Red Roof Inns	800-843-7663
Homewood Suites	800-225-5466	Regal Hotels	800-222-8888
Hotel Okura	800-526-2281	Regent Int'l Hotels	800-545-4000
Howard Johnson	800-446-4656	Registry Hotels	800-247-9810
Hyatt Hotels	800-233-1234	Relais & Chateaux	800-735-2478
Inter-Continental Hotels	800-327-0200	Renaissance Hotels	800-228-9898
International Travel		Reservation Network	800-255-6451
& Resorts	800-223-9815	Residence Inn	800-331-3131
Jack Tar Villages	800-999-9182	Resinter	800-221-4542
Jarvinen Worldwide		Ritz-Carlton Hotels	800-241-3333

Robert F. Warner	800-888-1199	Super 8 Motels	800-800-8000
Rockresorts	800-223-7637	Supranational Hotels	800-843-3311
Rodeway Inns	800-228-2000	Susse Chalet	800-524-2538
Royce Hotels	561-689-9970	Swissotel	800-637-9477
Sandals Resorts	800-726-3257	Taj Group	800-458-8825
Sandman Hotels	800-726-3626	Tara Hotels	800843-8272
Scottish Inns	800-251-1962	Travelodge	800-578-7878
Shangri-La Hotels	800-942-5050	Utell Hotels	800-448-8355
Sheraton Hotels	800-325-3535	Vacation Network	800-423-4095
Shiloh Inns	800-222-2244	Vagabond Inns	800-522-1555
Shoney's Inns	800-222-2222	Venture Inns	800-387-3933
Signature Inns	800-822-5252	Village Resorts	800-367-7052
Sleep Inns	800-753-3746	VIP Reservations	800-858-8471
Small Luxury Hotels	800-525-4800	Walt Disney Hotels	800-647-7900
Sofitel Hotels	800-763-4835	Warwick Int'l	800-203-3232
Sonesta Hotels	800-766-3782	Wellesley Ins	800-444-8888
SRS Hotels	800-223-5652	Westin Hotels	800-228-3000
Sterling Hotels	800-637-7200	Westmark Hotels	800-544-0970
Summerfield Suites	800-833-4353	World Hotels	800-821-0900
Summit Int'l Hotels	800-457-4000	Wyndham Hotels	800-822-4200

Additional Hotel Contacts

Rental Cars

ABC	800-464-6422	Europe by Car	800-223-1516
ACE	800-323-3221	European Car Reser-	
Advance	800-775-0774	vations (ECR)	800-535-3303
Advantage	800-777-5500	Hertz	800-654-3131
Airways	847-678-2300	Holiday Autos	800-422-7737
Alamo	800-327-9633	ITS	800-521-0643
Allstate	800-634-6186	Kemwel	800-678-0678
Auto Europe	800-223-5555	Kenning	800-227-8990
AutoNet	800-221-3465	Lloyd's International	800-654-7037
Avis	800-331-1212	Midway	800-643-9294
Bon Voyage by Car	800-272-3299	National	800-227-7368
Budget	800-527-0700	Pass	800-879-3737
Carey Limousine	800-336-4646	Payless	800-729-5377
DER Car	800-782-2424	Sears	800-527-0770
Dollar	800-800-4000	Thrifty	800-367-2277
Enterprise	800-325-8007	Town and Country	800-521-0643
Eurodollar	800-800-6000	U-Save Auto Rental	800-272-8728
Europcar	800-227-3876	Value	800-468-2583

Additional Rental Car Contacts

Tour Operators

206 Tours	800-345-2854	American Express	
AAT King's Australian		Vacations	800-241-1700
Tours	800-353-4525	American Media Tours	800-969-6344
Abaco Vacation Res.	800-633-9197	American Overland	
Abercrombie & Kent	800-323-7308	Expeditions	800-598-1325
Aberdeen Tours	800-282-8321	American Travel Abroad	800-228-0877
Above the Clouds		American Wilderness	800-444-0099
Trekking	800-233-4499	Amphitryon Holidays	800-424-2471
Abratours	800-227-2887	Anderson House Tours	800-325-2270
Abreu Tours	800-223-1580	Anglers Travel	800-624-8429
Absolute Asia	800-736-8187	Anthony's Travel	800-752-9034
Access Adventure Tours	800-821-1221	Any Mountain Tours	800-468-3455
Action Whitewater		Apollo Tours	800-228-4367
Adven.	800-453-1482	Apple Vacations	800-727-3400
Adriatic Tours	800-262-1718	APT International	800-290-8687
Adrift River Expeditions	800-874-4483	Aqua Trek Fiji	800-541-4334
Adventure Alaska	800-365-7057	Ariel Tours	800-262-1818
Adventure Assocs.	800-527-2500	Arizona River Runners	800-477-7238
Adventure Center	800-227-8747	Armadillo Tours	800-284-5678
Adventure Express	800-443-0799	Around Town Tours	800-468-0906
Adventure Tours USA	800-999-9046	Asensio Tours	800-221-7679
Adventure Unlimited	800-523-4135	Asia Trans Pacific	800-825-1680
Adventure Vacations	800-638-9040	Asian Pacific Adventures	800-825-1680
Adventures	800-231-7422	Aspen Ski Tours	800-525-2052
Adventures on Skis	800-628-9655	Astro Tours	800-543-7717
Adventureworld Tours	800-776-8747	ATA Vacations	800-442-8952
Aegean Holidays	800-368-6262	ATI Tours	800-533-2292
Aer Lingus Vacations	800-223-6537	Atlantic Tours	800-565-7173
AeroTours	800-223-4555	AtlanticGolf	800-443-8075
AESU	800-638-7640	Atlas Tours	800-634-1057
Afloat in France	800-313-2702	Atlas Travel Service	800-222-8060
Africa Travel Ctr.	800-220-2165	ATS Tours	800-423-2880
African Sun Safaris	800-856-6713	Atwood World Travel	800-944-8259
African Travel	800-421-8907	Australian Pacific Tours	800-290-8687
Africatours	800-235-3692	Auto Venture	800-426-7502
AIB Vacations	800-242-8687	AutoNet Int'l	800-221-3465
Air Jamaica Vacations	800-622-3009	Avanti Destinations	800-422-5053
Alaska Reel Adventures	800-877-2661	Avenir Travel	800-367-3230
Alaska Sightseeing/		Avia Tours	800-888-8167
Cruise West	800-426-7702	Aviatrade	800-950-0747
Alaska Travel Bureau	800-426-0082	Ayelet Tours	800-237-1517
Alaska Wildland	800-334-8730	AZ Travel Associates	800-987-2793
Alek's Travel	800-929-7768	B&V Associates	800-755-8266
Alken Tours	800-221-6686	Backroads	800-462-2848
All About Tours	800-274-8687	Bahia Tours	800-443-0717
All Charter Svcs & Tours	800-654-7967	Baja Expeditions	800-843-6967
Alta Tours	800-338-4191	Balkan Tourist	800-822-1106
Altura Tours	800-242-4122	Barbachano Tours	800-327-2254
Ambassador Tours	800-989-9000	Barcello Int'l	800-879-8687
Amelia Tours	800-742-4591	Barge Lady	800-252-9400
America West Vacations	800-356-6611	Baskin in the Sun	800-233-7938

Bennett Tours	800-221-2420	Network	800-423-4095
Bentley Tours	800-821-9726	Carriage Tours of	
Bermuda Travel		Savannah	800-442-5933
Planners	800-323-2020	Cartan Tours	800-422-7826
Best Golf	800-227-0212	CBN Tours	800-585-7261
Best in Tours	800-345-3502	CBT Bicycle Tours	800-736-2453
Best of Belize	800-735-9520	Cedok	800-800-8891
Bhutan Travel	800-950-9908	Celtic Int'l Tours	800-833-4373
Bicycle Adventures	800-443-6060	Central Holidays	800-935-5000
Big Bend River Tours	800-545-4240	Central Pacific Dive	800-846-3483
Big Five Tours	800-244-3483	Certified Vacations	800-233-7260
Blakes Vacations	800-628-8118	Changes in L'Attitudes	800-330-8272
Blue & White Tours	800-367-1789	Char-Tours	800-323-4444
Blue Danube Holidays	800-268-4155	CHAT Tours	800-268-1180
Blue Marble Travel	800-258-8689	Chateau Bike Tours	800-678-2453
Blue Planet Journeys	800-334-3782	China Connection	800-645-5484
Blue Sky Tours	800-678-2787	China Tours	800-252-4462
Bolder Adventures	800-642-2742	Chinasmith	800-872-4462
Bombard Balloon	800-862-8537	Christian Tours	800-476-3900
Borealis Outdoor		Christian Holidays	800-397-4608
Adventure	800-463-6399	Christian Traveler	800-323-6181
Born Free Safaris	800-372-3274	Ciclismo Classico	800-866-7314
Branson Vacation Tours	800-417-6122	CIE Tours	800-243-8687
Born Free Safaris	800-372-3274	CIT Tours	800-248-8687
Borton Overseas	800-843-0602	City Escape Holidays	800-222-0022
Bravo Tours	800-272-8674	Clark Malcolm Custom	800-688-3301
Brazil Nuts	800-553-9959	Classic Adventures	800-777-8090
Brazilian Vacation Ctr.	800-342-5746	Classic Golf & Leisure	800-283-1619
Brendan Tours	800-421-8446	Classic Custom Vacations	800-221-3949
Brennan Tours	800-237-7249	Classic Greece & Turkey	800-221-3949
Brewster	800-661-1152	Classic Holiday	800-225-4394
Brian Moore Int'l	800-982-2299	Classical Vacations	800-458-2863
British Air Tours	800-359-8722	Cloud Tours	800-223-7880
British Airways Holidays	800-247-9297	Club Med	800-258-2633
British Network	800-274-8583	Collette Tours	800-832-4656
Brroks Country Cycling	800-284-8954	Colorado Int'l Ski	800-487-1136
Butterfield & Robinson	800-678-1147	Columbus Travel	800-843-1060
Byrne & Proctor	800-441-3010	Complete Travel &	
Calif. Parlor Car Tours	800-227-4250	Leisure	800-446-3796
Calif. Tour Consultants	800-227-4276	Comtours	800-248-1331
Camino Tours	800-938-9311	Contiki	800-266-8454
CampAlaska	800-376-9438	Continental Vacations	800-634-5555
Canaan Tours	800-645-5732	Corliss Tours	800-456-5717
Canadian Mtn. Holidays	800-661-0252	Cosmopolitan Travel Svc.	800-633-4087
Canadian River		Costa Rica Connection	800-345-7422
Expeditions	800-898-7238	Costa Rica Experts	800-451-7111
Capricorn Leisure	800-426-6544	Country Walkers	800-464-9255
Caradonna Caribbean	800-328-2288	Cox & Kings	800-999-1758
Caravan Tours	800-227-2826	Creative Leisure Int'l	800-413-1000
Caribbean Adventures	800-934-3483	Creative Tours	800-289-8687
Caribbean Collection	800-969-8222	Crown Peters Travel	800-321-1199
Caribbean Concepts	800-423-4433	Custom Spa Vacations	800-443-7727
Caribbean Holidays	800-828-9204	Dailey-Thorp	800-988-4677
Caribbean Vacation		Dan Dipert Tours	800-433-5335

David Anderson Safaris	800-733-1789
Delta Dream Vacations	800-221-6666
Departures Int'l	800-509-5959
DER Tours	800-937-1235
Design Trav. & Tours	800-543-7164
Design-A-Tour	800-437-6469
Destination Ireland	800-832-1848
DFW Tours	800-527-2589
Diana Presents	800-441-3485
Diplomat Tours	800-727-8687
Direct Travel	800-275-4384
Discovery Tours	800-825-0699
Distinctive Journeys	800-922-2060
Distrav	800-334-7872
DMI Tours	800-553-5090
Dolphin Holiday	800-356-9742
Donna Franca Tours	800-225-6290
Down Under Connections	800-937-7878
Dream Voyages	800-320-2767
Dylan's Irish Golf	800-476-8547
Easy Rider Tours	800-488-8332
EBM Tours	800-234-3888
EC Tours	800-388-0877
Ecosummer Expeditions	800-465-8884
Ecotour Expeditions	800-688-1822
Ecoventures	800-743-8352
Edita Krunic	800-842-4842
Educational Field Studies	800-654-4750
Educational Tours	800-962-0060
Educational Travel Svcs.	800-929-4387
Edwards & Edwards	800-223-6108
EF Educational Tours	800-637-8222
Egyptian Connection	800-334-4477
Elegant Vacations	800-451-4398
Endless Beginnings	800-822-7855
Equestrian Holidays	800-625-2553
Esoteric Sports Tours	800-321-8008
Especially Britain	800-869-0538
Esplanade Tours	800-426-5492
Euro Bike Tours	800-321-6060
Euro Lloyd Tours	800-334-2724
EuroCruises	800-688-3876
Europe Train Tours	800-551-2085
European Connection	800-345-4679
European Culinary Adventures	800-852-2625
European Holidays	800-752-9578
European Tours Ltd.	800-722-3679
EuroSeven	800-890-3876
Exclusive Tours	800-828-8231
Experience Plus	800-685-4565
Experts in Greece	800-841-7107
Expo Garden Tours	800-448-2685
Extra Value Vacations	800-336-4668
Families Welcome	800-326-0724
Family Explorations	800-934-6866
Fantasy Holidays	800-645-2555
Fantasy Tours	800-772-6001
Far West Travel	800-533-1016
Fenwick & Lang	800-243-6244
Fishing Int'l	800-950-4242
FITS Equestrian	800-666-3487
Five Star Touring	800-792-7827
Fly AAway	800-321-2121
Foreign Indep. Tours	800-248-3487
FOS Tours	800-367-3450
Foundations of Faith	800-338-7075
Four Seasons Vacations	800-328-4298
Fourth Dimension Tours	800-343-0020
Frames Rickards	800-992-7700
France in Your Glass	800-578-0903
France Vacations	800-332-5332
FreeGate Tourism	800-223-0304
Friendly Holidays	800-221-9748
Friendly Planet Worldwide	800-555-5765
Friendship Int'l Tours	800-782-4597
Frontier Travel & Tours	800-647-0800
Frontiers Int'l	800-245-1950
Frontiers North	800-663-9832
Funjet Vacations	800-558-3050
Gadabout Tours	800-952-5068
Galapagos Network	800-633-7972
Galaxy Tours	800-523-7287
Galilee Tours USA	800-874-4445
Garuda Indonesia	800-342-7832
Gate 1	800-682-3333
General Tours	800-221-2216
Genesis Tours	800-888-8167
Geo Expeditions	800-351-5041
Geographic Expeditions	800-777-8183
Global Fitness Advent.	800-488-8747
Globetrotters	800-989-9960
Globus & Cosmos	800-221-0090
Go Classy Tours	800-329-8145
Go Diving	800-328-5285
GoGo Worldwide	800-899-2558
Golden West Tours	800-346-1625
Golf Getaways	800-423-3657
Golf Int'l	800-833-1389
Good Will Tours	800-244-3218
Grand Prix Tours	800-533-3503
Grand Slam Tennis	800-289-3333
Grandtravel	800-247-7651
Great Adventure Travel	800-874-2826
Great British Vacations	800-452-8434
Great Escape Tours	800-365-1833

Great Southern Island	
Adventures	800-748-8733
Great Spas of the World	800-772-8463
Great Times Out	800-877-5006
Great Western Ski	
Adventures	800-748-8733
Grecian Holidays Travel	800-554-6281
Greek Hotel & Cruise	800-362-7847
Greek Island Connection	800-241-2417
Group Tour Company	800-424-8895
Group Travel Enterprise	800-664-8259
GTI	800-868-7484
Guides for All Seasons	800-457-4574
GWT	800-868-7498
GWV	800-868-7498
Haddon Holidays	800-257-7488
Happy Tours	800-877-4277
Harwood Student Tours	800-972-7665
Health Travel Int'l	800-390-4964
Heavenly Int'l Tours	800-322-8622
Hellenic Adventures	800-851-6349
Hexatours	800-214-1148
Hidden Ireland	800-868-4750
Hiking Holidays	800-245-3868
Himalayan Int'l Tours	800-421-8975
Himalayan Travel	800-225-2380
HLO Tours	800-736-4456
Holbrook Travel	800-451-7111
Holiday Tours of America	800-677-6454
Holidaze Ski Tours	800-526-2827
Homeric Tours	800-223-5570
Hometours Int'l	800-367-4668
Horizon Tours	888-786-6726
HSA Voyages	800-927-4765
HTI	800-441-4411
Hudson Holidays	800-323-6855
Iberia/Discover Spain	800-227-5858
In the English Manner	800-422-0799
Insight Int'l	800-582-8380
Inter-Island Tours	800-245-3434
Int'l Curtain Call	800-669-9070
Int'l Diving Expeditions	800-544-3483
Int'l Group Travel	800-752-8090
Int'l Travel Planners	800-223-7406
Int'l Travel Alternatives	800-332-0482
Inter-Tours	800-959-4743
Intervac	800-992-9629
Irish-American Int'l	800-633-0505
Irish Links Tours	800-824-6538
Island Dreams Travel	800-326-6116
Island Flight Vacations	800-426-4570
Island Resort Tours	800-251-1755
Island Vacations	800-367-3450
Islands in the Sun	800-828-6877
Israel Tour Connection	800-727-1404
Israel Tours & Travel	800-769-6000
Isram	800-223-7460
IST Cultural Tours	800-833-2111
Italiatour	800-845-3365
ITC Golf Tours	800-257-4981
ITS Tours	800-533-8688
Jamaican Travel	
Specialists	800-544-5979
Japan & Orient	800-377-1080
JC Belize Resorts	800-881-3459
JC Travel	800-227-3920
Jefferson Tours	800-767-7433
Jet Vacations	800-538-0999
JetSet Tours	800-638-3273
Jetway Tours	800-421-8771
Journeys Thru Scotland	800-521-1429
Journeys Unlimited	800-486-8359
Journeyworld Int'l	800-635-3900
Kaplan Tours	800-999-5275
Katy Van Tours	800-525-6706
Kenny Tours	800-648-1492
Ker & Downey	800-423-4236
Key Holidays	800-783-0783
Key Tours	800-576-1784
Kingdom Tours	800-626-8747
Kirby Tours	800-521-0711
KLM/Northwest World	800-470-1111
Koala Tours	800-535-0316
Kompas Holidays	800-233-6422
Kwik Tours	800-826-8948
Ladatco Tours	800-327-6162
Lamers Tour & Travel	800-236-8687
L'Arc en Ciel	800-965-5272
Latitudes, Expeditions	
East	800-580-4883
Latour	800-825-0825
Legend Tours	800-333-6114
Leisure Resource	800-729-9051
Lemur Tours	800-735-3687
Lenzner Tours	800-342-2349
Lismore Tours	800-547-6673
Live/Dive Pacific	800-344-5662
LNT Associates	800-582-4832
Loire Tours	800-755-9313
Lord Addison Travel	800-326-0170
Lost World Adventures	800-999-0558
Lotus Travel	800-998-6116
Lynott Tours	800-221-2474
Maduro Dive Fanta-Seas	800-327-6709
Magnatours	800-856-2462
Magnum Belize	800-447-2931
Maiellano Tours	800-223-1616
Maitland & Assoc.	800-610-8687

Marathon Tours	800-444-4097
Marco Polo Vacations	800-421-5276
Mariah Wilderness Exp.	800-462-7424
Marketing Ahead	800-223-1356
Marnella Tours	800-937-6999
Matterhorn Travel Svc.	800-638-9150
Maupintour	800-255-4266
Maya World Tours	800-392-6292
Mayan Experience	800-403-7426
Mayflower Tours	800-323-7604
Mediterranean Dest.	800-247-3323
Megatrails	800-547-1211
Mena Tours & Travel	800-937-6362
Merano Tours	800-221-4551
Metro Tours	800-221-2810
Mexico Travel Advisors	800-876-4682
Mexitours	800-423-1004
Micato Safaris	800-642-2861
MILA/Perutours	800-367-7378
MISR Travel	800-223-4978
MLT	800-328-0025
Moore Tours	800-527-6366
Morocco Travel	800-428-5550
Mosaic Tours	800-525-7726
Mount Cook Tours	800-468-2665
Mountain Travel-Sobek	800-227-2384
MTI Vacations	800-535-6808
Munditour	800-327-7011
Myths & Mountains	800-670-6984
Naggar Tours of Egypt	800-443-6453
National Travel Vacations	800-525-5009
Natural Habitat Adventures	800-543-8917
Nature Expeditions	800-869-0639
New England Vacation Tours	800-742-7669
New Frontiers	800-366-6387
Niki Tours	800-487-9749
Oberammergau Tours	800-228-1590
Ocean Connection	800-365-6232
Ocean Voyages	800-299-4444
Oceans of Diving	800-466-1400
Oceanwide Expeditions	800-453-7245
Ole Travel	800-559-5192
Olson Travelworld	800-421-2255
Olympia Tours	800-367-6718
Omni Tours	800-962-0060
Open Road Tours	800-766-7117
Orbis Polish Travel	800-223-6037
Orbitair	800-847-1800
Orient Flexi-Pax	800-545-5540
Orientours	800-757-1772
Our Family Abroad	800-999-5500
Outer Edge Expeditions	800-322-5140
Overseas Adventure Travel	800-221-0814
Owenoak Castle Tours	800-426-4498
Pacific Bestour	800-688-3288
Pacific Delight	800-221-7179
Pacific Holidays	800-355-8025
Pacific Select	800-722-4349
Pacific Sun Spots	800-663-0755
Panama Discovery Tours	800-813-3115
Paradise Isl. Vacations	800-722-7466
Paris Vision	800-882-2344
Parker Tours	800-833-9600
Passports	800-332-7277
Path Tours	800-843-0400
Paul Laifer Tours	800-346-6314
Pearls of Scandinavia	800-806-8785
Pedersen World Tours	800-933-6627
Performing Arts Abroad	800-952-0643
Perillo Tours	800-431-1515
PerryGolf	800-344-5257
Petrabox USA	800-367-6611
PGA Travel	800-283-4653
Pharos Travel	800-999-5511
Photo Adventure Tours	800-821-1221
Pierbussetti World Trav.	800-621-1047
Pilgrimage Tours	800-669-0757
Pioneer Tours	800-288-2107
Places To Go	800-775-2237
Pleasant Holidays	800-242-9244
Pleasure Break	800-777-1566
Pleasure Travel & Tours	800-452-5494
Plus Ultra Tours	800-367-7724
Portuguese Tours	800-526-4047
Poseidon Ventures	800-854-9334
Presidential World Travel	800-874-1811
Prestige Villas	800-336-0080
Private Holidays	800-821-3690
Progressive Travels	800-245-2229
Provence Travel Res.	800-292-0219
Qantas Jetabout Holidays	800-641-8772
Queensway Tours	800-267-3483
Quest Tours	800-621-8687
Questers Tours	800-468-8668
R & H Voyages	800-862-2476
Rahim Tours	800-556-5305
Rail Europe	800-438-7245
Rama Tours	800-835-7262
Rascals in Paradise	800-872-7225
Ready Int'l	800-847-3239
Rebel Tours	800-227-3235
Red Sail Sports	800-255-6425

Redstone Tours	800-547-3323	Vacations	800-451-0341
Reggae Jam	800-873-4423	South Pacific Your Way	800-426-3610
Regina Tours	800-228-4654	South Sea Tour & Travel	800-546-7890
Rent-A-Home	800-488-7368	South Star Tours	800-654-4468
RFD Travel Corp.	800-365-5359	Southern Connections	800-635-3303
River Odysseys West	800-451-6034	Southwest Airlines Fun	
RMA Tours	800-841-9800	Pack	800-423-5683
Roatan Charter	800-282-8932	Sovereign Tourism	800-832-3228
Rockwell Tours	800-526-4910	Spa Finders	800-255-7727
Rod & Reel Adventures	800-356-6982	Spa Trek Int'l	800-272-3480
Romantik Travel & Tours	800-826-0015	Spanish Golf Adventures	800-772-6465
Rothschild Dive Safaris	800-359-0747	Spanish Heritage Tours	800-221-2580
Royal Northwest		Special Expeditions	800-762-0003
Holidays	800-818-7799	Specialty Tours	800-421-3913
Royal Travel Svc.	800-245-4990	Spectacular Sports Spcls.	800-451-5772
Runaway Tours	800-622-0723	Sport Stalker	800-525-5520
Rustin Group	800-787-8461	SporTours	800-660-2754
Sabra Tours	800-231-4111	Sports Empire of LA	800-255-5258
Sacca Tours	800-326-5170	Sportstours	800-879-8647
Safaricentre	800-223-6046	Starr Tours	800-314-8411
Saga Int'l Holidays	800-343-0273	Stepping Stone Environ-	
Sanborn Tours	800-395-8482	mental Education	
Sante Int'l Great Spas	800-772-8463	Tours	800-874-8784
Saranjan	800-858-9594	Sterling Tours	800-727-4359
Scantours	800-223-7226	Stoddard Int'l Travel	
Schwartz Tours	800-234-0303	Network	800-279-4454
Scuba Travel Ventures	800-298-9009	Student Travel Services	800-648-4849
Scuba Voyages	800-544-7631	Sue's Safaris	800-541-2011
Sea & Explore	800-345-9786	Sunburst Holidays	800-972-9795
Sea Air Holidays	800-732-6247	Sunmakers	800-841-4321
Sea Connections Center	800-367-1789	Suntrek Tours	800-786-8735
Sea Fiji Travel	800-854-3454	Sunny Land Tours	800-783-7830
Select Destinations	800-759-7727	Super Holiday Tours	800-327-2116
Select Int'l	800-842-4842	Surprising London	800-233-4459
Select Travel Service	800-752-6787	Swain Australia Tours	800-227-9246
Shamrock Travel Golf		Synagogue Travel	800-448-0399
Tours	800-376-7815	T For Travel	800-226-9992
Sheri Griffith Exped.	800-332-2439	Take A Guide	800-825-4946
Showcase Ireland	800-654-6527	TAL Tours	800-825-9399
Showline Tours	800-962-9246	Talmage Tours	800-825-6243
Silkway Travel	800-826-0770	Tara Tours	800-327-0080
Sino-American Tours	800-628-1168	Tauck Tours	800-468-2825
SITA World Travel	800-421-5643	TBI Tours	800-221-2216
Ski Pak	800-446-4688	Temasa Travel	800-331-9506
Ski Vacation Planners	800-822-6754	Terra Firma Adventures	800-524-1823
SkiCan Quality Ski		Terry Flynn Tours	800-678-7848
Holidays	800-268-8880	TFI Tours	800-745-8000
Skipper Travel Services	800-631-1030	That's The Ticket	800-648-8990
Skyline Travel Club	800-645-6198	The Best of Israel	800-982-9783
Smolka Tours	800-722-0057	Tierra Mar Travel	800-525-5524
Snow Tours	800-222-1170	Tiffany Tours	800-786-8772
Solar Tours	800-388-7652	TNT Vacations	800-262-0123
South American Fiesta	800-334-3782	Topline Travel	800-221-1289
South American		Toro Tours	800-246-9546

Tortuga Express	800-521-2346
Tour & Travel Managers	800-677-7411
Tour Arrangements	800-343-3487
Tour de France	800-261-2891
Tour Designs	800-432-8687
Tour Host Int'l	800-843-4678
Tourcrafters	800-621-2259
Touritalia	800-848-6276
Tourlite Int'l	800-272-7600
Tours by Andrea	800-535-2732
Tours in the Sun	800-987-8669
Tours Specialists	800-223-7552
Tours & Travel Dimensions	800-437-9085
Tourtech Int'l	800-882-2636
Towne Tours Holiday	800-523-8880
T.R. Int'l	800-327-4433
Tradesco Tours	800-833-3402
Trafalgar Tours	800-854-0103
Transglobal Vacations	800-328-6264
Travcoa	800-992-2003
Travel Arrangements	800-392-8213
Travel Bound	800-456-2004
Travel Center Tours	800-621-8188
Travel Charter	800-521-5267
Travel Impressions	800-284-0044
Travel Magic	800-883-6244
Travel Plans Int'l	800-323-7600
Travel Priorities	800-342-7300
Travel Specialists	800-458-5394
Travel With the Experts	800-595-9778
Travel Wizards	800-622-4868
Travelers Service Co.	800-232-2016
Traveline	800-268-1180
Traveltrends	800-634-4808
Travelvisions	800-550-0091
Travent Int'l	800-325-3009
Tread Lightly	800-643-0060
Triaena Tours	800-223-1273
Tricolor Int'l Tours	800-570-0730
Trip-N-Tour Micronesia	800-348-0842
Tristar Tours	800-325-7753
Tropical Adventures	800-247-3483
Tropical Travel Reps.	800-451-8017
TTI-Travel Inc.	800-446-5952
Tuchman Media Tours	800-772-1010
Tumbaco	800-247-2925
Turicum Int'l	800-451-4284
Tursem Tours Int'l	800-223-9169
TWA Getaway Vacations	800-438-2929
Twelve Island & Beyond	800-345-8236
U.E.T.	800-525-0525
Uliat Tours	800-248-5428
Ulysses Tours	800-431-1424
Underseas Expeditions	800-669-0310
Underwater Explorers	800-992-3483
Uniglobe Travel Int'l	800-999-8000
Uniontours	800-451-9511
Unique Journeys	800-421-1981
Unique Tours	800-543-5527
Unique World Travel	800-669-0757
Uniquely Europe	800-426-3615
United Touring Int'l	800-223-6486
United Tours Corp.	800-245-0203
United Vacations	800-328-6877
Unitours	800-621-0495
Universal City Travel	800-224-3838
Uniworld	800-733-7820
US Int'l Travel & Tours	800-759-7373
USAir Vacations	800-455-0123
Vacation Express	800-486-9777
Vacation Homes Abroad	800-727-0082
VacationLand	800-245-0050
Value Holidays	800-558-6850
Vantage Adventures	800-826-8268
VE Tours	800-222-8383
Vermont Bicycle Touring	800-245-3868
Victor Emanuel Nature	800-328-8368
Visit Italy Tours	800-255-3537
Visits Plus	800-321-3235
Vista Tours	800-248-4782
Walking the World	800-340-9255
Walt Disney Travel	800-327-2996
Wayfarers, The	800-249-4620
Wegiel Tours	800-333-3307
Weissman Teen Tours	800-942-8005
Western River Exped.	800-453-7450
Wide World of Golf	800-214-4653
Wild Women Adventures	800-992-1322
Wilderness Travel	800-368-2794
Wildland Adventures	800-345-4453
Wildlife Safari	800-221-8118
Wings Tours	800-869-4647
World Arrow FIT Tours	800-648-0004
World Arrow Tours	800-223-7396
World Dive Adventures	800-433-3483
World of Oz	800-248-0234
World Pilgrim Tours	800-438-8281
World Travelers	800-426-3610
World Wide Christian Tours	800-732-7920
WorldVentures	800-800-1775
Worldwide Holidays	800-327-9854
Worldwide Vacations	800-841-8222
WTI	800-243-3239
Yachts Are Us	800-913-9471
Yankee Holidays	800-225-2550
Zeus Tours	800-447-5667

Additional Tour Operator Contacts

Cruise Lines

Alaska Sightseeing	800-426-7702	Majesty Cruise Line	800-532-7788
Ambassador	800-255-5551	Norwegian Cruise Line	800-327-7030
America West Steamboat	800-4341232	Oceanic Cruises	800-545-5778
American Canadian		OdessAmerica	800-221-3254
Caribbean	800-556-7450	Orient Lines	800-333-7300
American Hawaii Cruises	800-765-7000	Palm Beach Cruise Line	800-841-7447
Bergen Line	800-323-7436	Paradise Cruise	800-334-6191
Carnival Cruise Lines	800-327-9501	Premier Cruise Lines	800-327-7113
Celebrity Cruises	800-437-3111	Prince of Fundy Cruises	800-341-7540
Classical Cruises	800-252-7745	Princess Cruises	800-421-0522
Clipper Cruise Line	800-325-0010	Quark Expeditions	800-356-5699
Club Med	800-258-2633	Radisson Seven Seas	
Commodore Cruise Line	800-237-5361	Cruises	800-333-3333
Costa Cruise Line	800-832-1122	Regency Cruises	800-734-3629
Crystal Cruises	800-446-6645	Renaissance Cruises	800-525-5350
Cunard Line	800-528-6273	Royal Caribbean Int'l	800-327-6700
Delta Queen Steamboat	800-458-6789	Royal Hawaiian Cruises	800-852-4183
Discovery Cruises	800-937-4477	Sea Escape Cruises	800-432-0900
Dirigo Cruises	860-669-7068	Seabourn Cruises	800-929-9595
Disney Cruise		Seawind Cruise Line	800-258-8006
Vacations	800-511-1333	Silversea Cruises	800-722-9955
Dolphin Cruise Line	800-222-1003	St. Lawrence Cruise	800-267-7868
Epirotiki Lines	800-872-6400	Star Clippers	800-442-0551
EuroCruises	800-688-3876	Sun Line Cruises	800-872-6400
European Waterways	800-438-4748	Swan Hellenic Cruises	800-426-5492
French Country		Tall Ship Adventures	800-662-0090
Waterways	800-222-1236	Temptress Cruises	800-451-4398
Galapagos Inc.	800-327-9854	Windjammer Barefoot	800-327-2601
Galapagos Cruises	800-421-5276	Windstar Cruises	800-258-7245
Holland America Line	800-426-0327	World Explorer Cruises	800-854-3835
Ivaran Lines	800-451-1639	Zeus Cruises	800-447-5667
KD River Cruises	800-346-6525		

Additional Cruise Line Contacts

Web Sites for Travel Agents

This section contains Universal Resource Locators (URLs) that will enable you to log on to sites on the Internet's World Wide Web. If you are not already familiar with the Internet, you will be. However, it is not our intention here to educate anybody about this exploding communications phenomenon. Suffice it to say that the Web (as it is invariably called) has the potential to revolutionize the way travel agents get information and do business.

In addition to listing web sites for suppliers of travel products — airlines, hotels, rental cars, tour operators, and cruise lines — we have also listed sites for associations, CRS suppliers, tourist bureaus, Internet search engines, and others. We have also listed so-called "**Super Sites**," whose main attraction is their listing of or links to other sites, usually within a specific category.

In these listings, we have omitted the "http://" that begins all Internet addresses. Be aware that, while most Internet addresses continue with "www.", many do not, especially ones on servers overseas. So the fact that an address does not begin "http://www." does not mean it is a typographical error.

We make no pretense to being encyclopedic. With the Internet growing exponentially, that would be impossible. The Super Sites we list should help you keep reasonably up to date.

Finally, we invite you to visit our web site at

http://www.intrepidtraveler.com

where you will find a continually updated list of links to many worthwhile sites along with updates to *The Intrepid Traveler's Complete Desk Reference* and other books published by The Intrepid Traveler.

Airlines

Adria Airlines	www.kabi.si/si21/aa/
Aer Lingus	www.hursley.ibm.com/aer
Aero Costa Rica	www.centralamerica.com/cr/tran/aero.htm
Aeroflot	www.aeroflot.org/Aeroflot.html
Aerolinas Argentinas	www.pinos.com/Aero/aero.html
AeroMexico	www.wotw.com/aeromexico/
Air Aruba	www.interknowledge.com/air-aruba/
Air Canada	www.aircanada.ca/
Air China	www.airchina.com
Air Europa	www.g-air-europa.es
Air France	www.airfrance.fr/
Air India	www.globalindia.com/airindia/airindia.htm
Air Mauritius	www.cyber.be/air-mauritius/
Air New Zealand	airnz.com/
Air Niugini	www.datec.com.au/airniugini/welcome.htm
Air South	www.airsouth.com
Air UK	www.airuk.co.uk/
Alaska Airlines	www.alaska-air.com/
Alitalia	www.alitalia.it/
All Nippon Airways	www.ana.co.jp/index-e.html
ALM Antillean Airlines	www.empg.com/alm/
Aloha Airlines	www.alohaair.com/aloha-air/
America West Airlines	www.americawest.com/
American Airlines	www.americanair.com
American Trans Air	www.ata.com
Ansett Australia	www.ansett.com.au/
Asiana Airlines	www.asiana.co.kr
Austrian Airlines	www.aua.co.at/aua/
Avianca	www.avianca.com
AVIATECA	www.flylatinamerica.com/acc_aviateca.html
Balkan-Bulgarian Airlines	www.balkanair.com
Bangkok Airways	www.bkkair.co.th
British Airways	www.british-airways.com
British Midland	www.iflybritishmidland.com
BWIA	www.bwiacaribbean.com
Canadian Airlines Int'l (CAI)	www.CdnAir.CA/
Carnival Air Lines	www.carnivalair.com
Cathay Pacific Airways	www.cathay-usa.com
Cayman Airways	www.caymanairways.com
China Airlines	www.china-airlines.com/
China Eastern Airlines	206.170.104.72
China Southern Airlines	www.chinasouthernair.com/
Comair	w3.one.net/~flypba/comair/comair.home.html
Conquest Airlines	www.conquestair.com/
Continental Airlines	www.fly-continental.com
COPA Airlines	www.copaair.com
CSA (Czechoslovak Airlines)	www.csa.cz/
Delta Air Lines	www.delta-air.com
Eastwind	pages.prodigy.com/X/S/A/XSNN68A/eastwind.htm

El Al Israel Airlines	www.elal.co.il/
Emirates Airlines	www.ekgroup.com/
EVA Airways	www.evaair.com.tw
Finnair	www.finnair.fi/
Frontier Airlines	www.flyfrontier.com
Garuda Indonesia	www.indonesianet.com/garudausa/
Gulf Air	www.gulfairco.com
Hawaiian Airlines	www.hawaiianair.com
Horizon Airlines	www.horizonair.com/
Iberia Airlines	www.iberiausa.com
Icelandair	www.centrum.is/icelandair/
Intercontinental de Aviacion	www.insite-network.com/Inter/
Iran Air	www.nether.net/~behzadx/homa.html
Japan Airlines	www.jal.co.jp/
Kiwi	users.aol.com/chnaclppr/airline/kiwi.htm
Kiwi Int'l (NZ)	www.kiwiair.co.nz/
KLM Royal Dutch Airlines	www.klm.nl/
Korean Air Lines (KAL)	www.koreanair.com/
Ladeco Airlines	www.ladeco.com/
Laker Airways	www.lakerair.com
Lan Chile	www.lanchile.com/
LOT Polish Airlines	www.lot.com/
LTU International Airways	www.iquest.net/ltu/
Lufthansa	www.Lufthansa.ch/
Mahalo Air	http://www.islander-magazine.com/
Malaysia Airlines	http://www.malaysiaairlines.com.my
Malev Hungarian Airlines	www.osgweb.com/airlines/ma.htm
Mandarin Air	www.mandarinair.com/
Manx Airlines	www.manx-airlines.com/
Mesa Airlines	www.mesa-air.com
Mexicana	www.mexicana.com
Middle East Airlines (AirLiban)	www.mea.com.lb
Midwest Express Airlines	www.midwestexpress.com/
Myrtle Beach Jet Express	www.myrtlebeachjetexp.com
New England Airlines	www.ids.net/flybi/
Northwest Airlines	www.nwa.com
Olympic Airways	agn.hol.gr/info/olympic1.htm
Pakistan International Airlines	www.piac.com/index.htm
Paradise Island Airlines	www.paradiseair.com
Philippine Airlines	www.sequel.net/PAL/
Qantas Airways	www.qantas.com.au/
Reno Air	www.renoair.com
Royal Air Maroc	www.kingdomofmorocco.com/html/ royal_air.html
Royal Jordanian	www.rja.com.jo
Sabena	www.sabena-usa.com/
SAETA (Ecuador)	www4.saeta.com.ec/
Saudi Arabian Airlines	www.saudiarabian-airlines.com/
Scandinavian Airlines System (SAS)	www.sas.se/
Silkair	www.singaporeair.com/silkair/default.htm
Singapore Airlines	www.singaporeair.com
Sky West Airlines	www.skywest.com.au
South African Airways (SAA)	www.saa.co.za/saa/notnet2.htm
Southwest Airlines	www.iflyswa.com

Spanair	www.spanair.com/
Sun Country Airlines	www.suncountry.com
Surinam Airways	www.surinamair.com
Swissair	www.swissair.com
Taca Int'l Airlines	www.flylatinamerica.com/acc_taca.html
TAESA	www.wotw.com/wow/mexico/city/taesa.html
TAP Air Portugal	www.tap-airportugal.pt
Thai Airways	www.thaiair.com/
Transbrasil	www.transbrasil.com.br
TWA (Trans World Airlines)	www.twa.com
United Airlines	www.ual.com
USAirways	www.usair.com
ValuJet Airlines	www.valujet.com
Varig	www.varig.com.br/
VASP Brazilian	www.vasp.com.br
Virgin Atlantic	www.fly.virgin.com/atlantic/
Western Pacific	www.westpac.com
World Airways	www.worldair.com/
Yugoslav Airlines	www.yurope.com/jat/

Airline 'Super Sites'

Airlines on the Web	www.itn.net/airlines/
Yahoo Airlines	www.yahoo.com/business/corporations/travel/airlines

Additional Airline Web Sites

Hotels

Adams Mark Hotels	www.travelx.com/adamsmark.html
ANA Hotels	www.ananet.or.jp/anahotels/e/
Aston Hotels & Resorts	www.amrcorp.com/amr_mgmt/teleserv/aston.htm
Barclay International	www.barclayweb.com
Best Western Int'l	www.travelweb.com/bw.html
Budgetel	www.budgetel.com
Canadian Pacific Hotels	www.cphotels.ca/
Choice Hotels	www.hotelchoice.com
Colony Resorts	www.colony-resorts.com
Concorde Hotels	www.concorde-hotels.com/
Conrad International	www.travelweb.com/thisco/conradin/common/conradin.html
Continental Plaza	www.wotw.com/wow/situr/cpl-main.html
Courtyard	www.marriott.com/courtyard/
Crown Plaza	www.crowneplaza.com/
Days Inns	www.daysinn.com
Delta Hotels	www.deltahotels.com/
Doubletree Hotels	www.doubletreehotels.com
Dusit & Kempinski	www.dusit-kempinski.com/
Embassy Suites	www.embassy-suites.com/
Fairfield Inn	www.marriott.com/fairfieldinn/
Family Inns of America	www.familyinnsofamerica.com
Forte Hotels	www.forte-hotels.com
Four Seasons	www.fshr.com/
Furama Hotels	www.furama-hotels.com
Hampton Inns	www.hampton-inn.com
Hilton Hotels	www.hilton.com
Holiday Inn Worldwide	www.holiday-inn.com
Homewood Suites	www.homewood-suites.com
Howard Johnson	www.hojo.com/
Hyatt Hotels	www.hyatt.com/
Inter-Continental Hotels	www.interconti.com
Leading Hotels	lhw.com/
Loews Hotels	www.loewshotels.com/
Mandarin Oriental	www.mandarin-oriental.com
Marriott Hotels	www.marriott.com
Meridien Hotels	www.forte-hotels.com/br_meri.htm
Minotel	www.minotel.com/
Movenpick Hotels	www.moevenpick.ch
New Otani Hotels	www.newotani.co.jp/index-e.htm
Novotel	www.novotel.com/welcome/
Omni Hotels	www.omnihotels.com
Orient Express Hotels	www.orient-expresshotels.com/oeh/
Outrigger Hotels	www.outrigger.com
Pan Pacific Hotels	www.panpac.com
Park Plaza Int'l	www.parkhtls.com
Preferred Hotels	www.travelweb.com/thisco/prefered/common/home.html
Prima Hotels	www.prima-hotels.com/

Princess Hotels	www.princess.com.tr
Radisson Hotels	www.radisson.com
Ramada Inns	ramada.com
Red Lion Hotels	www.travelweb.com/thisco/redlion/common/redlion.html
Red Roof Inns	www.travelweb.com/thisco/redlion/common/redlion.html
Relais & Chateaux	www.integra.fr/relaischateaux/
Renaissance Hotels	www.renaissance-asia.com/
Residence Inn	www.marriott.com/residenceinn/
Sandals Resorts	www.sandals.com
Shangri-La Hotels	www.shangrila.com
Sheraton Hotels	www.sheraton.com
Shoney's Inns	www.shoneysinn.com/
Small Luxury Hotels	www.slh.com/slh/
Sonesta Hotels	www.sonesta.com
Stakis Hotel Group	www.stakis.co.uk/stakis/hotels.html
Super 8 Motels	www.super8motels.com/
Susse Chalet	www.sussechalet.com
Travelodge	www.travelodge.com/
Utell Hotels	www.hotelbook.com
Westin Hotels	www.westin.com
Westmark Hotels	www.westmarkhotels.com
Wyndham Hotels	www.wyndham-recruiting.com/Hotel.htm

Hotel 'Super Sites'

All the Hotels on the Web	www.all-hotels.com/
E-Scope	www.escope.com
Hotel & Travel Index	www.traveler.net/htio/
Hotel Guide	www.hotelguide.ch/
Hotel Reservations Network	www.180096hotel.com
HotelsOnline	www.hotelsonline.com
Resorts On-Line	www.resortsonline.com
TravelWeb	www.travelweb.com

Additional Hotel Web Sites

Rental Cars

ABC Rent A Car	www.rentabc.com/
Advantage	www.arac.com
Alamo	www.goalamo.com
Auto Europe	www.auto-europe.com
Avis	www.avis.com
Budget	www.budget.com
Dollar	www.dollarcar.com
Eurodollar	www.eurodollar.co.uk/
Hertz	www.hertz.com
Holiday Autos	www.holidayautos.co.uk/
Kemwel	www.kemwel.com
National	www.nationalcar.com
Payless	www.paylesscar.com
Rent-A-Wreck	rent-a-wreck.com/
Thrifty	www.thrifty.com
Value	www.go-value.com

Additional Rental Car Web Sites

Tour Operators

Abaco Vacation Res.	www.acadia.net/abaco
Abercrombie & Kent	www.abercrombiekent.com
Abreu Tours	www.abreu-tours.com
Accent on Britain	www.englishtours.com
Accessible Journeys	www.disabilitytravel.com
Adventure Center	www.adventure-center.com
Adventures on Skis	www.advonskis.com
American Media Tours	www.amttours.com
American Overland Expeditions	ourworld.compuserve.com/homepages/a_o_e
Auto Venture	www.autoventure.com
Avanti Destinations	www.teleport.com/~avanti/
Backroads Int'l	www.backroadsinternational.com
Baja Expeditions	www.bajaex.com
Bicycle Africa	www.halcyon.com/fkroger/bike/bifeafr.htm
Brennan Tours	www.brennantours.com
Calif. Tour Consultants	www.tfa2.com/caltourcon/
Certified Vacations	www.leisureweb.com
Changes in L'Attitudes	www.changes.com/
City Escape Holidays	www.cityescapes.com/
Club America	www.clubamericatravel.com
Collette Tours	www.collettetours.com
Contiki	www.contiki.com
Country Walkers	www.countrywalkers.com
Cox & Kings	www.zenonet.com/cox-kings/
David Anderson Safaris	www.davidanderson.com
Delta Dream Vacations	www.leisureweb.com/DELTA/
Destination Mgmt.	www.new.orleans.com/index.html
DFW Tours	www.sojourner.com/wings/dfwtours.html
Ecotour Expeditions	www.naturetours.com
Egypt Tours & Travel	pages.prodigy.com/IL/ashraf/egypt.html
English Lakeland Ramblers	www.ramblers.com
European Walking Tours	www.walkingtours.com
Experience Plus	www.xplus.com
Far West Travel	www.astanet.com/get/farwest
Forum Travel Int'l	www.ten-io.com/forumtravel
Fourth Dimension Tours	www.4thdimension.com/
FreeGate Tourism	www.freegatetours.com
Friendly Holidays	www.ten-io.com/friendly/
Funjet Vacations	www.funjet.com
Galaxy Tours	www.galaxytours.com
Global Vacations	www.globalvacations.com
Globus/Cosmos	www.globusandcosmos.com
Go Ahead Vacations	ef.com/ga/
Golden Sports Tours	www.goldenint.com
Gray Line Worldwide	www.grayline.com
Greek Hotel & Cruise	www.cruiseair.com
Guides for All Seasons	gfas.com
Haddon Holidays	www.haddon.com
Heavenly Int'l Tours	www.heavenlytours.com/
Horizon Tours	www.horizontours.com
Isram	www.isram.com/

Italiatour	www.zenonet.com/italiatour/
Japan & Orient	www.jot.com
Japan Travel Bureau	www.jtbi.com
Jet Vacations	www.jetvacations.com
JetSet Tours	www.jetsettours.com/
Ker & Downey	www.kerdowney.com
Latitudes, Expeditions East	www.weblatitudes.com
Leisure Resource	www.escope.com
Lenzner Tours	www.motorcoach.com/lenzer
Lost World Adventures	www.gorp.com/lostworld.htm
Lotus Travel	lotustravel.com
Maitland & Assoc.	www.travelfile.com/get/maitland
MILA Travel Planner	www.a2z.com/a2z/mila/mila.html
Mount Cook Line	www.mtcook.co.nz/
Mountain Travel-Sobek	www.MTSobek.com
Open Road Tours	www.openroadtours.com
Pacific Holidays	www.travelfile.com/get/pacifhol
Performing Arts Abroad	www.paa-net.com
Perillo Tours	www.perillotours.com
Petrabax	www.petrabax.com/
Preferred Holidays	www.prefhol.com
Rail Travel Center	www.megacomp.com/railtvl/
Remote Odysseys	www.rowinc.com
Rocky Mountaineer Railtours	www.rkymtnrail.com
Rustin Group	www.rustingroup.com
Sacca Tours	www.saccatours.com
Sanborn Tours	www.sanborns.com/
Select Destinations	www.selectdestinations.com
Solar Tours	solartours.com
Southern Horizon	www.pacificnet.net/~sht/
Sports Tour Classics	www.sportstourclassics.com
SporTours	www.sportours.com
Star Tours	www.star-tours.com
Stoddard Int'l	www.ameriruss.com
Sunny Land Tours	www.sunny-land-tours.com
Suntrek Tours	www.sonic.net/suntrek
Super Holiday Tours	www.superholiday.com
Swain Australia Tours	www.swainaustralia.com
Thomas Cook Vacations	www.tch.thomascook.com/
Tourcrafters	www.tourcrafters.com
Tourlite Int'l	www.tourlite.com
Trans Global Vacations	www.tgvacations.com/
Travac Tours	www.travac.com
Triaena Travel	www.triaena.com
Tropical Adventures	ourworld.compuserve.com/homepages/ tropical_adventures/
Uliat Tours	www.uliattours.com
Uniontours	www.travelfile.com/get/uniontrs.html
Value Holidays	www.valhol.com
Value World Tours	www.vwtours.com/
VE Tours	www.vetours.com
Walt Disney Travel	www.disney.com
Wild Women Adventures	www.wildwomenadv.com
Wilderness Travel	www.wildernesstravel.com

Yachts Are Us   www.seatheworld.com
Zeus Tours   www.zeustours.com

Tour Operator 'Super Sites'

National Tour Association   www.ntaonline.com
Special Interest Travel
  Marketing Alliance   www.sitravel.com
USTOA   www.ustoa.com
Vacation Packager   www.vacationpackager.com

Additional Tour Operator Web Sites

Additional Tour Operator Web Sites

Cruise Lines

American Canadian	www.accl-smallships.com
American Hawaii Cruises	www.cruisehawaii.com
Carnival Cruise Liness	www.carnival.com
Celebrity Cruises	www.celebritycruises.com
Clipper Cruise Line	www.clippercruise.com
Club Med	www.clubmed.com
Commodore Cruise Line	www.commodorecruise.com/
Costa Cruise Line	www.costacruises.com
Cunard Line	www.cunardline.com
Delta Queen Steamboat	www.asource.com/deltaqueen/index.htm
Dirigo Cruises	www.uconect.net/~dirigo
Discovery Cruises	www.introweb.com/discovery/
Dolphin Cruise Line	mmink.com/dcl.htm
Dolphin Hellas	www-na.biznet.com.gr/tourism/dolphin/index.html
Epirotiki Lines	www.epirotiki.com
European Waterways	www.europeanwaterways.com
Hapag Lloyd/Hanseatic	www.hapag-lloyd.com/schiff/index.htm
Hellenic Mediterranean	www.hml.it/
Holland America Line	www.hollandamerica.com
Majesty Cruise Line	mmink.com/mcl.html
Norwegian Cruise Line	www.ncl.com/ncl
OdessAmerica	www.interknowledge.com/russia/odessa-america/odessa.htm
Paradise Cruise	www.bestcruise.com/
Premier Cruise Lines	www.inx.net/bigred
Radisson Seven Seas	www.asource.com/radisson/
Renaissance Cruises	www.rencruises.com/
Royal Caribbean International	www.royalcaribbean.com
Silversea Cruises	www.asource.com/silversea/
Star Clippers	www.globalint.com/mart/star.html
Swan Hellenic Cruises	www.swan-hellenic.co.uk/
Tall Ship Adventures	www.the-wire.com/torbrig/
Windjammer Barefoot	www.windjammer.com
Windstar Cruises	www.windstarcruises.com
World Explorer Cruises	www.wecruise.com

Additional Cruise Line Web Sites

Associations

Air Transport Association (ATA)	www.air-transport.org
American Recreation Coalition	www.funoutdoors.com/arc
American Society of Travel Agents	www.astanet.com
International Air Transport Association (IATA)	www.iata.org
International Airlines Travel Agent Network (IATAN)	www.iatan.org
International Association of Amusement Parks and Attractions	www.iaapa.org
International Association of Conference Centers	www.iacconline.com
National Association of Commissioned Travel Agents	www.nacta.com
National Motorcoach Network	www.motorcoach.com
National Tour Association	www.ntaonline.com
Outside Sales Support Network	www.ossn.com
Trade Show Exhibitors Association	www.tsea.org
Travel and Tourism Research Association	www.ttra.com
Vacation Rental Managers Association	www.vrma.com

Additional Association Web Sites

Other Web Sites of Interest to Travel Agents

Major CRSs

Amadeus	www.amadeus.com
Apollo	www.apollo.com
easySABRE	www.easysabre.com
SystemOne	www.sys1.com
Worldspan	www.worldspan.com

Proprietary Reservations Systems

Internet Travel Network	www.itn.com
Microsoft Expedia	expedia.msn.com
Travelocity	www.travelocity.com
Yahoo Air Travel	www.yahoo.flifo.com

Consolidators on the Web

Air Fares for Less	www.air4less.com
Airline Discount Store	www.airvalues.com/airfare_disc
Airplan	www.airplan.com
Global Discount Travel	www.lowestfare.com
Intransco	www.intransco.com
Jetset Tours	www.jetsettours.com
Online Discount Airline Tickets	www.airfare.com
Overseas Express	www.ovex.com
Travel Information System	www.tiss.com/
UniTravel Online	unitravel.com

Government

Consular Informations Sheets	travel.state.gov/travel_warnings.html
Department of Transportation	www.dot.gov
Federal Aviation Administration	www.faa.gov
Foreign entry requirements	travel.state.gov/foreignentryreqs.html
Passport Services	travel.state.gov/passport_services.html
State Department travel publications	travel.state.gov/travel_pubs.html
U.S. Customs	www.customs.ustreas.gov/

Miscellaneous

Currency Converter	www.xe.net/currency/
The Intrepid Traveler	www.intrepidtraveler.com
Hyde's Travel Agent Resource	www.hyde.com/hyde.htm

Sources of Tourist Information: United States

There are hundreds, if not thousands, of sources of free tourist information about states, cities, regions, and resort areas across the United States. We have listed some of them here.

First, we have listed all of the state tourist offices. These governmental organizations have the job of attracting tourists to their states. They all produce informational materials about the attractions and recreational activities their states have to offer. Some are more lavish or more helpful than others. Some are more prompt in responding to queries than others.

Many states publish guides which are targeted specifically at those in the travel industry, containing information of special interest to travel agents and tour operators. Make sure, when requesting information, that you identify yourself as a travel agent.

Within some of the states, we have listed, alphabetically by location, the names and addresses of major local sources of information, usually a convention and visitors bureau. Again, this listing is not exhaustive. We have limited ourselves to the major tourist destinations. Obviously, any selection of "major tourist destinations" will be somewhat subjective. We limited ourselves to major cities and areas which, according to industry statistics, are the most visited by tourists. So please don't take offense if your local area or favorite destination is not included. No slight was intended.

Finding sources of information on cities or areas not listed is an easy task. Start with 800-number information (1-800-555-1212) to see if there is a toll-free number for tourist information. Failing that, call directory information in the local area code, specify the city, and ask for the convention and visitors bureau or the chamber of commerce listing.

ALABAMA
Alabama Bureau of Tourism and Travel
P.O. Box 4927
Montgomery, AL 36103-4927
800-252-2262

ALASKA
Alaska Division of Tourism
P.O. Box 110801
Juneau, AK 99811-0801
907-465-2010

Anchorage Convention and Visitors
Bureau
524 West Fourth Avenue
Anchorage, AK 99501
907-276-4118

ARIZONA
Arizona Office of Tourism
2702 North Third Street
Suite 4015
Phoenix, AZ 85007
602-542-8687

Phoenix Convention and Visitors
Bureau
1 Arizona Center, Suite 600
400 East Van Buren Street
Phoenix, AZ 85004-2290
602-254-6500

Scottsdale Chamber of Commerce
7343 Scottsdale Mall
Scottsdale, AZ 85251-4498

Metropolitan Tucson Convention and
Visitors Bureau
130 South Scott Avenue
Tucson, AZ 85701
520-624-1817

ARKANSAS
Arkansas Department of Parks and
Tourism
One Capitol Mall, Dept. 7701
Little Rock, AR 72201
800-628-8725

CALIFORNIA
California Division of Tourism
P.O. Box 1499
Sacramento, CA 95812-1499
800-862-2543

Anaheim Area Convention and Visitors
Bureau
P.O. Box 4270
Anaheim, CA 92803
714-999-8999

Los Angeles Convention and Visitors
Bureau
633 West Fifth Street
Los Angeles, CA 90071
213-624-7300

Palm Springs Desert Resorts
Convention and Visitors Bureau
69-930 Highway 111
Rancho Mirage, CA 92270
619-770-9000

San Diego Convention and Visitors
Bureau
401 B Street
San Diego, CA 92101-4237
619-232-3101

San Francisco Convention and Visitors
Bureau
201 Third Street
San Francisco, CA 94103
415-974-6900

COLORADO
Colorado Tourism Board
340 Highway 340
Fruita, CO 81521
303-858-9335

Denver Metro Convention and Visitors
Bureau
225 West Colfax
Denver, CO 80202
303-892-1505

Vail Valley Tourism and Convention
Bureau
100 East Meadow Drive
Vail, CO 81657
970-476-1000

CONNECTICUT
Connecticut Department of Economic
Development, Tourism Division
865 Brook Street
Rocky Hill, CT 06067-3405
800-282-6863

DELAWARE
Delaware Tourism Office
99 Kings Highway
P.O. Box 1401, Dept. TIA
Dover, DE 19903
800-441-8846

DISTRICT OF COLUMBIA
Washington DC Convention and
Visitors Association
1212 New York Avenue NW
Washington, DC 20005-3992
800-422-8644
202-789-7000

FLORIDA
Florida Tourism Industry Marketing
Corp.
661 East Jefferson Street
Tallahassee, FL 32301
904-488-5667

Greater Fort Lauderdale Convention
and Visitors Bureau
1850 Eller Drive
Ft. Lauderdale, FL 33316
954-765-4466

Kissimmee-St. Cloud Convention and
Visitors Bureau
P.O. Box 422007
Kissimmee, FL 34742-2007
407-847-5000

Florida Space Coast Office of Tourism
2725 Judge Fran Jamieson Way
Melbourne, FL 32940
407-633-2110

Greater Miami Convention and Visitors
Bureau
701 Brickell Avenue
Suite 2700
Miami, FL 33131
305-539-3000

Orlando-Orange County Convention
and Visitors Bureau
6700 Forum Drive
Orlando, FL 32821
407-363-5800

St. Petersburg-Clearwater Convention
and Visitors Bureau

14450 46th Street North
Clearwater, FL 34662
813-464-7200

Tampa-Hillsborough Convention and
Visitors Bureau
400 North Tampa Street
Tampa, FL 33602
813-223-1111

GEORGIA
Georgia Department of Industry, Trade
and Tourism
P.O. Box 1776, Dept. TIA
Atlanta, GA 30301
800-847-8242

Atlanta Convention and Visitors
Bureau
233 Peachtree Street NE
Atlanta, GA 30303
404-521-6600

Savannah Area Convention and
Visitors Bureau
P.O. Box 1628
Savannah, GA 31402
912-944-0456

HAWAII
Hawaii Department of Industry, Trade
and Tourism
P.O. Box 2359
Honolulu, HI 96815
808-586-2423

IDAHO
Idaho Division of Tourism Development
700 West State Street, Dept. C
Boise, ID 83720
800-835-7520

ILLINOIS
Illinois Bureau of Tourism
100 West Randolph
Suite 3-400
Chicago, IL 60601
800-266-0121

Chicago Convention and Tourism
Bureau
2301 South Lake Shore Drive
Chicago, IL 60616-1490
312-567-8500

INDIANA
Indiana Department of Commerce/
Tourism
One North Capitol Street
Indianapolis, IN 46204-2288
800-289-6646

IOWA
Iowa Division of Tourism
Department of Economic Development
200 East Grand Avenue
Des Moines, IA 50309
800-528-5265
515-242-4705

KANSAS
Kansas Travel and Tourism Division
700 SW Harrison Street
Suite 1300
Topeka, KS 66603-3712
800-252-6727

KENTUCKY
Kentucky Department of Travel
Development
500 Mero Street
22nd Floor, Dept. DA
Frankfort, KY 40601
800-225-8747

LOUISIANA
Louisiana Office of Tourism
P.O. Box 94291
Baton Rouge, LA 70804
800-334-8626

New Orleans Metropolitan Convention
and Visitors Bureau
1520 Sugar Bowl Drive
New Orleans, LA 70112-1259
504-566-5011

MAINE
Maine Office of Tourism
33 Stone Street
State House, Station 59
Augusta, ME 04333
800-533-9595

MARYLAND
Maryland Office of Tourism
Development
217 East Redwood Street
Baltimore, MD 21202-0059

800-543-1036
207-287-5711

MASSACHUSETTS
Massachusetts Office of Travel and
Tourism
100 Cambridge Street
Boston, MA 02202
800-447-6277

Greater Boston Convention and
Visitors Bureau
P.O. Box 990468
Prudential Tower, Suite 400
Boston, MA 02199
617-536-4100

MICHIGAN
Michigan Travel Bureau
P.O. Box 3393
Livonia, MI 48151-3393
800-543-2937

MINNESOTA
Minnesota Office of Tourism
121 7th Place East
St. Paul, MN 55101
800-657-3700

MISSISSIPPI
Mississippi Division of Tourism
Development
P.O. Box 1705
Ocean Springs, MS 39566
800-927-6378

MISSOURI
Missouri Division of Tourism
P.O. Box 1055, Dept. TIA
Jefferson City, MO 65102
800-877-1234

MONTANA
Travel Montana
Room TIA
Deer Lodge, MT 59722
800-847-4868

NEBRASKA
Nebraska Division of Travel and
Tourism
P.O. Box 94666
Lincoln, NE 68509
800-228-4307

NEVADA
Nevada Commission on Tourism
Capitol Complex, Dept. TIA
Carson City, NV 89710
800-638-2328

Las Vegas Convention and Visitors
Authority
3150 Paradise Road
Las Vegas, NV 89109-9096
702-892-0711

NEW HAMPSHIRE
New Hampshire Office of Travel and
Tourism
P.O. Box 1856
Concord, NH 03302
800-386-4664, ext. 159
603-271-2343

NEW JERSEY
New Jersey Division of Travel and
Tourism
20 West State Street
Trenton, NJ 08625
800-537-7397

NEW MEXICO
New Mexico Department of Tourism
491 Old Santa Fe Trail
Santa Fe, NM 87503
800-545-2040

NEW YORK
New York State Division of Tourism
1 Commerce Plaza
Albany, NY 12245
800-225-5697

New York (City) Convention and
Visitors Bureau
2 Columbus Circle
New York, NY 10019
212-484-1200

NORTH CAROLINA
North Carolina Division of Travel and
Tourism
Department of Commerce
430 North Salisbury Street
Raleigh, NC 27603
800-847-4862

NORTH DAKOTA
North Dakota Department of Tourism
Liberty Memorial Building
604 East Boulevard
Bismarck, ND 58505
800-435-5663

OHIO
Ohio Division of Travel and Tourism
P.O. Box 1001
Columbus, OH 43216-1001
800-282-5393

OKLAHOMA
Oklahoma Tourism and Recreation
Department, Travel and Tourism
Division
2401 Lincoln Boulevard
Room 505-DA95
Oklahoma City, OK 73105-4492
800-652-8552

OREGON
Oregon Tourism Division
775 Summer Street NE
Salem, OR 97310
800-547-7842

PENNSYLVANIA
Pennsylvania Office of Travel
Marketing
453 Forum Building
Harrisburg, PA 17120
800-847-4872

Philadelphia Convention and Visitors
Bureau
1515 Market Street
Philadelphia, PA 19102
215-636-3300

RHODE ISLAND
Rhode Island Tourism Division
7 Jackson Walkway, Dept. TIA
Providence, RI 02903
800-556-2484

SOUTH CAROLINA
South Carolina Division of Tourism
P.O. Box 71
Columbia, SC 29202
803-734-0122

SOUTH DAKOTA
South Dakota Department of Tourism
711 East Wells Avenue
Pierre, SD 57501-3369
800-732-5682

TENNESSEE
Tennessee Department of Tourism
Development
P.O. Box 23170
Nashville, TN 37202
800-836-6200
615-741-2158

TEXAS
Texas Department of Commerce,
Tourist Division
P.O. Box 12728
Austin, TX 78711-2728
800-888-8839

Dallas Convention and Visitors Bureau
1201 Elm Street
Dallas, TX 75270
214-746-6677

San Antonio Convention and Visitors
Bureau
P.O. Box 2277
San Antonio, TX 78298
210-270-8700

UTAH
Utah Travel Council
Council Hall, Capitol Hill
Salt Lake City, UT 84114
800-200-1160
801-538-1030

Salt Lake Convention and Visitors
Bureau
90 South West Temple
Salt Lake City, UT 84101-1406
801-521-2822

VERMONT
Vermont Department of Travel and
Tourism
P.O. Box 1471
Montpelier, VT 05601-1471
800-837-6668
802-828-3236

VIRGINIA
Virginia Division of Tourism
901 East Byrd Street
Richmond, VA 23219
800-847-4882

Williamsburg Area Convention and
Visitors Bureau
P.O. Box 3585
201 Penniman Road
Williamsburg, VA 23185
804-253-0192

WASHINGTON
Washington State Tourism
Development Division
P.O. Box 42500
Olympia, WA 98504-2500
800-544-1800

Seattle Convention and Visitors
Bureau
520 Pike Street, Suite 1300
Seattle, WA 98101
206-461-5800

WEST VIRGINIA
West Virginia Division of Tourism
2101 Washington Street East
Charleston, WV 25305
800-225-5982

WISCONSIN
Wisconsin Division of Tourism
P.O. Box 7606
Madison, WI 53707
800-432-8747

WYOMING
Wyoming Division of Tourism
Frank Norris Jr. Travel Center
I-25 at College Drive
Cheyenne, WY 82002
800-225-5996

Sources of Tourist Information: International

This listing of international tourism information is very similar to the one in the last section, with one major difference. In this section we have also listed, in abbreviated form, the visa and entry requirements for each foreign country. More about visas will be found in the section on passports and visas beginning on page 205.

On the line immediately following the country name you will find one or more of the following codes:

US: Proof of U.S. citizenship and a photo ID required for entry.

P: Passport required for entry.

PV: Passport and visa required for entry. When a visa is required, the length of stay and cost of the *typical* tourist visa is given. Be aware that many countries that do not require a visa for short stays, require them for stays of longer than 15, 30, 90, or more days. Note, too, that some countries have different requirements for different types of visas (e.g. tourist, business, study, resident, etc.). That may mean that while no visa may be required for tourists, business trips may require a visa with a hefty fee. So we have provided contact information for the office issuing visas, even if no visa is required for tourists. Make sure you check on the applicable requirements so you can advise your client accordingly.

NT: No tourist visas issued. Some countries issue no tourist visas, but only admit visitors with a valid business visa and business reason for entry.

TC: Tourist card required. For more information, see the section on passports and visas beginning on page 205.

✈ : Proof of a return/onward ticket required. In other words, they want to make sure you won't wind up stranded in their country.

$: Proof of sufficient funds required. Many countries want some assurance you have enough money to support yourself during your stay. What constitutes "sufficient funds" will vary from country to country.

✚ : Vaccinations or other medical measures required.

In addition to this basic information on passports, visas, and other entry requirements, we have provided a contact for free tourist information about each country. Sometimes that will be the embassy, other times it will be a separate tourist bureau with separate offices.

When a country has more that one tourist office, we list the primary office and then give a list of other cities in which offices are located. When no source of tourist information is listed, you may be able to obtain tourist brochures from the embassy or consulates.

AFGHANISTAN
PV
(No tourist or business visas being issued at press time.)
Embassy of the Islamic State of Afghanistan
2341 Wyoming Avenue NW
Washington, DC 20008
202-234-3770

ALBANIA
P
For visa information:
Embassy of the Republic of Albania
1511 K Street NW
Washington, DC 20005
202-223-4942

ALGERIA
PV (90 days, $30) ✈ $
For visa information:
Embassy of the Democratic and Popular Republic of Algeria
2137 Wyoming Avenue NW
Washington, DC 20008
202-265-2800
(Travel by U.S. citizens not recommended.)

ANDORRA
P
For tourism information:
Andorra Bureau for Tourism and Information
6800 North Knox Avenue
Lincolnwood, IL 60646
847-674-3091

ANGOLA
PV ✚
For visa information:
Embassy of Angola
1819 L Street NW
Washington, DC 20036
202-452-1042
Consulates in:
New York
(Travel by U.S. citizens not recommended.)

ANTIGUA AND BARBUDA
P or **US** ✈ $
For visa information:
Embassy of Antigua and Barbuda
3216 New Mexico Avenue NW
Washington, DC 20016
202-362-5122

For tourism information:
Antigua & Barbuda Department of
Tourism
610 Fifth Avenue
New York, NY 10020
212-541-4117

ARGENTINA
P
For visa information:
Argentine Embassy
1718 Connecticut Avenue NW
Washington, DC 20009
202-797-8826
Consulates in:
Atlanta, Chicago, Houston, Los
Angeles, Miami, New York
For tourism information:
Argentina Government Tourist
Information
12 West 56th Street
New York, NY 10019
212-603-0443
Other offices in:
Coral Gables, Los Angeles

ARMENIA
PV (21 days, $50)
For visa information:
Embassy of the Republic of Armenia
2225 R Street NW
Washington, DC 20008
202-319-2983
Consulates in:
Beverly Hills

ARUBA
P or US ✈ **$**
For visa information:
Royal Netherlands Embassy
4200 Linnean Avenue NW
Washington, DC 20008
202-244-5300
Consulates in:
Chicago, Houston, Los Angeles, New
York
For tourism information:
Aruba Tourism Authority
1000 Harbor Boulevard
Weehawken, NJ 07087
800-862-7822
Other offices in:
Atlanta, Coral Gables

AUSTRALIA
P
For visa information:
Embassy of Australia
1601 Massachusetts Avenue NW
Washington, DC 20036-2273
800-242-2878
Consulates in:
Honolulu, Los Angeles, New York, San
Francisco, Toronto, Vancouver
For tourism information:
Australian Tourist Commission
2049 Century Park East
Los Angeles, CA 90067
310-229-4870
Other offices in:
New York

AUSTRIA
P
For visa information:
Embassy of Austria
3524 International Court NW
Washington, DC 20008
202-895-6767
Consulates in:
Chicago, Los Angeles, New York
For tourism information:
Austrian National Tourist Office
500 Fifth Avenue
New York, NY 10036
212-944-6880
Other offices in:
Los Angeles, Toronto

AZERBAIJAN
PV
For visa information:
Embassy of the Republic of Azerbaijan
927 15th Street NW
Washington, DC 20005
202-842-0001

AZORES
(See Portugal)

BAHAMAS
US ✈
For visa information:
Embassy of the Commonwealth of the
Bahamas
2220 Massachusetts Avenue NW
Washington DC 20008
202-319-2660

Consulates in:
Miami
For tourism information:
Bahamas Tourist Office
150 East 52nd Street
New York, NY 10022
212-758-2777
Other offices in:
Atlanta, Boston, Chicago, Dallas, Los
Angeles, Miami

BAHRAIN
PV ✈
For visa information:
Embassy of the State of Bahrain
3502 International Drive NW
Washington, DC 20008
202-342-0741
Consulates in:
New York

BANGLADESH
PV ($21) ✈
For visa information:
Embassy of the People's Republic of
Bangladesh
2201 Wisconsin Avenue NW
Washington, DC 20007
202-342-8372

BARBADOS
US ✈
For visa information:
Embassy of Barbados
2144 Wyoming Avenue NW
Washington, DC 20008
202-939-9200
Consulates in:
Los Angeles, New York
For tourism information:
Barbados Tourism Authority
800 Second Avenue
New York, NY 10017
800-221-9831
Other offices in:
Los Angeles, Toronto

BELARUS
PV (2 days, $30)
For visa information:
Embassy of Belarus
1619 New Hampshire Avenue NW
Washington, DC 20009
202-986-1604

Consulates in:
New York

BELGIUM
P
For visa information:
Embassy of Belgium
3330 Garfield Street NW
Washington, DC 20008
202-333-6900
Consulates in:
Atlanta, Chicago, Los Angeles, New
York
For tourism information:
Belgian Tourist Office
780 Third Avenue
New York, NY 10017
212-758-8130

BELIZE
P ✈ **$**
For visa information:
Embassy of Belize
2535 Massachusetts Avenue NW
Washington, DC 20008
202-332-9636
Consulates in:
New York
For tourism information:
Belize Tourist Board
421 Seventh Avenue
New York, NY 10001
212-563-6011

BENIN
PV (90 days, $20) ✈ ✚
For visa information:
Embassy of the Republic of Benin
2737 Cathedral Avenue NW
Washington, DC 20008
202-232-6656

BERMUDA
P or **US** ✈
For visa information:
British Embassy
19 Observatory Circle NW
Washington, DC 20008
202-588-7800
For tourism information:
Bermuda Department of Tourism
310 Madison Avenue
New York, NY 10017
212-818-9800

Other offices in:
Atlanta, Boston, Chicago, Toronto

BHUTAN
PV (15 days, $20) ✚
For visa information:
Bhutan Mission to the United Nations
2 United Nations Plaza, 27th floor
New York, NY 10017
212-826-1919
For tourism information:
Bhutan Travel
120 East 56th Street
New York, NY 10022
800-950-9908

BOLIVIA
P
For visa information:
Embassy of Bolivia
3014 Massachusetts Avenue NW
Washington, DC 20008
202-232-4828
Consulates in:
New York, Miami, San Francisco

BONAIRE
P or **US** ⇥
For visa information:
(See Netherlands Antilles)
For tourism information:
Bonaire Tourism Office
10 Rockefeller Plaza
New York, NY 10020
800-826-6247

BOSNIA AND HERZEGOVINA
P
For visa information:
Embassy of Bosnia-Herzegovina
1707 L Street NW
Washington, DC 20036
202-833-3612
(Travel by U.S. citizens not
recommended.)

BOTSWANA
P
For visa information:
Embassy of the Republic of Botswana
3400 International Drive NW
Washington, DC 20008
202-244-4990
Consulates in:

Houston, Los Angeles

BRAZIL
PV (90 days, $0-$10)
For visa information:
Brazilian Embassy
Consular Section
3009 Whitehaven Street NW
Washington, DC 20008
202-745-2820
Consulates in:
Boston, Chicago, Houston, Los Angeles,
Miami, New York, San Francisco, San
Juan
For tourism information:
Brazil Tourist Office
1050 Edison Street
Santa Ynez, CA 93460
800-544-5503

BRITISH VIRGIN ISLANDS
P or **US**
For visa information:
Chief Immigration Officer
Govt. of the British Virgin Islands
Road Town, Tortola
British Virgin Islands
809-494-3701
For tourism information:
British Virgin Islands Tourist Board
370 Lexington Avenue
New York, NY 10017
800-835-8530
Other offices in:
San Francisco

BRITISH WEST INDIES
US ⇥ **$**
For visa information:
British Embassy
19 Observatory Circle NW
Washington, DC 20008
202-588-7800
For tourism information:
(See various islands)

BRUNEI
P ⇥
For visa information:
Embassy of the State of Brunei
Darussalam
2600 Virginia Avenue NW
Washington, DC 20037
202-342-0159

Consulates in:
New York

BULGARIA
P

For visa information:
Embassy of the Republic of Bulgaria
1621 22nd Street NW
Washington, DC 20008
202-387-7969
Consulates in:
New York
For tourism information:
Balkan Tourist USA
20 East 46th Street
New York, NY 10017
800-822-1106
Other offices in:
Toronto

BURKINA FASO
PV (1 month, $25) ✦

For visa information:
Embassy of Burkina Faso
2340 Massachusetts Avenue NW
Washington, DC 20008
202-332-5577
Consulates in:
Decatur (GA), Los Angeles, New
Orleans

BURMA
(See Myanmar)

BURUNDI
PV (2 months, $40) ✈ ✦

For visa information:
Embassy of the Republic of Burundi
2233 Wisconsin Avenue NW
Washington, DC 20007
202-342-2574
Consulates in:
New York

CAMBODIA
PV (1 month, $20)

For visa information:
Royal Embassy of Cambodia
4500 16th Street NW
Washington, DC 20036
202-726-7742
Consulates in:
New York

CAMEROON
PV (90 days, $65.22) ✈ $ ✦

For visa information:
Embassy of the Republic of Cameroon
2349 Massachusetts Avenue NW
Washington, DC 20008
202-265-8790
Consulates in:
New York, San Francisco

CANADA
US

For visa information:
Canadian Embassy
501 Pennsylvania Avenue NW
Washington, DC 20001
202-682-1740
Consulates in:
Atlanta, Boston, Buffalo, Chicago,
Cincinnati, Dallas, Detroit, Los
Angeles, Minneapolis, New York,
Pittsburgh, Seattle
For tourism information:
Contact nearest consulate.

CAPE VERDE
PV ($11)

For visa information:
Embassy of the Republic of Cape Verde
3415 Massachusetts Avenue NW
Washington, DC 20007
202-965-6820
Consulates in:
Boston, New York

CAYMAN ISLANDS
US ✈ $

For visa information:
British Embassy
19 Observatory Circle NW
Washington, DC 20008
202-588-7800
For tourism information:
Cayman Islands Department of
Tourism
420 Lexington Avenue
New York, NY 10170
212-682-5582
Other offices in:
Atlanta, Baltimore, Boston, Chicago,
Dallas, Houston, Los Angeles, Miami,
Tampa, Toronto

CENTRAL AFRICAN REPUBLIC
PV ✈ ✚
For visa information:
Embassy of Central African Republic
1618 22nd Street NW
Washington, DC 20008
202-483-7800

CHAD
PV (2 months, $25) ✈ ✚
For visa information:
Embassy of the Republic of Chad
2002 R Street NW
Washington, DC 20009
202-462-4009

CHILE
P
For visa information:
Embassy of Chile
1732 Massachusetts Avenue NW
Washington, DC 20036
202-785-3159
Consulates in:
Boston, Chicago, Houston, Los Angeles,
Miami, New York, Philadelphia, San
Francisco, San Juan

CHINA
PV ($30)
For visa information:
Embassy of the People's Republic of
China
2300 Connecticut Avenue NW
Washington, DC 20008
202-328-2517
Consulates in:
Chicago, Houston, New York, Los
Angeles, San Francisco, Toronto,
Vancouver
For tourism information:
China National Tourist Office
333 West Broadway
Glendale, CA 91204
818-545-7505
Other offices in:
New York

COLOMBIA
P ✈
For visa information:
Embassy of Colombia
1825 Connecticut Avenue NW
Washington, DC 20009

202-332-7476
Consulates in:
Atlanta, Boston, Chicago, Coral Gables,
Houston, Los Angeles, New York, San
Francisco, San Juan

COMOROS ISLANDS
P ✈ ✚
For visa information:
Embassy of the Federal and Islamic
Republic of Comoros
336 East 45th Street
New York, NY 10017
212-972-8010

CONGO
PV (3 months, $70) ✈ ✚
For visa information:
Embassy of the Republic of the Congo
4891 Colorado Avenue NW
Washington, DC 20011
202-726-5500
Consulates in:
New York

COOK ISLANDS
P ✈
For visa information:
Consulate for the Cook Islands
Kamehameha Schools #16
Kapalama Heights
Honolulu, HI 96817
808-847-6377

COSTA RICA
P or US ✈
For visa information:
Embassy of Costa Rica
Consular Section
2112 S Street NW
Washington, DC 20008
202-328-6628
Consulates in:
Atlanta, Chicago, Houston, Los
Angeles, Miami, New Orleans,
New York, San Antonio, San Diego,
San Francisco

COTE D'IVOIRE
P
For visa information:
Embassy of the Republic of Cote
D'Ivoire
2424 Massachusetts Avenue NW

Washington, DC 20008
202-797-0300
Consulates in:
San Francisco
For tourism information:
Tourist Office of Cote D'Ivoire
2412 Massachusetts Avenue NW
Washington, DC 20008
202-797-0344

CROATIA
PV
For visa information:
Embassy of Croatia
236 Massachusetts Avenue NE
Washington, DC 20002
202-543-5580
Consulates in:
Cleveland, New York

CUBA
PV (90 days, $26) ✈
For visa information:
Cuban Interests Section
2639 16th Street NW
Washington, DC 20009
202-797-8609
(Treasury Dept. license required for
travel by U.S. citizens.)
For tourism information:
Cuba Tourist Board
55 Queen Street
Toronto, ONT M5C 1R6
CANADA
(416) 362-0700
Other offices in:
Montreal

CURACAO
P or US ✈ **$**
For visa information:
Royal Netherlands Embassy
4200 Linnean Avenue NW
Washington, DC 20008
202-244-5300
Consulates in:
New York
For tourism information:
Curaçao Tourist Board
475 Park Avenue South
New York, NY 10017
800-270-3350
Other offices in:
Miami

CYPRUS
P
For visa information:
Embassy of the Republic of Cyprus
2211 R Street NW
Washington, DC 20008
202-462-5772
Consulates in:
New York
For tourism information:
Cyprus Tourism Organization
13 East 40th Street
New York, NY 10016
212-683-5280

CZECH REPUBLIC
P
For visa information:
Embassy of the Czech Republic
3900 Spring of Freedom Street NW
Washington, DC 20008
202-274-9123
Consulates in:
Atlanta, Dallas, Fort Lauderdale,
Houston, Los Angeles, New York,
Philadelphia, Portland, San Francisco

DENMARK
P
For visa information:
Royal Danish Embassy
3200 Whitehaven Street NW
Washington, DC 20008
202-234-4300
Consulates in:
Atlanta, Chicago, Cleveland, Honolulu,
Los Angeles, Coral Gables, Montreal,
New Orleans, New York, Philadelphia,
San Francisco, Seattle, Toronto,
Vancouver
For tourism information:
Danish Tourist Board
655 Third Avenue
New York, NY 10017
212-949-2333

DJIBOUTI
PV (30 days, $30) ✈ **$**
Embassy of the Republic of Djibouti
1156 15th Street NW
Washington, DC 20005
202-331-0270
Consulates in:
New York

DOMINICA
US ✈
For visa information:
Consulate of the Commonwealth of
Dominica
820 Second Avenue
New York, NY 10017
212-599-8478
For tourism information:
Caribbean Tourism Association
20 East 46th Street
New York, NY 10017
212-682-0435

DOMINICAN REPUBLIC
P or **US TC** ($10)
For visa information:
Embassy of the Dominican Republic
1715 22nd Street NW
Washington, DC 20008
202-332-6280
Consulates in:
Boston, Chicago, Miami, New Orleans,
New York, Philadelphia, San Francisco,
San Juan
For tourism information:
Dominican Republic Tourist Office
1 Times Square
New York, NY 10022
212-575-4966

ECUADOR
P ✈
For visa information:
Embassy of Ecuador
2535 15th Street NW
Washington, DC 20009
202-234-7166
Consulates in:
Baltimore, Boston, Chicago, Dallas,
Detroit, Houston, Los Angeles, Miami,
New Orleans, New York, San
Francisco, Toronto, Vancouver
For tourism information:
Ecuador Trade Center
2600 Douglas Road
Coral Gables, FL 33134
305-461-2363

EGYPT
PV (3 months, $15-$20)
For visa information:
Embassy of the Arab Republic of Egypt
3521 International Court NW
Washington, DC 20008
202-996-6342
Consulates in:
Chicago, Houston, New York, San
Francisco
For tourism information:
Egyptian Tourist Authority
630 Fifth Avenue
New York, NY 10111
212-332-2570
Other offices in:
Beverly Hills, Chicago, Montreal

EL SALVADOR
PV
For visa information:
Consulate General of El Salvador
1010 16th Street NW
Washington, DC 20036
202-331-4032
Consulates in:
Chicago, Dallas, Houston, Los Angeles,
Miami, New Orleans, New York, San
Francisco

ENGLAND
(See United Kingdom)

EQUATORIAL GUINEA
PV
For visa information:
Embassy of Equatorial Guinea
1511 K Street NW
Washington, DC 20005
202-745-3680

ERITREA
PV (6 months, $25)
For visa information:
Embassy of Eritrea
1700 New Hampshire Avenue NW
Washington, DC 20009
202-319-1991

ESTONIA
P
For visa information:
Consulate General of Estonia
630 Fifth Avenue
New York, NY 10111
212-247-1450

ETHIOPIA
PV (2 years, $70) ✚

For visa information:
Embassy of Ethiopia
2134 Kalorama Road NW
Washington, DC 20008
202-234-2281
Consulates in:
New York
For tourism information:
Ethiopian Airlines
405 Lexington Avenue
New York, NY 10017
212-867-0095

FIJI
P ✈ $
For visa information:
Embassy of Fiji
2233 Wisconsin Avenue NW
Washington, DC 20007
202-337-8320
Consulates in:
New York
For tourism information:
Fiji Visitors Bureau
5777 West Century Boulevard
Los Angeles, CA 90045
800-932-3454

FINLAND
P
For visa information:
Embassy of Finland
3301 Massachusetts Avenue NW
Washington, DC 20008
202-298-5800
Consulates in:
Los Angeles, New York
For tourism information:
Finnish Tourist Board
655 Third Avenue
New York, NY 10017
212-370-5540
Other offices in:
Malibu (CA), Toronto

FRANCE
P
For visa information:
Embassy of France
4101 Reservoir Road NW
Washington, DC 20007
202-944-6200
Consulates in:
Atlanta, Boston, Chicago, Honolulu,

Houston, Los Angeles, Miami, New
Orleans, New York, San Francisco, San
Juan
For tourism information:
French Government Tourist Office
444 Madison Avenue
New York, NY 10022
212-838-7800
Other offices in:
Beverly Hills, Chicago, Montreal,
Toronto

FRENCH GUIANA
US
For visa information:
Embassy of France
4101 Reservoir Road NW
Washington, DC 20007
202-944-6200

FRENCH POLYNESIA
P
For visa information:
Embassy of France
4101 Reservoir Road NW
Washington, DC 20007
202-944-6200
For tourism information:
Tahiti Tourisme
444 Madison Avenue
New York, NY 10022
212-838-8663
Other offices in:
El Segundo (CA)

FRENCH WEST INDIES
US
For visa information:
Embassy of France
4101 Reservoir Road NW
Washington, DC 20007
202-944-6200
For tourism information:
French West Indies Tourist Board
444 Madison Avenue
New York, NY 10022
212-838-3486

GABON
PV (4 months, $60) ✚
For visa information:
Embassy of the Gabonese Republic
2034 20th Street NW
Washington, DC 20009

202-797-1000
Consulates in:
New York
For tourism information:
Gabon Tourist Information Office
347 Fifth Avenue
New York, NY 10016
212-447-6700

GALAPAGOS ISLANDS
(See Ecuador)

GAMBIA
PV (1 year, $30)
For visa information:
Embassy of the Gambia
1155 15th Street NW
Washington, DC 20005
202-785-1399
Consulates in:
New York

GEORGIA
PV
For visa information:
Embassy of the Republic of Georgia
1511 K Street NW
Washington, DC 20005
202-393-6060

GERMANY
P
For visa information:
Embassy of the Federal Republic of
Germany
4645 Reservoir Road NW
Washington, DC 20007
202-298-4000
Consulates in:
Atlanta, Boston, Chicago, Detroit,
Houston, Los Angeles, Miami,
Montreal, New York, San Francisco,
Seattle, Toronto, Vancouver
For tourism information:
German National Tourist Board
11766 Wilshire Boulevard
Los Angeles, CA 90025
310-575-9799
Other offices in:
New York, Toronto

GHANA
PV (30 days, $20) ✈ ✚
For visa information:

Embassy of Ghana
3512 International Drive NW
Washington, DC 20008
202-686-4520
Consulates in:
New York

GIBRALTAR
P
For visa information:
British Embassy
19 Observatory Circle NW
Washington, DC 20008
202-588-7800

GILBERT ISLANDS
(See Kiribati)

GREAT BRITAIN
(See United Kingdom)

GREECE
P
For visa information:
Embassy of Greece
2221 Massachusetts Avenue NW
Washington, DC 20008
202-939-5818
Consulates in:
Atlanta, Boston, Chicago, Houston, Los
Angeles, Montreal, New Orleans, New
York, San Francisco, Toronto
For tourism information:
Greek National Tourist Board
168 North Michigan Avenue
Chicago, IL 60601
312-782-1084
Other offices in:
Los Angeles, Montreal, New York,
Toronto

GREENLAND
(See Denmark)

GRENADA
P or US
For visa information:
Embassy of Grenada
1701 New Hampshire Avenue NW
Washington, DC 20009
202-265-2561
Consulates in:
New York
For tourism information:

Grenada Board of Tourism
820 Second Avenue
New York, NY 10017
800-927-9554

GUADELOUPE
US
For visa information:
Embassy of France
4101 Reservoir Road NW
Washington, DC 20007
202-944-6200
For tourism information:
French West Indies Tourist Board
444 Madison Avenue
New York, NY 10022
212-838-3486

GUATEMALA
P TC ($5)
For visa information:
Embassy of Guatemala
2220 R Street NW
Washington, DC 20008-4081
202-745-4952
Consulates in:
Chicago, Coral Gables, Houston, Los
Angeles, New York, Philadelphia,
Providence

GUINEA
PV (3 months, $25) +
For visa information:
Embassy of the Republic of Guinea
2112 Leroy Place NW
Washington, DC 20008
202-483-9420

GUINEA-BISSAU
PV (90 days, $20) $
For visa information:
Embassy of Guinea-Bissau
918 16th Street NW
Washington, DC 20006
202-872-4222

GUYANA
P +
For visa information:
Embassy of Guyana
2490 Tracy Place NW
Washington, DC 20008
202-265-6900

HAITI
P
For visa information:
Embassy of Haiti
2311 Massachusetts Avenue NW
Washington, DC 20008
202-332-4090
Consulates in:
Boston, Miami, New York

HONDURAS
P +
For visa information:
Embassy of Honduras
1612 K Street NW
Washington, DC 20006
202-223-0185
Consulates in:
Chicago, Houston, Los Angeles, Miami,
New York, San Francisco, Tampa
For tourism information:
Contact nearest consulate.

HONG KONG
P +
For visa information:
Embassy of the People's Republic of
China
2300 Connecticut Avenue NW
Washington, DC 20008
202-328-2517
For tourism information:
Hong Kong Tourist Association
10940 Wilshire Boulevard
Los Angeles, CA 90024
310-208-4582
Other offices in:
Chicago, New York, Toronto

HUNGARY
P + $
For visa information:
Embassy of the Republic of Hungary
3910 Shoemaker Street NW
Washington, DC 20008
202-362-6730
Consulates in:
Los Angeles, New York
For tourism information:
Hungarian Tourist Board
150 East 58th Street
New York, NY 10155
212-355-0240

ICELAND
P
For visa information:
Embassy of Iceland
1156 15th Street NW
Washington, DC 20005
202-265-6653
Consulates in:
New York
For tourism information:
Scandinavian Tourist Boards
655 Third Avenue
New York, NY 10017
212-949-2333

INDIA
PV (15 days, $25) ✈ **$**
For visa information:
Embassy of India
2536 Massachusetts Avenue NW
Washington, DC 20008
202-939-9839
Consulates in:
Chicago, New York, San Francisco,
Toronto, Vancouver
For tourism information:
Government of India Tourist Office
3550 Wilshire Boulevard
Los Angeles, CA 90010
213-380-8855
Other offices in:
New York, Toronto

INDONESIA
P ✈
For visa information:
Embassy of the Republic of
Indonesia
2020 Massachusetts Avenue NW
Washington, DC 20036
202-775-5200
Consulates in:
Chicago, Houston, Los Angeles, New
York, San Francisco, Toronto,
Vancouver
For tourism information:
Indonesia Tourist Office
3457 Wilshire Boulevard
Los Angeles, CA 90010
213-387-2078

IRAN
PV
For visa information:

Embassy of the Islamic Republic of
Iran
2209 Wisconsin Avenue NW
Washington, DC 20007
202-965-4990

IRAQ
PV
For visa information:
Iraq Mission to the United Nations
14 East 79th Street
New York, NY 10021
212-737-4433
(U.S. passports not valid for travel in
Iraq without State Dept.
authorization.)

IRELAND
P ✈
For visa information:
Embassy of Ireland
2234 Massachusetts Avenue NW
Washington, DC 20008
202-462-3939
Consulates in:
Boston, Chicago, New York, San
Francisco
For tourism information:
Irish Tourist Board
345 Park Avenue
New York, NY 10154
212-418-0800
Other offices in:
Toronto

ISRAEL
P ✈ **$**
For visa information:
Embassy of Israel
3514 International Drive NW
Washington, DC 20008
202-364-5500
Consulates in:
Atlanta, Boston, Chicago, Houston, Los
Angeles, Miami, Montreal, New York,
Philadelphia, San Francisco, Toronto
For tourism information:
Israel Ministry of Tourism
800 Second Avenue
New York, NY 10017
212-499-5600
Other offices in:
Chicago, Dallas, Los Angeles, Toronto

ITALY
P

For visa information:
Embassy of Italy
1601 Fuller Street NW
Washington, DC 20009
202-328-5500
Consulates in:
Boston, Chicago, Detroit, Houston, Los
Angeles, Miami, New Orleans, New
York, Philadelphia, San Francisco
For tourism information:
Italian Government Tourist Board
401 North Michigan Avenue
Chicago, IL 60611
312-644-0996
Other offices in:
Los Angeles, New York, Montreal

IVORY COAST
(See Cote D'Ivoire)

JAMAICA
P or US ✈ $

For visa information:
Embassy of Jamaica
1520 New Hampshire Avenue NW
Washington, DC 20036
202-452-0660
Consulates in:
New York
For tourism information:
Jamaica Tourist Board
801 Second Avenue
New York, NY 10017
800-233-4582
Other offices in:
Chicago, Coral Gables, Los Angeles,
Toronto

JAPAN
P ✈

For visa information:
Embassy of Japan
2520 Massachusetts Avenue NW
Washington, DC 20008
202-939-6800
Consulates in:
Anchorage, Atlanta, Boston, Chicago,
Honolulu, Houston, Kansas City (MO),
Los Angeles, Montreal, New Orleans,
New York, Portland (OR), San
Francisco, Seattle, Toronto, Vancouver
For tourism information:

Japan National Tourist Organization
401 North Michigan Avenue
Chicago, IL 60611
312-222-0874
Other offices in:
Los Angeles, New York, San Francisco,
Toronto

JORDAN
PV

For visa information:
Embassy of the Hashemite Kingdom of
Jordan
3504 International Drive NW
Washington, DC 20008
202-966-2664
Consulates in:
Chicago, Houston, New York
For tourism information:
Jordan Tourism Authority
Royal Jordanian Airlines
535 Fifth Avenue
New York, NY 10017
800-223-0470

KAZAKHSTAN
PV

For visa information:
Embassy of Kazakhstan
3421 Massachusetts Avenue NW
Washington, DC 20007
202-333-4507

KENYA
PV (6 months, $30) ✈ ✚

For visa information:
Embassy of Kenya
2249 R Street NW
Washington, DC 20008
202-387-6101
Consulates in:
Los Angeles, New York
For tourism information:
Kenya Tourist Office
424 Madison Avenue
New York, NY 10017
212-486-1300
Other offices in:
Beverly Hills

KIRIBATI
PV ($32)

For visa information:
British Embassy

19 Observatory Circle NW
Washington, DC 20008
202-588-7800

KOREA (NORTH)
(Treasury Dept. license required for
travel by U.S. citizens.)

KOREA (SOUTH)
P
For visa information:
Embassy of the Republic of Korea
2320 Massachusetts Avenue NW
Washington, DC 20008
202-939-5663
Consulates in:
Anchorage, Atlanta, Boston, Chicago,
Honolulu, Houston, Los Angeles,
Miami, Montreal, New York, San
Francisco, Seattle, Toronto, Vancouver
For tourism information:
Korea National Tourism Organization
2 Executive Drive
Fort Lee, NJ 07024
201-585-0909
Other offices in:
Chicago, Los Angeles, Toronto

KUWAIT
PV
For visa information:
Embassy of the State of Kuwait
2940 Tilden Street NW
Washington, DC 20008
202-966-0702
Consulates in:
New York

KYRGYZSTAN
PV
For visa information:
Embassy of Kyrgyz Republic
1732 Wisconsin Avenue NW
Washington, DC 20007
202-338-5143

LAOS
PV (15 days, $35) ✈ $ ✚
For visa information:
Embassy of the Lao People's
Democratic Republic
2222 S Street NW
Washington, DC 20008
202-667-0076

LATVIA
PV
For visa information:
Embassy of Latvia
4325 17th Street NW
Washington, DC 20011
202-726-8213

LEBANON
PV ($20)
For visa information:
Embassy of Lebanon
2560 28th Street NW
Washington, DC 20008
202-939-6300
Consulates in:
Detroit, Los Angeles, New York,
Montreal

LESOTHO
PV ($7.50-$15) ✈ $
For visa information:
Embassy of the Kingdom of Lesotho
2511 Massachusetts Avenue NW
Washington, DC 20008
202-797-5533
Consulates in:
Austin (TX), New Orleans

LIBERIA
PV (3 months, $20) ✈ ✚
For visa information:
Embassy of the Republic of Liberia
5303 Colorado Avenue NW
Washington, DC 20011
202-723-0437
Consulates in:
Chicago, New Orleans, Montreal
For tourism information:
Contact nearest consulate.

LIBYA
PV
(U.S. passports not valid here without
State Dept. authorization.)

LIECHTENSTEIN
P
For visa information:
Embassy of Switzerland
2900 Cathedral Avenue NW
Washington, DC 20008
202-745-7900

LITHUANIA

P

For visa information:
Embassy of Lithuania
2622 16th Street NW
Washington, DC 20009
202-234-5860
Consulates in:
Chicago, New York, Westlake Village
(CA)

LUXEMBOURG

P

For visa information:
Embassy of Luxembourg
2200 Massachusetts Avenue NW
Washington, DC 20008
202-265-4171
Consulates in:
Atlanta, Boston, Chicago, Los Angeles,
Miami, Montreal, New Orleans, New
York, San Francisco, Seattle, St. Paul
For tourism information:
Luxembourg National Tourist Office
17 Beekman Place
New York, NY 10022
212-935-8888

MACAU

P

For visa information:
Embassy of Portugal
2125 Kalorama Road NW
Washington, DC 20008
202-328-8610
For tourism information:
Macau Tourist Information Bureau
70A Greenwich Avenue
New York, NY 10011
212-206-6828
Other offices in:
Honolulu, Los Angeles, Kenilworth
(IL), Toronto

MACEDONIA

PV ($20)

For visa information:
Embassy of the Former Yugoslav
Republic of Macedonia
3050 K Street NW
Washington, DC 20007
202-337-3063
Consulates in:
New York

MADAGASCAR

PV (30 days, $33.45) ✈ $ ✚

For visa information:
Embassy of the Democratic Republic of
Madagascar
2374 Massachusetts Avenue NW
Washington, DC 20008
202-265-5525
Consulates in:
Berkeley (CA), New York, Philadelphia

MALAWI

P

For visa and dress code information:
Embassy of Malawi
2408 Massachusetts Avenue NW
Washington, DC 20008
202-797-1007
Consulates in:
New York

MALAYSIA

P ✚

For visa information:
Embassy of Malaysia
2410 Massachusetts Avenue NW
Washington, DC 20008
202-328-2700
Consulates in:
Los Angeles, New York
For tourism information:
Malaysia Tourism Promotion Board
818 West 7th Street
Los Angeles, CA 90017
213-689-9702

MALDIVES

P ✈ $ ✚

For visa information:
Permanent Mission of the Maldives to
the United Nations
820 Second Avenue
New York, NY 10017
212-599-6194

MALI

PV (1 month, $20) ✈ ✚

For visa information:
Embassy of the Republic of Mali
2130 R Street NW
Washington, DC 20008
202-332-2249

MALTA
P

For visa information:
Embassy of Malta
2017 Connecticut Avenue NW
Washington, DC 20008
202-462-3611
Consulates in:
Carnegie (PA), Garden City (MI),
Houston, Independence (MO), New
York, Pompano Beach (FL), San
Francisco, St. Paul
For tourism information:
Malta National Tourist Office
350 Fifth Avenue
New York, NY 10118
212-695-9520

MARSHALL ISLANDS
US ✈ $

For visa information:
Embassy Islands
2433 Massachusetts Avenue NW
Washington, DC 20008
202-234-5414
Consulates in:
Honolulu

MARTINIQUE
US

For visa information:
Embassy of France
4101 Reservoir Road NW
Washington, DC 20007
202-944-6200
For tourism information:
French West Indies Tourist Board
444 Madison Avenue
New York, NY 10022
212-838-3486

MAURITANIA
PV (3 months, $20) ✈ ✚
For visa information:
Embassy of the Republic of Mauritania
2129 Leroy Place NW
Washington, DC 20008
202-232-5700

MAURITIUS
P ✈ $
For visa information:
Embassy of Mauritius
4301 Connecticut Avenue NW
Washington, DC 20008
202-244-1491
For tourism information:
Mauritius Tourist Information
8 Haven Avenue
Port Washington, NY 11050
516-944-3763

MEXICO
US TC

For visa information:
Embassy of Mexico
2827 16th Street NW
Washington, DC 20009-4260
202-736-1000
Consulates in:
Laredo (TX), New York
For tourism information:
Mexican Government Tourism Office
405 Park Avenue
New York, NY 10022
212-755-7261
Other offices in:
Chicago, Houston, Los Angeles, Miami,
Montreal, Toronto, Washington

MICRONESIA
US ✈ $ ✚

For visa information:
Embassy of the Federated States of
Micronesia
1725 N Street NW
Washington, DC 20036
202-223-4383

MOLDOVA
PV

For visa information:
Embassy of the Republic of Moldova
1533 K Street NW
Washington, DC 20005
202-667-1130

MONACO
P

For visa information:
Consulate of Monaco
c/o Ambrose & Casselman
888 16th Street NW
Washington, DC 20008
202-296-8600
Consulates in:
Boston, Chicago, Dallas, Montreal,
New Orleans, New York, Philadelphia,

Palm Beach (FL), San Francisco
For tourism information:
Monaco Government Tourist and
Convention Office
542 South Dearborn Street
Chicago, IL 60605
312-939-7863
Other offices in:
New York

MONGOLIA
PV (90 days, $45) ✈
For visa information:
Embassy of Mongolia
2833 M Street NW
Washington, DC 20007
202-333-7117
Consulates in:
New York
For tourism information:
Mongolian Tourism Corporation
1 Deerpark Drive
Monmouth Junction, NJ 08852
908-274-0088

MOROCCO
P
For visa information:
Embassy of Morocco
1601 21st Street NW
Washington, DC 20009
202-462-7979
Consulates in:
New York
For tourism information:
Moroccan National Tourist Office
Epcot Center, Box 22663
Lake Buena Vista, FL 32830
407-827-5337
Other offices in:
Montreal, New York

MOZAMBIQUE
PV (30 days, $20) ✚
For visa information:
Embassy of the Republic of
Mozambique
1990 M Street NW
Washington, DC 20036
202-293-7146

MYANMAR (Burma)
PV (28 days, $10)
For visa information:

Embassy of the Union of Myanmar
2300 S Street NW
Washington, DC 20008
202-332-9044
Consulates in:
New York

NAMIBIA
P ✈ **$**
For visa information:
Embassy of Namibia
1605 New Hampshire Avenue NW
Washington, DC 20009
202-986-0540

NAURU
PV ✈
For visa information:
Consulate of the Republic of Nauru
Ada Professional Building
Marine Drive
Agana, Guam 96910
671-649-7106

NEPAL
PV (30 days, $40)
For visa information:
Royal Nepalese Embassy
2131 Leroy Place NW
Washington, DC 20008
202-667-4550
Consulates in:
New York

NETHERLANDS
P ✈ **$**
For visa information:
Royal Netherlands Embassy
4200 Linnean Avenue NW
Washington, DC 20016
202-244-5300
Consulates in:
New York, Montreal, Toronto,
Vancouver
For tourism information:
Netherlands Board of Tourism
225 North Michigan Avenue
Chicago, IL 60601
800-598-8500
Other offices in:
Los Angeles, New York, Toronto

NETHERLANDS ANTILLES
(Aruba, Bonaire, Curaçao, Saba, Statia,

St. Maarten)
US P ✈ $
For visa information:
Royal Netherlands Embassy
4200 Linnean Avenue NW
Washington, DC 20008
202-244-5300
Consulates in:
Chicago, Houston, Los Angeles, New
York
For tourism information:
Caribbean Tourism Organization
20 East 46th Street
New York, NY 10017
212-682-0435
(See also, Aruba, Bonaire, Curaçao)

NEW ZEALAND
P ✈ $
For visa information:
Embassy of New Zealand
37 Observatory Circle NW
Washington, DC 20008
202-328-4800
Consulates in:
Los Angeles, Vancouver
For tourism information:
New Zealand Tourism Board
501 Santa Monica Boulevard
Santa Monica, CA 90401
800-388-5494
Other offices in:
Vancouver

NICARAGUA
P ✈
For visa information:
Embassy of Nicaragua
1627 New Hampshire Avenue NW
Washington, DC 20009
202-939-6531

NIGER
PV ($31) **✈ $ ✚**
For visa information:
Embassy of the Republic of Niger
2204 R Street NW
Washington, DC 20008
202-483-4224

NIGERIA
PV ($20-$40) **✈ ✚**
For visa information:
Embassy of the Republic of Nigeria

2201 M Street NW
Washington, DC 20037
202-822-1500
Consulates in:
New York

NIUE
P ✈
For visa information:
Embassy of New Zealand
37 Observatory Circle NW
Washington, DC 20008
202-328-4800

NORFOLK ISLAND
PV
For visa information:
Embassy of Australia
1601 Massachusetts Avenue NW
Washington, DC 20036-2273
800-242-2878

NORWAY
P
For visa information:
Royal Norwegian Embassy
2720 34th Street NW
Washington, DC 20008
202-333-6000
Consulates in:
Chicago, Houston, Minneapolis, New
York, San Francisco
For tourism information:
Norwegian Tourist Board
655 Third Avenue
New York, NY 10017
212-949-2333
Other offices in:
San Francisco

OMAN
PV
For visa information:
Embassy of the Sultanate of Oman
2535 Belmont Road NW
Washington, DC 20008
202-387-1980

PAKISTAN
PV ($20) **✈**
For visa information:
Embassy of Pakistan
2315 Massachusetts Avenue NW
Washington, DC 20008

202-939-6295
Consulates in:
New York

PALAU, REPUBLIC OF
P or **US** ✈
For visa information:
Representative Office
444 North Capitol Street
Washington, DC 20001
202-452-6814

PANAMA
P TC (30 days, $5) ✈
For visa information:
Embassy of Panama
2862 McGill Terrace NW
Washington, DC 20008
202-483-1407
Consulates in:
Beverly Hills, Houston, Miami,
Montreal, New Orleans, New York, San
Diego, San Francisco, Tampa

PAPUA NEW GUINEA
P ✈ **$**
For visa information:
Embassy of Papua New Guinea
1615 New Hampshire Avenue NW
Washington, DC 20009
202-745-3680
Consulates in:
New York
For tourism information:
Air Niugini
500 Birch Street
Newport Beach, CA 92660
714-752-5440

PARAGUAY
P
For visa information:
Embassy of Paraguay
2400 Massachusetts Avenue NW
Washington, DC 20008
202-483-6960
Consulates in:
Huntington Beach (CA), Miami, New
York

PERU
P ✈
For visa information:
Embassy of Peru

1700 Massachusetts Avenue NW
Washington, DC 20008
202-833-9860
Consulates in:
Chicago, Houston, Los Angeles, Miami,
New York, Paterson (NJ), San
Francisco

PHILIPPINES
P ✈
For visa information:
Embassy of the Philippines
1600 Massachusetts Avenue NW
Washington, DC 20036
202-467-9300
Consulates in:
Chicago, Honolulu, Houston, Los
Angeles, New York, San Francisco,
Toronto, Vancouver
For tourism information:
Philippine Department of Tourism
556 Fifth Avenue
New York, NY 10036
212-575-7915
Other offices in:
Los Angeles, San Francisco

POLAND
P
For visa information:
Embassy of the Republic of Poland
2224 Wyoming Avenue NW
Washington, DC 20008
202-232-4517
Consulates in:
Chicago, Los Angeles, Montreal, New
York, Toronto, Vancouver
For tourism information:
Polish National Tourist Office
275 Madison Avenue
New York, NY 10016
212-338-9412
Other offices in:
Montreal

PORTUGAL
P
For visa information:
Embassy of Portugal
2125 Kalorama Road NW
Washington, DC 20008
202-328-8610
Consulates in:
Boston, Coral Gables, Houston, Los

Angeles, Montreal, New Bedford (MA),
Newark (NJ), Philadelphia,
Providence, San Francisco, Toronto,
Vancouver, Waterbury (CT)
For tourism information:
Portuguese National Tourist Office
590 Fifth Avenue
New York, NY 10036
212-354-4403

QATAR
PV (10 years, $22)
For visa information:
Embassy of the State of Qatar
4200 Wisconsin Avenue NW
Washington, DC 20016
202-274-1600

ROMANIA
P
For visa information:
Embassy of Romania
1607 23rd Street NW
Washington, DC 20008
202-232-4747
Consulates in:
Los Angeles, New York
For tourism information:
Romanian National Tourist Office
342 Madison Avenue
New York, NY 10173
800-621-8687

RUSSIA
PV ($40-$80)
For visa information:
Embassy of Russia
2650 Wisconsin Avenue NW
Washington, DC 20007-4601
202-628-7551
Consulates in:
New York, San Francisco
For tourism information:
Intourist USA
610 Fifth Avenue
New York, NY 10020
212-757-3884

RWANDA
PV (1 month, $30) **✛**
For visa information:
Embassy of the Republic of Rwanda
1714 New Hampshire Avenue NW
Washington, DC 20009

202-232-2882
Consulates in:
Northbrook (IL)

ST. KITTS AND NEVIS
US ✈
For visa information:
Embassy of St. Kitts and Nevis
3216 New Mexico Avenue NW
Washington, DC 20016
202-686-2636
Consulates in:
New York
For tourism information:
St. Kitts and Nevis Tourist Board
414 East 75th Street
New York, NY 10021
800-582-6208

SAINT LUCIA
P or **US** ✈
For visa information:
Embassy of Saint Lucia
3216 New Mexico Avenue NW
Washington, DC 20016
202-364-6792
Consulates in:
New York
For tourism information:
St. Lucia Tourist Board
820 Second Avenue
New York, NY 10017
800-456-3984

SAINT MAARTEN
P or **US** ✈ **$**
For visa information:
Royal Netherlands Embassy
4200 Linnean Avenue NW
Washington, DC 20008
202-244-5300
Consulates in:
New York
For tourism information:
St. Maarten Tourist Bureau
675 Third Avenue
New York, NY 10017
212-953-2084

SAINT MARTIN
US
For visa information:
Embassy of France
4101 Reservoir Road NW

Washington, DC 20007
202-944-6200
For tourism information:
French West Indies Tourist Board
444 Madison Avenue
New York, NY 10022
212-838-3486

SAINT VINCENT
US ✈ $
For visa information:
Embassy of Saint Vincent and the
Grenadines
3216 New Mexico Avenue NW
Washington, DC 20016
202-342-6730
Consulates in:
New York
For tourism information:
St. Vincent Tourism Information
801 Second Avenue
New York, NY 10017
800-729-1726
Other offices in:
Dallas

SAN MARINO
P
For visa information:
Honorary Consulate of the Republic of
San Marino
1899 L Street NW
Washington, DC 20036
202-223-3517
Consulates in:
Detroit, New York

SAO TOME AND PRINCIPE
PV (3 months, $25) **✚**
For visa information:
Permanent Mission of Sao Tome and
Principe to the United Nations
122 East 42nd Street
New York, NY 10168
212-697-4211

SAUDI ARABIA
PV NT ✈ ✚
For visa information:
Royal Embassy of Saudi Arabia
601 New Hampshire Avenue NW
Washington, DC 20037
202-944-3126
Consulates in:

Houston, Los Angeles, New York

SENEGAL
P ✈ ✚
For visa information:
Embassy of the Republic of Senegal
2112 Wyoming Avenue NW
Washington, DC 20008
202-234-0540
For tourism information:
Senegal Tourist Office
310 Madison Avenue
New York, NY 10017
800-443-2527

SERBIA AND MONTENEGRO
P
For visa information:
Embassy of the Former Federal
Republic of Yugoslavia
2410 California Street NW
Washington, DC 20008
202-462-6566

SEYCHELLES
P ✈ $
For visa information:
Permanent Mission of Seychelles to the
United Nations
820 Second Avenue
New York, NY 10017
212-687-9766
For tourism information:
Seychelles Tourist Office
235 East 40th Street
New York, NY 10016
212-687-9766

SIERRA LEONE
PV (3 months, $20) **✈ $ ✚**
For visa information:
Embassy of Sierra Leone
1701 19th Street NW
Washington, DC 20009
202-939-9261

SINGAPORE
P ✈
For visa information:
Embassy of Singapore
3501 International Place NW
Washington, DC 20008
202-537-3100
For tourism information:

Singapore Tourist Promotion Board
8484 Wilshire Boulevard
Beverly Hills, CA 90211
213-852-1901
Other offices in:
Chicago, New York, Toronto

SLOVAK REPUBLIC
P

For visa information:
Embassy of the Slovak Republic
2201 Wisconsin Avenue NW
Washington, DC 20007
202-965-5164
For tourism information:
Slovakia Travel Service
10 East 40th Street
New York, NY 10016
212-213-3865

SLOVENIA
P

For visa information:
Embassy of Slovenia
1525 New Hampshire Avenue NW
Washington, DC 20036
202-667-5363
Consulates in:
New York
For tourism information:
Slovenian Tourist Office
122 East 42nd Street
New York, NY 10168-0072
212-682-5896

SOLOMON ISLANDS
P ✈ $

For visa information:
British Embassy
19 Observatory Circle NW
Washington, DC 20008
202-588-7800

SOMALIA
P

For visa information:
Consulate of the Somali Democratic
Republic
425 East 61st Street
New York, NY 10021
212-688-9410

SOUTH AFRICA
P ✚

For visa information:
Embassy of South Africa
3201 New Mexico Avenue NW
Washington, DC 20016
202-966-1650
Consulates in:
Chicago, Los Angeles, Montreal, New
York, Toronto
For tourism information:
South African Tourism Board
500 Fifth Avenue
New York, NY 10110
800-822-5368
Other offices in:
Los Angeles

SPAIN
P

For visa information:
Embassy of Spain
2375 Pennsylvania Avenue NW
Washington, DC 20037
202-452-0100
Consulates in:
Boston, Chicago, Houston Los Angeles,
Miami, New Orleans, New York, San
Francisco, San Juan, Toronto
For tourism information:
Tourist Office of Spain
845 North Michigan Avenue
Chicago, IL 60611
312-642-1992
Other offices in:
Los Angeles, New York, Miami, Toronto

SRI LANKA
P ✈ $

For visa information:
Embassy of Sri Lanka
2148 Wyoming Avenue NW
Washington, DC 20008
202-483-4025
Consulates in:
Honolulu, New Orleans, New York

SUDAN
PV (3 months, $50) ✈ $ ✚

For visa information:
Embassy of the Republic of the Sudan
2210 Massachusetts Avenue NW
Washington, DC 20008
202-338-8565
Consulates in:
New York

SURINAME
PV
For visa information:
Embassy of the Republic of Suriname
4301 Connecticut Avenue NW
Washington, DC 20008
202-244-7488
Consulates in:
Miami

SWAZILAND
P +
For visa information:
Embassy of the Kingdom of Swaziland
3400 International Drive NW
Washington, DC 20008
202-362-6683

SWEDEN
P
For visa information:
Embassy of Sweden
1501 M Street NW
Washington, DC 20005-1702
202-467-2600
Consulates in:
Chicago, Houston, Minneapolis, San
Francisco, Toronto, Vancouver
For tourism information:
Scandinavian Tourist Board
P.O. Box 4649
New York, NY 10163-4649
212-949-2333

SWITZERLAND
P
For visa information:
Embassy of Switzerland
2900 Cathedral Avenue NW
Washington, DC 20008
202-745-7900
Consulates in:
Atlanta, Chicago, Houston, Los
Angeles, New York, San Francisco,
Montreal, Toronto, Vancouver
For tourism information:
Switzerland Tourism
608 Fifth Avenue
New York, NY 10020
212-757-5944
Other offices in:
Chicago, Los Angeles, Toronto

SYRIA
PV (3-6 months, $35)
For visa information:
Embassy of the Syrian Arab Republic
2215 Wyoming Avenue NW
Washington, DC 20008
202-232-6313
Consulates in:
Houston

TAHITI
(See French Polynesia)

TAIWAN
P
For visa information:
Taipei Economic and Cultural
Representative
4201 Wisconsin Avenue NW
Washington, DC 20016-2137
202-895-1800
Other offices in:
Atlanta, Boston, Chicago, Honolulu,
Houston, Kansas City (MO), Los
Angeles, Miami, New York, San
Francisco, Seattle
For tourism information:
Taiwan Visitors Association
333 North Michigan Avenue
Chicago, IL 60601
312-346-1038
Other offices in:
New York, San Francisco

TAJIKISTAN
PV
For visa information:
Embassy of Russia
2650 Wisconsin Avenue NW
Washington, DC 20007-4601
202-628-7551

TANZANIA
PV (30 days, $45) **+**
For visa information:
Embassy of the Republic of Tanzania
2139 R Street NW
Washington, DC 20008
202-939-6125
For tourism information:
Tanzania Tourist Corp.
205 East 42nd Street
New York, NY 10017
212-972-9160

THAILAND

P ✈

For visa information:
Embassy of Thailand
1024 Wisconsin Avenue NW
Washington, DC 20007
202-944-3608
Consulates in:
Chicago, El Paso (TX), Honolulu, Los
Angeles, Montgomery (AL), New
Orleans, New York, Toronto, Vancouver
For tourism information:
Tourism Authority of Thailand
303 East Wacker Drive
Chicago, IL 60601
312-819-3990
Other offices in:
Los Angeles, New York

TOGO

P ($20) ✚

For visa information:
Embassy of the Republic of Togo
2208 Massachusetts Avenue NW
Washington, DC 20008
202-234-4212
For tourism information:
Togolese Tourist Information
112 East 40th Street
New York, NY 10016
212-490-3455

TONGA

P ✈

For visa information:
Consulate General of Tonga
360 Post Street
San Francisco, CA 94108
415-781-0365

TRINIDAD AND TOBAGO

P

For visa information:
Embassy of Trinidad and Tobago
1708 Massachusetts Avenue NW
Washington, DC 20036
202-467-6490
For tourism information:
Tourism and Industry Development
Corp. of Trinidad and Tobago
7000 Boulevard East
Guttenberg, NJ 07093
800-748-4224

TUNISIA

P ✈

For visa information:
Embassy of Tunisia
1515 Massachusetts Avenue NW
Washington, DC 20005
202-862-1850
Consulates in:
New York, San Francisco

TURKEY

P

For visa information:
Embassy of the Republic of Turkey
1714 Massachusetts Avenue NW
Washington, DC 20036
202-659-0742
Consulates in:
Chicago, Houston, Los Angeles, New
York
For tourism information:
Turkish Tourism Information Office
821 UN Plaza
New York, NY 10017
212-687-2194
Other offices in:
Washington

TURKMENISTAN

PV

For visa information:
Embassy of Turkmenistan
2207 Massachusetts Avenue NW
Washington, DC 20008
202-588-1500

TURKS AND CAICOS

(See British West Indies)

TUVALU

P ✈ $

For visa information:
British Embassy
19 Observatory Circle NW
Washington, DC 20008
202-588-7800

UGANDA

P ✚

For visa information:
Embassy of the Republic of Uganda
5909 16th Street NW
Washington, DC 20011
202-726-7100

UKRAINE
PV ($50-$140)
For visa information:
Embassy of Ukraine
3550 M Street NW
Washington, DC 20007
202-333-7507
Consulates in:
Chicago, New York

UNITED ARAB EMIRATES
PV
For visa information:
Embassy of the United Arab Emirates
3000 K Street NW
Washington, DC 20007
202-338-6500
Consulates in:
New York
For tourism information:
Dubai Commerce and Tourism
Promotion Board
8 Penn Center
Philadelphia, PA 19103
(215) 751-9750

UNITED KINGDOM
P
For visa information:
British Embassy
19 Observatory Circle NW
Washington, DC 20008
202-588-7800
Consulates in:
Atlanta, Boston, Chicago, Cleveland,
Houston, Los Angeles, New York, San
Francisco
For tourism information:
British Tourist Authority
551 Fifth Avenue
New York, NY 10019
800-462-2748

URUGUAY
P
For visa information:
Embassy of Uruguay
1918 F Street NW
Washington, DC 20008
202-331-4219
Consulates in:
Coral Gables, New Orleans, New York,
Rio Pedras (PR), San Francisco, St. Paul

UZBEKISTAN
PV
For visa information:
Embassy of the Republic of Uzbekistan
1746 Massachusetts Avenue NW
Washington, DC 20036
202-293-6803
Consulates in:
New York
For tourism information:
Uzbekistan Tourist Board
60 East 42nd Street
New York, NY 10165
212-983-0382

VANUATU
P ✈
For visa information:
British Embassy
19 Observatory Circle NW
Washington, DC 20008
202-588-7800

VENEZUELA
P TC
For visa information:
Embassy of Venezuela
1099 30th Street NW
Washington, DC 20007
202-342-2214
Consulates in:
Boston, Chicago, Hato Rey (PR),
Houston, Miami, New Orleans, New
York, San Francisco
For tourism information:
Venezuelan Tourism Association
P.O. Box 3010
Sausalito, CA 94966
415-331-0100

VIETNAM
PV (6 months, $25)
For visa information:
Embassy of Vietnam
1233 20th Street NW
Washington, DC 20036
202-861-2293

WALES
(See United Kingdom)

WESTERN SAMOA
P ✈
For visa information:

Western Samoa Mission to the United
Nations
820 Second Avenue
New York, NY 10017
212-599-6196

YEMEN
PV (30 days, $50) ✈ $ ✚
For visa information:
Embassy of the Republic of Yemen
2600 Virginia Avenue NW
Washington, DC 20037
202-965-4760
Consulates in:
New York
For tourism information:
Yemen Airways
191 Court Street
Brooklyn, NY 11201
718-522-0692

ZAIRE
PV (1 month, $75) ✈ ✚
For visa information:
Embassy of the Republic of Zaire
1800 New Hampshire Avenue NW
Washington, DC 20009
202-234-7690

ZAMBIA
PV (3 months, $25) ✚
For visa information:
Embassy of the Republic of Zambia
2419 Massachusetts Avenue NW
Washington, DC 20008
202-265-9717
For tourism information:
Zambia National Tourist Board
800 Second Avenue
New York, NY 10017
212-972-7200

ZIMBABWE
P ✈ $ ✚
For visa information:
Embassy of Zimbabwe
1608 New Hampshire Avenue NW
Washington, DC 20009
202-332-7100
For tourism information:
Zimbabwe Tourist Office
1270 Avenue of the Americas
New York, NY 10020
212-332-1090

Consortiums

Consortiums and co-ops offer small, independent agencies a chance to match the clout wielded by major chains and franchises. It is even possible for outside sales reps operating as independent contractors to join a consortium in their own name. By pooling the selling power of a large number of small agencies, consortiums can provide the preferred pricing and commission overrides enjoyed by the "big boys."

While the major attraction in joining a consortium is the good deals you can get for both your clients and yourself, many consortiums offer additional benefits, such as marketing aids, sales training, and advertising. On top of all that, the cost of belonging can be surprisingly modest.

ABC Corporate Services
500 Plaza Drive
Secaucus, NJ 07096
800-722-5179
201-902-7923

Action 6
237 Church Street
Lowell, MA 01852
508-459-2104

Allied Percival International
500 Main Street
Suite 400
Fort Worth, TX 76102
817-870-0300

Aloha Marketing Group, Inc.
370 Whooping Loop
Suite 1184
Altamonte Springs, FL 32701-3451
800-733-2048
407-831-8700

Aura, Inc.
5 East County Road B
St. Paul, MN 55117
800-326-2872
612-487-3223

BTI Americas, Inc.
400 Skokie Boulevard
Northbrook, IL 60062
847-480-8400

BTS Travel Network
5435 Scotts Valley Drive
Scotts Valley, CA 95067
800-358-2355
408-438-6662

Condominium Travel Associates
2001 West Main Street
Suite 140
Stamford, CT 06902
203-975-7714

Consolidated Travel Services
9800 Centre Park Lane
Suite 860
Houston, TX 77036
800-969-9311
713-776-0775

Corp-Net International
3040 Riverside Drive
Columbus, OH 43221
614-488-0600

Crown Travel Group
2701 East Camelback Road
Suite 440
Phoenix, AZ 85016
800-848-8756
602-266-5577

The Cruise Consortium
254 South Main Street
New City, NY 10956
800-285-0111
914-639-9330

Cruise Shoppes America
701 Metairie Road
Suite 1A-208
Metairie, LA 70005
800-375-0199
504-833-0340

Cruiselink
7 West Main Street
Bay Shore, NY 11706
800-253-4242
516-665-2222

Gem
754 Montauk Highway
West Islip, NY 11795
800-843-0733
516-422-7700

Giants
(Greater Independent Association of
National Travel Services)
2 Park Avenue
New York, NY 10016
800-442-6871
212-545-7460

Hickory Travel Systems
Park 80
Plaza East
Saddle Brook, NJ 07663-5291
800-448-0350
201-843-0820

International Tours
5810 East Skelly Drive
Suite 1800
Tulsa, OK 74135
800-777-9691
918-655-2300

Leisure Travel Group
4640 Admiralty Way
Suite 306
Marina Del Rey, CA 90292
310-574-0883

Marketing Alliance for Retail Travel
(MART)
1175 Herndon Parkway
Suite 100
Herndon, VA 20170
888-577-7627

Riverside Travel Group
6645 NE 78th Court
Suite C1
Portland, OR 97218
503-255-2950

Space & Leisure Time
15 Front Street
Rockville Centre, NY 11570
800-223-4523
516-764-6767

Thor 24
382 South Arthur Avenue
Louisville, CO 80027
800-862-2111
303-661-3000

TIME
(Travel Industry Marketing
Enterprises)
200 West Main Street
Babylon, NY 11702
800-321-1060
516-321-1030

The Travel Authority
100 Executive Way
Suite 202
Ponte Vedra, FL 32082
904-285-9796

Travel Design Associates
2005 De La Cruz Boulevard
Suite 171
Santa Clara, CA 95050-3030
800-927-7444
408-727-8787

Travelhost Consortium
10701 Stemmons
Dallas, TX 75220
800-446-3644
972-556-0541

Travelsavers
71 Audrey Avenue
Oyster Bay, NY 11771
800-755-8222
516-624-0500

ValuTravel Marketing
3313 Superior Lane
Bowie, MD 20715
800-432-8258
301-262-2384

Woodside Travel Trust
4330 East West Highway
Suite 1100
Bethesda, MD 20814
301-718-9500

Travel Associations

There are many, many organizations that involve themselves with the travel industry in one way or another, as this list proves. Some represent travel agents, some represent suppliers, others represent business travelers who deal with travel agents and suppliers, some represent people who work in the travel industry, some provide services to the trade. Some are non-profit associations, some are for-profit corporations, some are government agencies.

There will probably be a number of associations and organizations listed here that you will want to contact for one reason or another — part of any trade organization's mission, after all, is to dispense information about its area of expertise to the general public. There may well be some organizations listed here that you will want to join.

Adventure Travel Society
6551 South Revere Parkway
Suite 160
Englewood, CO 80111
303-649-9016
303-649-9017 fax
"Promotes adventure travel and ecotourism while integrating responsible natural resource management."

Academy of Travel and Tourism
235 Park Avenue South
New York, NY 10003
212-420-8400
A non-profit organization that develops travel career prep programs for high school students.

Africa Travel Association (ATA)
347 Fifth Avenue
Suite 610
New York, NY 10016
212-447-1926
212-725-8253 fax
A "nonprofit, nonpolitical" educational organization that promotes "the tourist attractions of the continent of Africa to the travel industry in North America."

African-American Travel and Tourism Association (AATTA)
P.O. Box 870712
New Orleans, LA 70187-0712
504-241-8464
504-522-0785 fax
A national association of local organizations promoting African-American tourism.

Air Line Pilots Association (ALPA)
1625 Massachusetts Avenue NW
Washington, DC 20036
202-797-4010
As a labor union, ALPA represents 41,000 pilots of 44 American airlines. It also works to promote airline safety.

Air Transport Association of America (ATA)
1301 Pennsylvania Avenue NW
Suite 1100
Washington, DC 20004-1707
202-626-4000
202-626-4181 fax
A lobbying and trade organization which represents the interests of the airline industry. "Its members collectively account for 97 percent of the revenue passenger miles flown in

the United States and over 95 percent of the freight ton miles."

Airlines Reporting Corporation (ARC)
1530 Wilson Boulevard
Suite 800
Arlington, VA 22209
703-816-8000
A separate corporate entity established by the major airlines to administer the accreditation of travel agencies, the collection of payments for fares, and the disbursement of commissions to agents.

Airports Council International, North America (ACI-NA)
1775 K Street NW
Suite 500
Washington, DC 20006
202-293-8500
202-331-1362 fax
A trade organization representing "143 local, regional, and state governing bodies that own and operate approximately 300 commercial service airports in the United States, Canada, and Bermuda. ACI-NA member airports service more than 90 percent of the U.S. domestic scheduled air passenger and cargo traffic and virtually all U.S. scheduled international travel."

Alliance of Canadian Travel Associations (ACTA)
1729 Bank Street
Ottawa, ON K1V 7Z5
CANADA
613-521-0474
613-521-0805 fax
Represents the interests of its members (primarily retail travel agents and tour operators) to the public, the government, and other bodies.

American Aid Society of Paris
2, Avenue Gabriel
75008 Paris
FRANCE
011-33-1-4312-2222
Provides aid, in the form of loans, to financially strapped Americans living or traveling in France.
American Association of Airport

Executives (AAAE)
4212 King Street
Alexandria, VA 22302
703-824-0500
703-820-1395 fax
Represents those who manage "airports which enplane 99 percent of passengers in the United States."

American Association of Travel Agents (AATA)
40 Commerce Drive
Wyomissing, PA 19610
800-523-8020
A fee-based insurance program that enables participating travel agencies to automatically cover their clients.

American Automobile Association (AAA)
1000 AAA Drive
Heathrow, FL 32746-5063
407-444-7000
407-444-7380 fax
A vast membership organization providing services to and representing the interests of the American motorist. AAA provides emergency road service, maps, guide books, and trip planning services.

American Bed & Breakfast Association
10800 Midlothian Turnpike
Richmond, VA 23235
800-769-2468
804-379-2222
804-379-1469 fax
A membership organization for operators of bed and breakfast hostelries. Offers continuing education, property inspections, and marketing services.

American Bus Association (ABA)
1100 New York Avenue NW
Suite 1050
Washington, DC 20005-3934
800-283-2877
202-842-1645
202-842-0850 fax
A lobbying organization representing the interests of the commercial bus industry. "The oldest bus association in the United States."

American Car Rental Association
(ACRA)
1225 I Street NW
Suite 500
Washington, DC 20005
202-682-4778
202-789-4512 fax
A nonprofit trade association for those
in the business of short-term renting
and leasing of vehicles.

American Hotel and Motel Association
(AHMA)
1201 New York Avenue NW
Suite 600
Washington, DC 20005-3931
202-289-3100
202-289-3199 fax
A federation of associations in the hotel
and motel industry. Represents the
industry's interests to Congress and
the public. Publishes a directory of
every hotel, motel, and resort chain
with more than three units.

American Public Transit Association
(APTA)
1201 New York Avenue NW
Suite 400
Washington, DC 20005
202-898-4000
202-898-4070 fax
An international industry group
representing more than 1,100 private
businesses providing public transit.
"More than 95 percent of the people
who use transit in the U.S. and Canada
are carried by APTA members."

American Recreation Coalition
1225 New York Avenue NW
Suite 450
Washington, DC 20005
800-257-6370
202-682-9530
202-682-9529 fax
A non-profit educational organization
serving the recreation industry and
recreation enthusiasts.

American Sightseeing International
490 Post Street
Suite 1701
San Francisco, CA 94102

415-986-2082
415-986-2703 fax
A nonprofit sales and marketing
association for the sightseeing industry.
Will help travel agents arranging
multi-destination tours for groups by
putting them in touch with appropriate
suppliers.

American Society of Travel Agents
(ASTA)
1101 King Street
Alexandria, VA 22314
800-275-2782
703-739-2782
703-684-8319 fax
The largest travel trade organization
with 20,000 members seeks "to
enhance the professionalism and
profitability of member agents through
effective representation ... education
and training, and by identifying and
meeting the needs of the traveling
public."

American Tourism Society
419 Park Avenue South
Suite 505
New York, NY 10016
212-532-8845
212-545-9641 fax
A nonprofit association of travel
agencies, tour operators and hotels
promoting tourism between the
United States and Russia, Central
and Eastern Europe, and the Baltic
states.

Assist Card International (ACI)
1001 South Bay Shore Drive
Suite 2302
Miami, FL 33131
800-874-2223
305-381-9959
305-375-8135 fax
Provides assistance for travelers from
South America.

Association of American Railroads
(AAR)
50 F Street NW
Washington, DC 20001
202-639-2100
202-639-2558 fax

A lobbying and research group representing the railroad industry. "AAR's corporate members haul 91 percent of the nation's rail carloads and 100 percent of the rail passengers."

Association of British Travel Agents (ABTA)
55-57 Newman Street
London, WlP 4AH
UNITED KINGDOM
011-44-171-637-2444
011-44-171-637-0713 fax
The British equivalent of ASTA.

Association of Certified Travel Agents (ACTA)
1209 Park Avenue
New York, NY 10128
212-427-6938
212-427-6931 fax
A nonprofit travel trade school association.

Association of Corporate Travel Executives (ACTE)
608 Massachusetts Avenue NW
Washington, DC 20002
800-228-3669
202-546-5746
A professional association offering "educational and networking opportunities for those involved with the business travel industry."

Association of Flight Attendants (AFA)
1625 Massachusetts Avenue NW
Washington, DC 20036
202-328-5400
202-328-5424 fax
This labor union is "the collective bargaining agent for 33,000 flight attendants on 21 air carriers. AFA is the largest flight attendant union in the world."

Association of Group Travel Executives (AGTE)
424 Madison Avenue
Suite 705
New York, NY 10017
212-486-4300
212-755-2135 fax

Association of Latin American Travel Agents
150 Nassau Street
Suite 1605
New York, NY 10038
212-964-5500
212-385-4087 fax
A membership organization of individual travel agents. The group's primary purpose is to provide its members with better commission rates from suppliers serving the Latin American market.

Association of Retail Travel Agents (ARTA)
845 Sir Thomas Court
Suite 3
Harrisburg, PA 17109
800-969-6069
717-545-9613 fax
A feisty trade and lobbying organization representing travel agents. "The Association that fights for the rights and dignity of travel."

Association of Travel Marketing Executives (ATME)
305 Madison Avenue
Suite 2025
New York, NY 10165
800-526-0041
800-525-3087 fax

California Coalition of Travel Organizations (CCTO)
c/o Desmond & Desmond
925 L Street
Suite 220
Sacramento, CA 95814
916-441-4166
916-441-3520 fax
A government watchdog group and political action committee which seeks to insure that the California legislature will enact laws "favorable" to the travel industry. They were instrumental in the passage of California's oppressive Sellers of Travel Law.

Canadian Institute of Travel Counsellors (CITC)
55 Eglinton Avenue East
Suite 209

Toronto, ON M4P 1G8
CANADA
800-589-5776
416-239-4891
The Canadian equivalent of the
Institute of Certified Travel Agents
(ICTA).

Caribbean Hotel Association (CHA)
18 Marseilles Street
San Juan, PR 00907-1672
787-725-9139
787-725-9166 fax
A marketing organization which
promotes the tourism interests of the
entire Caribbean area.

Caribbean Tourism Organization
(CTO)
20 East 46th Street
New York, NY 10017-4258
212-682-0435
212-697-4258 fax
This association promotes travel and
tourism to the Caribbean area as a
whole.

Center for Responsible Tourism
P.O. Box 827
San Anselmo, CA 94979
415-258-6594
CRT seeks "to open the minds of North
American travelers toward an
appreciation of cultural and
environmental differences and
encourage their use of responsible
alternate forms of travel."

Central Ohio Travel Professionals
c/o McMurray Travel Service
787 South State Street
Westerville, OH 43081
614-899-1979
614-899-1970 fax
A professional educational, networking,
and support group for travel
professionals in the central Ohio
region, including outside sales reps.

Citizens Emergency Center
U.S. State Department
2201 C Street NW
Room 4811
Washington, DC 20520

202-647-5225
202-647-6201 fax
Acts as a liaison between Congress and
citizens overseas, providing assistance
in cases of illness, legal problems, and
destitution of Americans traveling
abroad. Also issues periodic Consular
Information Sheets (formerly called
"Travel Advisories") alerting the public
to potential dangers and hazards in
foreign countries.

Commercial Travelers Association
(CTA)
P.O. Box 76400
Atlanta, GA 30358-1400
800-392-2856
770-993-1155
Representing the "average business
traveler," CTA describes itself as "a
non-profit contract negotiation and
advocacy group." It is seeking, among
other things, to end the airlines'
requirement of a Saturday stay-over to
qualify for the lowest fares.

Convention Liaison Council
1575 I Street NW
Suite 1190
Washington, DC 20005
202-626-2764
202-408-9652 fax
A federation of 23 groups representing
the convention and meeting industry.
Sponsors the Certified Meeting
Planner (CMP) program.

Council on Hotel, Restaurant and
Institutional Education (CHRIE)
1200 17th Street NW
Washington, DC 20036-3097
202-331-5990
202-785-2511 fax
A nonprofit educational association
which brings together educational
institutions offering degrees in the
hospitality industry with
representatives of the industry they
serve. CHRIE seeks to "establish an
accreditation process for education
programs and identify skills standards
or outcomes required for success in
positions throughout the industry,"
which is broadly defined as comprising

the food, lodging, travel and tourism segments.

Council on International Educational Exchange (CIEE)
205 East 42nd Street
New York, NY 10017
888-268-6245
212-822-2600
212-822-2699 fax
An information clearinghouse and sponsoring organization for student travel and international student exchanges.

Cruise Lines International Association (CLIA)
500 Fifth Avenue
Suite 1407
New York, NY 10110
212-921-0066
212-921-0549 fax
An organization sponsored by the cruise industry, providing training and marketing support to travel agents.

Department of Commerce
International Trade Administration
Trade Development, Tourism
Industries
Room 1860
14th Street & Constitution Avenue NW
Washington, DC 20230
202-482-4028
202-482-2887 fax
This office has taken over some of the functions of the defunct United States Travel and Tourism Administration.

Department of Transportation (DOT)
400 7th Street SW
Room 3248
Washington, DC 20590
202-554-1716
202-488-7876 fax
The United States government agency responsible for handling consumer complaints about the travel industry.

Dive Travel Industry Association (DTIA)
27041 SW 119 Court
Miami, FL 33032
305-257-3113
305-257-2072 fax
A trade group that promotes dive travel, that is, travel for the purposes of scuba diving. Yearly dues are $25.

Dude Ranchers' Association
P.O. Box 471
LaPorte, CO 80535
970-223-8440
970-223-0201 fax

East Asia Travel Association (EATA)
c/o Japan National Tourist Organization
One Rockefeller Plaza
Suite 1250
New York, NY 10020
212-757-5640
212-307-6754 fax
A marketing association which promotes travel to its member countries — Japan, Korea, Hong Kong, Macau, Thailand, and Taiwan.

The Eco-Tourism Society
P.O. Box 755
North Bennington, VT 05257
802-447-2121
802-447-2122 fax
An association promoting responsible, environmentally sensitive practices in the tourism industry.

Elderhostel
75 Federal Street
Boston, MA 02110-1941
617-426-8056
Elderhostel sponsors educational travel programs for senior citizens with accommodations provided by colleges and universities worldwide.

European Travel Commission (ETC)
c/o Donald N. Martin Company
One Rockefeller Plaza
Suite 214
New York, NY 10020
800-863-8767
212-307-1200
212-301-1205 fax
This association promotes travel and tourism to Europe and provides information to U.S. media.

Federal Aviation Administration (FAA)
APA 200 - FAA
800 Independence Avenue SW
Washington, DC 20591
800-322-7873
202-366-4000

Florida-Caribbean Cruise Association
(FCCA)
2701 Ponce de Leon Boulevard
Suite 203
Coral Gables, FL 33134
305-446-7297
305-448-0931 fax
A trade association of 16 cruise lines
"created to discuss and exchange views
on issues relating to legislation,
tourism development, ports, safety,
security and other cruise industry
issues."

Foundation for Access by the Disabled
P.O. Box 356
Malverne, NY 11565
516-887-5798 phone and fax
This group is building an international
computer network of companies and
resources serving the needs of the
disabled traveler.

Globetrotters' Club
BCM/Roving
London WC1 3XX
UNITED KINGDOM
A club for those interested in
"economical international travel and
opportunities to meet people of other
countries."

Greater New Orleans Black Tourism
Network
1520 Sugar Bowl Drive
New Orleans, LA 70112
800-725-5652
504-523-5652
504-522-0785 fax
Functions like a convention and
visitors bureau, seeking to bring more
African-American groups to New
Orleans. Also provides tourist
information to visitors with an interest
in African-American culture.

Group Leaders of America (GLAMER)
P.O. Box 129
Salem, OH 44460
800-628-0993
330-337-1027
330-337-1118 fax
"The only national organization for
leaders of traveling senior groups" with
a membership of 38,000.

Helicopter Association International
(HAI)
1635 Prince Street
Alexandria, VA 22314
703-683-4646
703-683-4745 fax
A trade association "with over 1,100
member organizations in 51 nations.
HAI is dedicated to promoting the
helicopter as a safe and efficient
method of transportation."

Highway Users Federation
1776 Massachusetts Avenue NW
Suite 500
Washington, DC 20036
202-857-1200
202-857-1220 fax

Hospitality Sales and Marketing
Association International (HSMAI)
1300 L Street NW
Suite 800
Washington, DC 20005
202-789-0089
202-789-1725 fax
An educational and informational
association servicing the hotel industry.
Seeks to educate hotel executives "to
better service hotel users."

Hotel Electronic Distribution Network
Association (HEDNA)
303 Freeport Road
Pittsburgh, PA 15215
412-784-8433
412-781-2871 fax
HEDNA is a trade association of more
than 100 member companies that seeks
to "promote the use of electronic
distribution systems for hotel
reservation sales . . . enhance
automated applications and use [and]
provide support to members on

electronic distribution functionality and operational issues."

Independent Travel Technology Association (ITTA)
303 Freeport Road
Pittsburgh, PA 15215
412-781-3255
412-781-2871 fax
An association of technology firms and travel agents working toward industry-wide technical standards.

Institute of Certified Travel Agents (ICTA)
148 Linden Street
P.O. Box 812059
Wellesley, MA 02181-0012
800-542-4282
617-237-0280
617-237-3860 fax
A professional organization dedicated to excellence in the travel agent profession. Administers the rigorous Certified Travel Counselor (CTC) certification program.

InterAmerican Travel Agents Society
c/o Almeda Travel
1020 Holcombe Street
Suite 1306
Houston, TX 77030
800-992-5112
713-799-1001
713-799-8022 fax
An association of some 300 minority travel agents founded in 1953. Seeks to assist minorities in increasing their business.

International Airline Passengers Association (IAPA)
P.O. Box 700188
Dallas, TX 75370-0188
800-821-4272
972-404-9980
972-233-5348 fax
A membership organization "dedicated to the concerns and safety of frequent travelers." IAPA helps members resolve problems with suppliers, runs a full-service travel agency, and publishes *Travel Safety Alert*.

International Air Transport Association (IATA)
International Airlines Travel Agents Network (IATAN)
2000 Peel Street
Montreal, Quebec
CANADA H3A 2R4
514-844-6311
514-844-5286 fax
U.S. Office:
300 Garden City Plaza
Suite 342
Garden City, NY 11530
516-747-4716
516-747-4462 fax
This association, founded by a consortium of international airlines, administers the codes which identify all the world's airports and air carriers. They also certify travel agencies and issue an identification card which has become the de facto mark of the "professional travel agent."

International Association for Medical Assistance to Travellers (IAMAT)
417 Center Street
Lewiston, NY 14092-3633
716-754-4883
519-836-3412 fax
A membership association that provides members with access to medical care around the world at fixed rates. With sufficient notice, members can contact IAMAT and receive a wide variety of health-related information. Their information is especially helpful on the health hazards of foreign countries to which your clients might be traveling. Membership is free, although donations are welcomed.

International Association of Amusement Parks and Attractions
1448 Duke Street
Alexandria, VA 22314
703-836-4800
703-836-4801 fax

International Association of Conference Centers (IACC)
243 North Lindbergh Boulevard
St. Louis, MO 63141
314-993-8575

314-993-8919 fax
"IACC is a not-for-profit association whose mission is to promote a greater awareness of conference centers as a distinct and unique segment of the training, education, hospitality and travel industries."

International Association of Convention and Visitor Bureaus (IACVB)
200 L Street NW
Washington, DC 20036-4990
202-296-7888
202-296-7889 fax
Promotes "an awareness of the convention and visitor industry's contribution to communities around the world." Works to improve professionalism within the industry.

International Association of Fairs and Expositions
P.O. Box 985
Springfield, MO 65801
417-862-5771
417-862-0156 fax
The trade association for the agricultural fair industry.

International Association of Tour Managers
397 Walworth Road
London SE17 2AW
UNITED KINGDOM
011-44-171-703-9154
011-44-171-703-0358 fax

International Council of Cruise Lines (ICCL)
1211 Connecticut Avenue NW
Suite 800
Washington, DC 20036
800-595-9338
202-296-8463
202-296-1676 fax
A trade organization founded to fight perceived government over-regulation of the cruise industry. "ICCL membership represents over 90% of the ocean-going, overnight, deep-sea passenger cruise line industry."

International Ecotourism Education Foundation
P.O. Box 676
Falls Church, VA 22040
703-534-5430
703-534-5109 fax
"An international nonprofit alliance of tourism and environmental educators." Conducts ecotourism workshops for travel agents and tour operators.

International Federation of Women's Travel Organizations (IFWTO)
13901 North 73rd Street
Suite 210B
Scottsdale, AZ 85260-3125
602-596-6640
602-596-6638 fax

International Festivals Association
P.O. Box 2950
Port Angeles, WA 98362-0336
800-432-4304
360-457-3141
360-452-4695 fax
A professional development and educational group serving the sponsored and special events industry. "Our membership ranges from the Kentucky Derby Festival and Pasadena Tournament of Roses . . . to the Barbecue Goat Cook-off in Brady, Texas."

International Food, Wine and Travel Writers Association
P.O. Box 13109
Long Beach, CA 90803
310-433-5969
Members are professional food and travel writers. Associate members represent the travel and hospitality industry. Presents awards and offers scholarships.

International Forum of Travel and Tourism Advocates (IFTTA)
693 Sutter Street
6th Floor
San Francisco, CA 94102-1076
415-673-3333
415-673-3548 fax
This association of lawyers and travel professionals provides information, to

its members and others, about legislation and regulations affecting the travel industry. It seeks to "foster research on the legal aspects of travel and tourism [and] foster a spirit of collegiality amongst the members."

International Gay Travel Association (IGTA)
P.O. Box 4974
Key West, FL 33041
800-448-8550
305-296-6633 fax
IGTA is "dedicated to encouraging and assisting in the promotion of gay and lesbian travel. Membership is open to all travel and travel-related businesses."

International Hotel Association (IHA)
251, rue du Faubourg Saint Martin
75010 Paris
FRANCE
011-33-1-4489-9400
011-33-1-4036-7330 fax
An association of hotel associations, hotel chains, and individuals from 140 countries. "Works to raise the standards and reputation of the international hotel industry."

International Society of Travel and Tourism Educators (ISTTE)
19364 Woodcrest
Harper Woods, MI 48225
313-526-0710 phone & fax
An association of those teaching and providing training in and to the tourism industry.

Long Island Travel Agents
c/o Here and There Travel
1249 Melville Road
Farmingdale, NY 11735
516-777-1790
516-777-1791 fax
A regional association of approximately 125 owners of local retail travel agencies.

Meeting Professionals International (MPI)
4455 LBJ Freeway
Suite 1200
Dallas, TX 75244
972-702-3000
972-702-3070 fax
A trade association for those who organize meetings and conventions and the companies that supply them.

Metropolitan Association of Professional Travel Agents (MAPTA)
337 West 57th Street
Suite 151
New York, NY 10019
212-332-1256
212-332-1251 fax
A continuing education and networking association of travel industry professionals in the metropolitan New York area.

Midwest Agents Selling Travel (MAST)
15 Spinning Wheel Road
Suite 336
Hinsdale, IL 60521
800-762-9657
630-323-0770
630-323-2662 fax
A regional association of travel agencies that promotes "professionalism and ethical conduct in the travel agency industry" and provides "educational programs for travel agents on industry issues."

Mobility International USA (MIUSA)
P. O. Box 10767
Eugene, OR 97440
541-343-1284
541-343-6812 fax
This nonprofit membership organization, affiliated with Mobility International in London, seeks to "promote and facilitate opportunities for people with disabilities to participate in international educational exchange and travel."

National Air Carrier Association (NACA)
1730 M Street NW
Suite 806
Washington, DC 20036
202-833-8200
202-659-9479 fax
"NACA represents U.S. certificated

airlines which specialize in low-cost scheduled and charter services . . . in domestic and international markets."

National Air Transportation Association (NATA)
4226 King Street
Alexandria, VA 22302
800-808-6282
703-845-9000
703-845-8176 fax
A lobbying organization representing "the business interests of the aviation service industry." Members are "general aviation service companies providing fueling, flight training, maintenance and repair, and on-demand charter service by more than 1,700 member companies with more than 100,000 employees."

National Association of Commissioned Travel Agents (NACTA)
P.O. Box 2398
Valley Center, CA 92082-2398
800-759-5738
619-751-1197
619-751-1309 fax
Formed in 1990 to "furnish a voice in the industry for the outside sales agent." Publishes a quarterly newsletter, offers fam trips, group insurance, and other benefits for its membership.

National Association of Cruise Only Agencies (NACOA)
7600 Red Road
Suite 128
South Miami. FL 33143
305-663-5626
305-663-5625 fax
"A nonprofit trade association ... founded in 1985 to provide a forum to address the needs and concerns of cruise only agencies." Open to full-service agencies and independent contractors, NACOA offers educational and networking opportunities as well as errors and omissions insurance.

National Association of Railroad Passengers

900 Second Street NE
Suite 308
Washington, DC 20002
202-408-8362
202-408-8287 fax
A nonprofit educational group founded in 1967 that seeks to increase government spending for rail transportation to create a more balanced mix of transportation alternatives.

National Association of RV Parks and Campgrounds
8605 Westwood Center Drive
Suite 201
Vienna, VA 22182
703-734-3000
703-734-3004

National Association of Senior Travel Planners
44 Cushing Street
P.O. Box 212
Hingham, MA 02043
617-740-1185
617-749-4099 fax
An association of "pied pipers" and others who plan travel for senior citizens.

National Business Travel Association (NBTA)
1650 King Street
Suite 401
Alexandria, VA 22314-2747
703-684-0836
703-684-0263 fax
A lobbying and educational organization servicing corporate business travel managers "involved in $130 billion [in] travel and entertainment expenses annually."

National Council of Area and Regional Tourism Organizations
1004 Main Street
Stroudsburg, PA 18360
717-421-5791
717-421-6927 fax

National Council of Travel Attractions
Six Flags Fiesta Texas
17000 I-10 West

San Antonio, TX 78257
800-697-4258
210-697-5457
210-697-5444

National Council of Urban Tourism
Organizations
P.O. Box 4270
Anaheim, CA 92803
714-999-8999
714-991-8963 fax

National Golf Foundation
1150 South US Highway 1
Jupiter, FL 33477
800-733-6006
561-744-6006
561-744-6107 fax
The major trade association of the golf
industry. Members comprise facilities,
country clubs, and manufacturers.

National Motorcoach Network, Inc.
Patriot Square
10527C Braddock Road
Fairfax, VA 22032
800-822-6602
703-250-7897
703-250-1477 fax
A for-profit marketing support group of
"leading independent motorcoach
operators throughout the United
States." Publishes the *National
Motorcoach Directory*.

National Park Foundation
1101 17th Street NW
Suite 1102
Washington, DC 20036
202-785-4500
202-785-3539 fax
The National Park Foundation
describes itself as "the official nonprofit
partner of the National Park Service."
They award "more than $2 million in
grants each year to support education,
visitor services, volunteer activities,"
and other services for the Parks.

National Tour Association (NTA)
546 East Main Street
Lexington, KY 40508
800-682-8886
606-226-4444

606-226-4404 fax
Trade organization of operators of
escorted bus tours in the United States
and Canada. Publishes a consumer's
guide and offers a Consumer Protection
Plan which protects travelers in case of
default of a member.

National Travel and Tourism
Awareness Council
1133 21st Street NW
Suite 800
Washington, DC 20036
202-293-1433
An industry coalition which promotes
and publicizes the economic
contribution of travel and tourism.

National Trust for Historic
Preservation (NTHP)
1785 Massachusetts Avenue NW
Washington, DC 20036
800-944-6847
202-588-6000
202-588-6038 fax
A nonprofit membership organization
leading the national preservation
movement. The NTHP funds
preservation activities and operates
historic house museums.

Outside Sales Support Network
(OSSN)
1061 East Indiantown Road
Suite 410
Jupiter, FL 33477
407-575-7327
407-575-4371 fax
"The national association for
independent contractors and outside
sales travel agents." Provides cruise
fam/seminars to educate outside reps.

Pacific Asia Travel Association (PATA)
Telesis Tower, Suite 1000
1 Montgomery Street
San Francisco, CA 94104
415-986-4646
415-986-3458 fax
A trade organization which promotes
travel and tourism to the nations of the
Pacific Rim.

Passenger Vessel Association
1600 Wilson Boulevard
Suite 1000A
Arlington, VA 22209
703-807-0100
703-807-0103 fax
A trade association representing
American-owned tour boats.

Pegasus Fear of Flying Foundation
6671 West Indiantown Road
Suite 384
Jupiter, FL 33458-3983
800-332-7668
407-744-5683 fax

Recreation Vehicle Dealers Association
of North America (RVDA)
3930 University Drive
Fairfax, VA 22030-2515
800-336-0355
703-591-7130
703-591-0734 fax
An association of RV dealers who rent
vehicles to the consumer. Publishes a
directory of its members for travel
agents and other interested parties.

Recreational Vehicle Industry
Association (RVIA)
1896 Preston White Drive
P.O. Box 2999
Reston, VA 20195-0999
703-620-6003
703-620-5071 fax
The trade association for RV
manufacturers and parts suppliers.
RVIA provides industry statistics to
government and promotes RV travel to
the general public.

Regional Airline Association (RAA)
1200 19th Street NW
Suite 300
Washington, DC 20036-2401
202-857-1170
202-429-5113 fax
A trade association representing
"airlines engaged in short and medium
haul scheduled airline transportation
of passengers and cargo, as well as
suppliers of products and services for
the industry."

RV Rental Association
3930 University Drive
Fairfax, VA 22030
703-591-7130
A division of the RV Dealers
Association, this organization
represents companies that rent and
lease recreational vehicles for a variety
of uses including tourism.

Society for the Advancement of Travel
for the Handicapped (SATH)
347 Fifth Avenue
Suite 610
New York, NY 10016
212-447-7284
212-725-8253 fax
An association promoting the needs and
interests of disabled travelers. Provides
information on facilities available to the
disabled in foreign countries.

Society of American Travel Writers
(SATW)
4101 Lake Boone Trail
Suite 201
Raleigh, NC 27607
919-787-5181
919-787-4916 fax
A professional organization for
published travel writers. Conducts
continuing education programs and
upholds the standards of the
profession.

Society of Corporate Meeting
Professionals
1819 Peachtree Street NE
Suite 620
Atlanta, GA 30309
404-355-9932
404-351-3348 fax
A networking and professional
development association for those in
the meeting planning and convention
services field.

Society of Incentive Travel Executives
(SITE)
21 West 38th Street
10th Floor
New York, NY 10018-5584
212-575-0910
212-575-1838 fax

Provides "a network, research, professional development and ethics" to the $5 billion incentive travel industry. Members range from travel agents, to official tourist organizations, to incentive houses, and cruise lines.

Society of Travel Agents in Government (STAG)
6935 Wisconsin Avenue NW
Suite 200
Bethesda, MD 20815
301-654-8595
301-654-6663 fax
STAG describes itself as "a non-profit educational forum [of] travel agencies, suppliers, federal and other government travel managers and contractors throughout the U.S." Government travel is a $15 billion market, according to STAG.

Tourism Industry Association of Canada (TIAC)
130 Albert Street
Suite 1016
Ottawa, ON K1P 5G4
CANADA
613-238-3883
613-238-3878 fax
A lobbying group representing the interests of the tourism industry to all levels of Canadian government.

Tourism Works for America Council
1133 21st Street NW
Suite 800
Washington, DC 20036
202-293-1433
An industry coalition that promotes and publicizes the economic contribution of travel and tourism.

Trade Show Exhibitors Association (TSEA)
5501 Backlick Road
Suite 105
Springfield, VA 22151
703-941-3725
703-941-8275 fax
An association "representing exhibit marketing managers domestically and abroad." Offers educational and informational services, sponsors a

certification program and an annual trade show.

Travel Agents of Suffolk County (TASC)
P.O. Box 49
Bohemia, NY 11716
516-363-9522
A professional and networking association of travel agents on Long Island, NY.

Travel Agents of the Carolinas
P.O. Box 99398
Raleigh, NC 27624-9398
919-676-0400
919-676-8211 fax
A regional association of travel agencies.

Travel and Tourism Government Affairs Council
1100 New York Avenue NW
Suite 450
Washington, DC 20005-3934
202-408-9600
202-408-1255 fax
ASTA, the National Tour Association, and other trade groups comprise the membership of this lobbying group, affiliated with the Travel Industry Association of America (see below), that represents the official position of the travel industry to Congress.

Travel and Tourism Research Association (TTRA)
546 East Main Street
Lexington, KY 40508
606-226-4344
606-226-4355 fax
The goal of this association is "to increase the quality, value, effectiveness and use of research in travel marketing, planning and development . . . by bringing together both producers and users of information in the travel and tourism field."

Travel Industry Association of America (TIAA)
1100 New York Avenue NW
Suite 450
Washington, DC 20005-3934

202-408-8422
202-408-1255 fax
Promotes travel to and within the
United States. Membership consists of
hotels, attractions, state travel
councils, and other members of the
travel industry. Publishes a useful
series of special reports and directories.

Travel Information Service (TIS)

215-456-9600
A public relations service of an
internationally known hospital
dispensing accessibility information, by
phone only, for disabled travelers on
tourist attractions, accommodations,
and places of interest.

Travel South USA
3400 Peachtree Road NE
Atlanta, GA 30326
404-231-1790
404-231-2364 fax
Promotes travel to and within eleven
Southern states. Sponsors periodic
"Showcases" in which travel buyers
meet with Southern suppliers.

United Motorcoach Association
113 South West Street
Alexandria, VA 22314
703-838-2929
703-838-2950

United States Tour Operator's
Association (USTOA)
342 Madison Avenue
Suite 1522
New York, NY 10173
212-599-6599
212-599-6744 fax
A trade association of many of the
larger tour operators, including such
heavyweights as Colette, Contiki and
Globus. Represents the interests of the
industry and insures travelers against
member default.

United States Travel Data Center
(USTDC)
1100 New York Avenue NW
Suite 450
Washington, DC 20005

202-408-1832
202-408-1255
The research arm of the Travel
Industry Association of America.
Publishes informative reports on the
economics of and trends in travel and
tourism.

Universal Federation of Travel Agents
Associations (UFTAA)
Avenue du Prince Hereditaire Albert
Stade Louis II - Entree H
MC-98000
MONACO
011-33-92-052829
011-33-92-052987 fax
An association of travel agency
organizations, individual travel
agencies, and tourism enterprises from
81 countries. Promotes ethical conduct
and helps members collect
commissions.

Vacation Rental Managers Association
P.O. Box 1202
Santa Cruz, CA 95061-1202
408-458-3573
408-458-3637 fax
This association was formed to
"increase awareness of vacation rental
lodging and enhance members'
business through education,
professional standards, marketing,
political involvement and networking."
Publishes a free directory of members.

Women's Travellers Center and
Information Bank (WTCIB)
3918 W Street NW
Washington, DC 20007
202-333-9696
202-337-9096 fax

World Association of Travel Agencies
(WATA)
37, rue Ferrier
1202 Geneve
SWITZERLAND
011-41-22-731-4760
011-41-22-732-8161 fax
WATA exists "to bring local (preferably
privately-owned) travel agencies into
an international network." They have
196 members in 83 countries.

World Federation of Travel Writers
(FIJET)
1 Ballinswood Road
Atlantic Highlands, NJ 07716
908-291-2840
908-291-9272
An association of travel writers and
columnists in 40 countries.

World Tourism Organization
Calle Capitan Haya 42
E-28020 Madrid
SPAIN
011-34-1-571-0628
011-34-1-571-3733 fax
"Promotes tourism and its contribution
to economic development, international
understanding, peace, and prosperity."

World Travel and Tourism Council
(WTTC)
181 Chausée de la Hulpe, Box 10
1170 Brussels
BELGIUM
011-32-2-6602067
011-32-2-6609170 fax
"A global coalition of 70 chief executive
officers from all sectors of the travel
and tourism industry. Its goals are to
convince governments of the strategic
and economic importance of travel and
tourism [and] promote environmentally
compatible development."

Part Three:

Reference
Section
&
Bibliography

Getting Passports & Visas

United States government travel booklets and documents advise readers to ask their travel agent what documentation — passport, etc. — is needed for the countries they plan to visit. Amazingly, only ten percent of American citizens have passports. So you'd better be prepared to advise your clients on such matters. You'll also want to be able to direct them if they ask for your help in obtaining a passport or visa.

U.S. citizens bound for foreign lands must get a passport or other proof of citizenship (see below) before they go. They may also need a tourist card or visa. Like passports, many visas must be acquired before a citizen leaves the U.S.; tourist cards, however, are issued by the foreign nation's Customs when the tourist enters the country. Here are some guidelines on getting passports and visas:

Passports

Most countries, including the U.S., require travelers to prove their identity and citizenship when they enter or leave the country. The most common proof is a valid passport. Travelers have to show one in order to get their boarding passes for most international flights.

Note: U.S. citizens do not need passports to visit Mexico, Canada, and some Caribbean countries; they merely need valid proofs of citizenship and identity. A valid driver's license or government ID card plus an expired passport, a certified copy of a U.S. birth certificate, a Certificate of Naturalization or a Certificate of Citizenship will do. However, your clients might be well advised to take a passport anyway, because a valid U.S. passport is the best proof of citizenship and identity for U.S. citizens.

Getting a first passport

Know where to apply. U.S. citizens who are 13 or older must apply in person to get their first passport. Passports are issued by 13 U.S. passport agencies (see below) and thousands of U.S. post offices and federal or state courts. To find the office nearest you, check the government listings in your telephone book. This information is also available on the Internet at the State Department's Passport Services home page. The URL is

http://travel.state.gov.passport_services.html

A parent or legal guardian must accompany 13- to 18-year old applicants. Children under 13 needn't apply in person; they can be represented by their parent or legal guardian. The adult must simply bring the required photos and documentation (see below).

What to bring. Passport applicants have to prove their identity and citizenship. To prove identity, they may use:

- A valid driver's license,
- A military or government ID card (federal, state, or local), or
- A certificate of naturalization or citizenship — provided that the document contains their signature and a photo or physical description that readily identifies them.

Note that any document that has been altered or changed in any manner is unacceptable. Ditto for Social Security cards, credit cards, or any temporary or expired ID card or driver's license.

As proof of citizenship, the passport office will accept any of the following:

- A certified copy of a U.S. birth certificate, bearing the registrar's signature and a raised, impressed, embossed or multicolored seal. Such certificates are normally available from the Bureau of Vital Statistics in the city, state, county, or territory where you were born.
- A Certificate of Naturalization.
- A Certificate of Citizenship.
- A Report of Birth Abroad of a Citizen of the United States of America (Form FS-240).
- A Certification of Birth (Form FS-545 or DS-1350).

If your client was born in the U.S. but has no birth certificate — because, say, the courthouse where it was filed burned down or she was a foundling and her adoption papers were mishandled — she or he may submit a notice from a state registrar stating that no birth record exists, along with the best secondary evidence possible. That might be a baptismal certificate, a hospital birth record, affidavits of persons having personal knowledge of the facts of the birth, or other documentary evidence, such as school records or newspaper files. Personal knowledge affidavits must be supported by at least one public record reflecting birth in the U.S., the State Department says.

Along with proofs of identity and citizenship, applicants need:

- A completed, but unsigned, passport application (DSP-11). Passport applications may be downloaded from the State

Department's Passport Services home page (see above).

- Two identical photos of themselves that are recent enough to be good likenesses. The State Department has very specific regulations about the size of the photos and the image. These are posted at just about any place that takes passport photos. Most vending machine prints are not acceptable for passport use, so your clients should plan on going to a local photo shop.

Note: Dress is important. State Department regulations require a person to appear hatless, in street clothes, and without dark glasses in passport photos (unless dark glasses must be worn for medical reasons or head coverings for religious reasons).

- The fee — $65 for applicants 18 and over; $40 for applicants younger than 18. The former are issued passports good for 10 years, the latter, for 5 years. Passport offices accept checks, bank drafts, and money orders in payment of the fee. Passport agencies and post offices accept cash in the exact amount of the fee, but court houses are not required to do so. Check before applying.

Getting subsequent passports

Once you have a passport, you may apply in person or by mail for a renewal, provided all of the following are true:

- You were issued your previous passport within the past 12 years.
- You can submit your previous passport with your new application.
- Your previous passport was issued on or after your 18th birthday.
- You use the same name as that on your previous passport or you have had your name changed by marriage or court order and can submit the original or certified copy of the court order or marriage certificate showing the change of name.

Failing any of the above, you must apply for your new passport in person.

To apply by mail, your client should:

- Obtain Form DSP-82, Application for Passport by Mail, from a passport office or agency.
- Complete the application, then sign and date it.
- Include the date of departure. Passport agents will otherwise assume that the applicant's trip is not imminent and will process the application in two to three weeks (or

sometimes longer in the rush summer season).

- Enclose the previous passport, two identical 2x2-inch photos that meet passport requirements, and a $55 fee. Applicants may pay the fee by bank draft, cashier's check, money order or certified, personal, or travelers check. They should not send cash.
- If your client has changed his or her name since the old passport was issued, an original or certified copy of the court order — or marriage or divorce certificate — that shows the change of name must also be included.
- Mail the above to one of the 13 passport offices listed on page 217.

Advise your clients to sign their new passports as soon as they get them and also fill in the personal notification data page. The old passport and the documents they submitted with their application will be returned with the new passport.

Note: Lost or stolen passports should be reported immediately. If lost or stolen in the U.S., report them to Passport Services, Department of State, 1425 K St., NW, Washington, DC 20524 or your local passport agency. If lost abroad, inform the local police and nearest U.S. embassy or consulate.

Advise clients to follow the State Department's recommendation that they photocopy the data page of their passports before traveling abroad. It suggests that travelers make two copies — one to carry along on their trip (stashed separately from their passports) and one to leave in the U.S. with a relative or friend. State Department officials say that information speeds up the replacement process considerably should the passport be lost or stolen.

To change the name on a valid passport, advise clients to pick up or send for Form DSP-19, Passport Amendment/Validation Application. They simply submit it, along with their passport and certified proof of the name change (an original marriage certificate, divorce decree, or certified court order) to the nearest passport agency. There is no fee for this service. The original documents are returned with the amended passport.

Getting a passport in a hurry

Suppose your client is all set to travel abroad and suddenly discovers that his passport has expired or will expire before he gets back. Or suppose that you are journeying to countries that require a visa and you've got less than six months left before your passport expires. Some countries won't place a visa in a passport with less than six months of validity. What do you do?

Passport agencies will expedite issuance in cases of genuine, documented emergencies. If you are leaving within five days and need a passport, you can pay to have it delivered to you by express mail — provided you arrange and pay for this service in advance. Your local passport agency can give you the details.

Note: As a service to your clients, you may wish to lay in a small supply of passport forms DSP-11 (for initial applications), DSP-82 (for renewals), and DSP-19 (for name changes). You can get them from either a local passport office or the nearest passport agency (see below).

Getting more information

The cheapest way to get more information or answers to your questions is on the Passport Services home page, mentioned earlier. If you do not have access to the Internet, or if your visit to the home page did not answer your specific question, you can get help by telephone — for a fee.

The National Passport Information Center (NPIC) is now the only source of telephone information about passports. You can visit one of the Passport Agencies listed below in person with your questions, but you can't phone them. You can request an application, get additional information, or check on the status of an application by calling 1-900-225-5674. Between 8 a.m. and 8 p.m. Eastern Standard Time you can speak with an operator; otherwise, you will be connected to an automated attendant. The cost is $0.35 per minute for the automated system and $1.05 per minute for a live operator.

If 900 number access has been blocked from your phone, you can call 1-888-362-8668. The fee is a flat $4.95 per call, which must be charged to a credit card.

Passport agencies

Boston Passport Agency
Thomas P. O'Neill Federal Building
Room 247
10 Causeway Street
Boston, MA 02222-1094

Chicago Passport Agency
Kluczynski Federal Building
Suite 380
230 South Dearborn Street
Chicago, IL 60604-1564

Honolulu Passport Agency
First Hawaii Tower
Suite 500
1132 Bishop Street
Honolulu, HI 96813-2809

Houston Passport Agency
Mickey Leland Federal Building
Suite 1100
1919 Smith Street
Houston, TX 77002-8049

Los Angeles Passport Agency
11000 Wilshire Boulevard
Room 13100
Los Angeles, CA 90024-3615

Miami Passport Agency
Claude Pepper Federal Office Building
3rd Floor
51 Southwest First Avenue
Miami, FL 33130-1680

New Orleans Passport Agency
Postal Services Building
701 Loyola Avenue
Room T-12005
New Orleans, LA 70113-1931

New York Passport Agency
Rockefeller Center
Room 270
630 Fifth Avenue
New York, NY 10111-0031
212-399-5290
(This number is to be used only to
make an appointment by residents of
the New York City area who are
traveling in less than 14 days.)

Philadelphia Passport Agency
U.S. Customs House
Room 103
200 Chestnut Street
Philadelphia, PA 19106-2970

San Francisco Passport Agency
95 Hawthorne Street
5th Floor
San Francisco, CA 94105-3901

Seattle Passport Agency
Federal Office Building
Room 992
915 Second Avenue
Seattle, WA 98174-1091

Stamford Passport Agency
One Landmark Square
Broad and Atlantic Streets
Stamford, CT 06901-2667

Washington Passport Agency
1111 19th Street NW
Washington, DC 20522-1705

Getting visas

Many of the countries that U.S. citizens visit most frequently require no special advance warning that your clients are coming. The traveler simply shows his or her passport on arrival and is welcomed as a tourist for a visit of anywhere from one week to a year.

Other countries like to keep closer tabs on who is visiting their country. To do this, they require that prospective visitors obtain a visa before leaving home. Some countries require visas of U.S. citizens because the U.S. requires them of their citizens. For some countries, visas are no doubt another way of levying a tax on foreigners and getting some hard currency in the process.

A visa is the vehicle whereby a country grants formal permission for a specific individual to enter for a specific purpose and stay for a predetermined period of time. At the end of that time, or before, the visitor must get an extension, leave the country, or face penalties, which can range from the inconvenient to the uncomfortable, depending on the host country's tolerance for foreigners.

Types of visas include:

- Tourist visas.
- Transit visas.
- Business or commercial visas.
- Student visas.
- Residence visas.
- Diplomatic visas.

Usually, your clients will need tourist or transit visas; less frequently they may need business or student visas.

Most frequently, a visa takes the form a rubber stamp placed in a passport by a foreign government. Less frequently, the traveler might also be required to carry additional documents during the visit. When required, visas should be obtained before leaving the U.S., although some countries allow visitors to acquire the necessary documentation at the border.

Most countries that do not require a visa for a short stay by a tourist — and the definition of "short" varies widely from country to country — will require a visa for longer stays. Generally speaking, if your client plans to stay more than 15 days in a country, it's a good idea to check the country's visa requirements. Sometimes a visa for a lengthier stay can be obtained in the foreign country. However, it will usually be easier to take care of the paperwork before leaving.

Procedures for obtaining visas

Applying for a visa is usually a quick and easy procedure. However, you should be aware that getting visas for some obscure countries or even getting permission to travel in remote areas of more open countries can be an adventure in itself.

Needless to say, procedures vary from country to country. Among the things you will most likely need are:

- A completed application form (or forms).
- Passport sized photos.
- A check or money order for the correct amount of the visa fee.
- Your U.S. passport, in which the visa will be placed.
- A return postage certificate, typically certified (to insure the safe return of your passport).

You may also be required to produce one or more of the following pieces of documentation:

- Proof of vaccinations for or immunizations against specific diseases.
- Proof that you have a return ticket.
- Proof that you have sufficient funds, which might take the form of a letter from your bank or a line of credit.

- A letter from your employer, detailing the purpose of your visit, if this is a business trip.

If at all possible it is best to apply for a visa in person at either the embassy in Washington, DC (where all embassies are located), or at a consulate. If you are not in or near Washington, you might find a consulate in your own city or one nearby. A consulate is simply a branch office of the embassy. Consulates tend to be located in major cities, or in cities where the foreign country does a great deal of business.

You will also find consulates in cities in which there is a large population with blood ties to the foreign country. For example, Portugal has a consulate in New Bedford, MA, and Sweden has one in Bloomington, MN, reflecting the immigration of Portuguese and Swedes to these regions.

If you are near New York City, you also might be able to obtain a visa from the offices of the country's Mission to the United Nations. Some, but not all of these offices, provide consular services.

Remember that passport agencies cannot help your clients obtain visas. They have to apply directly to the consular section of the embassy, the nearest consulate, or permanent mission to the U.N. of the countries they plan to visit.

In the section titled *Sources of Tourist Information: International*, you will find a listing of countries, their embassies, and cities in which their consulates are located. This section also provides brief information about visa requirements (at press time) for short tourist visits. For stays of over 15 days, or when in doubt, it is always wise to doublecheck with the embassy or consulate.

The State Department publishes an extremely helpful publication, *Foreign Entry Requirements* (Publication M-264), updated annually, which is available for fifty cents from the Consumer Information Center, Pueblo, CO 81009. It is also posted on the Internet at http://travel.state.gov/foreignentryreqs.html. You may want to have this information on hand so as to better advise your clients about visa requirements for countries they may wish to explore.

Time Zones at a Glance

From time to time, you will find it helpful to know what time it is in Hong Kong. Or Paris. Or wherever. This chart will help you do that. To use it, first locate, in the left column, the country you are interested in. Then find the column for your time zone. Reading from left to right, as you would see them on a map of the United States, they are Pacific Standard Time (PST), Mountain Standard Time (MST), Central Standard Time (CST), and Eastern Standard Time (EST).

The number in the appropriate time zone column opposite the appropriate country will tell you how many hours to add or subtract to determine the corresponding time in the foreign country. An equal sign (=) indicates that there is no difference in time.

For larger countries, which span several time zones, we have listed major cities to assist you in determining the correct local time.

COUNTRY	PST	MST	CST	EST
Albania	+9	+8	+7	+6
Algeria	+9	+8	+7	+6
American Samoa	-3	-4	-5	-6
Andorra	+9	+8	+7	+6
Angola	+9	+8	+7	+6
Antigua	+4	+3	+2	+1
Argentina	+5	+4	+3	+2
Armenia	+12	+11	+10	+9
Aruba	+3	+2	+1	=
Australia				
Sydney, Melbourne	+18	+17	+16	+15
Perth	+16	+15	+14	+13
Austria	+9	+8	+7	+6
Azerbaijan	+12	+11	+10	+9
Bahamas	+3	+2	+1	=
Bahrain	+11	+10	+9	+8
Bangladesh	+14.5	+13.5	+12.5	+11.5
Barbados	+4	+3	+2	+1
Belarus	+10	+9	+8	+7
Belgium	+9	+8	+7	+6

COUNTRY	PST	MST	CST	EST
Belize	+2	+1	=	-1
Benin	+9	+8	+7	+6
Bermuda	+4	+3	+2	+1
Bhutan	+13.5	+12.5	+11.5	+10.5
Bolivia	+4	+3	+2	+1
Bonaire	+4	+3	+2	+1
Bosnia	+9	+8	+7	+6
Botswana	+10	+9	+8	+7
Brazil	+5	+4	+3	+2
British Virgin Is.	+3	+2	+1	=
British W. Indies	+3	+2	+1	=
Brunei	+16	+15	+14	+13
Bulgaria	+10	+9	+8	+7
Burkina Faso	+8	+7	+6	+5
Burundi	+10	+9	+8	+7
Cambodia	+15	+14	+13	+12
Cameroon	+9	+8	+7	+6
Canada				
St. Johns	+4.5	+3.5	+2.5	+1.5
Toronto, Quebec	+3	+2	+1	=
Winnipeg	+2	+1	=	-1
Calgary	+1	=	-1	-2
Vancouver	=	-1	-2	-3
Cape Verde	+7	+6	+5	+4
Cayman Islands	+3	+2	+1	=
Central African Rep.	+9	+8	+7	+6
Chad	+9	+8	+7	+6
Chile	+4	+3	+2	+1
China (People's Rep.)	+16	+15	+14	+13
Colombia	+3	+2	+1	=
Comoros Islands	+11	+10	+9	+8
Congo	+9	+8	+7	+6
Cook Islands	-2	-3	-4	-5
Costa Rica	+2	+1	=	-1
Cote D'Ivoire	+8	+7	+6	+5
Croatia	+9	+8	+7	+6
Cuba	+3	+2	+1	=
Curaçao	+4	+3	+2	+1
Cyprus	+10	+9	+8	+7
Czech Republic	+9	+8	+7	+6
Denmark	+9	+8	+7	+6
Djibouti	+11	+10	+9	+8
Dominica	+4	+3	+2	+1

COUNTRY	PST	MST	CST	EST
Dominican Republic	+4	+3	+2	+1
Ecuador	+3	+2	+1	=
Egypt	+10	+9	+8	+7
El Salvador	+2	+1	=	-1
Equatorial Guinea	+9	+8	+7	+6
Eritrea	+11	+10	+9	+8
Estonia	+10	+9	+8	+7
Ethiopia	+11	+10	+9	+8
Fiji	+20	+19	+18	+17
Finland	+10	+9	+8	+7
France	+9	+8	+7	+6
French Guiana	+5	+4	+3	+2
French Polynesia	-2	-3	-4	-5
French West Indies	+4	+3	+2	+1
Gabon	+9	+8	+7	+6
Galapagos Islands	+2	+1	=	-1
Gambia	+8	+7	+6	+5
Georgia	+12	+11	+10	+9
Germany	+9	+8	+7	+6
Ghana	+8	+7	+6	+5
Gibraltar	+9	+8	+7	+6
Greece	+10	+9	+8	+7
Greenland	+5	+4	+3	+2
Grenada	+4	+3	+2	+1
Guadeloupe	+4	+3	+2	+1
Guatemala	+2	+1	=	-1
Guinea	+8	+7	+6	+5
Guinea-Bissau	+8	+7	+6	+5
Guyana	+4	+3	+2	+1
Haiti	+3	+2	+1	=
Honduras	+2	+1	=	-1
Hong Kong	+16	+15	+14	+13
Hungary	+9	+8	+7	+6
Iceland	+8	+7	+6	+5
India	+13.5	+12.5	+11.5	+10.5
Indonesia	+15	+14	+13	+12
Iran	+11.5	+10.5	+9.5	+8.5
Iraq	+11	+10	+9	+8
Ireland	+8	+7	+6	+5
Israel	+10	+9	+8	+7
Italy	+9	+8	+7	+6
Jamaica	+3	+2	+1	=
Japan	+17	+16	+15	+14

COUNTRY	PST	MST	CST	EST
Jordan	+10	+9	+8	+7
Kazakhstan	+14	+13	+12	+11
Kenya	+11	+10	+9	+8
Kiribati	-3	-4	-5	-6
Korea, North & South	+17	+16	+15	+14
Kuwait	+11	+10	+9	+8
Kyrgyz Republic	+14	+13	+12	+11
Laos	+16	+15	+14	+13
Latvia	+10	+9	+8	+7
Lebanon	+10	+9	+8	+7
Lesotho	+10	+9	+8	+7
Liberia	+8	+7	+6	+5
Libya	+9	+8	+7	+6
Liechtenstein	+9	+8	+7	+6
Lithuania	+10	+9	+8	+7
Luxembourg	+9	+8	+7	+6
Macau	+16	+15	+14	+13
Macedonia	+9	+8	+7	+6
Madagascar	+11	+10	+9	+8
Malawi	+10	+9	+8	+7
Malaysia	+16	+15	+14	+13
Maldives	+13	+12	+11	+10
Mali	+8	+7	+6	+5
Malta	+9	+8	+7	+6
Marshall Islands	+20	+19	+18	+17
Martinique	+4	+3	+2	+1
Mauritania	+8	+7	+6	+5
Mauritius	+12	+11	+10	+9
Mexico				
Cancun, Mex. City	+2	+1	=	-1
La Paz	+1	=	-1	-2
Micronesia	+18	+17	+16	+15
Moldova	+10	+9	+8	+7
Monaco	+9	+8	+7	+6
Mongolia	+16	+15	+14	+13
Morocco	+8	+7	+6	+5
Mozambique	+10	+9	+8	+7
Myanmar	+14.5	+13.5	+12.5	+11.5
Namibia	+10	+9	+8	+7
Nauru	+20	+19	+18	+17
Nepal	+13.5	+12.5	+11.5	+10.5
Netherlands	+9	+8	+7	+6
Netherlands Antilles	+4	+3	+2	+1

COUNTRY	PST	MST	CST	EST
New Zealand	+20	+19	+18	+17
Nicaragua	+2	+1	=	-1
Niger	+9	+8	+7	+6
Nigeria	+9	+8	+7	+6
Norway	+9	+8	+7	+6
Oman	+12	+11	+10	+9
Pakistan	+13	+12	+11	+10
Palau, Republic of	+17	+16	+15	+14
Panama	+3	+2	+1	=
Papua New Guinea	+18	+17	+16	+15
Paraguay	+4	+3	+2	+1
Peru	+3	+2	+1	=
Philippines	+16	+15	+14	+13
Poland	+9	+8	+7	+6
Portugal	+8	+7	+6	+5
Qatar	+11	+10	+9	+8
Romania	+10	+9	+8	+7
Russia				
Moscow	+11	+10	+9	+8
Vladivostok	+15	+14	+13	+12
Rwanda	+10	+9	+8	+7
St. Kitts & Nevis	+4	+3	+2	+1
St. Lucia	+4	+3	+2	+1
St. Maarten	+4	+3	+2	+1
St. Martin	+4	+3	+2	+1
St. Vincent	+4	+3	+2	+1
San Marino	+9	+8	+7	+6
Sao Tome & Principe	+9	+8	+7	+6
Saudi Arabia	+11	+10	+9	+8
Senegal	+8	+7	+6	+5
Serbia & Montenegro	+9	+8	+7	+6
Seychelles	+12	+11	+10	+9
Sierra Leone	+8	+7	+6	+5
Singapore	+16	+15	+14	+13
Slovak Republic	+9	+8	+7	+6
Slovenia	+9	+8	+7	+6
Solomon Islands	+19	+18	+17	+16
Somalia	+11	+10	+9	+8
South Africa	+10	+9	+8	+7
Spain	+9	+8	+7	+6
Sri Lanka	+13.5	+12.5	+11.5	+10.5
Sudan	+10	+9	+8	+7
Suriname	+5	+4	+3	+2

COUNTRY	PST	MST	CST	EST
Swaziland	+10	+9	+8	+7
Sweden	+9	+8	+7	+6
Switzerland	+9	+8	+7	+6
Syria	+11	+10	+9	+8
Tahiti	-2	-3	-4	-5
Taiwan	+16	+15	+14	+13
Tajikistan	+14	+13	+12	+11
Tanzania	+11	+10	+9	+8
Thailand	+16	+15	+14	+13
Togo	+8	+7	+6	+5
Tonga	+21	+20	+19	+18
Trinidad & Tobago	+4	+3	+2	+1
Tunisia	+9	+8	+7	+6
Turkey	+10	+9	+8	+7
Turkmenistan	+13	+12	+11	+10
Turks & Caicos	+3	+2	+1	=
Tuvalu	+20	+19	+18	+17
Uganda	+11	+10	+9	+8
Ukraine	+10	+9	+8	+7
United Arab Emirates	+12	+11	+10	+9
United Kingdom	+8	+7	+6	+5
Uruguay	+5	+4	+3	+2
Uzbekistan	+13	+12	+11	+10
Vanuatu	+19	+18	+17	+16
Venezuela	+4	+3	+2	+1
Vietnam	+16	+15	+14	+13
Western Samoa	-3	-4	-5	-6
Yemen	+11	+10	+9	+8
Zaire				
Kinshasa	+9	+8	+7	+6
Kisangani	+10	+9	+8	+7
Zambia	+10	+9	+8	+7
Zimbabwe	+10	+9	+8	+7

Note: Many countries adopt "daylight savings" time (or its equivalent) for a part of each year. Be aware that the starting and stopping dates vary from country to country. The time differences shown above apply to standard time in both the U.S. and the applicable country. Tourist information sources can tell you if and when daylight savings time applies in a given country.

Glossary of Travel-Related Terms & Abbreviations

This glossary is intended to serve as a ready reference for all the varied and sundry bits of industry jargon, CRS abbreviations, and organizational acronyms you might come across in the course of your business as a travel agent.

We have not attempted to define the thousands of geographical terms that you might come across from time to time; specialized geographical dictionaries exist should you want to expand your knowledge in that area.

Abbreviations used

The following abbreviations are used in this glossary:

Abr.   Abbreviation.
adj.   Adjective.
Brit.   British English.
CRS.   Code used in computerized reservation systems.
Fr.   French.
Ger.   German.
It.   Italian.
Lat.   Latin.
n.   Noun.
Sp.   Spanish.
qv   See separate entry.
v.   Verb

—A a

A. *CRS.* 1. Availability; will display flights with seats available. 2. An arunk (qv) or surface segment of a trip. 3. American plan (qv). 4. Code for a class of service, usually superior.

a la carte. *Fr.* Literally, "from the menu." Indicates that each dish ordered will have a separate price. Also, used in tour literature to indicate a choice of dishes will be available.

AA. 1. American Airlines. 2. Alcoholics Anonymous.

AAA. American Automobile Association.

AAAE. American Association of Airport Executives.

AAD. *CRS.* Agent automated deduction.

AAR. Association of American Railroads.

AARP. American Association of Retired Persons.

AATTA. African-American Travel and Tourism Association.

ABA. American Bus Association.

ABC. 1. *CRS.* Advanced booking charters. 2. *Slang.* The islands of the Netherlands Antilles — Aruba, Bonaire, and Curaçao.

abeam. Off to the side of a ship or at right angles to its length.

above board. On a cruise ship, cabins above water level.

ABTA. Association of British Travel Agents.

AC. 1. *Abr.* Alternating current. 2. *CRS.* Access card.

a/c. *Abr.* 1. Air conditioned. 2. Additional collection.

acceleration clause. A provision in a promissory note (qv) calling for the immediate payment of the balance in the event of a default (qv) by the borrower.

access code. Password to gain entry into a computer or a computer file.

ACCL. American Canadian Caribbean Line.

accommodation. Any seat, berth, room, or service sold to a passenger.

accommodation ladder. A portable, external ladder on the side of a ship, used for shore or tender (qv) access.

accountable document. Any piece of paper that, when validated by a travel agency, has a monetary value and which must be accounted for to the ARC (qv).

accreditation. Approval given by various trade associations to a travel agency allowing the sale of tickets and other accommodations.

accrual method. An accounting system in which the recording of income and expenses is adjusted to reflect the time periods to which they apply, as opposed to the time monies were received or disbursed. *See also* cash method.

ACI. Assist Card International.

ACI-NA. Airports Council International, North America.

ACK. *CRS.* Acknowledge.

ACON. *CRS.* Air conditioned.

ACRA. American Car Rental Association.

acrophobia. Fear of heights.

ACTA. Alliance of Canadian Travel Associations.

ACTE. Association of Corporate Travel Executives.

actual flying time. Total time spent in the air, as opposed to scheduled flight time or time spent waiting on the ground.

ACV. *Abr.* Air cushioned vehicle. Hovercraft (qv).

AD. 1. *CRS.* Agent's discount. When followed by a number, indicates the percentage amount of the discount. For example: AD75 indicates a discount to travel agents of 75% off unrestricted coach fares. 2. *Abr. Lat.* Anno Domini, "year of our Lord."

ad hoc. *Lat.* Of tours, put together on a customized or one-time basis, usually from existing options.

ADB. *CRS.* 1. Advise if duplicate booking. 2. Air discount bulletin.

add/coll. *Abr.* Additional collection.

add-on fare. Amount added to a gateway fare (qv) to arrive at a through fare (qv). Sometimes called a proportional fare.

add-on(s). Anything optional purchased by a passenger, as in tour arrangements.

adiabatic rate. Rule of thumb which holds that temperature decreases as altitude increases (3.5°F per 1,000 ft.).

adjoining rooms. Hotel rooms which, while next to each other, have no connecting doors. *See also* connecting rooms.

ADNO. *CRS.* Advise if not okay.

ADOA. *CRS.* Advise on arrival.

ADR. *CRS.* Average daily rate.

ADT. *Abr.* Atlantic Daylight Time; Alaska Daylight Time.

ADTK. *CRS.* Advise if ticketed.

aduane. *Fr.* Customs.

ADV. *CRS.* Advise.

advertised tour. Specifically, a travel package meeting the airline requirements needed to be assigned an IT (inclusive tour) number.

ADVN. *CRS.* Advise as to names.

ADVR. *CRS.* Advise as to rate.

aerospace. Concerning the earth's atmosphere and its immediate environs, as in "Aerospace Museum."

AF. *CRS.* Added phone.

AFA. Association of Flight Attendants.

affinity card. A credit card marketed by a company, charity, or other group in association with the credit card company.

affinity charter. A charter (of an airplane, ship, etc.) arranged by or for an affinity group.

affinity group. A group of people linked by a common bond, such as ethnicity or membership in an organization.

affinity group airfare. A fare set aside specifically for affinity groups.

AFT. *CRS.* Actual flying time (qv).

aft. Toward the rear of a ship.

agency. 1. A legal relationship in which one person acts for another in a business dealing with a third party. 2. A travel agency.

Agency Agreement, The. The contract used by IATAN (qv) to govern its dealings with travel agencies.

agency check. A check drawn on the business account of a travel agency and bearing the agency's name.

agency list. The list maintained by ARC (qv) and IATAN (qv) of appointed travel agencies.

agency manager. The person in a travel agency who holds appointment from ARC (qv), IATA (qv), etc. The person who runs an agency's day-to-day affairs.

agent. 1. A person who represents another to a third party. 2. A travel agent.

agent bypass. The practice of suppliers dealing directly with the public *See also* agentless booking.

agent eligibility list. A list prepared by the travel agency and submitted to ARC (qv) or IATAN (qv) of agency employees eligible for travel benefits. Also referred to as "the ARC list."

Agent Reporting Agreement, The. The contract used by ARC (qv) to govern its dealings with travel agencies.

agent sine. *CRS.* An agent's two-letter personal identification code.

agentless booking. A booking made by a consumer using an automated system and bypassing a travel agent.

agoraphobia. Fear of open spaces or public places.

AGT. *CRS.* Agent.

ahead. In front of the ship's bow.

AHMA. American Hotel and Motel Association.

air courier. A person who accompanies time-sensitive cargo being shipped as passengers' baggage, usually in exchange for a deep discount on the air fare.

air mile. A unit of distance measuring approximately 6,076 feet.

air piracy. The forcible appropriation or hijacking of an aircraft.

air taxi. An aircraft with a limited seating capacity (19 or fewer), operating within a limited range (250 miles).

Air Travel Card. An airline-sponsored credit card, good for airline tickets only. Also known as the Universal Air Travel Plan Card.

air walls. Moveable panels used to subdivide a larger area, such as a hotel ballroom, into smaller rooms.

airdrome. Airport, now generally obsolete.

AIRIMP. *CRS*. ARC/IATAN reservations interline message procedures/passenger.

airline designator. Two- or three-digit alphanumeric code for an air carrier, administered by IATA (qv).

airline plate. A metal plate given to travel agencies by airlines for the purpose of imprinting and thereby validating tickets. *See also* plates.

Airlines Reporting Corporation (ARC). An autonomous corporation created by the domestic airlines. Appoints travel agencies to sell airline tickets and oversees the financial details of tracking payments to airlines and the disbursement of commissions to travel agencies.

airport access fee. The fee paid to an airport management by a car rental company for the privilege of operating its vans and buses on the airport grounds, usually passed on to the consumer.

airport codes. Three-letter codes used to uniquely identify all airports.

airport tax. A local tax imposed on air tickets and passed along to passengers, ostensibly used to fund airport maintenance, expansion, and similar expenditures.

airport transfer. Transportation provided by a tour operator to a passenger from an airport, usually to a hotel.

air/sea. Trips, tickets, or fares that include both air and sea components, as in a cruise package.

airsickness. Nausea or other discomfort caused by the motion of an aircraft.

airworthy. Capable of being flown. Safe, of an aircraft.

aka. *Abr.* Also known as.

alcove. A small section of a room, indented into the wall or otherwise set apart.

all inclusive. One price covers all listed elements of the package.

alleyway. A corridor or passage on a ship.

all-in. *Slang*. All inclusive, as a tour.

allotment. The number of seats, cabins, berths, etc. available for sale by a supplier or agent.

all-terrain vehicle. A one- or two-person motorized vehicle with large wheels designed for recreational use on uneven ground or sand.

aloha. The Hawaiian word for both "hello" and "good-bye."

alongside. Describing a ship when next to a pier or another vessel.

ALPA. Airline Pilots Association.

alphanumeric. Composed of both letters and numbers, as in a record locator number (qv).

alternate distribution system. Any system that bypasses travel agencies in selling travel arrangements. Usually used to refer to the distribution of tickets through personal computers and ETDNs (qv).

altiport. An airport or airstrip in a high, mountainous region.

altitude. Height above sea level.

a.m. *Abr. Lat.* Ante meridian. Morning; between midnight and noon.

Amadeus® . A computerized reservations system (qv).

ambassador. The highest ranking diplomatic representative of one country to the government of another. The executive in charge of an embassy, typically located in the capitol city.

amenities. The facilities and features of a property, usually a hotel.

American plan. A meal plan at a hotel or resort in which three meals a day are included in the price. Sometimes referred to as Full American Plan.

AMEX, AMEXCO. American Express.

amidships. Toward the middle of a ship; the imaginary line that runs down the center of a ship.

amphibious. Capable of operating on land as well as sea.

Amtrak. Trade name of the U. S. National Railroad Passenger Corporation.

amusement park. A recreational attraction featuring mechanical rides and other forms of active entertainment. *See also* theme park.

AN. *CRS.* Added name.

anchor ball. A black ball hoisted over a ship's bow to indicate that it is anchored.

antebellum. Built or in existence prior to the American Civil War. Used primarily to describe historic buildings.

antipodean day. The day gained by crossing the International Date Line (qv). Also, called meridian day.

AP. *Abr.* American plan (qv).

apartheid. The former racist policy of South Africa, mandating the rigid separation of peoples by race.

APEX. *CRS.* Advance purchase excursion fare.

APHIS. Animal and Plant Health Inspection Service.

Apollo. A computerized reservation system owned by United Airlines and the Covia Corp.

appointment. The process whereby an air carrier or other supplier certifies a travel agency to act as its agent.

apres-ski. *Fr.* Any activity that is scheduled after skiing.

APT. *CRS.* Airline passenger tariff.

aqueduct. A bridge-like structure, usually raised, designed to carry water or a canal.

arbiter, travel agent. An individual selected by a committee representing travel agents and air carriers and charged with the responsibility of settling disputes between travel agents and ARC (qv) and enforcing terms of the Agent Reporting Agreement (qv).

arbitrary fare. *See* add-on fare.

arbitration. A method of dispute resolution intended to avoid the high costs of legal action, typically conducted under rules established by the American Arbitration Association.

arbitration clause. A provision in a contract requiring any disputes between the parties involved to be submitted to arbitration, typically under rules established by the American Arbitration Association.

ARC. Airlines Reporting Corporation (qv).

ARC list. A list prepared by a travel agency and submitted to ARC (qv) or IATAN (qv) of agency employees eligible for travel benefits. Also referred to as "the agent eligibility list."

architectural bias. The tendency of a CRS (qv) to make it easier to find and book the flights of its sponsor by virtue of the way the system is designed.

archive. 1. *v.* To store in computerized form, as travel records. 2. *n.* A repository for documents or records.

area bank. *See* Area Settlement Plan.

Area Settlement Plan. System administered by ARC on a regional basis to handle the processing of airline tickets, payments, and the disbursement of commissions to travel agencies. Also referred to as a Bank Settlement Plan.

ARNK. *CRS.* (Pronounced "arunk.") Arrival unknown. Used to indicate the land portion of an air itinerary.

ARR. *CRS.* Arrival.

ARTA. Association of Retail Travel Agents.

articles of incorporation. The formal legal description of a business' activities required for registration by the state.

arunk. Pronunciation of the acronym, ARNK (qv).

AS. *CRS.* Added segment.

ASAP. *Abr.* As soon as possible.

ASC. *CRS.* Advising schedule change.

ASP. *Abr.* Area Settlement Plan.

asset. Any property, real (i.e. real estate), personal, or intellectual (e.g. a trademark or copyright), which has a cash value.

AST. *Abr.* 1. Atlantic Standard Time (qv). 2. Alaska Standard Time.

ASTA. American Society of Travel Agents.

ASTAPAC. ASTA Political Action Committee.

astern. Toward the back of a ship.

asylum. *See* political asylum.

AT. *CRS.* Travel to be via the Atlantic Ocean.

ATA. Air Transport Association.

ATB. *Abr.* Automated ticket/boarding pass. An electronically generated ticket which also includes the boarding pass.

ATC. Air Traffic Conference of America, the predecessor to ARC.

ATFDS. *Abr.* Automated ticket and fare determination system.

Atlantic Standard Time. A Canadian time zone. Also called Provincial Standard Time.

ATM. Automated teller machine.

ATME. Association of Travel Marketing Executives.

ATO. *Abr.* Airline ticket office.

ATP. Airline Tariff Publishing Company.

atrium. A large open space in a building, usually topped by a glass roof, sometimes containing elaborate landscaping and ponds. A popular style of hotel lobby.

ATV. *Abr.* All-terrain vehicle (qv).

ATW. Around the world.

au pair. *Fr.* A young person, usually foreign, hired to provide child care and household help in exchange for room, board, a modest salary, and a chance to learn a new language.

audit. 1. *v.* To examine financial or performance records. 2. *n.* Any such examination.

auditorium style. In a meeting, a configuration in which seats are arranged in rows, facing front, as in a theater.

aurora australis. "The Southern Lights." A colorful geomagnetic and electric display visible near the South Pole.

aurora borealis. "The Northern Lights." The Northern hemisphere's equivalent of the aurora australis.

Australasia. The region including Australia, New Zealand, and the major South Pacific islands.

auto drop PNR. A passenger name record (PNR) that has been flagged for automatic queuing on a CRS.

Autobahn. A network of high-speed superhighways in Germany and other European countries.

automated reservation system. Computerized reservation system (qv).

avail. *Slang.* Availability.

available rooms. In a hotel, the number of rooms actually available for use on a given day, eliminating rooms not available due to damage, repairs, and so forth.

available seat miles. One seat, occupied or not, moved one mile. Used as a measure of airline capacity.

average daily rate. Statistical unit used to measure a hotel's pricing scale. Figure derived by dividing actual daily revenue by the total number of available rooms (qv).

Aviation Trust Fund. A federal reserve of tax monies levied on airline tickets and operations and set aside to improve the U.S. air transportation system.

AVIH. *CRS.* Animal in hold.

AVS. *CRS.* Availability status messages.

AWOL. *Abr.* Absent without leave. Pronounced both as individual letters and as an acronym. Term used to indicate the unauthorized absence of a crew member, as on a cruise ship.

AX. *CRS.* American Express.

— *B b*

B&B. *n.* Bed and breakfast. Traditionally, a private home which takes in guests, with breakfast included in the price of lodging. B&Bs can range from modest homes with one spare room to elaborately restored historic houses with luxury prices. Used increasingly to describe any lodging arrangement that includes breakfast, even in a hotel.

BA. *CRS.* BankAmericard.

back office. *adj.* Describing business activities, such as accounting, that typically take place out of the view of customers.

back to back. Sequential booking of two different tours, so that the traveler has a continuous journey. Also used to describe arrangements in which one group arrives as another departs.

back to back ticketing. A strategy used to reduce the cost of a round trip involving no Saturday stay when the cost of two excursions is less than the cost of one unrestricted fare. For example, if a traveler wants to fly from New York to Denver on Monday and return Thursday, he would purchase two excursions, one from New York to Denver beginning on the Monday and the other from Denver to New York departing on the Thursday. The traveler then uses only the outbound portion of each excursion. The itinerary can be designed in such a way that the return portions of each excursion can be used on another trip. A technically illegal practice discouraged by the airlines. Also called "nested excursions."

backhaul. 1. The movement of an airliner, or other vehicle, from a destination to the point of origin. 2. The shipment of cargo on a returning vehicle.

backwash. 1. A disturbance of the water caused by a ship's propellers turning in reverse. 2. The turbulence caused by the exhaust of a jet plane.

baggage. All of a passenger's or traveler's personal belongings, whether checked or unchecked. *See also* checked baggage and unchecked baggage.

baggage check. The claim check (qv) or receipt, usually numbered, issued to a passenger for his or her luggage.

bait and switch. An illegal sales tactic in which a consumer is lured by a low price only to be told that the "special offer" is no longer available and steered to a higher priced product.

baksheesh. *Arabic.* Literally, "gift." A constant refrain of street beggars, the word is also used to refer to "gifts" or bribes paid to facilitate business.

balance sheet. A financial report detailing a company's assets and liabilities as of a specific date.

balcony. An open-air space or platform off a room. The uppermost level of a theater.

bank rate. The official rate at which currency trades between banks. Usually more favorable that the rate that can be obtained by the traveler from the bank.

bankruptcy. A legal proceeding in which a company seeks protection from its creditors while it either reorganizes in the hope of surviving or liquidates its assets. Thus, a bankrupt company may or may not still be conducting business.

banquet event order. A document providing complete and precise instructions to a hotel for the running of a banquet, meeting, or other event to be held in the hotel. Also called a function sheet.

bar. 1. A retail establishment or a counter in a restaurant which sells or dispenses alcohol. 2. In navigation, a sandbar.

bareboat charter. A charter of a boat or yacht which does not include supplies or crew.

barge. A low draft (qv) vessel, often towed or pushed, used to transport cargo. A vessel designed for use on inland waterways and canals.

barge cruising. Pleasure cruises along canal systems, using converted commercial barges or new vessels built to resemble them.

barometer. A instrument which measures air pressure. Used to forecast weather.

barometric pressure. The density of the atmosphere, which varies according to altitude and weather conditions.

barter. Buying and selling without the exchange of money. Purchasing by means of the exchange of goods or services. Typically, airlines will exchange airline seats for goods or services rendered by various suppliers.

base fare. The fare, as of an airline ticket, before tax has been added. Commissions are calculated on the base fare.

bassinet. A small, portable crib for an infant.

batch mode. A computer operation in which a specific task, ticketing, for example, is performed on a group of records.

BB. *CRS.* Buffet breakfast.

BBML. *CRS.* Baby meal.

BBR. *CRS.* Bank buying rate.

BCHFT. *CRS.* Beachfront.

beam. A measurement of a ship's width at its widest point.

bearing. The compass direction in which a vessel is traveling.

Beaufort Scale. A scientific scale from zero to seventeen measuring wind force.

bed and breakfast. *See* B&B.

bed night. In the hotel industry, a measurement of occupancy. One person for one night.

bedienung. *Ger.* Gratuity included.

bedroom. A railway compartment for two, with toilet and sink.

beeper. A paging device which alerts the user that a telephone message has been received.

bell captain. The person in charge of a shift of a hotel's bellhops (qv).

bellhop. In a hotel, the person who carries a guest's luggage to or from the room and performs sundry other services. The term, short for "bell-hopper," derives from the bell used in hotels to summon someone to carry a guest's luggage.

bellman and **bellstaff.** See "bellhop."

below. *n.* On a ship, any area underneath the main deck.

benchmarking. The practice of studying the methods of an acknowledged leader in an industry as a way of setting standards for one's own operation.

Benelux. Nickname for the area comprised by Belgium, the Netherlands, and Luxembourg.

BEO. *Abr.* Banquet event order (qv).

bereavement fare. A lower airline fare offered to those traveling due to a death or illness in their immediate family.

Bermuda Plan. A hotel arrangement which includes a full breakfast with the room rate.

Bermuda Triangle. A triangular area of the Atlantic whose apices are Bermuda, Miami, and the Lesser Antilles. Reputed to be the site of numerous mysterious disappearances of planes and ships.

berth. 1. A bed on a ship, usually attached to the bulkhead (qv). 2. By extension, a passenger's stateroom. 3. The space on a dock at which a ship or boat is moored. *See also* slip.

beyond rights. *See* freedom rights.

BHC. *CRS.* Backhaul check (qv).

bicentenary. The 200th anniversary.

bidet. A porcelain bathroom fixture, common in European hotels, designed to bathe a woman's external genitalia and for douching.

BIKE. *CRS.* Bicycle.

bilateral agreement. A treaty or other agreement, usually between sovereign nations, detailing their mutual understanding, policies, and obligations on a particular matter, such as trade or airline landing rights.

bilge. The bottommost part of a ship's interior. In seaman's slang, worthless talk.

bilingual. Written in or speaking two languages.

bill of fare. A menu.

binnacle. On a ship, the holder for the compass.

biodegradable. Capable of being broken down into its constituent elements by natural processes. Used to describe "environmentally friendly" products.

biorhythms. The natural cycles of the human body, said to vary from person to person and to be affected by travel. *See also* jet lag.

bird dog. *n.* A person who drums up or brings in business for a travel agency.

bistro. *Fr.* A small restaurant, featuring simple fare, sometimes with entertainment.

black market. Illegal trade, commerce, or currency exchange which evades taxes, governmental oversight, or both.

blacked out. Not available. *See also* blackout dates.

blackout dates, blackout periods. Dates on which tickets or certain fares are not available. Blackout dates usually coincide with holidays and peak travel seasons.

BLCY. *CRS.* Balcony (qv).

blimp. A lighter-than-air airship. Used primarily as an advertising vehicle or a camera platform for sporting events; occasionally used for tourist excursions.

BLND. *CRS.* Passenger is blind.

block(ed) space. *n.* Seats, berths, or rooms set aside for group sale. Also, *v.*, to reserve such space.

board. 1. To get on a plane, train, or ship. 2. Meals, as in a hotel stay.

board of directors setup. Configuration of a meeting room in which chairs are placed around rectangular or oval conference tables.

boarding pass. A ticket-like form or stub, usually containing a seat assignment, issued to a boarding passenger. Serves as an additional check in the boarding process.

boat station. A ship's passenger's assigned space during lifeboat drills or an actual emergency.

boatel. Combining "boat" and "hotel." A motel for boaters.

bodega. *Sp.* A wine cellar. By extension, a winery. In some Spanish speaking countries, a bar or grocery store.

bon voyage. *Fr.* Literally, "good voyage." The traditional farewell for those departing by ship.

bond. A sum of money held in escrow to assure full payment or to indemnify a party against financial loss. An insurance agreement that accomplishes the same ends.

bonded. Protected or guaranteed by a bond.

bonnet. *Brit.* The hood of a car.

booking. A reservation.

booking code. The code used to make a booking on a CRS (qv) for a specific fare. Also called a fare code (qv).

booking fee. The charge levied by a CRS on a supplier for handling a reservation.

boot. *Brit.* The trunk of a car.

booth. An exhibit area at a trade show. A covered-over stall in a market.

bottom line. The net profit or result in a transaction. By extension, the final word or the outcome.

boutique hotel. A small property, typically offering an enhanced level of service and marketed to the affluent.

boutique operation. Any business venture that seeks to provide an enhanced level of service, at a premium price, to a select clientele.

bow. The front of a ship.

BP. *CRS.* Breakfast plan or Bermuda Plan (qv).

BPR. *CRS.* Boarding Pass Reserved or Boarding Pre-Reserved. A boarding pass with seating assignment arranged at the time of booking.

brasserie. *Fr.* A restaurant serving hearty fare, usually with a liquor and coffee bar.

breakdown. The process of clearing and cleaning a meeting room, as in a hotel, after a function.

break-even point. The dollar figure at which an enterprise begins to show a profit. The amount of sales that must be reached for a project to become worthwhile.

break-out room. A smaller room, near a larger meeting room, for use when a larger group breaks into sections.

bridge. On a ship, the navigational center. Where the captain stands.

bridge officers. On a cruise ship, the personnel charged with the navigation of the ship.

briefing. An informational talk, usually given to those with a professional need to know the information being dispensed.

briefing tour. A tour, usually for travel agents and other industry personnel, intended to acquaint them with a new destination or new procedures.

brioche. *Fr.* A type of breakfast roll.

Brit. *Slang.* A Briton. A citizen of the British Isles.

Britannia. The mythical female personification of Britain.

BritRail. British Railways.

brochure. Any piece of promotional literature.

brown bagging. Bringing one's own food. In a restaurant, bringing wine or liquor when the restaurant is not licensed to serve alcohol.

browser. A software program enabling users to navigate the World Wide Web and the Internet.

BSI. *CRS.* Basic Sine In.

BSO. *CRS.* Basic Sine Out.

BSP. *CRS.* Bank Settlement Plan. *See* Area Settlement Plan.

BTD. Business Travel Department, usually of a large corporation.

BTH. *CRS.* Bath.

bubble car. A train car with a domed plexiglass top for sightseeing. Also called a dome car (qv).

bucket shop. *Brit. slang.* A consolidator (qv). Any retail outlet dealing in discounted airfares.

budget. 1. *adj.* Accommodations, tours, restaurants, etc. which are low in price and appeal to the frugal traveler. 2. A written plan outlining limits on expenditures. 3. *v.* To cost out an itinerary or trip.

budget fare. Any of a number of heavily restricted airline fares offering a substantial discount off the normal fare (qv).

buffer zone. 1. A demilitarized zone between two countries, intended to decrease the likelihood of hostilities. 2. An imaginary area extending 225 miles north and south of the United States border. Flights within this area are subject to US tax.

buffet. A serve-yourself meal featuring several choices in each course.

bug. A defect or malfunction in a computer program. By extension, any glitch in a system.

bulk contract. An agreement whereby an airline sells large blocks of seats at a discount for resale by a third party.

bulk fare. A fare available only when buying blocks of seats.

bulk mail. A US Post Office category of presorted third-class mail mailed at a special low rate.

bulkhead. The walls on a ship or airplane, dividing the vessel into sections or compartments.

bulkhead seats. On an airplane, the seats immediately aft (qv) of a bulkhead, usually with limited legroom.

bumping. The practice of denying seats, usually on an airline, to ticketed passengers due to overbooking or in favor of other passengers with a higher priority.

bungalow. A cottage. A small house. In hotels, a room or suite that is a separate building.

buoy. A floating navigational marker, used to mark channels or warn of danger.

-burg. *Ger. suffix.* A fortified place. A medieval city.

burgher. A resident of a town. A solid citizen.

burgomaster. In several European countries, a mayor or chief magistrate of a town.

burro. A small pack animal, a donkey.

bus. 1. *n.* A multi-seated vehicle used for inter- and intracity transportation. Sometimes called a "motorcoach," especially when specially designed for carrying tourists. 2. *v.* To transport by bus. 3. *v.* To clear tables, as in a restaurant.

busboy. A low-level restaurant employee who clears tables, serves water, etc. Sometimes "busman" or "busperson."

Bushman. 1. A member of a nomadic tribe in Southern Africa. 2. In Australia, one who lives in "the bush," the rural areas of the country.

business class. A relatively new class of airline service, positioned in marketing as between first-class and coach. Designed to appeal to the business traveler. The amenities provided in business class vary from carrier to carrier.

business mix. In a travel agency, the percentage of corporate to leisure travel booked.

bust-out, bust-out operation. A scheme in which an ARC-appointed agency sells large numbers of airline tickets in a short period but does not deposit the funds with ARC. The agency then goes out of business and the owners abscond with the funds.

buyback agreement. In the rental car industry, a practice in which automobile companies repurchase their cars at a set price after a negotiated period of time.

buyer's market. An economic condition in which supply exceeds demand, resulting in very favorable prices for buyers.

buyer's remorse. A tendency to have second thoughts about a purchase, which often leads to cancelling the sale.

buying market share. A practice in which a company offers goods or services at extremely low prices or at a loss to attract large numbers of customers, in the expectation that many of these customers will remain loyal even when prices move upwards in the future.

BVI. British Virgin Islands.

BWI. British West Indies. Sometimes pronounced "BeeWee."

bypass. 1. A route that goes around a city or other congested area. 2. v. To skip or avoid a destination on a trip. 3. The practice of marketing or selling direct to the public, without travel agents. *See also* agent bypass.

– C c

C. *Abr.* Celsius. *See* Celsius scale.

CAA. Civil Aeronautics Authority.

CAB. Civil Aeronautics Board. Absorbed into the DOT (Department of Transportation) in 1985.

cab. 1. A taxi (qv). 2. The driver's compartment of a vehicle.

cabana. *Sp.* 1. A hotel room which is a separate building, typically near the beach or a pool. 2. A private changing room near a hotel beach or pool.

cabaret. 1. A type of entertainment performed in a club or restaurant, usually small-scale featuring singing and/or comedy sketches. 2. A club or restaurant offering such entertainment.

cabin. 1. The passenger compartment of an airplane. 2. A ship's stateroom. 3. A rustic hotel room separate from the main building.

cabin attendant. 1. A flight attendant (qv). 2. A cabin steward (qv).

cabin steward. A ship's employee responsible for cleaning staterooms.

cable car. 1. A trolley operated by underground cables. 2. An aerial tramway.

cable length. On ships, a distance of 600 feet (100 fathoms).

cablegram. An overseas telegram, specifically one transmitted by undersea cables.

cabotage. 1. Trade between two points in a country, usually prohibited to carriers of another nation. 2. The right to engage in such trade. *See also* freedom rights.

cabriolet. A one-seat, horse-drawn carriage.

cache. 1. A hiding place for supplies, as on a hiking trip, or any supplies so hidden. 2. Supplies suspended in the air to prevent animals from getting to them.

cachet. *Fr. adj.* Possessed of charm, allure, or attraction. Enjoying a good reputation.

caddy. A person who carries a golfer's clubs.

cafe. 1. *Fr.* and *Sp.* Coffee. 2. A small restaurant serving coffee. Sometimes with outdoor seating, as in "sidewalk cafe."

cafe au lait. *Fr.* Coffee with milk.

cafe noir. *Fr.* Black coffee.

CAI. Computer-assisted instruction.

call sign. A code identifying a ship's radio.

cambio. *Sp.* Literally, "change." By extension, a currency exchange bureau.

canal. An artificial inland waterway originally built to connect one body of water with another and allow commercial barge traffic.

Now also used for recreational purposes.

canal barge. A vessel designed to carry freight on a canal, now often converted to passenger use for leisure cruising.

cancel. 1. To void, as a reservation. 2. To indicate an item has been processed, as a check.

cancellation clause. In a contract, a provision which allows for cancellation by one of the parties, usually upon payment of a penalty.

cancellation penalty. An amount deducted by a supplier from a refund of prepaid funds when a reservation is cancelled.

canoe. 1. *n.* A slender oared vessel of Native American origin. 2. *v.* To travel by or navigate a canoe.

canton. An administrative district in Switzerland or France.

capacity controlled. With limited space or seating at a specific price.

capital. The seat of government of a state, province, or country.

capitol. 1. A building housing and symbolizing a seat of government. 2. The decorative portion surmounting a column.

caps. *See* commission cap.

capsule hotel. A Japanese lodging featuring small, coffin-like sleeping compartments. Often found near railway stations and usually accepting men only. Pronounced "capseru hoteru" in Japanese.

captain. 1. The commanding officer on a ship. 2. The pilot of an airplane.

car class. The specific size, style, and rental price of a rental car.

car ferry. A ship transporting automobiles and passengers.

car for hire. *Brit.* A rental car.

caravan. 1. *Brit.* A mobile home or van. 2. A group traveling together. Typically, Arab merchants and their camels. 3. By extension, a convoy of vehicles traveling together, especially military vehicles.

card mill. Derogatory term for a travel agency that recruits outside salespeople with the lure of instant travel benefits said to be obtainable with the photo ID card the agency issues.

carfare. 1. Money given, as to an employee, to cover the cost of local transportation. 2. The fare charged on a municipal transportation system.

cargo. Freight carried by a ship or airplane.

cargo liner. A ship which transports freight. *See also* freighter.

carhop. A waiter or waitress at a drive-in restaurant, where people eat in their cars.

Caribbean Basin Initiative. A U.S. government program established in 1983 to promote economic growth in the region through lower tariffs.

carnet. A customs document authorizing the transport of a car or other motor vehicle from one country to another.

carnival. 1. *U.S.* A traveling show featuring rides, games of chance, and displays of oddities. 2. A celebration preceding Lent, celebrated most prominently in New Orleans and Rio de Janeiro. 3. By extension, any large party-like outdoor celebration.

carousel. 1. A circular amusement park ride, typically with wooden horses which go up and down. 2. A mechanized device at airports to which passenger baggage is delivered and on which it is displayed while awaiting pickup.

carrier. Any company which transports passengers or freight.

carry-on. A piece of luggage designed to be taken aboard an airplane and fit into the space allotted for such luggage.

carry-on baggage or luggage. Baggage which is carried aboard an airplane by the passenger, as opposed to being checked and carried in the hold.

cartographer. A person who creates maps.

cartography. The art and science of map-making.

CAS. *Abr.* Computer-assisted selling.

casbah. Traditionally, the old (or "native") quarter of a North African city.

cash advance. An amount given to an employee prior to a trip to cover anticipated cash outlays.

cash bar. An arrangement at a party where guests must pay for their drinks.

cash method. An accounting system in which income and expenses are recorded at the actual time received or disbursed. *See also* accrual method.

cash stipend. An amount paid by some educational tour operators to tour organizers as compensation for signing up passengers over and above those needed to qualify for a free ticket for the organizer.

cashless cruising. A system in which all purchases made on a cruise ship are signed for, with the bill presented for payment, by cash or credit card, at the end of the cruise.

casino. A gambling establishment offering a variety of gaming choices.

castaway. A person who has been shipwrecked.

casual courier. A person serving as an air courier (qv) on a one-time basis.

category. On a cruise ship, a class of cabin or fare level.

caveat emptor. *Lat.* Literally, let the buyer beware.

cay. A small island. A term used primarily in the Caribbean and pronounced "key."

CBBG. *CRS.* Cabin baggage.

CBI. *Abr.* Computer-based instruction.

CBN. *CRS.* Cabin (qv).

CCAR. *CRS.* Compact car.

CCRN. *CRS.* Credit card return notice.

CCS. *CRS.* Change segment status.

CCTE. *Abr.* Certified Corporate Travel Executive.

CCTV. Closed circuit television.

CDC. Centers for Disease Control and Prevention.

CD-ROM. *Abr.* Compact disc, read-only memory. A high-density storage medium for computer programs and data.

CDT. Central Daylight Time.

CDW. Collision Damage Waiver (qv).

ceiling. 1. The altitude of the lowest clouds. 2. The upper limit of operation of an aircraft. 3. By extension, any limit, as on expenditures.

Celsius scale. The metric scale for measuring temperature in which zero is the freezing point of water and 100 is the boiling point. Used in most countries of the world instead of the Fahrenheit scale (qv).

centralization. The process of consolidating certain types of activities or decision making in one place, as opposed to spreading them across corporate divisions or geographical locations.

centralized billing. A system in which a travel agent sends a single bill for travel by several or many people, as when a corporation is billed once for travel by all its employees.

centralized commissions. A system in which a supplier such as a hotel chain sends commission payments from a central office, rather than having individual properties pay commissions separately.

centralized payment plan. *See* centralized commissions.

CEO. Chief Executive Officer.

certification. A document attesting that a person or organization meets minimum standards or qualifications in a specified area. Usually issued by an organization with recognized expertise in the area.

Certified Travel Counselor (CTC). One who has passed a series of rigorous tests of professional competency administered by the Institute of Certified Travel Agents.

certified mail. A premium category of mail delivery which provides proof of receipt by the addressee. Notifications required by contract are often sent certified mail, as are airline tickets.

CFCs. Chlorofluorocarbons, chemical compounds found in aerosol spray cans, refrigerators, air conditioners, and styrofoam cups among other products. In their gaseous forms they are said to be responsible for the depletion of the ozone layer (qv).

CFMD. *CRS.* Confirmed.

CFO. Chief Financial Officer.

CFY. *CRS.* Clarify.

CH. *CRS.* Child.

CHA. Caribbean Hotel Association.

chain. 1. A group of hotels, or other businesses, sharing a common name and ownership. 2. A group of islands.

chair. 1. *n.* The gender-neutral version of "chairman." The head of a committee or similar group. 2. *v.* To head such a group.

chair lift. A motor-driven cable from which hang chair-like seats for passengers. Typically found at ski resorts and used to transport people up steep inclines.

chalet. 1. A style of house associated with the ski regions of Europe. 2. By extension, any accommodation at a ski or mountain resort, especially if detached from the main building.

Chamber of Commerce. An association of businesses in a city, region, or state, devoted in part to promoting the business interests of its members. Chambers of commerce are often active in promoting tourism to their areas.

chambermaid. In hotels, a woman who cleans the rooms.

change of equipment. A change of aircraft that occurs without a change in the flight number.

change of gauge. *See* change of equipment.

channel. 1. A designated passage in a harbor, often dredged to allow safe passage of ships. Any navigable ship route. 2. A relatively narrow sea lane between two land masses.

charge d'affaires. *Fr.* A diplomatic rank below ambassador but accredited to the host government. The charge d'affaires often handles embassy business in the ambassador's absence.

chargeback. An amount of money deducted from monies otherwise due a merchant from a credit card company to cover the amount of disallowed charges.

chart. 1. *n.* A "map" of coastal or open waters, showing depths and hazards, used for navigation. 2. *v.* To plan, as to chart a course. 3. *n.* A graphical display of information or statistics.

charter. 1. *v.* To lease an aircraft or other mode of transport for the use of a group. 2. *n.* Any craft so used or any trip taken by such means. 3. *n.* A written document setting forth the governing principles of a group or organization.

chauffeur. A hired driver, usually of a limousine.

CHD. *CRS.* Child.

check. *v.* To place in the care of another, usually a carrier (qv), for retrieval at a later time upon presentation of a receipt, as in "to check luggage."

checked baggage. Baggage which a traveler has given over to the care of the carrier or other responsible party. An important distinction when liability for loss or damage is to be determined. *See also* unchecked baggage.

checker. 1. A person who receives baggage, coats, or other items to be checked. 2. *Cap.* A roomy make of New York taxicab, now obsolete.

check-in. A procedure whereby a hotel guest or airline passenger is registered as having arrived. Check-in may require the presentation of payment, reservations, or other documentation or identification.

check-in time. 1. In hotels, the earliest time at which a room will be available. 2. At airline terminals, the latest time at which a passenger may arrive for the flight without risk of losing his seat.

check-out. A procedure whereby a hotel guest formally leaves the hotel and settles his or her bill.

check-out time. In hotels, the latest time a guest may leave without being charged for another night's lodging.

checkpoint. A place on a road or at a terminal at which vehicles or people are stopped for inspection.

chevron setup. In a meeting, an arrangement in which chairs are aligned in a "V" along a central aisle.

child. In the travel industry, a designation used to determine fares and other rates. The precise definition varies from carrier to carrier and hotel to hotel. Generally, a "child" is at least two years old, as opposed to an "infant" (qv) who is younger. The upper limit can be anywhere from 11 to 18 years of age.

chit. A piece of paper or voucher (qv) which can be exchanged for food, drink, or other amenities. A raincheck (qv).

CHNG. *CRS.* Change.

CHNT. *CRS.* Change name to.

CHRIE. Council on Hotel, Restaurant, and Institutional Education.

Christian name. *Brit.* First name, of a person.

chronological order. Arranged in sequence by time of occurrence.

chronology. A list of events in their order of occurrence.

chronometer. Any instrument that measures time. A watch.

CHTR. *CRS.* Charter (qv).

Chunnel. *Slang.* Nickname for the railway tunnel beneath the English Channel linking Britain and France.

ciao. *It.* Word for both hello and good-bye.

CIEE. Council on International Educational Exchange.

circle trip. Any trip that involves more than one destination, returning to the point of departure, as opposed to a "round trip" (qv).

circle trip minimum. The lowest allowable fare for a circle trip, which cannot be less than any round trip fare between any two cities on the itinerary.

circumnavigate. To sail around, as an island or the world.

citadel. A fort in a city used for the city's defense.

CITC. Canadian Institute of Travel Counselors.

city codes. Three-letter codes used to uniquely identify cities and/ or their airports.

city pair. In airline bookings, the departure and arrival cities on an itinerary. The number of city pairs served by an airline is sometimes used as a measure of its size.

city terminal. *See* city ticket office.

city ticket office. An airline sales and ticketing office located anywhere other than the airport.

civil aviation. Any flight activity conducted by the private sector, as opposed to military aviation.

civil law. The law regulating non-criminal activities between and among individuals and corporations.

claim check. The receipt or stub, usually numbered, issued to a passenger for his or her luggage.

claim PNR booking. A booking that occurs when a travel agency issues a ticket for a reservation made by the passenger and entered into the CRS by the airline reservationist.

clearance. 1. Permission, as for an airplane to take off. 2. The height of a bridge or overpass. 3. The distance between the highest point on a vessel and a bridge.

CLIA. Cruise Lines International Association.

client. A term used for a customer, usually to indicate an on-going relationship.

climate. The prevailing weather conditions in a geographical region.

close. 1. *v.* To finalize or complete a sale. 2. *v.* To ask a closing question (qv). 3. *n. Brit.* A dead-end street.

closed dates. Dates on which travel or hotel rooms are unavailable due to prior sale or booking.

closing question. Any question that requires the client to make a commitment or decision that leads them closer to making a purchase.

club car. A car on a train serving liquor and refreshments.

club floor. In a hotel, a separate floor providing a higher level of service and security for a premium price. Also called Concierge Floor or Level

clustering. In the hotel industry, a business strategy in which a number of properties are located in the same geographic area.

CMP. *Abr.* 1. Certified Meeting Professional. 2. Complete meeting package.

CNL. *CRS.* Cancel.

coach. 1. The economy class on an airline. Also referred to as "economy" or "tourist." 2. The section of the plane designated for this class of passenger. 3. A motorcoach (qv).

COC. *CRS.* Country of commencement (i.e. where travel begins).

cockpit. The pilot's compartment in a plane.

COD. *Abr.* Cash on delivery.

code sharing. An agreement whereby airlines permit the use of their CRS code in the flight schedule displays of other airlines.

cog railway. A railway system, usually used on short, very steep grades, in which a series of teeth on the rail mesh with the vehicle to insure traction.

co-host carrier. An airline that pays another to display its flights on a CRS.

COLA. *Abr.* 1. Cost of living allowance (qv). 2. Cost of living adjustment (qv).

cold call. A sales call to a prospective client with whom you have no prior contact.

cold wave. A period of abnormally cold weather.

collision damage waiver. Daily insurance which covers damage to a rental car.

colors. The flag or ensign flown from the mast or stern of a ship.

COMM. *CRS.* Commission.

commercial agency. A travel agency that specializes in corporate travel.

commercial airline. An airline that carries passengers.

Commercial Sabre®. Term used to distinguish the full version of the Sabre® CRS from Eaasy Sabre®. a simplified version.

commission. 1. A percentage of a sale price paid to a salesperson as payment for making a sale. 2. An official investigative body. 3. *v.* To contract for the production of something, as to commission a work of art.

commission cap. The maximum dollar amount an airline, or other supplier, will pay as commission regardless of the actual price of the ticket or the standard commission rate.

commission split. An agreed upon division of commission income between two entities, such as a travel agency and an outside salesperson.

commissionable. Denoting the portion of total cost on which a travel agent can receive a commission.

commode. A portable toilet, usually one containing a removable bed pan or other receptacle.

common carrier. Any company engaged in the transport of people or goods for profit.

common law. Unwritten law which has become generally accepted by the formal legal system through long-standing practice.

Common Market. Obsolete term for the European Economic Community (qv).

common rated. Describing two identical fares to geographically close destinations.

commonwealth. A political entity with representative government. A voluntary association of sovereign states.

commuter. 1. *n.* A person who travels to work each day. 2. *adj.* Used to describe short-haul airlines.

comp. *Slang.* A free ticket or other complimentary extra.

comp rooms. Free rooms provided to a group of hotel guests based on total occupancy by the group.

companionway. A stairway connecting two decks on a ship.

compartment. A distinct section on a railroad car, airplane, ship, or other vehicle.

compass. A magnetic device used to determine direction aboard ship.

computer virus. A malicious and destructive program designed to be passed unwittingly from machine to machine via floppy disks, downloading, or other means.

computerized reservation system. Any of several proprietary computer systems allowing real-time access to airline fares, schedules, and seating availability and offering the capability of booking reservations and generating tickets.

complimentary. Free. Without charge.

concentrated hub. An airport where a single airline controls most of the passenger capacity.

concession. A shop or other place of business within a larger area, such as an airport or cruise ship, which has paid a fee in exchange for exclusivity.

concierge. A hotel employee charged with providing advice and additional services to the guests.

concierge level. *See* club floor.

Concorde. The supersonic jet jointly developed by Britain and France.

concourse. 1. A public area in an airport. 2. The section of the airport containing the gates.

COND. *CRS.* Conditional.

conditional fare. A fare which guarantees passage on the next available flight if the flight for which the ticket was purchased is full.

condo. Short for condominium (qv).

condo vacation. A travel product featuring lodging in a condominium (qv), typically one in a resort area, and providing additional amenities such as pools, tennis courts, golf courses, and so forth.

condominium. A form of ownership of real estate. In travel, generally used to refer to accommodations that are similar to or identical to furnished, private apartments or townhouses and which are available for rent by the day or week. Such properties are frequently rented out when the owner is not present. *See also* time sharing.

conductor. 1. A railway employee who collects tickets on board. 2. The person nominally in charge of a tour group. 3. The director of a symphony orchestra.

conductor's ticket. On a cruise ship, a free ticket awarded based on the size of a group booking. The ticket can be used by the travel agent who put the group together or given to a person in the group who was instrumental in making the booking happen.

conference center. A hotel-like property designed specifically for hosting conventions and meetings.

confidential tariff. Wholesale rates intended for markup (qv) to retail pricing.

configuration. Arrangement or layout, as of an airplane's interior.

confirmation. The official acceptance of a booking by the supplier.

confirmation number. An alphanumeric code used to identify and document the confirmation of a booking.

confiscate. Take away or seize, as contraband goods.

congress. *See* convention.

conjunction tickets. Two or more tickets used on a single itinerary.

connecting flight. A flight that requires a passenger to change from one plane to another. *See also* connection.

connecting rooms. Hotel rooms which are next to each other and have a connecting door, in addition to the doors which give out onto the hallway.

connection. A stop on a journey that requires a change of planes or other mode of transportation. *See also* connecting flight.

consent decree. A legal document whereby the target of a government lawsuit ends the suit by agreeing to take or refrain from specific actions specified in the decree.

consignment. 1. An arrangement whereby a supplier allots merchandise to a retailer who needs pay for it only upon sale. 2. Goods allotted under such an arrangement.

consolidation. 1. A business tactic in which a company concentrates its purchases with fewer suppliers to effect cost savings. 2. The process in which an industry comes to be served by fewer and fewer suppliers as companies merge or succumb to bankruptcy and competitive pressures; the airline industry is a prime example.

consolidator. A company or individual who negotiates bulk contracts (qv) with an airline (or other travel supplier) and sells that space to the general public, usually at a discount.

consortium. A group of companies that enter into a voluntary association to share resources in order to gain a market advantage. In travel, usually used to refer to groups of suppliers that offer higher commissions and other incentives to travel agencies that enter into "preferred supplier" (qv) relationships with them.

consul. A diplomatic representative of one country to another. The executive in charge of a consulate (qv).

Consular Information Sheet. One of a series of publications of the United States Department of State, providing essential travel information for each of the world's countries.

consulate. A subsidiary office of a foreign government, usually in a location other than the host nation's capital. Consulates typically handle visa applications and other business affairs of the foreign government.

consultant. An expert in a particular field who provides technical and other forms of assistance to companies on a fee basis.

continental breakfast. A breakfast of rolls, fruit and coffee or tea. Often provided on a complimentary basis by hotels and motels.

continental code. International Morse code (qv).

continental plan. A hotel rate that includes a continental breakfast (qv).

contour map. A map showing gradations in altitude.

contraband. Merchandise or substances which are illegal to import or export.

contract. A legal and enforceable agreement between two or more parties.

contract of carriage. The small print on the passenger's coupon of an airline ticket detailing the legal relationship, rights, and liabilities of the passenger and the carrier.

control tower. A central, raised operational center which supervises and directs all traffic into and out of an airport.

CONV. *CRS.* Convertible (car).

convention. A gathering of professionals or others to discuss matters of common interest.

conventioneer. A person participating in a convention.

conversion. 1. In the hotel industry, the change of a property from one brand to another. 2. The process of switching from one vendor to another. *See also* convert.

conversion agency. A formerly independent travel agency that has joined a chain. Typically, the conversion agency's name will be changed to or blended with the name of the chain.

conversion payment. A fee paid by a travel agency to a consortium upon joining.

conversion rate. The rate at which one currency is exchanged for another.

convert. *v.* 1. To switch vendors, as when an agency moves from one CRS to another. 2. To convince a customer to switch vendors.

converter. An electrical device which allows appliances designed for one type of current to be used with another.

convoy. 1. *n.* A group of ships (or other vehicles) traveling together, usually for purposes of mutual safety or defense. 2. *v.* To accompany or lead a group of vehicles to assure safe passage.

COO. *Abr.* Chief Operating Officer.

co-op advertising. An arrangement in which a supplier underwrites a portion of a travel agency's advertising expenses when such advertising features the supplier's products.

cooperative. A group of individuals or organizations that have joined together, usually to increase their buying or negotiating power.

cork charge, corkage. A fee charged by a restaurant for opening a bottle of wine, especially one not purchased on the premises.

corporate agency. 1. A travel agency physically located on the premises of a corporation which it services. 2. A travel agency that specializes in corporate clients.

corporate apartment. A condominium owned by a corporation for the exclusive use of its employees and guests.

corporate rate. 1. A lower hotel rate negotiated by a specific corporation for the use of its employees and guests. 2. A rate extended by a hotel to all business travelers.

corporate travel manager. A middle management position. Corporate travel managers are tasked with setting corporate travel policy and standardizing and overseeing all travel by corporate employees on company business. Many corporate travel managers function as in-house travel agents.

cost of living allowance. An additional sum provided to a corporate employee to offset higher prices in certain countries or cities.

cost of living adjustment. The percentage by which Social Security recipients' monthly benefits are increased each year to adjust for increases in the cost of living. Intended to ensure that beneficiaries don't lose purchasing power due to inflation.

cost-reimbursable contractor. A person or company working as an independent contractor for a governmental agency, whose costs, including travel, are reimbursed by the contracting agency.

cot. 1. *Abr.* Cottage. 2. A small folding bed used to provide additional sleeping space in a hotel room.

coterminous. Sharing a common boundary.

couchette. *Fr.* A sleeping compartment on a train with up to six beds.

counterfeit. 1. *adj.* False, forged. 2. *n.* An illegal copy, as of paper currency.

country of registry. The nation in which a ship's ownership is formally registered. The country of registry need not reflect the nationality of the crew or the cruise area in which the ship operates and is often chosen for tax reasons.

coup d'etat. *Fr.* The usually quick overthrow of a country's government, typically by assassination or forcible removal from office of the top leaders.

coupon. 1. The portion of an airline ticket collected from the passenger at the time of boarding. 2. A pre-paid voucher (qv) which can be exchanged for certain specified goods or services, as a hotel room. 3. Any printed voucher providing for free or reduced cost services or goods.

coupon broker. A person or company that buys and resells airline frequent flyer awards in contravention of airline regulations.

courier. 1. Any person who accompanies cargo or hand-delivered documents. 2. *Brit.* A guide or tour escort.

course. The direction in which a ship or plane is headed. Expressed in degrees of the compass.

cover charge. An admission charge, especially to a nightclub or cabaret (qv).

cover letter. A business letter which accompanies other documents or goods and explains the contents and purpose of what is being sent.

CP. *CRS.* Continental plan (qv).

CPM. *Abr.* Cost per thousand.

CPU. *Abr.* Central processing unit. Your computer's "brain."

CR. *CRS.* Change record.

credit memo. An informal document indicating that one company has a specific dollar amount credit with another, typically as a result of overpayment.

crew. All the members of the staff of a ship, airplane, or other form of transportation.

crew to passenger ratio. The number of passengers on a cruise ship divided by the number of crew members. In theory, the lower the number, the higher the level of service.

CRN. *CRS.* Cash refund notice.

croak fare. *Slang.* An airline's bereavement fare (qv) or other fare based on compassionate reasons. The implication is that one has to die to qualify for the fare.

cross-border ticketing. Writing a ticket in such a way that it appears that the travel commences in a different country than is actually the case. Used to take advantage of lower fare structures.

crossing. A cruise journey across an ocean.

Crown Colony. *Brit.* A colonial territory over which Great Britain still exerts some degree of direct control.

crow's nest. A lookout's station at the top of a ship's highest mast.

CRS. *Abr.* Computerized reservation system.

CRT. *Abr.* Cathode ray tube. The screen of a computer.

cruise. In travel, a round-trip ocean voyage undertaken for pleasure.

cruise broker. Term used for a travel agent or other person who specializes in the sale of last-minute cruise berths.

cruise director. The person on a cruise ship charged with ensuring the enjoyment of all the passengers.

cruise fare. The actual cost of a cruise, excluding any extras, such as port taxes and gratuities.

cruise host. A gentleman recruited by the cruise ship, and usually traveling at a reduced cost, to serve as a dancing and social partner for single ladies on the cruise.

cruise to nowhere. A cruise, typically of short duration and with an emphasis on partying and gambling, with no ports of call.

CSM. *Abr.* Convention services manager.

CSML. *CRS.* Child's meal.

CST. *Abr.* Central Standard Time.

CT. *CRS.* 1. Circle trip (qv). 2. Central time.

CTA. Condominium Travel Associates.

CTC. 1. *Abr.* Certified Travel Counselor (qv). 2. *CRS.* Contact.

CTCA. *CRS.* Contact's address.

CTCB. *CRS.* Contact's business phone.

CTCH. *CRS.* Contact's home phone.

CTG. *CRS.* Cottage.

CTM. 1. *CRS.* Circle trip minimum (qv). 2. *Abr.* Consolidated tour manual.

CTO. *CRS.* City ticket office (qv).

culture shock. The state of being overwhelmed by the differences in customs and behavior in a foreign place.

curator. The person in charge of one or more of a museum's collections.

curfew. A police or military regulation requiring people to be off the streets during a certain period, generally at night.

currency adjustment. A discontinued method of figuring fares in local currency using fare construction units (qv).

currency restriction. Any rule or law imposed by a country to regulate the flow of currency into or out of its territory.

customer-activated ticketing. A vending machine that allows passengers to purchase airline tickets with a credit card.

customs. 1. A government agency which monitors the flow of goods, commodities, and substances into and from its territory and levies fees, fines, and other charges according to posted regulations. 2. The inspection area maintained by such an agency at an airport or other port of entry.

customs declaration. A form completed by an arriving passenger on which are listed the dutiable goods being imported.

customs duty. *See* duty.

customs user fee. A fee added to international airline tickets to benefit the U.S. customs service.

cut-off date. A date beyond which an offer, fare, request, or availability will no longer apply or be honored.

CV. *Abr.* Container vessel.

CVB. *Abr.* Convention and Visitors Bureau.

CWGN. *CRS.* Compact station wagon.

CWO. *Abr.* Cash with order.

_D d

dabble agent. Derogatory term for a part-time travel agent. Sometimes applied to any outside agent or independent contractor as a slur on their professionalism.

daily program. On a cruise ship, a listing of the day's activities.

dais. Raised platform in a room or hall on which a speaker's lectern or table for VIPs is situated.

DAPO. *CRS.* Do all possible.

database. 1. Any collection of information on a specific subject or area. Specifically, a computerized collection of such information. 2. A computer program designed to store such information.

DATAS II. A computer reservation system which is now part of Worldspan.

Davey Jones' locker. *Slang.* The bottom of the ocean.

davit. A crane on a ship that's used to raise and lower anchors, lifeboats, and cargo.

day rate. 1. In hotels, the fee charged for a stay of limited duration, typically during daylight hours. 2. A fee charged for the use of a facility during a twenty-four hour period.

day tripper. *Brit.* A person whose round-trip travel will be completed on the same day. On a longer leisure trip, a day tripper will make a series of one-day excursions to different locales to avoid changing hotels.

daylight savings time. An artificial forward adjustment of the clock in the Spring. Instituted to increase business by adding more hours of daylight in the evening.

d.b.a. *Abr.* Doing business as (qv).

dbl. *Abr.* Double (qv).

DBLB. *CRS.* Double room with bath.

DBLN. *CRS.* Double room without shower or bath.

DBLS. *CRS.* Double room with shower.

DC. *Abr.* Direct current.

DCSN. *CRS.* Decision.

DEA. Drug Enforcement Agency.

dead ahead. Straight in front of the ship's bow.

dead calm. No wind. Zero on the Beaufort scale (qv).

dead reckoning. In navigation, a way of calculating a ship's or plane's position without reference to sun or stars, based on speed, direction, and drift.

deadend booking. A booking that is completed on a CRS but never ticketed. Deadend bookings can result from training new hires, forgetfulness, or fraud on the part of the travel agent.

deadhead. *v.* To return without paying cargo, whether freight or passengers. Used of commercial vehicles.

deadlight. A ventilated porthole cover that prevents light from entering.

DEAF. *CRS.* Deaf passenger.

debark. To get off a plane or ship.

debit memo. An informal invoice (qv) from a supplier showing an additional amount due. ARC (qv) will issue a debit memo when it feels the agency has made an error.

debug. A computer term meaning to identify and correct mistakes in a computer program. By extension, to correct mistakes in other contexts.

deck. The floor of a ship. A level on a ship.

deck chair. On a cruise ship, a reclining chair designed for lounging.

deck plan. Drawing or "map" that shows the layout of a ship's decks, cabins, and other areas.

deck steward. Member of a ship's crew who provides passengers with drinks, towels, deck chairs, etc.

decode. Translate from code into ordinary language.

decommission. To remove a ship from active service.

dedicated line. A telephone line that is used for ("dedicated to") a single purpose, such as a fax machine. May also refer to an electrical line.

deductible. 1. *n.* In insurance, the amount the customer must pay before the insurance kicks in. 2. *adj.* Used to describe business and other expenditures that you may subtract from your gross income in figuring your income tax liability.

deep six. *Slang.* To throw overboard. By extension, to throw away anything, usually with the motive of concealing its existence.

default. 1. *v.* To fail to supply contracted goods or services or refund the money paid for them. 2. *n.* In a computer program, a pre-programmed setting, which can sometimes be changed or modified by the user.

deluxe. *Fr.* Literally, "of luxury." Room or hotel in an excellent location with luxurious furnishings or accommodations.

demi-pension. *Fr.* Half pension (qv).

demo. 1. *Slang.* Demonstration. 2. Video or other visual or hands-on unit used in a sales demonstration.

demographics. Age, income, marital status, ethnicity, and other statistical characteristics of populations. Used in marketing to analyze and identify markets.

denied-boarding compensation. Payment given passengers who've been bumped from a flight, cruise, or land-tour. May be a free trip, money, or accommodations.

dep. *Abr.* 1. Departure. 2. Deposit (qv).

DEP. *CRS.* 1. Scheduled departure time. 2. After departure, the time the flight departed.

departure tax. Tax levied on travelers when they leave a country.

deplane. *v.* To get off a plane.

deplate. *v.* Withdraw the right of a travel agency to issue tickets for an airline.

deposit. Payment made to hold space on a tour or accommodations. May be fully or partially refundable if the passenger cancels with enough advance notice.

depot. 1. Bus or train station. 2. Storage place for goods or motor vehicles.

depreciable asset. Any property owned by a business that is subject to depreciation (qv) for tax purposes.

depreciation. In taxation, a deduction taken to account for the decline in value of assets, such as machines used in a business, over a period of time. Used to offset the cost of acquiring the asset. *See also* expensing.

dereg. *Slang.* Deregulation (qv).

deregulation. Elimination of regulation. Usually used to refer to the U.S. government's elimination of restrictions on airlines' fares, routes, etc. Enacted in 1978.

designated driver. Member of a group who refrains from drinking alcoholic beverages in order to drive the group home safely.

designator, designator code. A two- or three-digit alphanumeric code uniquely identifying airlines and airports throughout the world. Administered by IATA (qv).

destination. Place to which a person is traveling or a thing is sent.

destination management company. A local company that handles arrangements for tours, meetings, transportation, and so forth, for groups originating elsewhere.

DET. *CRS.* Domestic escorted tour. A packaged tour, with guide, that takes place in your own country.

detached interface. A computer configuration that allows additional functions (such as accounting) to be performed while primary functions (such as ticketing) are in progress.

detente. *Fr.* A state of lessened tension or hostility between nations.

devaluation. The decrease in value of one currency in relation to another, usually by action of the government. When a currency is devalued, it buys less in foreign markets.

DEW Line. *Abr.* Distant Early Warning line. A line of radar stations set up to give advance warning of enemy air attack.

differential. 1. The difference in price, quality, etc. between comparable products or services. 2. The amount of the difference. 3. Amount owed or credited due to a change in the class of service.

dig. *Slang.* An area of archeological excavation.

digs. *Brit. slang.* Living accommodations.

dine-around plan. Prepaid plan (such as a modified American plan) that allows guests to choose among a number of restaurants. Typically, the restaurants will all be owned by the same company.

diner. 1. The restaurant car on a train. 2. A small, usually very informal restaurant. 3. Person eating in a restaurant.

dinghy. A small oared boat.

diplomatic immunity. A provision of international law which exempts the diplomats of one country from the laws of a country to which they are assigned.

diplomatic plates. Automobile license plates, usually of a distinct design, issued to the vehicles of accredited diplomats.

direct access. System or program that gives the user the capability of tapping directly into a vendor's computer system to get last-minute information about seat or product availability.

direct billing. System in which a corporation's travel agency bills employees for their business travel. The employee must then submit an expense accounting and be reimbursed by the corporation.

direct flight. Any flight between two places that carries a single flight number. Unlike a nonstop, a direct flight will make one or more stops between the two places. The passenger may have to change planes or even change airlines. This is a change in meaning. In the past, direct flights made stops but required no change of plane.

direct mail. 1. A form of marketing in which sellers offer their products or services to buyers by mail, instead of (or in addition to) through agents or stores. 2. A form of advertising in which sellers promote their products or services by mail. Many recipients consider direct mail ads "junk mail."

directional selling. Booking with suppliers with whom the agency has a preferred supplier relationship.

directional tariff. A lower fare for one segment of an itinerary, usually requiring round-trip travel or available only during certain time periods.

dirigible. A blimp (qv).

dis. *Abr.* Discontinued.

disburse. To pay out (money).

disclaimer, disclaimer of liability. A formal denial of legal and financial responsibility for monetary losses or other injury incurred as a result of advice given or products or services sold. Example: A travel agent would use a disclaimer to ward off claims for injuries or losses a client might incur while traveling, as a result, say, of a charter cancellation or an accident while white-water rafting.

disclosure. The act of making something known. Example: By law, airline ads must disclose all the restrictions on the special fares they advertise.

discotheque. Nightclub for dancing.

discount fare. A special fare, usually offered for a limited time and in a limited quantity.

discretionary income. The amount a person has left to spend, save, or invest after paying all bills.

disembark. To get off a plane, ship, or train.

disk. A magnetic file used in computers.

display bias. A discontinued practice in which a CRS (qv) would display it's owners' flights first. *See also* architectural bias.

distribution. 1. The process of delivering products or services to customers. 2. The full extent of a supplier's distribution network.

district sales manager. The individual responsible for managing sales at the district level for a hotel, airline, cruise line, or other supplier. Depending on the company, may be primarily a salesperson or a manager of salespeople.

DIT. *CRS.* Domestic Independent Tour/Traveler.

divestiture. The compulsory transfer of title or disposal of interests (for example, in a corporation or real estate) upon government order, often to satisfy antitrust legislation and ensure competition. Example: In the early eighties, the federal government required the divestiture of the regional telephone companies by AT&T.

DLX. *CRS.* Deluxe room.

DM. *Abr.* District manager.

D-Mark. *Abr.* Deutschemark.

DMC. 1. *CRS.* Directional Minimum Check. The check a travel agent must make to be sure that the fare (charged) isn't lower than the minimum applicable fare (in either direction). 2. Destination management company (qv) or consultants.

DMO. *Abr.* 1. Destination marketing organization. 2. District marketing office.

DO. *CRS.* Drop-off.

docent. A guide in a museum or art gallery.

dock. 1. *n.* The waterway between piers (qv) for the reception of ships. 2. *n.* A place for loading or unloading cargo or other materials. 3. A berth, pier, or quay. 4. *v.* To come into dock; to become docked.

docs. *Slang.* Documents.

docs rec'd. *Abbr.* Documents received.

dog and pony show. *Slang.* A derogatory term for a sales presentation.

doing business as. A phrase indicating that a corporation has registered with the state to conduct business under a name other than its official corporate name. Typically abbreviated dba. A corporation might have several dba's.

dom. *Abr.* Domestic.

dome car. A train car with a domed plexiglass top for sightseeing. Also called a bubble car (qv).

domestic airline. An air carrier that provides service within its own country. Also called a domestic carrier.

domestic escorted tour. Escorted tour (qv) for traveling within one's own country, typically used to refer to U.S. tours.

domestic fare. Fare charged for travel within a country.

domicile. Place of residence, home.

dormette. An airline seat that reclines to sleeping position. Used on some carriers for long-distance runs. Also called a sleeperette.

DOT. Department of Transportation.

dot-matrix printer. A printer, used with a computer, that forms letters and numbers with a series of ink dots. Dot-matrix printers produce a lower print quality than laser printers.

double. A room designed to be shared by two people. It may have one double (or larger) bed, two twin beds, or two double (or larger) beds. Rooms with two double beds are sometimes called a "double double."

double booking. The practice of booking and confirming two or more reservations when only one will be used.

double occupancy rate. The rate charged when two people will occupy a room, suite, apartment, etc. For example, a hotel might charge an individual $100 per night for a room (single occupancy) but charge two people only $130 for double occupancy of the same room.

double-decker. A bus, or other conveyance, with two levels; used as public transportation in some cities, and exclusively for sightseeing and other special uses in other areas.

down. *Slang.* Inoperable (as in "The computer is down."). Often used of computers and computer networks when they shut down as a result of power failures, system crashes, operator errors, quirks in the system, or downtime (qv) on networks or reservation systems.

Down East. *Slang.* Extreme northeast New England. Maine.

Down under. An affectionate term for Australia and, to a lesser extent, New Zealand.

downgrade. To move to a lower grade or quality of services or accommodations.

downline. 1. All segments, legs, or cities listed below the originating or headline city (on a schedule or CRS). 2. The members, in rank order, of a multi-level marketing program.

download. *v.* To transfer a file or files from a remote computer to a local computer electronically.

downsizing. A corporate restructuring aimed at making the organization smaller, more efficient, and more profitable by selling ("spinning off") various product lines and/or business units and permanently eliminating many jobs.

downtime. 1. Time during which production is stopped for repairs or alterations to a system, network, machine, or program. 2. *Slang.* Time a person spends sleeping or vegging out.

downtown. The business district of a city.

DPLX. *CRS.* Duplex (qv).

DPP. Default protection plan. An insurance policy that protects the holder against a supplier's failure to deliver products or services or refund the money paid for them.

DPST. *CRS.* Deposit.

dptr. *Abr.* Departure.

draft. (*Brit.* draught) Measurement in feet from a ship's waterline (qv) to the lowest point of its keel (qv).

drag. The aerodynamic force that slows a plane in flight.

draw. An amount paid to a salesperson on a regular basis and deducted from his or her commission earnings. Also referred to as a "draw against commission."

drayage. The charge assessed for transporting goods.

dress circle. The mezzanine (qv) or first balcony of a theater, especially an opera house.

drive-away company. A company that transports automobiles and other vehicles by finding people who will drive them to their destination.

drive-in. 1. *n.* An outdoor movie theater where people watch from their cars. 2. *adj.* Any service designed to be provided to customers in their cars.

drop-off charge. An add-on fee that may be assessed when a rental car or other rental vehicle is dropped off at a location other than the one where it was rented. Usually a flat amount.

DRS. *CRS.* Direct reference system.

dry dock. 1. *n.* Dock (qv) that can be emptied of water while a ship is being repaired. 2. *v.* To put into dry dock.

dry lease. The rental of a boat, or other vehicle, without a crew or supplies.

DSM. *Abr.* District sales manager.

DSO. *Abr.* District sales office. May also be called a DMO (qv).

DSPL. *CRS.* Display.

DTIA. Dive Travel Industry Association.

dual designated carrier. Air carrier that uses another airline's code in flight schedule displays. *See also* code sharing.

DUI. Abr. Driving under the influence (of alcohol or another drug).

dumbwaiter. A small, hand-operated elevator system used to transport food and dishes from one level to another, as between the kitchen and dining room.

dungeon. A prison or chamber that's dark and usually underground.

duplex. 1. A two-family house. A house that contains two separate dwelling units. 2. An apartment with rooms on two floors. 3. Separate accommodations that share walls.

dutiable. Subject to duty (qv).

duty. A tax; most often applied to imported goods.

duty-free. *adj.* Being exempt from import tax. Most often applied to goods bought in special airport shops just before boarding for a trip to another country.

DWB. *CRS.* Double (qv) room with bath.

DXA. *CRS.* Deferred cancellation area.

–E e

easySABRE. A simplified version of the Sabre CRS (qv).

EATA. East Asia Travel Association.

EB. *CRS.* 1. Eastbound. 2. English breakfast.

ECAR. *CRS.* Economy car.

eclipse. The partial or total obscuring of one heavenly body by another, especially of the sun by the moon.

ecology. 1. The study of the environment and the interaction of its various elements. 2. The flora, fauna, climate, etc. of a region or location.

economy class. 1. Coach class. 2. Y class.

economy hotel. A hotel offering few amenities (qv).

ecosystem. *See* ecology, def. 2.

ecotourism. A style of travel in which an emphasis is placed on unspoiled, natural destinations and on disturbing the environment as little as possible.

ECU. *Abr.* European currency unit. The some-day common currency of Europe.

EDI. *Abr.* Electronic data interchange.

EDT. *CRS.* Eastern daylight time.

EEC. European Economic Community (qv).

eff. *Abr.* Effective.

efficiency. A hotel room with a small kitchen area and dining table.

elapsed flying time. Actual time an airplane spends in the air, as opposed to time spent taxiing to and from the gate and during stopovers.

elderhostel. 1. Hostel that caters to senior citizens. 2. Special travel-study program for seniors offered by a college or university. Participants stay in college dormitories and may generally take a short course of study if they so desire.

electronic mail. A communications system that allows people on the same computer network to exchange messages. Frequently referred to as "e-mail." Systems also exist that allow people to exchange e-mail messages between networks.

electronic ticket delivery network. A network, national or regional, of ticket printing machines that are not operated by an ARC-accredited agency but instead by a company that sells its ticket distribution services. Also called "electronic ticket distribution network." An ETDN delivers flight and passenger coupons after an agent generates the ticket.

electronic ticketing. A computerized system used by airlines in which no physical ticket or boarding pass is generated.

EMA. *Abr.* Extra mileage allowance.

e-mail, email. *See* electronic mail.

EMAN. *CRS.* Economy car with manual transmission.

embargo. A government order forbidding the departure of a commercial vehicle from an airport, port, or whatever or prohibiting commerce. Example: an embargo on rice shipments.

embark. 1. To board a ship, plane, or other transportation vehicle. 2. To start out.

EMER. *CRS.* Emergency travel.

emigrant. A person who leaves the country where he or she lives to settle in another. *See also* immigrant.

emigrate. *v.* To leave one country to assume permanent residence in another.

emissary. A person who is sent out on a mission on behalf of another person or a country.

EMS. 1. *Abr.* Emergency medical service. 2. *CRS.* Excess mileage surcharge.

en suite. *Fr.* In the hotel industry, a phrase indicating that an amenity or feature is in the room itself or immediately adjacent.

enclave. A small area of a country or city, usually occupied by people ethnically or culturally distinct from their neighbors.

encode. To put into code. To substitute a short set of letters or numbers for a longer word or words.

encroach. 1. To gradually advance beyond the usual limits or take possession of what belongs to another. Example: A forest might encroach on a meadow; a lion might encroach on a jackal's kill.

ENDI. *CRS.* End item.

English breakfast. A breakfast of cereal or juice, eggs, meats, breads, and beverages.

English Channel. The body of water separating England from France.

enhancement. 1. An added feature to a product, as a tour. 2. In a software program, added capabilities.

enplane. To board an airplane.

enroute. On the way; while one is traveling.

ensign. The flag flown by a cruise ship.

entree. 1. In the U.S., the main dish of a meal. 2. In France, the appetizer (qv) course.

entrepreneur. A person who starts and runs a usually small business, risking capital.

entry. An input into a computer program, such as a data entry or a request for information.

entry fee. 1. The price charged for admission to a place, a competition, or an attraction. 2. The duty levied on a person entering a country.

entry requirements. 1. The payments required of and the official documents needed by a traveler entering a country for business or pleasure. Examples: passport, visa, proofs of inoculation, proofs of duty (qv) paid.

environs. The area around a place.

EP. *CRS.* European plan. Accommodations that do not include meals.

equator. Imaginary line around the center of the earth, dividing it into northern and southern hemispheres.

equinox. Either of the two times a year (around March 21 and September 23) when the sun crosses the equator and day and night are equally long.

EQUIV. *Abr.* Equivalent amount.

ERQ. *CRS.* Endorsement request.

errors and omission insurance. Insurance that pays for damages incurred by a client because of an agent's mistake or omission. Example: listing the wrong departure time on an itinerary or forgetting to check whether pets are allowed.

escort. 1. A person who accompanies an individual or group to protect or guide the other party or parties. 2. A guide who travels with a tour group. 3. A woman's date. 4. Euphemistically used of a prostitute.

escort service. A company that provides "dates" for social engagements. Often, thinly disguised call girl operations.

escorted tour. A tour offering an escort's services.

escrow account. A special account opened with a bank or other financial institution to hold funds in trust until some condition is met by the person or company for whom the funds are designated; for example, until a service has been rendered or a legal dispute settled. Example: Tenants on a rent strike to protest inadequate heat or maintenance would open an escrow account to hold their rent payments until their grievance with the landlord was settled. By paying into the escrow account, the tenants would be legally protected from eviction for nonpayment of rent.

EST. *CRS.* Eastern standard time.

ETA. *CRS.* Estimated time of arrival.

ETC. European Travel Commission.

ETD. *CRS.* Estimated time of departure.

ETDN. *Abr.* Electronic ticket delivery (distribution) network (qv).

E-ticket. Electronic ticket. *See* electronic ticketing.

EU. *CRS.* A global indicator meaning via Europe.

Eurailpass. A special-fare train ticket that entitles the purchaser to unlimited train travel in many European countries for a specified number of days or weeks.

European Economic Community. A bloc of European countries that have adopted common trading rules.

European plan. A hotel rate that includes no meals.

Eurotunnel. *See* Chunnel.

EWGN. *CRS.* Economy station wagon.

excess baggage. Luggage that exceeds the allowed limits for weight, size, or number of pieces. Carriers usually charge extra for excess baggage and, in some cases, may have to ship it later rather than with the passenger.

exchange order. A voucher issued by a carrier or travel agent requesting that a ticket be issued. The ARC document which entitles a travel agent to receive a commission.

excursion. A side trip, usually optional and at an additional cost, from a main destination.

excursion fare. A special-price fare that comes with restrictions, such as advance purchase requirements and a minimum stay. Usually a round-trip fare.

excursionist. A traveler spending less than 24 hours in a country.

exhibit or **exhibition.** A display of art, artifacts, or skill open to the public. A public showing.

expatriate. A person living in a foreign country.

expedition. In tourism, a journey with few amenities, usually to a remote area, sometimes for a scientific purpose.

expense. *v.* To elect to deduct, for the purposes of taxation, the entire cost of an asset in the current tax year, rather than depreciating it over a period of years. *See also* depreciation.

expense account. Funds allocated to cover the travel and entertainment expenses of an employee.

export. *n.* A product shipped from one country for sale in another.

exposition. A large exhibit, usually sponsored by a government or trade group, to showcase the products and services of a particular company, region, or country.

expressway. A limited-access highway or toll-road.

EXST. *CRS.* Extra seat.

extended stay. A hotel stay of more than seven days.

extension ladder. A form used on a manual airline ticket to extend the fare area when more than 13 cities must be listed on an itinerary.

extension tours. Tours that can be added to an existing tour, before or after, to create a longer trip.

extra section. A second aircraft used on a given flight schedule to accommodate additional passengers, usually during peak travel periods such as holidays.

EZS. *Abr.* easySABRE.

— *F f* ———————————————

F. *Abr.* Fahrenheit. *See* Fahrenheit scale.

FAA. Federal Aviation Administration.

Fahrenheit scale. A method of measuring temperature in which water boils at 212 degrees above zero and freezes at 32 degrees above zero under normal atmospheric pressure. Commonly used in the United States.

fair market value. The price something is actually worth, assuming a free market of willing buyers and sellers acting in their own best interests.

fait accompli. *Fr.* An accomplished fact. Something that has been done and seemingly may not be reversed.

false booking. *See* deadend booking.

fam, fam trip. *Abr.* Familiarization trip or tour (qv).

familiarization trip or tour. A low-cost trip or tour offered to travel agents by a supplier or group of suppliers to familiarize the agents with their destination and services. Example, a resort property or group of hotels and restaurants in Aruba might team up with an airline or tour operator to offer a discount fam trip to the resort or to Aruba. Generally referred to as a "fam trip."

family plan. Arrangement under which family members traveling together are entitled to discounts. Example: Many motels let children under 12 stay free in their parents' room.

family style. A style of serving meals in which food is brought to the table in serving dishes, for people to help themselves, rather than put on individual plates in the kitchen.

fantail. The rear or overhang of a ship.

FAP. *Abr.* Full American plan. *See* American plan.

fare. 1. The price charged for transportation. 2. A paying passenger on a plane, train, or other public means of transport. 3. Range of food, for example, the fare served by a restaurant.

fare basis. The specific fare for a ticket at a designated level of service; specified by one or more letters or by a combination of letters and numbers. Example: The letter "Y" designates coach service on an airline.

fare break point. The destination where a given fare ends. Example: The fare break point for a passenger flying from Washington DC to Kansas City via Cleveland is Kansas City.

fare code. The code used to make a booking on a CRS (qv) for a specific fare. *See also* booking code.

fare construction unit or **point.** *See* fare break point.

fathom. *n.* A unit of length equalling six feet, primarily used to measure the depth of water.

FCCA. Florida-Caribbean Cruise Association.

FCU. *Abr.* Fare construction unit (qv).

FDOR. *CRS.* Four-door car.

feasibility study. Research carried out to determine whether to go ahead with a project that is under consideration, based on such factors as the marketplace, the competition, available technology, manpower, and financial resources.

Federal Aviation Administration. An agency of the federal government that administers and monitors airline safety regulations.

Federal Trade Commission. An agency of the federal government that monitors and regulates trade within the United States.

fee-based pricing. A compensation plan in which a corporation pays its travel agency a portion of the commissions generated by the corporation's travel volume, according to a negotiated schedule.

feeder airline. An air carrier that services a local market and "feeds" traffic to the national and international carriers.

ferry. 1. *n. Abr.* Ferryboat. A boat that carries people, and/or vehicles and other cargo across a body of water. 2. *v.* To carry by boat over a given body of water. 3. *v.* To cross a body of water by ferryboat.

FET. *Abr.* Foreign escorted tour. *See* escorted tour.

fete. *Fr.* A party.

FFP. *Abr.* Frequent flyer program (qv).

FHTL. *CRS.* First-class hotel.

fictitious point principle. A technique used in constructing international fares, whereby the travel agent uses a fare to a city to which the passenger is not actually traveling in order to obtain a lower fare.

fiduciary. *adj.* Relating to financial guardianship, as in "a fiduciary relationship."

field. In computer programs, an area for recording specific information, such as the client's name, address, phone number, destination, travel date, and so on. The software generally provides one field for each item of information.

fifth freedom. *See* freedom rights.

FIJET. French acronym of the World Federation of Travel Writers.

file. 1. *n.* A collection of related information, for example, about a specific client or destination. 2. *n.* A PNR (qv) in a CRS (qv). 3. *n.* An item of furniture designed to hold files. 4. *v.* To put records into a file.

final payment. A payment that brings the balance owed to zero. Example: If a client pays a deposit and then two installments, the second installment is the final payment.

firm up. To confirm what has been discussed. Example: A travel agent will "firm up" the itinerary for an upcoming trip before booking space for the client or ticketing transportation.

first class. Top quality seats or services. Generally, first-class service is the best (and the most expensive) the supplier has to offer. However, some vendors offer an even more expensive "luxury class" (qv).

first sitting. On shipboard and in some restaurants, the earlier of two times a given meal is served.

first-class hotel. A hotel offering top quality services and, usually, a prime location and extensive amenities (qv).

fiscal year. A twelve-month period used for accounting or taxation purposes, which may or may not coincide with the calendar year.

FIT. *Abr./CRS.* Foreign independent tour. Now generally used to indicate any independent travel, domestic or international, that does not involve a package tour.

FITYO. Federation of International Youth Travel Organizations.

fixed costs. Costs that remain constant independent of income. Example: Rent and utilities are fixed costs for business owners, while the cost of processing orders varies with the number of orders received. To stay in business, the owner must be able to cover his or her fixed costs.

fjord. A narrow inlet from the sea, usually bounded by cliffs.

flagstaff. On a ship, a pole at the stern (qv) where the flag of the ship's country of registry is flown.

flambé. *Fr.* Literally, "flaming." A cooking technique in which liquor is added at the last minute and then lit before serving.

flaps. Surfaces on the wing of an airplane that can be raised or lowered during takeoff or landing to increase lift (qv) or drag (qv).

flat. *Brit.* Apartment.

flat rate. A fixed rate that may include fees for several different services.

fleabag. *Slang.* An inferior hotel or motel.

FLIFO. *Abr.* Flight information.

flight attendant. 1. A trained person who is responsible for looking after the passengers on an aircraft. In addition to serving food and drinks, the flight attendant is responsible for seeing that safety regulations are obeyed and passengers know what to do in case of emergency. 2. A gender-neutral alternative to "steward" or "stewardess" (qv).

flight coordinator. An employee of a cruise line responsible for arranging air travel for cruise passengers paying air-inclusive fares.

flight crew. All the employees — pilot, co-pilot, and flight attendants — working on an aircraft.

float. *n.* 1. A floating platform that's anchored near the shore for the use of boats or swimmers. 2. The sum of money represented by checks outstanding that have not yet been cashed. 3. The time between writing a check or charging a purchase on a credit card and the actual withdrawal of funds to cover it.

floodplain. 1. An area of flat land that may be covered by flood waters. 2. A land area built up by deposits from a stream or river.

floppy disk. A small, portable magnetic disk that is used to store and transport computer data. Sometimes called a diskette.

flotilla. A fleet of ships.

flowchart. A diagram that's used to illustrate the logical or chronological sequence of tasks in a job or process. May also be referred to as a "flow sheet."

flt or FLT. *CRS/Abr.* Flight.

fly-by-night. 1. *adj.* Shifty, shady; operating on the fringes of or outside the law. As in "a fly-by-night operation." 2. *n.* A company or person that exhibits such traits or conducts business in such a manner.

fly-drive package. An offering that bundles airfare, car rental, and sometimes, land accommodations into a single package, offered for a fixed price.

flyer. A single-sheet, printed advertisement.

FMC. Federal Maritime Commission.

F.O.B. *Abr.* Freight on board (qv).

foghorn. Any device that emits a deep booming sound as a warning to shipping.

folio. The written record of a hotel guest's account.

FONE. *CRS.* Telephone.

FOP. *CRS.* Form of payment.

force majeure. *Fr.* Literally, "superior force." An occurrence that cannot be anticipated or controlled by the travel agent, airline, cruise ship, or whatever and for which, therefore, the agent, etc. is not legally responsible.

fore and aft. *adv.* Lengthwise of a ship: from stem to stern.

foredeck. The forward part of a ship's main deck.

foreign exchange rate. *See* exchange rate.

foreign independent tour. A foreign itinerary that is individually constructed and does not involve a package tour. *See also* FIT.

foreign-flag vessel. A ship owned by or registered in a country other than the United States.

fortnight. *Brit.* A period of two weeks.

fortress. A fortified place, especially a large, permanent fortification.

fortress hub. *See* concentrated hub.

forum. 1. A public place or marketplace in an ancient Roman city. 2. A public meeting place, radio or TV program, or area in a newspaper or computer bulletin board in which two or more people may openly discuss ideas.

FP. *CRS.* Final payment (qv) or full pension (qv).

FQTV. *CRS.* Frequent traveler.

FRAG. *Abr.* Fragile.

franchise. A business contract in which an independent business (the franchisee) sells or markets the products and/or services of a larger firm (the franchisor). The franchisee receives training and marketing support from the franchisor and pays a fee for ongoing support.

FRAV. *CRS.* First available.

free hits. The number of times an agency can access and query a CRS before triggering per-use charges.

free port. A port where no customs duty or regulations are imposed on goods shipped in and out.

free sale. Indicates that reservations may be made without checking the availability.

free trade. The untrammeled international exchange of products and commodities with tariffs used to produce reasonable revenue and not to hinder commerce.

freebie. A product or service that is given away without charge.

freedom of the seas. The right of a commercial ship to cruise any waters, except territorial waters of other nations, in either peace or war.

freedom rights. A set of guiding principles governing air-service rights under international agreements. The seven freedom rights are: 1. The right to overfly another country. 2. The right to land in another country. 3. The right to carry revenue traffic to another country. 4. The right to carry revenue traffic from another country. 5. The right to carry revenue traffic between two foreign countries. 6. The right to use one's own country as a transit point when exercising other freedom rights. 7. Cabotage. (qv).

freedoms of the air. *See* freedom rights.

freestanding. *adj.* Describing an independent organization or business that is not affiliated with another establishment.

freight. 1. Cargo; goods to be shipped. 2. Shipment by common carrier as opposed to by an express service, as in "Ship it freight."

freight on board. A term used in shipping to refer to the place where the buyer becomes responsible for the shipment and the shipping charges. Example: If the buyer lives in Des Moines and buys a product F.O.B. New York, the buyer must pay the shipping charges from New York to Des Moines and is responsible for seeing that it is properly insured during that shipment.

freighter. A ship designed primarily to carry cargo. Some also carry passengers.

French service. A style of serving meals in which the waiter brings the serving dishes to the table and dishes up the food there, rather than serving plates prepared in the kitchen.

frequency. The number of flights by a given airline or other carrier on a given route during a given period of time.

frequency marketing, frequency marketing program. Any marketing plan designed to reward customers who buy on a regular basis or to encourage customers to do so, as in a frequent flyer program (qv).

frequent flyer. A person who flies frequently. Specifically, a person who is enrolled in an airline's frequent flyer program (qv).

frequent flyer program. A program offered by various airlines to promote passenger loyalty. Participants earn credits good for free travel or upgraded service based on the number of miles they fly with the carrier. They are also entitled to special services. Participation is optional.

frequent lodger. A person who frequently stays at a property or at properties belonging to a particular hotel chain. Specifically, a person who is enrolled in a hotel's frequent lodger program (qv).

frequent lodger program. A program offered by various hotels and hotel chains to promote customer loyalty. Participants earn credits good for free lodging or upgraded service based on the number of nights they stay at the hotel. They are also entitled to special services. Participation is optional.

front office. *adj.* Referring to those activities that take place with customers or the general public. *See also* back office.

FS. *CRS.* Free sale (qv).

FTC. Federal Trade Commission (qv).

fuel charge. The amount charged by a rental car company to refill the tank of a returned vehicle.

full house. 1. A theater, restaurant, or lodging in which all the seats or rooms are taken. 2. A poker hand consisting of three of a kind and a pair.

Full Pension. *See* American plan.

full service agency location. A branch of an agency that provides customers both reservations and ticketing.

full service hotel. A hotel with a restaurant.

fully appointed agency. A travel agency that is accredited to sell airline, cruise, and other travel services.

function book. In a hotel or conference center, the official record that controls room assignments for meetings and other events.

function sheet. *See* banquet event order.

funnel. A ship's chimney or smokestack

funnel flight. 1. A flight on a feeder airline (qv) that connects with another flight on a larger aircraft. *See also* change of gauge. 2. The use of a single flight number for an itinerary that actually involves an online connection (qv) with two separate flight numbers, with the presumed intent to make the itinerary appear to be a direct flight with a change of aircraft as opposed to a connection.

fuselage. The main body of an aircraft to which the wings, tail, and landing gear are attached.

FYI. *Abr.* For your information.

–G g

Galileo. A computerized reservation system (qv).

galley. The kitchen in a ship.

gangway. A movable ramp or stairway between a ship and a pier; used for boarding and deboarding. Also called a "gangplank."

garni. *Fr. adj.* Designates a hotel without meal service.

gate. Area in an airport where passengers board an airplane.

gateway city. 1. A city that serves as a departure or arrival point for international flights. 2. A city that serves as an airline's entry or departure point to or from a country.

gateway fare. The fare to a major foreign city, or "gateway."

Gay Nineties. The 1890s. Used to refer to a style of entertainment, costume, or decoration evocative of that period.

gazebo. A small, open-sided structure designed for sitting and taking in the view.

gazetteer. 1. A geographical dictionary. 2. A directory in which the entries are arranged by geographical location. For example, a gazetteer of restaurants.

GDN. *CRS.* Room with a garden or a garden view. Also designated GDNVW.

GDP. *Abr.* Gross domestic product (qv).

GDS. *Abr.* Global distribution system.

Gemini®. A computerized reservation system (qv).

genealogy. 1. The study of family history. 2. A listing of a person's ancestors.

gentleman's agreement. An unwritten agreement backed solely by the honor of the participants.

GETS. *Abr.* Gabriel Extended Travel Services. A global system for booking air travel, car rentals, hotels, and some ferry services that is unaffiliated with any airline or other travel provider.

GFAX. *Abr.* General facts.

GG rate. Guaranteed group rate (qv).

GI. *Abr.* Global indicator (qv).

GIANTS. Greater Independent Association of National Travel Services.

GIT. *Abr.* Group inclusive tour. A group tour that is offered only if a minimum number of people book for it.

GIT fares. Airfares that apply when sold in conjunction with a group inclusive tour.

GLAMER. Group Leaders of America.

glider. An aircraft without an engine that is towed to a given height and then set free to glide on air currents. Used for sport and sightseeing.

global distribution system. A computer reservation system (CRS), typically owned jointly by airlines in different countries, that includes reservation databases of suppliers in many countries.

global indicator. A code that appears next to the fare and tells what route the travel must take.

global positioning system. A system using satellites and cellular communication to pinpoint a vehicle's or aircraft's location. Now being introduced in rental cars and about to be tested by the FAA.

G.M. *Fr. Abr.* "Gentil membre." A guest at a Club Med resort.

GM. *Abr.* General manager.

GMT. *Abr.* Greenwich mean time (qv).

GNP. Gross national product (qv).

GNR. *CRS.* Guest name record.

G.O. *Fr. Abr.* "Gentil organisateur." A staff member at a Club Med resort.

GO. *CRS.* Value car rental company.

Golden Age Passport. An identification card sold by the U.S. National Park Service that gives persons who are 62 or older unlimited access/entrance to the sites it operates.

gondola. 1. Passenger car suspended from a cable; used to transport skiers and sightseers. 2. Flat-bottomed Venetian boat with a high bow and stern.

GPS. *Abr.* Global positioning system (qv).

GPST. *CRS.* Group seat request.

gradient. A measure, in degrees, of how steep a slope is.

Gran Prix. *Fr.* One of several automobile races.

grand tour. A lengthy journey which takes in the major sights of a continent. Usually used to refer to "The Grand Tour of Europe," on which people of means saw all of the best the continent had to offer.

grandfather. *v.* To exempt a person or company from new laws or regulations based on circumstances that existed in the past. Example: A travel agency might decide to cut outside agents' share of total commissions earned from 60% to 50%, but grandfather those agents with whom it is already working. If that were the case, agents already on the books would continue to earn 60%, while new agents would be paid 50%.

gratuity. A voluntary payment above the stated cost of a product or service given in appreciation for the service rendered. A tip.

graveyard shift. The late-night or overnight work shift.

greasy spoon. A inexpensive restaurant or coffee shop that doesn't look particularly clean.

green card. Identity card issued by the U.S. government to noncitizens who are permanent residents of the United States.

greenback. Any denomination of U.S. paper money.

Greenwich mean time. Solar time in Greenwich, England, which is used as the basis of standard time throughout the world. Also called "Greenwich time."

gringo. A foreigner, especially an English or American person, in Spain or Latin America. Sometimes used as a slur.

grogshop. *Brit.* Bar, usually low class.

gross. The total amount (usually of money), before any deductions have been made.

gross domestic product. The total value of the products and services a nation produces for its own use during a given time period, say one year.

gross national product. The total value of the products and services a nation produces during a given time period, including exports.

gross profit. Net sales minus the cost of goods or services sold and before payment of taxes and operating expenses.

gross registered tonnage. A measurement of the enclosed space in a ship. Port officials use it to calculate harbor dues.

gross sales. Total sales receipts before subtracting any expenses or deductions for returns or other post-sale adjustments.

ground arrangements. Services covering the land portion of a trip, such as lodging, visits to museums, sightseeing tours, and transfers between airport and hotel.

ground operator. A company that provides land services such as sightseeing tours, transfers from airport to hotel, limos, taxis, and so on.

group desk. The department or counter of an airline, travel agency, hotel, or other supplier that handles group reservations.

group rate. The fare or room rate offered to a group of travelers.

group sales. 1. The act of marketing travel to affinity groups. 2. A department of an agency devoted to this type of sale.

GRPS. *CRS.* Groups.

GRT. *Abr.* Gross registered tonnage (qv).

GST. *Abr.* Goods and services tax.

GTIA. Golf and Travel Industry Association.

gtd. *Abr.* Guaranteed.

guar. *Abr.* Guarantee or guaranteed.

guarantee. 1. *n.* An assurance that a product or service will be provided at an agreed-upon time and/or meet stated specifications, often with a promise that the purchaser will be reimbursed if the product or service fails to meet the guarantee. 2. *v.* To answer for a product or service meeting agreed-upon conditions. 3. *v.* To pay for a guarantee of product or service performance.

guaranteed group rate. On a cruise ship, a group rate extended to a travel agency on a negotiated basis which will be honored regardless of the number of bookings made.

guaranteed reservation. A reservation that will be held all night, whether or not the party arrives on time. Generally, the buyer pays for the privilege by guaranteeing payment whether or not the reservation is used.

guaranteed share. A cruise line rate for a single passenger based on the line's promise to find the passenger a roommate to share a cabin. The rate will be honored even if no roommate is found.

guest house. A home that offers rooms to travelers. *See also* bed and breakfast.

guide. A person who takes visitors on tours of sites, such as museums, cities, wilderness areas, etc. and shares his knowledge about places, objects, or flora and fauna of interest.

Gulf Stream. A warm-water current that flows from the Caribbean North and East to the British Isles.

gunwale. The upper edge of the side of a boat.

— H h

hacienda. *Sp.* A country house or estate.

HAI. Helicopter Association International.

half pension. Hotel rate that includes breakfast and one additional meal, typically dinner. Also called Modified American Plan and demi-pension.

halo effect. The extra business an agency gives the airline that owns the CRS system it uses, above and beyond what that airline might expect to get based on it's share of the overall market. Industry observers consider the halo effect a result of the agent's tendency to trust the CRS system's accuracy, as well as what critics call the CRS system's "architectural bias" (qv). The system lists the owner-airline's flights first, which some say leads to more bookings of those flights.

hand luggage. Baggage carried by the passenger, as on a plane. Often defined and limited by airline regulations.

hansom cab. A horse-drawn carriage, typically used for sightseeing.

harbor. A naturally or artificially protected area where ships dock.

harbor master. The official who oversees port operations.

hard copy. A printed version of a document, as opposed to the data in the computer.

hard-dollar savings. Easily identifiable savings, such as free tickets, reduced rates, or revenue-sharing (qv). *See also* soft dollar savings.

hatch. A hinged door covering an opening in a ship's deck.

hawker stand. In Singapore, an outdoor or indoor stall serving cooked food.

hawser. A heavy rope used to tow or tie up a ship to a dock.

HCC. Hotel Clearing Corporation.

head. A toilet on a boat or ship.

head count. The physical counting of passengers, as by a flight attendant, to compare a manifest with the actual number of passengers. *See also* nose count.

head tax. A fee assessed by some cities and countries on every passenger who arrives or leaves.

HEDNA. Hotel Electronic Distribution Network Association.

heliport. A landing pad for helicopters.

heli-skiing. An excursion by helicopter to remote, pristine skiing areas.

helm. The apparatus for steering a ship. A ship's steering mechanism.

herringbone setup. *See* chevron setup.

hidden-city ploy, hidden city ticketing. A stratagem used to get

a lower airfare when the fare for a flight from A to C with a stop
in B is cheaper than a fare directly from A to B. The passenger
who wants to travel to B, buys a ticket from A to C and then gets
off at B. Considered unethical by airlines and many travel agencies.

high season. The season of the year when travel to an area peaks
and rates are at their highest.

higher intermediate point. When a city between the city of origin
and the fare break point (qv) has a higher fare than the destination city, the higher fare must be used.

hijack. *v.* To take over a vessel or airplane by force.

HIP. *Abr.* Higher intermediate point.

hire car. *Brit.* A rented car.

history. In bookings, a detailed record of what has been done.

HK. *CRS.* Hold confirmed.

HL. *CRS.* Holds list.

HMS. *Abr.* Her (or His) Majesty's Ship.

HNML. *CRS.* Hindu meal.

hold. 1. *v.* Reserve or set aside. 2. *n.* The storage compartment of a
ship.

Holocaust. 1. The murder of six million Jews by the Nazis during
World War II. 2. Generically, any great loss of human life or any
almost total destruction, especially by fire.

hologram. A laser-generated image with three-dimensional properties, increasing used to deter counterfeiting of currency, credit
cards, and identification.

hollow square setup. A seating arrangement for meetings in which
tables or chairs are arranged in a square (or rectangle) with an
open space in the center.

home exchange. The swapping of personal residences by people in
different cities or countries as a strategy to reduce the costs of
vacation travel.

home port bonus. An additional commission, typically 5%, paid by
cruise lines on cruise-only bookings made by agents in Florida.
The commission, now being phased out by some cruise lines, is
ostensibly justified by the fact that Florida-based agents receive
no commissions on related airfares, as do agents in other states.

homepage. The first "page" or screen you see at a web site, typically containing a table of contents for the site.

homesickness. An intense longing for home experienced by some
travelers, especially on extended journeys.

honor system. A unsupervised system in which customers help
themselves to goods and services, and then are expected to pay
for what they used.

honorarium. A fee paid to a guest speaker or lecturer.

hooker. *Slang.* A prostitute or streetwalker.

hors d'oeuvres. *Fr.* Light snacks or finger food served before a meal or at the beginning of the meal.

horseshoe setup. A seating arrangement for meetings in which tables or chairs are arranged in a U shape.

hospitality industry. Term applied to the hotel, restaurant, entertainment, and resort industry.

hospitality suite. A hotel room, or suite, reserved by a company or group in which to greet customers or others. Typically, refreshments are served.

host. 1. Person leading or in charge of a tour. 2. In computer lingo, the system to which an agent's terminal is connected for CRS services. In some cases, the host is an airline's central computer system.

hosted tour. A tour that features the services of a person, sometimes a hotel employee, who is available to perform certain services for members of the group.

hostel. An inexpensive accommodation, typically in dormitory style. Usually used by younger travelers, as in "youth hostel."

hostelry. A hotel or inn.

hot air ballooning. An increasingly popular form of excursion in which a small number of people are carried aloft in a basket suspended from a large balloon made lighter than the surrounding air by being filled with heated air.

hot line. Any phone number used to provide fast help or customer service.

hotel. Any establishment offering overnight accommodations.

hotel register. A book, or other record, which guests sign and which becomes the permanent record of an establishment's guests.

hotel representative. A booking agent or agency for hotels.

hotel voucher. A pre-paid coupon that can be exchanged at certain hotels for a night's lodging.

hotelier. The owner or manager of a hotel. Someone in the hotel business.

house flag. The flag denoting the company to which a ship belongs. A shipping company's flag.

house limit. 1. In a casino, the maximum wager permitted. 2. In a hotel or other establishment, the maximum extent to which credit will be extended before payment is requested. 3. In restaurants and bars, the maximum number of alcoholic beverages that will be served to a single customer.

house plan. 1. A diagram of a property's function spaces. 2. A property's floor plan.

houseboat. A flat-bottomed or twin hulled recreational boat that resembles a small house or apartment.

housekeeping. The department of a hotel charged with cleaning and maintaining rooms and public spaces.

hovercraft. A water-borne vessel that floats on a cushion of air.

HRU. *Abr.* Hydrostatic release units (qv).

HSMA. Hospitality Sales and Marketing Association International.

HTL. *CRS.* Hotel.

hub. A city or an airport in which an airline has major operations and many gates. For example: American has a hub in Dallas, United in Chicago, Delta in Atlanta, TWA in St. Louis.

hub-and-spoke. *adj.* A system many airlines have adopted to maximize the amount of time their planes spend in the air, thus make money for them. They designate certain cities as hubs, schedule many flights to them, and offer connecting flights from the hubs to smaller cities, which can be served by smaller aircraft.

hub and spoke tour. The hub and spoke concept applied to tours. Tour members travel out of an return to a central point each day.

hull. A ship's frame or body, not including masts and rigging.

hurricane. A tropical storm (qv) with winds in excess of 75 mph.

hurricane season. A period in which hurricanes are most likely to occur, roughly from August to October in the Northern hemisphere..

hush kit. *Slang.* Added equipment used to make existing aircraft engines quieter.

HX. *CRS.* Have cancelled.

hydrofoil. 1. A ship or boat design that lifts the hull above the water as speed increases, thereby lessening friction and increasing speed. 2. Any ship or boat so designed.

hydrostatic release units. Automatically deployed life rafts used on cruise ships.

–*I i*

IACC. International Association of Conference Centers.

IACVB. International Association of Convention and Visitors Bureaus.

IAFE. International Association of Fairs and Expositions.

IAMAT. International Association for Medical Assistance to Travellers.

IAPA. International Air Passenger Association.

IAS. *CRS.* Insert a segment.

IATA. International Air Transport Association.

IATAN. International Airlines Travel Agency Network.

IATAN card. Photo identification issued by IATAN. Widely accepted as the only identification for travel agents. Sometimes called, erroneously, "IATA card."

IATAN list. A record maintained by a travel agency listing those employees and independent contractors who qualify for travel benefits, as determined by IATAN.

IAWT. International Association of World Tourism.

IC. *Abr.* Independent contractor. An outside sales representative for a travel agency.

ICAO. International Civil Aviation Organization.

ICAR. *CRS.* Intermediate-size car.

ICTA. Institute of Certified Travel Agents.

ID. *Abr.* Identification.

IDL. *Abr.* International date line (qv).

IFTAA. International Forum of Travel and Tourism Advocates.

IFUN. *CRS.* If unable.

IFWTO. International Federation of Women's Travel Organizations.

IGN. *CRS.* Ignore.

immigrant. A person who enters a country of which he is not native to settle. *See also* emigrant.

immigrate. *v.* To enter a country to assume permanent residence in it.

immunity. 1. Exemption from the laws of a country, as in "diplomatic immunity." 2. An acquired state of resistance to a disease.

import. 1. *v.* To bring goods from one country into another. 2. *n.* A product brought into one country from another.

IN. *CRS.* 1. International. 2. Infant. 3. Check-in.

in bond. Held until departure, as duty-free goods which, once purchased, are not delivered to the buyer until departure from the airport.

in plant. *adj.* Referring to a travel agency physically located on the premises of a corporation it services, and limited to 3% commissions. An outdated ARC (qv) term. *See also* corporate agency.

in season. Available only at certain times of the year. For example, "fresh fruit, in season."

in transit. En route. Traveling.

INAD. *CRS.* Inadmissible passenger.

inaugural. The first, as in "the inaugural sailing."

inbound. 1. Arriving. 2. Of an airline itinerary, the return leg. 3. Relating to travel services provided to passengers arriving to a travel agent's location from elsewhere.

incentive. Merchandise, travel, cash, service, or intangible offered to an employee or customer as a reward for taking a specified action.

incentive house. A company that runs incentive programs, often including travel programs, for other companies.

incentive travel. Travel that is given to employees as a reward for outstanding performance.

incidentals. Small items or miscellaneous expenditures.

inclusive tour. A tour package that bundles transportation and lodging along with additional services such as transfers, sightseeing, museum admissions, and so forth.

inclusive tour fare. A fare, as on an airline, that is based on the purchase of an inclusive tour.

independent contractor. An independent individual who performs services for a company for an agreed-on fee. Legally distinct from an employee.

independent tour. A tour that does not include a guide or a host or a set routine of daily activities.

indirect tax. Any tax or fee that is levied on one entity but passed along to another.

INF. *CRS.* Infant.

infant. In the travel industry, a designation used to determine fares and other rates. Generally, an infant is less than two years of age. Infants often travel for free.

inflation. In simplest terms, the tendency of prices to go up.

in-flight. *Adj.* Describing goods or services provided during an airline flight, as in-flight magazines, in-flight duty-free shopping, and so forth.

infrastructure. 1. The underlying framework of an enterprise. 2. The network of transportation services provided by a government — roads, bridges, and so forth.

in-house sales. Sales made to the employees of a company. *See also* self-sales.

inlet. A narrow expanse of water, hemmed in by land. A small bay.

inn. A small hotel or guest house. Generally, used to describe accommodations possessing a certain intimacy and charm. A tavern.

inner city. An urban slum, as distinct from downtown (qv).

innkeeper. A person who owns or manages an inn.

in-out dates. Dates on which a guest arrives and leaves.

in-room messaging. System that allows hotel guests to receive electronic mail and faxes on their room televisions.

INS. Immigration and Naturalization Service.

intercontinental. Spanning more than one continent.

interface. The juncture between two computer systems or between a user and a computer system. Generically, the juncture between any two systems or organizations.

interline agreements. Contractual or formal agreements between airlines governing such matters as ticketing, baggage transfers, and so forth.

interline connection. A change of planes that also involves a change of airlines.

intermodal. Combining two forms of transportation. For example, air and sea.

International Date Line. 180 degrees of longitude. The date is different on either side of this imaginary line located in the Pacific Ocean.

Internet. A world-wide network of computers linked by telephone lines, allowing for the global dissemination of information.

interstate. Involving travel or trade between states of the United States.

intl. *Abr.* International.

intranet. A private computer network.

intrastate. Referring to travel or commerce that doesn't cross a state line.

in-vehicle travel information (safety) systems. Any of a number of interrelated technologies such as cellular phones, global positioning systems (qv), digital mapping, and others offered in rental cars.

invoice. A business document detailing goods or services provided and requesting payment.

IRC. *CRS.* International route charge.

Iron Curtain. Now obsolete term used to refer to the border between the Communist states of Eastern Europe and the West.

iron horse. Affectionate term for railroad locomotives.

IS. *CRS.* If not holding, sell.

I/S. *Abr.* Inside, as of a ship's cabin.

ISDN. Integrated services digital network. A high-speed telephone line capable of sending large amounts of data quickly.

island hopping. Visiting a number of islands in quick succession, as on a cruise.

ISLVW. *CRS.* Island view.

ISO. International Standards Organization.

ISP. Internet service provider.

isobar. A line on a weather map separating areas of different barometric pressure.

ISTTE. International Society of Travel and Tourism Educators.

IT. *CRS*. Inclusive tour.

IT fare. Inclusive tour fare (qv).

IT number. Number used in airline CRS systems to indicate that a tour has met certain requirements.

itinerary. The route of travel. In an airline booking, a list of flights, times, etc.

ITTA. Independent Travel Technology Association.

ITX. *CRS*. Inclusive tour excursion fare.

IWGN. *CRS*. Intermediate-size station wagon.

—Jj—

jai alai. (pronounced "high-lie") A ball game of Basque origin, played on an indoor court. Players hurl the ball from wicker baskets. A popular sport for betting in some regions.

jamboree. 1. *Cap.* A national or international gathering of the Boy Scouts of America. 2. Any festivity featuring music, dancing, and refreshments; typically held outdoors.

jargon. The informal or technical language used by members of the same profession or industry.

JATO. *Abr.* Jet-assisted takeoff.

jaunting car. A small horse-drawn carriage, used for tourist excursions in Ireland.

jaywalk. To cross the street in the middle of the block or against traffic signals.

jeepney. In the Philippines, a converted jeep used for public transportation. The term is a corruption of jitney (qv).

jet lag. A physiological condition caused by the disorientation of a person's biological clock due to travel across several time zones. Characterized by irritability, lethargy, insomnia, and other symptoms.

jet loader. *See* jetway.

jet port. A synonym for airport. Seldom used.

jet ski. A one-person, motorized water vehicle on which the driver stands upright on ski-like pads.

jet stream. 1. Any high-altitude, strong wind current which can aid or hinder jet flight depending on its direction. 2. The trail of condensation left by a jet flying at high altitude.

jetliner. A passenger jet.

jetty. A wooden or stone platform, projecting into the water, used for the docking of boats and ships.

jetway. An enclosed gangway that provides access from the terminal to an aircraft.

jitney. Any small motorized vehicle used for public transportation.

joint fare. The fare charged for travel that utilizes more than one airline. This fare is agreed on by the airlines involved.

joint notice of change. A form submitted to IATA (qv) when the ownership of a travel agency changes hands.

joint tenancy. A legal form of ownership involving two people, typically spouses.

Jones Act. A protectionist law of 1886 forbidding foreign flag vessels from carrying passengers between United States ports.

JRSTE. *CRS.* Junior suite (qv).

JT. *CRS.* Joint. Joint fare (qv).

jumbo jet. Any large, wide-body jet aircraft.

junior suite. A hotel room that features a separate living-sitting area (although not a separate room), in addition to the bedroom.

junket. 1. A trip ostensibly taken for business purposes, which is primarily for pleasure. Usually used to refer to trips taken by elected officials. 2. A legitimate sponsored trip in which the expenses of the travelers are paid for by the sponsors, as when a foreign destination invites travel writers to visit.

Kk

K. *Abr.* Kilobyte. A measure of memory size in computers.

karaoke. (Pronounced "carry-okey.") Japanese name for a form of entertainment in which patrons take turns singing the lyrics to prerecorded music.

karaoke bar. A bar featuring karaoke entertainment.

karaoke system. The equipment needed to provide karaoke.

keel. The structural element that runs the length of a ship's bottom.

kg. *Abr.* Kilogram.

kilo. Short for kilogram. A metric unit of weight, approximately 2.2 pounds.

kilobyte. A measure of memory size in computers. A kilobyte can store the equivalent of 1,000 typewritten characters.

kilometer. A metric measure of distance, approximately five-eighths of a mile. The standard measure of distance and speed (kph) in most foreign countries.

king room. A hotel room with a king-size bed.

kiosk. 1. A small vendor's stall or cart. 2. A public booth dispensing information, usually via an interactive television interface.

KIP. *CRS.* Keep alone if possible.

KK. *CRS.* Confirmed.

KL. *CRS.* Confirmed waitlist.

km. *Abr.* Kilometer (qv).

knot. A nautical measure of speed, approximately 1.5 miles per hour.

kosher. Conforming to Jewish dietary laws.

KP. *CRS.* Commission percentage.

kph. *Abr.* Kilometers per hour.

Kremlin. The offices of the Russian government in Moscow.

KSML. *CRS.* Kosher meal.

– L l

lanai. In Hawaii and other tropical destinations, a porch or patio.

land arrangements. All travel elements provided to a client after arrival at the destination, such as hotel, sightseeing, and so forth.

land only. A fare rate that doesn't include air transportation.

landau. A four-wheeled, horse-drawn carriage.

landfall. The first sight of land, as on a cruise.

landing strip. A basic, often unpaved, runway for small planes.

landlocked. *adj.* Having no access to the sea.

landlubber. A person new to ships and sailing.

landmark. 1. A famous historical building or location. 2. A prominent geographical feature used for finding one's way.

larboard. *See* port.

last-room availability. A feature of a CRS allowing up-to-the minute information on the number of rooms available at a hotel.

last-seat availability. A CRS capability similar to last-room availability but pertaining to airline seats.

late booking fee. An additional charge levied by some tour operators for reservations made shortly before departure.

latitude. Angular distance measured in degrees North or South of the equator.

launch. *n.* A small boat that ferries cruise passengers to and from the shore.

lavatory. A toilet. Rest room.

layover. A stop on a trip, usually overnight and usually associated with a change of planes or other transportation.

LCAR. *CRS.* Luxury car.

LDW. *Abr.* Loss damage waiver (qv).

lead time. The amount or period of time before the announcement of an event and its occurrence, or between the notification that a task must be undertaken and the time at which it must be completed.

league. A measure of distance, primarily nautical, of approximately three miles.

lectern. A small stand used by speakers at formal meetings to hold notes and such. *See also* podium.

lee. The side of a ship or island away from the wind direction.

leeward. (Pronounced "LOO-erd") *See* lee.

leg. A single segment of an itinerary.

lei. In Hawaii, a flower necklace given in greeting.

leisure travel. Travel undertaken for pleasure, as opposed to business travel.

letter of agreement. A contract in the form of a letter from one person or company to another; both parties must sign for the agreement to become binding.

letter of credit. A document issued by a bank or other financial institution attesting to an individual's or company's ability to borrow money within specific limits.

letter of intent. Typically, a letter from a potential buyer to a seller indicating the seriousness of the potential buyer's interest and agreeing to hold in strict confidence any data provided by the seller to assist the buyer in evaluating the property or business being sold. Usually required by the owner of an agency from a prospective buyer before sharing proprietary information.

LHTL. *CRS.* Luxury hotel.

liability. Exposure to damage, legal or financial.

liability coverage. Insurance providing protection from claims by third parties.

license. 1. A permit obtained from local government authorities to conduct certain types of business activities, such as a restaurant, or events, such as a parade. 2. An agreement under which one company may use the logo or other property of another, as on a tee shirt.

lido deck. On a cruise ship, the area around the swimming pool.

lifeboat drill. A required test of a cruise ship's emergency procedures to be carried out before or within 24 hours of sailing.

lift. 1. The maximum number of airline seats available to a specific destination during a specific period. 2. The aerodynamic force that makes it possible for a plane to fly. 3. *Brit.* An elevator.

limited purpose card. A credit card that can be used only for travel expenditures, for example, and not for general purchases.

limited service agency location. A branch of a travel agency that takes reservations but doesn't provide ticketing.

limited service hotel. A hotel without a restaurant.

limousine. A large chauffeured vehicle for hire, as opposed to a taxi.

line. A rope on a ship.

linen. In a hotel, sheets and towels that are changed daily.

liner. A large passenger-carrying ship.

liquidated damages clause. In a contract between a travel agency and a CRS vendor, a stipulation that should the agency switch vendors before the contract expires, the original vendor will be due payment for the fees it would have received had the contract remained in effect for its full length.

liveried. In uniform, as a liveried chauffeur.

livery. The uniform worn by some employees, such as chauffeurs and doormen.

llama. A long-necked animal native to South America; used as a pack animal on some trekking and hiking vacations.

LNI. *CRS.* Lanai (qv).

load factor. The percentage of available space on a plane or other mode of transportation that has been sold to date.

local fare. 1. The fare on a direct flight. 2. A fare for transportation on a single carrier.

lodge. A type of hotel, typically of a rustic character in a national park or similar setting.

lodging. Any accommodation. A room in a hotel.

log. An official record of events on a minute-by-minute or hour-by-hour basis, as a ship's log.

logo. The trademarked symbol of a business.

longitude. Angular distance measured in degrees East or West of the prime meridian (qv).

longshoreman. A dock worker.

loo. *Brit.* A toilet.

loss damage waiver (LDW). Daily insurance that covers theft and vandalism of a rented car in addition to damage caused by accident.

low fare search. A continuous, computerized search for the lowest current available fares designed to lower the cost of trips already booked but not yet taken.

low season. The time of year when travel to a destination is at its lowest and prices decline.

lower bed. On a ship, the lower of two bunk beds, placed at the conventional height from the floor.

lowest logical airfare. The lowest fare that is consistent with a corporation's travel policy.

loyalty marketing. Term applied to frequent flyer and similar programs designed to create repeat business.

LSF. *CRS.* Local selling fare.

LUX. *CRS.* Luxury.

luxury class. The most expensive accommodations or fare category.

– *M m* —————————————————————————

MAAS. *CRS.* Meet and assist.

maglev. *Abr.* Magnetic levitation. A technology used in high-speed trains.

maid service. Room cleaning services, such as those provided in a hotel, that are offered separately as in a condo (qv) or villa (qv).

maiden voyage. The first voyage of a ship.

maitre d'. *Fr.* The host or head waiter at a restaurant; supervises the waiters. Also maitre d'hotel.

management contract. An arrangement whereby a hotel's owner contracts with a separate company to run the hotel.

management report. A report prepared by a travel agency for a corporate client detailing all travel activity and expenditures during the reporting period. Used to analyze patterns of travel usage.

manifest. A document listing the contents of a shipment or the passengers on a ship.

manual. 1. A book of instructions, computer documentation. 2. A car with a manual transmission.

MAP. *Abr.* Modified American plan (qv).

MAPTA. Metropolitan Association of Professional Travel Agents.

market share. The volume of sales, expressed as a percentage, achieved by one company in a specific geographic area, compared to all sales of similar products or of similar companies.

market share override program. An enhanced commission system in which a supplier (typically an airline) will pay a travel agency an override (qv) only when the agency's percentage of sales of the supplier's product exceeds by a specified amount the supplier's market share in the travel agency's market. In other words, a travel agency's sales of an airline's tickets might have to reach 33% of the agency's total airline sales before the airline, with a market share of 30% in the agency's market, would pay the agency an override.

marketing. The process of identifying and reaching specific segments of a population for the purposes of selling them a product or service.

markup. The sum of money or percentage added to a wholesale or purchase price to arrive at the retail or resale price.

marquee. 1. A sign over a theater entrance listing the current attraction. 2. A large tent, usually without some or all the sides, used during outdoor events.

MARS. *Abr.* Multi-access reservations system.

martial law. The suspension of normal civil law and its replacement by strict military control. Often declared during times of civil unrest.

Mason-Dixon line. The boundary between Pennsylvania and Maryland. The traditional boundary between the Northern and Southern United States.

masseur, masseuse. *Fr.* The male and female variants for a person who gives massages.

MAST. Midwest Agents Selling Travel.

maximum authorized amount. The largest sum of money a bank can withdraw from a travel agency's account to settle its weekly sales report.

Mayday. 1. A radio signal word used to denote a distress call. 2. By extension, a distress call.

MCO. *CRS. Abr.* Miscellaneous charge order.

MCT. *CRS.* Minimum connecting time (qv).

meal sitting. *See* sitting.

meet and greet. *Slang.* Term for a service that greets and assists members of a group on their arrival at the airport.

meeting fare. Special fare negotiated with an airline for passengers traveling to attend a specific meeting or convention.

meeting planner. A person who specializes in the planning and organization of conventions and other business meetings.

meeting rate. Special rate offered by a hotel for guests attending a meeting, usually one being held at the hotel.

mega-agency. *Slang.* A very large travel agency with nationwide operations. There are currently about seven such agencies in the United States.

megalopolis. An extended urban area caused by the tendency of large cities to grow together.

merchant marine. 1. The commercial shipping industry of a given nation. 2. Those involved in that industry.

merger. The legal process whereby one corporation acquires or joins with another.

meridians. The imaginary lines of longitude on a globe.

metal detector. A hand-held or walk-through device, such as those used at airport security checkpoints, used to detect concealed metal objects.

metro. A public rail transportation system. A subway system.

Metroliner. An Amtrak train running between New York and Washington, offering faster service at a higher fare.

mezzanine. The first balcony level above the orchestra in a theater. *See also* dress circle.

mid-office system. The management information (or MIS) portion of a travel agency's computer system, as distinct from the CRS (front office) and accounting functions (back office).

midship(s). *See* amidships.

migration. 1. The periodic movement of animals from one location to another. 2. The movement of large groups of ethnically similar peoples from one area to another.

mileage allowance, mileage cap. The mileage a rental car may be driven on a single day without additional charge.

mileage charge. The per mile fee charged by a car rental company.

mileage system, mileage based pricing. An airfare system allowing stopovers up to a specific maximum permitted mileage.

milk run. *Slang.* A trip, usually by a train and late at night, that makes many stops along the way.

millennium. 1. A period of 1,000 years. 2. Informally, January 1, 2000, expected to be a record-breaking time for tourism.

millibar. A measure of atmospheric pressure.

MIN. *CRS.* Minimum room (qv).

minibar. A hotel room amenity consisting of a small, stocked refrigerator containing beverages and snacks which are inventoried daily and paid for as they are used.

minimum connecting time. The legally defined minimum time necessary to change planes at a given airport.

minimum land package. The minimum cost of land arrangements that must be purchased to qualify for a special air fare.

minimum room. An inexpensive hotel room booked with the understanding that the booking can be upgraded if other rooms are available on arrival.

minshuku. An inexpensive Japanese inn, with fewer amenities and a lower level of service than a ryokan (qv).

MINR. *CRS.* Minimum rate.

MIS. *Abr.* Management information system.

miscellaneous charge order. An ARC document used to process the payment of travel arrangements other than airfares.

MLM. *Abr.* Multi-level marketing (qv).

M/M. *CRS.* Mr. and Mrs.

MOD. *CRS.* Moderate room.

modem. A device that allows computers to exchange data over phone lines.

modified American plan. A hotel rate that includes two meals daily, usually breakfast and dinner.

MODR. *CRS.* Moderate rate.

modular. In sections. Designed for easy expansion, as a modular computer system.

MOML. *CRS.* Muslim meal.

Montezuma's revenge. *Slang.* Traveler's diarrhea (qv), especially when experienced in Mexico. Named after the Aztec king of Mexico conquered by the Spanish. Considered derogatory by Mexicans.

moor. To secure a ship to a dock.

Morse code. A communications system consisting of letters coded into dots and dashes, and used in telegraphs.

mortality rate. 1. Of humans, the rate of deaths per thousand or hundred thousand of population. 2. Of businesses, the rate at which they cease operations or the amount of time between inception and failure.

motel. A type of hotel in which parking is provided at or near the room and the room door gives out onto the parking lot.

motor court, motor hotel. *See* motel.

motor home. A recreational vehicle that is self-driving (as opposed to towed) and which contains complete living accommodation.

motorbike. A small, easily-operated motorcycle.

motorboat. A power boat. A boat with an inboard or outboard gasoline or diesel engine.

motorcoach. A bus specifically designed for touring, featuring large windows and a large luggage compartment. May include toilet facilities.

moving sidewalk. A motorized, belt-like people mover which operates flush to the floor. Often found in long corridors at airports.

MPH. *Abr.* Miles per hour.

MPI. Meeting Professionals International, formerly Meeting Planners International.

MPM. *Abr.* Maximum permitted mileage. *See also* mileage system.

MS. *Abr.* Motor ship. A designation for many cruise liners.

MSCN. *CRS.* Misconnection.

MST. *Abr.* Mountain Standard Time.

MT. *Abr. CRS.* Mountain Time.

MTS. *Abr.* Motor turbine ship.

multi-access system. A CRS that can directly access the computers of several airlines or other travel suppliers.

multi-level. Having more than one floor or level.

multi-level marketing. A distribution scheme in which individuals are compensated for sales volume generated by people they have recruited into the distribution network; often a feature of referral agencies (qv).

mural. A large-scale painting on an interior or exterior wall.

Murphy bed. A bed designed to fold up into the wall when not in use. Found in some hotel rooms.

MV. *Abr.* Motorized vessel.

MY. *Abr.* Motorized yacht.

– N n

NA. *Abr.* Not available. Not applicable. No answer. Need alternative.

NABTA. National Association of Business Travel Agents.

NAC. *CRS.* No action taken on communication.

NACA. National Air Carrier Association.

NACOA. National Association of Cruise Only Agencies.

NACTA. National Association of Commissioned Travel Agents.

NAFTA. North American Free Trade Agreement.

NAOAG. *North American Official Airline Guide.*

NAR. *CRS.* New arrival information.

narrow body. *adj.* Referring to any aircraft with a single center aisle.

NATA. National Air Transportation Association.

national park. An area set aside by a country for preservation and recreation due to its outstanding natural beauty.

nautical mile. A measure of distance used in air and sea transportation of approximately 1.1 miles.

navigable. Open to commercial shipping.

navigation lights. *See* running lights.

NB. *CRS.* Northbound.

NBR. *CRS.* Number.

NBTA. National Business Travel Association.

NC. *CRS.* No charge.

nested excursions. *See* back-to-back ticketing.

Net. Informal term for the Internet (qv).

net amount. The amount due the supplier after commissions have been deducted.

net fare, net rate. 1. The wholesale price that is marked up for sale to the customer. 2. The fare after commission. 3. The price at which a consolidator sells a ticket to a travel agent.

net profit. Profit after all expenses have been taken into account.

netiquette. From "net etiquette," the unwritten code of what is acceptable in e-mail communication.

networking. The process of using one contact to gain others.

neutral unit of construction. A common denominator used to calculate a total when adding fares in different currencies.

NIBS. *Abr.* Neutral Industry Booking System.

NO. *CRS.* No action taken (on segment).

no go. *Slang.* 1. Not possible. 2. A cancelled flight or other service.

no name. *v.* To make a reservation even though you don't have the passenger's name yet.

no frills. *adj.* Bare bones. A service, as an airline flight, providing only the basics with no additional amenities.

no show. *n.* A passenger who doesn't arrive for a flight or a hotel guest who reserves but never arrives.

NOCN. *CRS.* No connection.

non-commissionable. *adj.* Referring to elements of a travel product for which the passenger must pay but for which the travel agent receives no commission. For example, port fees.

non-compete agreement, non-compete clause. A clause in an employment contract which prevents the employee from establishing a competing business for a period of time after leaving the company's employ. Often unenforceable.

non-refundable. Of a ticket, no moneys will be returned should the trip be cancelled. The amount of the ticket, minus a service fee, may be applied to another trip in many cases.

non-scheduled. Of an airline or other carrier, having no fixed timetable of operations. Operating on an irregular schedule. Non-scheduled carriers may have lower fares than scheduled ones.

non-sked. *See* non-scheduled.

non-transferable. Cannot be used by anyone other than the person to which it was issued, as a ticket.

nonstop. Transportation comprising a single segment. Without intermediate stops.

NOOP. *CRS.* Not operating.

NOREC. *CRS.* No record.

normal fare. An airline fare for a completely unrestricted ticket.

Northern Lights, The. *See* aurora borealis.

nose count. The physical counting of passengers, as by a flight attendant, to compare a manifest with the actual number of passengers. *See also* headcount.

NOSH. *CRS.* No show.

notarize. To have a document or a signature verified as genuine.

notary public. A person who has been authorized by the courts to attest to the authenticity of documents and signatures, usually for a fee. Sometimes referred to as a "notary."

NOTR. *CRS.* No traffic rights.

NPS. National Park Service.

NPTA. National Passenger Traffic Association.

NR. *CRS.* No rate. No payment required.

NRC. *CRS.* No record.

NRCF. *CRS.* Not reconfirmed.

NRP. *CRS.* Non-revenue (i.e. not paying) passenger.

NRS. *CRS.* No rate specified. (i.e. none available at time of reservation.)

NSML. *CRS.* No-salt meal.

NSST. *CRS.* Non-smoking seat.

NTA. National Tour Association.

NTBA. 1. *CRS.* Name to be announced (i.e. name will be provided later). 2. *Abr.* National Tour Brokers Association. *See* NTA.

NTHP. National Trust for Historic Preservation.
NTI. *CRS*. Need ticketing information.
NTSB. National Transportation Safety Board.
NUC. *Abr.* Neutral unit of construction (qv).
NV. *Abr.* Nuclear vessel.

— O o

O. *CRS.* Stopover.

O&D traffic. Origin and destination traffic. The passengers on a flight who are either boarding or deplaning at a particular stop, as distinct from those remaining on the plane to go to another destination.

OAG. *Official Airline Guide.*

occupancy rate. The percentage of hotel rooms occupied during a specific time period, omitting rooms not available for one reason or another.

OCNFT. *CRS.* Oceanfront.

OCNVW. *CRS.* Ocean view.

off airport location. A car rental company that does not have a counter in the terminal building. *See also* on airport location.

offline airline, offline carrier. Any airline other than the one or ones that own and/or control a particular computerized reservation system.

offline connection. A change of planes that also involves a change of airlines.

offline point. A destination with no service from a particular airline or other carrier.

off-peak. *adj.* Occurring or applicable during a period of less travel or demand, as in a flight or a fare.

off-season. *n.* A period of the year when demand for a destination decreases and prices go down. Also used as an adjective, as to describe a price or fare applicable during such a period.

OHG. *Official Hotel Guide.*

OJ. *CRS.* Open jaw (qv).

OK. *CRS.* Confirmed.

Old Glory. Nickname for the U.S. flag.

OMFG. Official Meeting Facilities Guide.

omnibus. Obsolete term for a bus, motorcoach, or similar mode of transportation.

on airport location. A rental car company with a counter in the terminal building. *See also* off airport location.

one-way trip. Any trip for which a return leg has not been booked.

online carrier. An airline that can provide immediate access through a computerized reservation system (qv).

online connection. A change of planes that does not involve a change of airlines.

OP. *CRS.* Other person.

open bar. Beverage service which is free for guests.

open jaw. A trip that has no air travel between two points on the itinerary. *See also* arunk.

open jaw with side trip. An open jaw itinerary with an additional roundtrip from one of the cities on the itinerary.

open pay, open rate. A rate of payment or compensation that is subject to or will be determined by negotiation.

open segment, open ticket. An airline ticket with no date specified.

open seating, open sitting. Seats or tables are not assigned and will be occupied on a first-come basis.

open skies. Referring to an agreement between two countries allowing unrestricted air services between them.

open ticket. A valid ticket that does not specify flight numbers, dates, or times. The holder of the ticket makes arrangements at a later date.

operator. Any company providing airline, cruise, hotel, or other services.

OPNS. *CRS.* Operations.

OPT. *CRS.* Option (qv). Option date (qv).

option. 1. An additional excursion or other element that need not be taken. 2. Option date (qv).

option date. The date by which payment must be made to secure a reservation.

ORG. *Official Recreation Guide.*

orientation. A meeting or training session designed to provide a basic understanding or overview of a subject.

ORIG. *CRS.* Origin. Originating. Originated.

origin. The starting point of travel.

origin and destination traffic. *See* O&D traffic.

ORML. *CRS.* Asian meal.

O/S. *Abr.* On a ship, an insider cabin.

OS. *Abr.* Outside sales. Outside sales representative.

OSI. *CRS.* Other service information (qv).

OSSN. Outside Sales Support Network.

OTC. *Abr.* One-stop inclusive tour charter.

OTD. *Official Tour Directory.*

other service information. Notes attached to a PNR (qv) which do not require attention by the airline.

OTHS. *CRS.* Other services. Other service information (qv).

OUT. *CRS.* Departure date, as from a hotel.

out plant. *adj.* Referring to a travel agency office on the premises of a corporate client at which reservations may be made. The actual ticketing is handled at another location.

outbound. *adj.* Referring to the leg of the journey departing the city of origin to the destination or destinations.

outrigger canoe. A Polynesian style, oared vessel with an extending arm that provides stability.

outside sales. A department or activity devoted to developing business through direct solicitation of potential customers away from a retail location.

outside sales representative. A person engaged in outside sales. May be an employee or an independent contractor.

outskirts. The outlying areas of a city.

outsource. To retain a separate specialist company to handle certain internal business functions.

overbooking. The practice of taking more reservations than there are seats, rooms, or space in the expectation that no shows (qv) will bring the number of reservations actually used below maximum occupancy.

overhead. 1. A storage compartment located above head level, as on an airplane. 2. The fixed expenses, such as rent and utilities, of a business.

overland. 1. Taking place on land. 2. Referring to travel that takes place off roads.

overlook. A turnoff on a highway or other location offering a scenic view.

override, override commission. An additional commission percentage paid when a certain volume level is achieved.

oversale. *See* overbooking.

oversell. 1. *See* overbooking. 2. *v.* To sell too aggressively; to exaggerate the features or benefits of a product.

oversupply. Excess capacity, as of airline seats or hotel rooms.

OW. *CRS.* One-way.

OX. *CRS.* Cancel if requested segment is available, otherwise hold.

ozone layer. A high atmosphere phenomenon providing shielding from the sun's ultra-violet rays. Degradation of the ozone layer in some areas (such as extreme southern South America) requires travelers to take additional precautions against overexposure to the sun.

Pp

PA. *CRS.* Via the Pacific.

PAC. *CRS.* Personal accident coverage. *See also* PAI, PIP.

pacing. The practice of making travel arrangements in such a way that sufficient time will be allotted for various activities.

package. A travel product bundling several distinct elements, such as air travel, a rental car, and a hotel. A package is distinguished from a tour by virtue of the fact that it combines fewer elements.

page. *v.* To call for a person, especially over a public address system in a public place, as an airport.

PAI. *CRS.* Personal accident insurance (qv).

P&L. *Abr.* Profit and loss.

Pan-American. *adj.* Embracing North, Central, and South America, as the Pan-American Highway.

panhandle. A section of a nation, state or territory that resembles a panhandle when viewed on a map, as the panhandle of Oklahoma.

par. 1. Equality or a level of equality. 2. A standard commonly accepted in most instances. 3. The number of strokes allotted to complete a hole in golf.

parador. *Sp.* A hotel, especially one that has been converted from a historic building such as a castle or monastery, providing luxury accommodations. Common in Spain.

parcel. 1. A piece of undeveloped land. 2. A package.

parish. A geopolitical division, equivalent to a county.

parliamentary procedure. A system for running meetings patterned on the rules of Britain's Parliament.

parlor car. On a train, a car providing more comfortable seating and/or food service.

PARS®. A former computerized reservation system (qv).

partnership. A legal form of business ownership comprising two or more individuals.

passenger facility charge. A fee imposed by a facility owner, as an airport, on those using the facility; typically added to the cost of a fare.

passenger mile. A statistical norm comprising one passenger traveling one mile. Passenger mileage is determined by multiplying the total number of miles flown (for airlines) by the total number of passengers carried.

passenger name record. A file on a computerized reservation system containing all the information relating to a specific booking. Also called "personal name record."

Passenger Network Services Corporation. Former name of International Airlines Travel Agent Network (IATAN).

passenger sales agent. Travel agent.

passenger service agent. An airline employee assigned to assist passengers checking in and boarding.

passenger service representative. An airline employee assigned to providing information and other services, such as wheelchair assistance.

passenger terminal indicator. A one- or two-digit code, administered by IATA, which identifies specific passenger terminals at airports having more than one such terminal.

passenger traffic manager. 1. An airport-based airline manager. 2. Individual in a company who handles travel arrangements for other employees.

passive booking, passive segment. A segment entered in a CRS (qv) that does not result in a ticket being issued. Typically used by agents to generate itineraries or make notes.

passport. A document identifying an individual as a citizen of a specific country and attesting to his or her identity and ability to travel freely.

password. Any alphanumeric string used to identify a specific individual to a computer, computer program, computer network, or similar system.

PATA. Pacific Asia Travel Association.

pavilion. 1. An exhibit hall at an exposition. 2. Any open sided building or tent. 3. A section of a building projecting out from that building.

PAWOB. *Abr.* Passenger arriving without baggage.

pax. *Abr.* Passenger. Passengers.

payload. 1. The percentage of total weight, as in an airplane, that represents revenue-producing passengers or cargo.

PC. *Abr.* Public charter (qv).

PDM. *CRS.* Possible duplicate message.

PDQ. *Abr.* Immediately, as soon as possible. (Literally, "pretty darn quick.")

PDR. *Abr.* People's Democratic Republic (of China).

PDW. *Abr.* Personal damage waiver. *See* collision damage waiver.

peak fare. A higher fare that applies during periods of maximum demand for a destination.

penalty fare. Fare subject to a deduction or other fee should the passenger change the itinerary or cancel.

pension. *Sp.* A small hotel or boarding house.

penthouse. 1. An apartment or suite on the top floor of a hotel or top deck of a cruise ship. 2. The top floor of a hotel.

people mover. Any motorized device for moving people over short distances. Typically, a flat escalator-like rubber mat in the corridors of an airport terminal. *See also* moving sidewalk.

per diem. 1. *Lat.* by the day. 2. A sum of money paid or given to an employee to cover daily expenses. 3. In the cruise industry, the daily cost of a cruise to the passenger.

perk. *Abr.* Short for perquisite. A privilege or extra benefit associated with a person's position in a company.

personal accident insurance. Individual coverage for accidents. Also called personal injury protection (PIP) or personal accident coverage (PAC).

personal effects coverage. Insurance covering the loss of personal property from a rented car.

personal name record. *See* passenger name record.

PETC. *CRS.* Pet in cabin.

petit dejeuner. *Fr.* Breakfast.

petrol. *Brit.* Gasoline.

PF. *Fr. Abr.* Prix fixe (qv).

PFC. *Abr.* Passenger facility charge (qv).

photo safari. An excursion designed to bring tourists close to wildlife, a staple of tours to African game parks.

piazza. *It.* An open square.

pidgin, pidgin English. Any of a number of dialects combining English and a local language, spoken in various parts of the world.

pier. A dock for the mooring of ships or boats.

pilgrimage. A journey undertaken to a religious shrine or for a religious purpose.

pilot. 1. *n.* The person in control of an aircraft. 2. The person who steers a ship; helmsman. 3. Port official responsible for guiding ships into and out of the harbor. 4. *v.* To control a plane in flight or a ship in water. 5. *n. See* pilot program.

pilot house. The enclosed area from which the steering mechanism of a ship is operated.

pilot program. A test or trial of a system or methodology used to detect and correct flaws or to determine suitability.

PIP. *Abr.* Personal injury protection. *See* personal accident protection.

pitch. 1. *n.* The measurement between identical points on seats of an airplane; the greater the pitch, the greater the degree of comfort. 2. *v.* To move sharply up or down, as in an airplane or boat. 3. *n.* The sharp, uncomfortable up or down motion of a plane or ship.

plate. A metal stamp used to impress the name of an airline on a manual ticket when issuing a ticket for that carrier.

plates. Imprints, usually specific to a supplier, which are distributed to travel agencies and used to create tickets. *See also* airline plate.

plating away. The practice of avoiding issuing tickets for a particular carrier in the belief that the carrier may be financially unstable and cease flight operations.

Plimsoll line. A line on the hull of a ship indicating the ship has reached its maximum cargo load.

plunge pool. A small pool in a hotel room or in a private courtyard adjacent to a hotel room.

PLVW. *CRS.* Pool view.

p.m. *Abr.* Post meridian. Afternoon or evening. The time between 12 noon and 12 midnight.

PNR. *Abr.* Passenger name record (qv). Passenger now recorded. Personal name record.

PNSC. Passenger Network Services Corporation (qv).

podium. 1. A lectern. 2. A raised platform, specifically one used in a public meeting for the speaker or speakers.

POE. *CRS.* Point of embarkation (qv).

point. A city or other stop on an itinerary.

point of embarkation, point of origin. Where a journey begins.

point to point. *adj.* 1. Referring to fares between two cities. 2. Referring to service between two cities only, without any additional segments or continuation.

political asylum. Sanctuary given by one country to a citizen of another to protect that person from arrest or persecution.

polyglot. A person who speaks many languages.

pontoon. 1. A hollow compartment used to float a flat-bottomed boat. 2. Any boat so designed. 3. The landing pad of a seaplane.

pool route. A route on which two carriers equally share revenues and facilities and exchange equipment and crew on an as-needed basis.

port. 1. The complex of buildings and facilities where ships dock. 2. In nautical parlance, left. The left side of a ship.

port charges, port tax. A fee levied by the local government on departing or visiting cruise passengers. Typically, listed as a separate charge in cruise brochures.

port of call. Any of the ports at which a ship will be stopping on a cruise.

port of entry. 1. The point at which a person or vessel enters a country. 2. A port or city designated as one at which a foreign ship or other vessel can enter a country's territory.

portal. Door. Tunnel entrance.

porter. A baggage handler. *See also* skycap.

porterage. The act or process of baggage handling.

porthole. A window, usually round, on a ship.

posada. *Sp.* A small country hotel.

posh. *Brit.* Elegant, high-class, as in a posh hotel. Its origins lie in the abbreviation for "port out, starboard home," indicating the best berths on sailings from England to India.

position, positioning. The act of moving aircraft or ships from one location to another so as to utilize them more efficiently or for greater revenue. *See also* repositioning.

positive space. Seating or rooms that can actually be occupied, as opposed to space reserved on a standby or if-available basis.

post audit. A detailed review of a company's employee's completed travel to determine whether or not the billed amount is accurate. Sometimes conducted by a third party which retains a percentage of any overbilled amount detected.

postal code. *Brit.* Zip code (qv).

postdate. To place a date on a document, as a check, later than the current date.

POT. *CRS.* Point of turnaround.

potable. Safe to drink.

pow wow. 1. A Native American meeting or festivity, now frequently a tourist attraction. 2. By extension, any meeting, especially one involving high level people, arranged to conclude business or make decisions.

PP. *Abr.* Per person.

PPDO. *CRS.* Per person, double occupancy.

PPR. *CRS.* Passenger profile record.

PRC. *Abr.* People's Republic of China.

pre- (or post-) convention tour. A tour or excursion sold in conjunction with attendance at a convention or meeting.

predesignated point. A system of unique telecommunications addresses, administered by IATA, used to ensure that reservations to specific airlines are properly routed.

preferred supplier. A supplier with which a travel agency has negotiated or earned a higher commission rate.

preferred supplier agreement. An arrangement between a corporation and supplier in which, in return for discounts or other advantages, the corporation requires its employees to use the products and services of the supplier.

premiere class. First-class or an elaboration thereof. The precise definition varies according to supplier.

prepaid. Paid in full in advance.

prepaid ticket advice. The form used when a person is buying a ticket that will be issued at the airport of the same or another city.

preregistration. A service offered for some conventions, whereby room assignments and other arrangements can be made prior to arrival.

preserve. An area set aside by the government, or other entity, specifically to conserve animal life or vegetation.

press release. A formal printed announcement by a company about its activities that is written in the form of a news article and given to the media to generate or encourage publicity.

pre-trip auditing. Review of proposed travel itineraries, usually by a corporate travel manager, to spot potential savings or avoid excessive or unauthorized expenditures.

PRF. *CRS.* Partial refund message.

price fixing. An illegal practice in which competing companies agree, formally or informally, to restrict prices within a specified range.

price signaling. The practice, now declared illegal, in which competing companies alert each other to proposed changes in their pricing structure, in order to control pricing within an industry. *See also* price fixing.

prime meridian. The imaginary line through Greenwich, England, designated as zero degrees longitude.

prix fixe. *Fr.* Literally, "fixed price." A meal of several courses, with no substitutions allowed, offered for a special price.

PRM. *CRS.* Premium.

productivity based pricing. An incentive provided by a CRS vendor to encourage maximum use of its service and discourage the agency from using more than one CRS.

professional liability insurance. *See* errors and omissions insurance.

profile. A record of information about a travel agent's customer used for qualifying (qv).

profit and loss statement. An accounting report detailing revenue and expenses.

promenade. 1. A leisurely stroll. 2. A place designed for taking such strolls. 3. A deck on a ship.

promissory note. A written promise to pay a specified sum either on demand or on a specific date.

promo. 1. *Abr.* Promotion, promotional. 2. *Slang.* A promotional announcement or advertisement.

promotional fare. A discount fare designed to increase volume.

proof of citizenship. Any documentation that indicates the citizenship of an individual, including birth certificates, voter's registration cards, or passports.

prop. 1. *Abr.* Property, proprietor. 2. A propeller. 3. *adj.* Describing a propeller driven aircraft.

proportional fare. *See* add-on fare.

proposal. 1. A formal written document soliciting business and spelling out what will be delivered, the costs, terms, conditions, and so forth. 2. A suggestion for a course of action.

prorate. 1. *v.* Adjust proportionally. 2. *n.* In the educational tour market, the number of paying customers required to earn a tour conductor's pass.

prospect. 1. *n.* A potential customer who meets certain minimum qualifications. *See also* suspect. 2. *v.* To search for potential customers.

prospecting cycle. The period of time after which a travel agent will recontact individuals or groups previously contacted to solicit business.

PROT. *CRS.* Protected reservation.

protected commission. A commission that will be paid even if the passenger cancels and the travel doesn't occur.

protocol. *n.* 1. A series of software conventions enabling computers to communicate with one another. 2. The proper form and format for conducting business, ceremonies, and so forth, as in *diplomatic protocol.*

prototype. A single or limited-edition working version of an aircraft or other device used for testing and demonstration purposes.

Provincial Standard Time. Canadian term for Atlantic Standard Time.

provisioned charter. A charter, as of a boat, that includes food and other supplies but no crew.

prow. The foremost part of a ship.

PSA. *Abr.* Passenger service agent (qv).

pseudo ARC number. An alphanumeric designator, often a telephone number, used by suppliers to identify travel agencies that do not have an ARC number.

pseudo city, pseudo city code. A CRS code used to identify a travel agency location.

pseudo PNR. A record stored in a CRS that does not contain an airline reservation. *See also* passenger name record.

pseudo-agent. 1. Someone who claims to be a travel agent but isn't. 2. Derogatory term for an outside sales representative not deemed to have sufficient training in travel.

psgr. *Abr.* passenger.

PSR. *Abr.* Passenger service representative (qv).

PST. *Abr.* Pacific Standard Time. Provincial Standard Time.

PT. *Abr.* Port taxes. Pacific Time. Physical training.

PTA. *CRS.* Prepaid ticket advice (qv).

PTHSE. *CRS.* Penthouse.

PTM. Passenger traffic manager (qv).

PTP. *Abr.* Point-to-point (qv).

P/U. *Abr.* Pick up.

public charter. An aircraft or other vessel that may be leased by the general public.

published fare. Any fare specifically listed in the carrier's tariff (qv).

pullman. A sleeping car on a railroad.

PUP. *CRS*. Pick up.

purser. On a ship, the person responsible for providing a wide array of passenger services, including mail, information, check cashing, safety deposit boxes, and so forth.

PWCT. *CRS*. Passenger will contact.

Q q

QADB. *CRS.* Quad (qv) with bath.

QADN. *CRS.* Quad without bath or shower.

QADS. *CRS.* Quad with shower.

qd. *Abr.* Quad.

QINB. *CRS.* Quin (qv) with bath.

QINN. *CRS.* Quin without bath or shower.

QINS. *CRS.* Quin with shower.

QTD. *Abr.* Quarter to date.

quad. Hotel room for four people.

qualifying. In sales, the process of determining if a prospect will make a good customer. Determining which travel product is right for a customer by asking questions.

quality assurance. In travel agency operations, the process of checking an itinerary, PNR (qv), or other reservation to insure its completeness and accuracy.

quarter deck. The stern section of the upper deck, traditionally officers' quarters.

quay. (Pronounced "key.") A pier.

queen room. A hotel room with a queen size bed.

query letter. A business letter requesting information.

queue. (Pronounced "cue.") *Brit.* 1. *v.* To line up to await service in turn, as at a bus stop. 2. *n.* A line of people waiting for service or admittance. 3. *n.* A communications area or subsystem within a networked computer system. 4. *v.* To route a communication, such as a PNR (qv), on a CRS to a specific destination, such as a travel agency.

quid. *Brit.* A pound sterling.

quin. Hotel room for five people.

quota. 1. The maximum number allowed. 2. A target number to be achieved, as a sales quota.

_R r_

R&R. *Abr.* Rest and relaxation/rehabilitation/recreation.

RAA. Regional Airline Association.

rack rate. The price a hotel charges for a room before any discount has been taken into account. The published rate for a room, sometimes set artificially high and used to calculate a variety of discounts. *See also* run of the house, walk-up rate.

raincheck. A slip or chit given to a customer in compensation for services promised but not received, usually redeemable for the identical service at a later date. For example, patrons of a rained-out sporting event will receive a coupon good for admission to a game later in the season.

ramp. 1. *n.* Any sloping surface accommodating foot or vehicular traffic.

ramp agent. An employee of an airline charged with bringing cargo, luggage, and food supplies to the aircraft.

range. The maximum distance an aircraft can fly or a ship cruise without refueling.

ranger. An official of a National Park. A Park Ranger.

rate and service structure. The prices a carrier charges and the services and amenities it provides, considered as a whole system.

rate desk. The office of an airline that calculates fares for travel agents and passengers.

rate hike. An increase in fares or other costs.

RCVD. *CRS.* Received.

RDB. *CRS.* Reply to duplicate booking enquiry.

re. *Abr.* Regarding, about.

rebate. 1. *v.* To deduct or return a portion of moneys otherwise due, as a portion of a travel agent's commission. 2. *n.* A sum so returned.

recall commission statement. An ARC document generated by an airline to retrieve a commission paid on a ticket which the airline has refunded to the passenger.

receivership. The state of being in the control of a court, as a business in bankruptcy.

receiving agent. A contractor that provides services to incoming passengers, as those on a tour.

reception. 1. The front desk of a hotel. 2. A party or event to greet a person or persons.

receptive service operator. *See* receiving agent.

receptive services. Services provided by a receiving agent, including transfers, currency exchange, interpreters, and so forth. *See also* meet and greet.

recheck system. An automated feature of a CRS or a separate software package that continuously checks the lowest fares on a route.

reconciliation. Matching one set of records against another. For example, an employee's expense account against credit card slips and other receipts.

reconfirm. To check again, as an airline reservation. Some reservations may be cancelled unless reconfirmed.

record. *n.* In a CRS, all the information about a single booking. A PNR (qv).

record locator, record locator number. An alphanumeric string which serves as a unique identifier of a booking or a PNR in a CRS.

recreational vehicle. 1. A self-contained, self-driven motor home. 2. Any vehicle, such as a dune buggy or all-terrain vehicle, used primarily for enjoyment.

red and green. A system used by customs in which passengers with nothing to declare follow the green symbols, while passengers with dutiable items to declare follow the red symbols through the customs area.

Red Book, The. A now-defunct hotel reference guide. The term is commonly used to refer to any hotel reference guide.

red light district. A part of a city set aside, either by municipal ordinance or informal custom, for prostitution and other sex-related businesses.

red-eye, red-eye flight. 1. A late-night flight, usually of some length and usually offering a lower fare. 2. An overnight flight that arrives at the destination early in the morning.

referral. A prospect (qv) recommended to a travel agent by another person, usually a present customer. The act of recommending such a person.

referral agency. A travel agency using a network of outside sales agents to funnel travel requests to an inside sales force that makes the actual sale. Typically, these agencies seek to recruit as large an outside sales force as possible. *Se e also* card mill.

refund/exchange notice. An ARC form and process for making an adjustment in money owed to the travel agency or due ARC.

regatta. A boat race.

regional carrier. An airline that serves only one clearly defined area of a country.

registry. A ship's formal registration of ownership. *See also* country of registry.

regular fare. An unrestricted, full-price fare, such as "coach" (Y class) or "first" (F class).

reissue. Write or generate a new ticket due to changes in itinerary or fare.

remittance. The sending of money to pay for a product or service. Any sum sent for this purpose.

REML. *CRS.* Reference my letter.

remote ticketing. Refers to the practice of making a reservation at one location and generating the ticket at another.

REMT. *CRS.* Reference my telegram.

REN. *Abr.* Refund/exchange notice (qv).

rent a plate. *Slang.* An off premises travel agency operated by employees of the corporation at which it is located.

repeat customer. Any customer who buys again. Generally used to refer to a customer who buys repeatedly or frequently.

replacement cost. The current price of a piece of equipment if it were to be purchased new, as opposed to the present, depreciated value of the equipment.

repositioning. The act of moving a vessel, such as a cruise ship, from one area to another, usually at a specific time of year, to maximize efficiency of use. *See also* positioning.

REQ. *CRS.* Request.

request for information. A preliminary step to a request for proposal (RFP) (qv), in which a company solicits a number of potential vendors for information about their products and services.

request for proposal. A formal request by a company, containing detailed specifications, to a potential vendor asking for a bid on satisfying those specifications.

res. (Pronounced "rez.") *Abr.* Reservation.

res vendor. 1. A computerized reservation system company. 2. A sales representative of such a company.

residential. *adj.* Consisting of private homes rather than commercial buildings, as a section of a city.

resort. 1. A city or other destination known for its leisure attractions. 2. A hotel featuring a broad range of amenities, sports facilities, and other leisure attractions, designed to provide a total vacation experience.

responsibility clause. *See* disclaimer.

rest area. On a limited-access highway, a parking area allowing drivers to rest without leaving the highway. May have amenities such as rest rooms, vending machines, full restaurant service, tourist information booths, picnic tables, and so forth.

restaurateur. A person who owns and operates restaurants.

restricted access. Not open to everyone, as a travel agency that is not open to the public.

retailer. 1. Anyone who sells goods or services to the general public. 2. In the travel industry, used to refer to a travel agent or travel agency.

retroactive. Encompassing a time period prior to execution or announcement, as a retroactive fare increase.

retrofit. Add machinery or equipment to an existing piece of equipment or system to correct a defect or add capability.

revalidation sticker. A self-adhesive form placed over the coupon portion of an airline ticket and used to record a change in carrier, flight number, date, time, class, and so forth.

revenue passenger mile. A statistical unit in the airline industry; one fare-paying passenger carried one mile.

revenue sharing. A term used to describe rebating (qv) to a corporation by a travel agency. *See* rebate.

REYL. *CRS.* Reference your letter.

REYT. *CRS.* Reference your telegram.

RFD. 1. *CRS.* Refund. 2. *Abr.* Rural free delivery.

RFI. 1. *CRS.* Request further information. 2. *Abr.* Request for information (qv).

RFP. *Abr.* Request for proposal (qv).

RHYA. *CRS.* Release for handling by your agency.

Richter scale. A logarithmic scale recording the severity of earthquakes. Because the scale is logarithmic, a 4.2 quake is ten times stronger than a 4.1 quake.

right of search. The right, under international maritime law, to stop a merchant ship to determine if it is in violation of revenue laws.

right of way. 1. The order of precedence in passing or proceeding, as of ships in a channel. 2. The right of one person to cross land owned by another.

riptide. A strong current flowing outward from the shore, endangering swimmers.

RLNG. *CRS.* Releasing.

RLOC. *CRS.* Record locator (qv).

RLSE. *CRS.* Release.

RMKS. *CRS.* Remarks.

RMS. *Abr.* Royal mail steamship.

RNP. *CRS.* Reduce number in party.

road rat. *Slang.* A person who makes his or her living delivering recreational vehicles.

ROC. 1. *CRS.* Record of charge. 2. *Abr.* (People's) Republic of China.

rodeo. An entertainment featuring displays of cowboy riding and roping skills.

ROE. *CRS.* Rate of exchange.

ROH. *CRS.* Run of the house (qv).

ROK. *Abr.* Republic of Korea.

roll. 1. A list of those present. 2. The side to side motion of a ship.

rollaway. In a hotel, a cot-like bed that can be folded and rolled from place to place.

rollover clause. A now-disallowed provision of CRS contracts that triggered a new contract term any time a new piece of equipment was purchased from the vendor.

room block. In a hotel, a number of rooms set aside or reserved for a group.

room night. One hotel room occupied for one night; a statistical unit of occupancy.

room service. Meal service to a hotel room.

room tax. Local and state taxes on hotel rooms that are added to the guest's bill.

roomette. On a train, a single compartment with a fold-down bed and a toilet.

rooming list. A roster of guests and their lodging needs presented to a hotel by a group prior to a meeting.

rope tow. A continuous, moving rope used to pull skiers up a slope.

roster. A list, as of those on duty at a particular time.

rostrum. *See* podium.

rotary phone. An old type of telephone with a circular dial which when turned produces pulses corresponding to the number dialed. *See also* touch-tone phone.

round trip. *n.* A trip, as on an airline, to a single destination and back. *adj.* Referring to fares, typically indicates that the fare is the same regardless of which of the two cities is the departure point.

roundabout. *Brit.* A traffic circle.

routing. The sequence of cities used to construct a fare.

royalty. A payment made to a company or individual for the use of its/her property, usually an intellectual property.

RPM. *Abr.* Revenue passenger mile (qv).

RPT. *CRS.* Repeat previous transaction.

RQ. *CRS.* On request.

RQID. *CRS.* Request is desired.

RQR. *CRS.* Request for reply.

RQST. *CRS.* Request seat.

RR. *CRS.* Reconfirmed.

RS. *CRS.* Reserved seat.

RSO. *Abr.* Receptive service operator (qv).

RSVP. *Fr. Abr.* Respondez s'il vous plait. Literally, "respond if you please." Often included in written invitations, and when included, etiquette demands a response.

RT. *CRS.* Round trip.

rudder. The steering device of a ship.

run of the house. *See* rack rate.

running lights. A series of colored lights required on a ship during the night to prevent collisions.

Ruta Maya. *Sp.* Literally, "Mayan route" or "road." Used to denote the Mayan areas of Mexico, Belize, Honduras, and Guatemala and the tourist sites therein.

RV. *Abr.* Recreational vehicle (qv).

ryokan. A traditional Japanese inn.

– S s

S&T. *CRS.* Shower and toilet.

SA. *CRS.* Space available.

Sabre®. A computerized reservation system (qv).

safari. 1. An adventure trip, typically in Africa, using off-road vehicles and tent-like accommodations for the purpose of viewing and photographing wildlife. 2. Originally, a hunting trip.

SAI. *Abr.* System assisted instruction.

sail 'n' stay program. A travel product combining a cruise to a destination with a one- or two-week stay at that destination, after which the passenger rejoins the cruise ship for the remainder of the cruise or to return to the point of departure.

salon. 1. An elegantly appointed reception room, as aboard a cruise ship. 2. A beauty parlor.

sampan. A small river vessel common in China.

satellite ticket printer. 1. A branch of an ARC-accredited agency that contains a ticket printer, either attended or unattended. 2. The printer in any such branch.

satellite ticket printer network. A network of attended ticket printers, typically in hotels, maintained by an ARC-accredited entity which sells its ticket distribution services to other ARC agencies. When an agent requests a ticket to be delivered through such a system, the STPN issues the ticket, receives money from the customer, deducts the appropriate commission, and sends it to ARC.

SATH. Society for the Advancement of Travel for the Handicapped.

SATO. *Abr.* Scheduled airline ticket offices.

SATW. Society of American Travel Writers.

sauna. 1. A dry heat bath in which steam can be produced by pouring water on hot coals. 2. A cabinet or room for such a bath.

SB. *Abr.* Steamboat.

SC. *CRS.* Schedule change.

SCAR. *CRS.* Standard (full-size) car.

scenic route. A secondary road designated as being especially scenic and, typically, longer.

scheduled carrier. An airline or other carrier that operates according to a regular and published timetable.

schoolroom setup. In a meeting a configuration in which tables are lined up on either side of an aisle, with all chairs on one side of the tables, facing front.

scooter. A small motor bike available for rental in some resort areas.

screw. The propeller of a ship.

script. 1. A CRS feature which leads and prompts an agent through the booking process. 2. An outline or word-for-word script used by someone making a telemarketing sales call.

SDR. *CRS.* Special drawing right (qv).

sea legs. *Slang.* The ability to move easily around a ship, without seasickness or loss of balance.

seaboard. The coast. The area near the ocean.

seagate. A small channel opening onto the sea.

seagoing. Capable of and safe for travel on the open seas.

seaplane. An airplane equipped with pontoons for landing on water.

search engine. An Internet-based computer program that enables users to locate information on the World Wide Web.

seasickness. Nausea and allied discomfort caused by the effect of a ship's motions on an individual's inner ear.

seat pitch. *See* pitch.

seat rotation. A practice on tours in which passengers are moved from seat to seat so as to give all travelers equal access to the "good seats."

seatmate. One's next-door neighbor on an airplane.

seatrain. A ship that transports railway cars.

seaward. In the direction of the ocean.

seaway. 1. A designated traffic lane in the ocean. 2. An inland waterway.

seaworthy. Able to float. Safe for sea travel.

second sitting. The later of two meal seatings on a cruise ship.

second-tier airports. Airports that are not located in major cities, which are not major hubs of any airline, and which traditionally enjoy only limited service.

sector bonus. An extra commission for certain airline segments, usually international, offered for limited periods of time.

security surcharge. An additional fee levied on an airline ticket to pay for increased security measures at airports.

SEDM. *CRS.* Schedule exchange data message.

segment. 1. A discreet portion of a trip, typically between two cities. *See also* leg. 2. A portion of the total market. 3. *v.* To divide the total market into demographic groups, so as to offer a slightly different product or product mix to each one.

self sales. Sales of a company's products or services made to employees of that company.

self-catering. *Brit.* Referring to an apartment or efficiency (qv) in which guests can take care of their own meal and laundry needs.

self-drive. *Brit.* A rental car.

selling fare. The unrestricted coach fare.

selling up. The practice of selling a more expensive alternative or selling more optional elements of a product. Not to be confused with bait and switch (qv).

senior, senior citizen. In the travel industry, a designation used to determine fares and other rates. The age at which a customer becomes a "senior" varies with the supplier and can range from 50 to 62 to 65 years of age.

server. A computer on which files and data are stored for retrieval by other computers.

servi-bar. A European term for minibar (qv).

service bureau. Typically, a company offering computer services on a contract basis.

service charge. 1. An additional charge, usually levied in lieu of a tip. 2. A fee charged by travel agencies for providing non-commissionable services.

service compris. *Fr.* Literally, "service included," that is, there is no need for an additional tip.

service non compris. *Fr.* Literally, "service not included," that is, an additional tip is expected.

set ups. Non-alcoholic mixers, glasses, ice, and garnishes provided by an establishment, such as a hotel or restaurant, with alcohol to be provided either by the guest or by the establishment for an extra charge.

SFML. *CRS.* Sea food meal.

sgl. *Abr.* Single (qv).

SGLB. *CRS.* Single room with bath.

SGLN. *CRS.* Single room without bath.

SGLS. *CRS.* Single room with shower.

SGMT. *CRS.* Segment.

shakedown cruise. A cruise undertaken to test a ship's systems, mechanical and human, sometimes made with passengers traveling at a discount.

Shangri-la. A fictional paradise where people live without care and never age. Used to describe any especially beautiful vacation destination.

shared code carrier. An airline which is listed on a CRS under the code of another airline.

sheikdom. A country or territory ruled by a sheik.

shell. A pre-printed brochure or flyer produced by a supplier which has empty space in which a travel agency may have its own logo and address imprinted.

Sherpa. 1. A Tibetan ethnic group. 2. Informally, a member of this group working as an aide or porter to a mountaineering expedition.

ship to shore. The radio system used to communicate with ships at sea.

shoji screen. A sliding rice-paper and wood room divider found in Japanese style hotels.

shore excursion. A sightseeing excursion offered in conjunction with a cruise, often for an additional charge.

shortest operated mileage. Under the mileage system (qv) of computing fares, the shortest distance between two points on an itinerary, omitting any intermediate connections.

short-haul. Of airline routes, of limited length and duration, often to, from, or between second-tier airports (qv).

shoulder season. An abbreviated season that falls between the high and low seasons (qv) and offers fares and rates between those of the other seasons.

showboat. A paddle steamer on which musical entertainment, often with a "Gay Nineties" (qv) theme, is provided.

SHTL. *CRS.* Second-class hotel.

shuttle. A short-run conveyance, sometimes provided free of charge, operating on a frequent schedule, usually between two points, such as a hotel and the airport, the airport and a car rental agency, and so forth.

SI. *CRS.* Service information.

sic. *Lat.* Literally, "thus it is written," usually used to indicate that a misspelling or other questionable element in a quotation is exactly as it appeared in the original.

siesta. An afternoon nap or rest period observed in many Spanish-speaking countries. Shops and other businesses are typically closed during this period.

simplified commissions. Supplier doublespeak for commission structures which, effectively, lower the amount of money due travel agents.

sine. A code used to identify a user or a travel agency in a CRS.

single. 1. A hotel room for one person, which may actually be able to accommodate more people. 2. One empty seat or one ticket in a theater.

single entity charter. An airplane, vessel, or other carrier that is chartered to a single company or group for the exclusive use by its employees or members.

single supplement. A charge added to a per-person occupancy rate that is based on an assumption of double occupancy, as on a cruise ship.

SIPP. *CRS.* Standard interline passenger procedures.

SITA. Societe Internationale Telecommunications Aeronautiques.

SITE. Society of Incentive Travel Executives.

site inspection. 1. A visit to a hotel property or other establishment for the purpose of evaluation, as on a fam trip (qv). 2. A fam trip.

SITI. *CRS.* Sold inside, ticketed inside. A ticket sold and issued in the same country.

SITO. *CRS.* Sold inside, ticketed outside. A ticket sold in one country and issued in a country not included in the itinerary.

sitting. On a cruise ship, one of the designated meal times. There are generally two sittings for each meal.

sixth freedom. *See* freedom rights

SKD. *CRS.* Schedule. Schedule change.

SKED. *CRS.* Schedule.

ski lift. A series of seats or bars suspended from a moving overhead cable, used to move skiers up a slope.

skid row. An inner city area of seedy hotels and bars.

skidoo. A brand name for a jet ski (qv), often used generically.

skiff. A small sailboat.

skipper. *Slang.* The captain of a vessel.

skycap. A baggage carrier or porter at an airport.

skyjacking. The forcible takeover of an airplane, as by terrorists. Air piracy (qv).

sleeper. 1. Sleeping compartment on a train. *See also* sleeperette. 2. *Slang.* In the hotel industry, a room marked as occupied when it was actually available for sale.

sleeper berth. *See* sleeperette.

sleeperette. 1. On an aircraft, a seat designed to recline nearly horizontally so as to approximate a bed. 2. On a train, a small sleeping compartment.

sleeping policeman. *Brit. slang.* A speed bump (qv).

slip. A docking space, as at a marina.

sloop. A one-masted sailing vessel, rigged fore and aft.

slot. 1. *Slang.* A slot machine (qv). 2. A parking space for planes at an airport. 3. A takeoff or landing time for a plane. 4. *v.* To schedule or fit into a schedule of events.

SLPR. *CRS.* Sleeperette (qv).

SM. *Abr.* Sales manager.

smokestack. A ship's funnel (qv).

smorgasbord. A Swedish-style buffet. By extension, any buffet service.

SMST. *CRS.* Smoking seat.

smuggle. To transport contraband or concealed dutiable items across an international border.

snail mail. Derogatory term for regular postal service mail, as opposed to the much faster e-mail.

snowbird. *Slang.* A person from a northern country or area who travels south during the winter.

snowboard. A surf board-like device used on ski slopes.

soft adventure. An outdoor or adventure travel experience that is not overly demanding physically.

soft class. In certain Far Eastern countries, a designation for first class.

soft departure, soft sailing. A departure date for which there are relatively few bookings.

soft opening. A period of time when a new hotel, which may not be fully complete, is open for business but has not formally announced its opening.

soft-dollar savings. Savings realized by not spending money or by saving time. *See also* hard-dollar savings.

soiree. *Fr.* A dance party. Any evening function.

SOLAS. Safety of life at sea. A set of international procedures designed to enhance safety aboard ships.

sole proprietorship. A legal definition of ownership in which the owner's profits are taxed as personal income.

solstice. The precise moment at which the sun is the farthest North or South from the Equator. There are two solstices each year (December 22 and June 22) marking, respectively, the shortest and longest days of the year (as measured from sunrise to sunset).

SOM. *CRS.* Shortest operated mileage (qv). Start of message.

sommelier. *Fr.* Wine steward, responsible for the opening, decanting, and serving of wine in a restaurant.

son et lumière. *Fr.* Literally, "sound and light." A form of entertainment in which the history of a tourist attraction is told through recorded dialogue and music and the artful lighting of the attraction itself.

SOS. *Abr.* "Save our souls," the international Morse code distress signal.

SOTI. *CRS.* Sold outside, ticketed inside. A ticket sold in one country but issued in another country on the itinerary.

SOTO. *CRS.* Sold outside, ticketed outside. A ticket sold and issued in a country not included in the itinerary.

souk. *Arabic.* A traditional North African marketplace.

Southern Lights, The. *See* aurora australis.

spa. 1. Traditionally, a resort town or area centered around mineral springs believed to have restorative powers; named after the town of Spa in Belgium. 2. A resort specifically designed to appeal to the health- or diet-conscious. 3. A room or area in a hotel or resort property offering such amenities as steam baths, saunas, massage, and so forth.

space. Generic term for any room, seat, table, and so forth available for sale.

space available. Term used to refer to any remaining seating or lodging sold at the last minute, generally at a discount.

SPCL. *CRS.* Special class (of rental car).

spec book. A document used by a meeting planner to record all the specifications and detailed supplier instructions for a specific event.

special drawing right. A fictitious unit of currency used to devise international air fares.

special fare. Any fare other than those normally offered.

special interest tour. A tour that combines elements designed to appeal to those with certain narrow interests.

special service requirement. A request to an airline for services or amenities other than standard, such as wheelchair usage, meals for special diets, and so forth.

specialty vehicle. Typically, any form of conveyance other than an automobile available for rental to tourists, including all-terrain vehicles, jet skis, and so forth.

specification. A detail of a product or service included in a written document detailing the features of such a product or service.

speed bump. A raised asphalt or concrete ridge in a road used to discourage excessive speeds.

speed trap. 1. An effort by local police to catch speeding motorists, ostensibly motivated more by a desire to raise cash than a concern for safety. 2. By extension, any town or location on a highway where such efforts are mounted on a regular basis.

spinner. *Slang.* A passenger, as on an airplane, who finds his seat already taken because a duplicate boarding pass has been issued.

split. An agreed-on division, as of a commission between a travel agency and an outside sales representative.

split payment transaction. A transaction in which full payment is made in two parts, each by a different method. For example, by cash and credit card or by two separate credit cards.

split ticketing. 1. Creating two separate tickets for a single journey, usually to obtain a lower fare. 2. A ticket issuing procedure in which the flight coupon goes to one location, while the auditor's and agency coupons go to another, usually a host agency.

SPML. *CRS.* Special meal.

SQ. *CRS.* Space requested.

SRO. *Abr.* Standing room only, as in a theater.

SRVS. *CRS.* Serves. Servicing.

SS. 1. *CRS.* Sold segment. 2. *Abr.* Steamship.

SSM. *CRS.* Segment status message.

SSR. *CRS.* Special service requirement (qv).

SST. *Abr.* 1. Supersonic transport. The Concorde. 2. Self-service terminal.

stabilizer. A fin-like projection from a ship's hull designed to reduce roll.

staff captain. The second in command on a cruise ship.

STAG. Society of Travel Agents in Government.

staging guide. *See* spec book.

stalls. The orchestra seats of a British theater.

standard hotel. A tourist or economy class hotel.

standard room. A lesser quality, lower priced room at a hotel.

standby. 1. *adj.* Available at a reduced cost on a space-available basis, as an airline fare. 2. *n.* A person traveling on a standby basis or waiting for a seat to open up on a flight.

starboard. A nautical term for the right-hand direction or side of a ship.

stateroom. A berth or cabin aboard a ship.

statute mile. A mile (5,280 feet).

STCR. *CRS.* (Passenger on a) stretcher.

STD. 1. *CRS.* Standard room (qv). 2. *Abr.* Sexually-transmitted disease.

steamer. A steam-powered ship.

steeplechase. A horse race across open country with obstacles.

steerage. An extremely low-cost and uncomfortable class of sea travel, typically well below decks with few if any amenities.

step-on guide. A guide who joins a tour bus for a local sightseeing excursion.

stern. The rear portion of a ship.

steward. A ship's employee responsible for the care of passengers. *See also* cabin steward.

stewardess. Name given to flight attendants in the days when all flight attendants were women.

stiff. *Slang. v.* To deliberately not tip a waiter or other service person.

STO. *CRS.* Studio (qv).

stopover. A planned overnight (or longer) stop on a ticketed journey.

stowaway. 1. *n.* An illegal, non-paying passenger on a ship or airplane. 2. *v.* To hide on a ship so as to avoid paying.

STP. *Abr.* Satellite ticket printer (qv).

STPN. *Abr.* Satellite ticket printer network (qv).

streetcar. An electrified light rail vehicle used for public transportation.

stretched vessel. A cruise ship that has been retrofitted with a new midsection to increase its length and passenger capacity.

strip. *Slang.* A street or area of town featuring a concentration of nightclubs, casinos, bars, and other forms of adult-oriented entertainment.

strip mall. A shopping center consisting of a continuous line of one-story shops.

stripped package. A tour product that meets the minimum qualifications for an IT (inclusive tour) designation on a CRS.

STTE. Society of Travel and Tourism Educators. Now the International Society of Travel and Tourism Educators.

student visa. A visa issued to those attending an accredited educational institution.

studio. An efficiency (qv). A one-room apartment.

STVR. *CRS.* Stopover (qv).

subchapter S corporation. A form of incorporation in which profits are taxed on the owner's or owners' individual tax returns, much as they would be in a sole proprietorship (qv) or partnership (qv).

subsidiary. A company wholly controlled by another through stock ownership.

subtropical. *adj.* Describing an area near the tropics but enjoying four distinct seasons.

subway. 1. An underground urban rail system. 2. *Brit.* An underground walkway or pedestrian passageway.

suite. In a hotel, an accommodation comprising more then one room; occasionally a single large room with clearly defined sleeping and sitting areas.

summit. *v.* To climb to the top of a mountain.

sun deck. 1. An open area on an upper story of a building for sunbathing. 2. A similar area on a ship.

sundries. Personal toiletries or grooming items.

sunstroke. Heat stroke caused by over-long exposure to the sun.

SUP. *CRS.* Superior room (qv).

superior room. In a hotel, a more desirable and more expensive room, perhaps with a better exposure, view, or other amenities.

superliner. 1. A large luxury cruise vessel. 2. A luxury train.

supersonic transport. A plane capable of exceeding the speed of sound. The Concorde.

supertax. A surtax (qv).

supl. info. *Abr.* Supplementary information.

supplement. An additional charge or payment, as a single supplement (qv).

supplemental liability coverage. Insurance coverage providing protection from injury and damage claims which is not automatically provided under a rental car contract.

supplier. In the travel industry, any company providing travel services to the public.

SUR. *CRS.* Surface.

surcharge. An additional charge levied for the provision of certain additional features or because of special or extenuating circumstances.

surety. A bond that guarantees performance or completion, as of a contract.

surface. On land. In an itinerary, referring to travel over land that does not involve an aircraft.

surname. *Brit.* Last name, of a person.

surtax. An additional tax levied on certain categories of goods or transactions or during a limited period of time. In some cases, funds raised by a surtax will be earmarked for specific purposes.

survey. *n.* A series of verbal questions or a questionnaire used to gather data about consumer attitudes or behavior.

suspect. An individual who may or may not meet the minimum qualifications necessary to make him a good prospect (qv).

SV. *Abr.* Sailing vessel.

SVW. *CRS.* Sea view.

SWAP. *Abr.* Severe weather avoidance procedure.

SWATH. *Abr.* Small waterplane area twin hull. A twin-hulled ship design said to reduce turbulence and, thus, seasickness.

SWB. *CRS.* Single room with bath.

swing shift. The work period from 4 p.m. until 12 midnight. Any work shift that overlaps the day and night shifts.

System One®. A computerized reservation system (qv).

system-wide revenue. In the hotel industry, the total amount of revenue realized at all of a hotel company's locations, company-owned and franchises.

_T t_

T&D. *Abr.* Training and development.

T&E. *Abr.* Travel and entertainment.

TA. *Abr.* Travel agent.

TAAD. *Abr.* Travel agent automated deduction.

tab. The bill, as in a restaurant.

table d'hote. *Fr.* Literally, "table of the host." A meal option, as on a tour, offering a full meal with a limited choice of dishes for a fixed price.

table tent. A folded place card on a restaurant table used to list specials, advertise a featured brand, or provide other information.

TAC. *CRS.* Travel agency commission.

tandem bicycle. A bicycle built for two.

tapas. *Sp.* Snacks or hors d'ouevres served at a bar.

tariff. A schedule of fares or prices.

tarmac. The paved area of an airport.

TASC. Travel Agents of Suffolk County (NY).

TAT. *CRS.* Transitional automated ticket.

taxi. 1. *n.* A vehicle with driver available for hire in metropolitan areas, which usually charges a mileage-based fare. A taxicab. 2. *v.* To drive an airplane on the ground.

TBA. *Abr.* To be announced.

T-bar. A type of ski lift (qv) in which skiers grasp or lean on a horizontal bar while keeping their skis on the ground.

TC1, TC2, TC3. Traffic conference areas (qv).

TCP. *CRS.* To complete party.

TD. *Abr.* Ticket designator (qv).

TDOR. *CRS.* Two-door car.

TEE. Trans-European Express.

telecommute. *v.* To work at home using a computer link to the office. Hence, *telecommuter*, one who works in this manner.

teleconference. A meeting in which some or all of the participants are in different locations linked by telephone.

teleferic. A cable car system.

telemarketing. Selling via the telephone.

teleticketing. A now-discontinued automated method of ticketing used by the airlines.

temperate zone. In the Northern hemisphere, the area between the Arctic Circle and the Tropic of Cancer. In the Southern hemisphere, the area between the Antarctic Circle and the Tropic of Capricorn.

TEN. *Abr.* Ticket exchange notice.

tender. A small boat used to supply a larger vessel. A boat used to ferry passengers between a cruise ship and the shore.

tercentenary. The 300th anniversary.

terminal. An airport, train station, or bus station. Of train and bus stations, one at which routes end and vehicles are stored.

terms and conditions. The section of a tour or cruise document in which legal details of liability and responsibility are spelled out.

terra firma. *Lat.* Dry land.

terra incognita. *Lat.* Unknown territory.

TFC. *CRS.* Traffic.

TGC. *Abr.* Travel group charters.

TGV. *Fr. Abr.* Initials for the French phrase, "train a grand vitesse." High speed French train system.

theater setup. In a meeting, a configuration in which seats are arranged in rows, facing front, as in a theater.

theme cruise. A cruise designed to appeal to a specific clientele with specific interests.

theme park. An amusement park that follows a particular motif or which incorporates rides based on characters or situations proprietary to the owner of the park.

thermal neutron analysis. A baggage screening technology.

third world. 1. Term applied to any undeveloped nation or area of the world. 2. (now generally obsolete) As distinct from the first world (non-Communist, developed nations) and the second world (the Communist nations of the world).

through fare. Fare to a foreign destination reached via a gateway city (qv).

through passenger. Any passenger who is not disembarking at a particular stop.

through service. An airline flight which makes stops but does not require a change of planes.

throwaway. An element of a travel product or package which is purchased but not used.

THRU. *CRS.* Through.

THTL. *CRS.* Tourist hotel.

TIA. Travel Industry Association.

TIAA. Travel Industry Association of America. (Same as TIA.)

TIAC. Travel Industry Association of Canada.

TIAG. Travel Industry Association of Georgia.

ticket. A formal travel document representing a contract between the traveler and the supplier.

ticket designator. An airline code, usually indicating a discounted fare.

ticket stock. Blank airline tickets.

ticketed. Having purchased and issued travel documents.

ticketed point mileage. The actual distance between two cities on an itinerary.

ticketless travel. *See* electronic ticketing.

tickler file. A reminder system that links activities or deadlines and dates.

tidal wave. An abnormally large and destructive wave caused by a storm, earthquake, or other natural event.

tie-in. The linking one product or promotion with another, as when frequent flyer miles can be earned by using a credit card.

tier. 1. A quality ranking, as of hotels. 2. A balcony in a theater.

tie-up. 1. A place to secure a small boat. A boat slip. 2. A temporary halt in business or traffic caused by accident or congestion.

time share, time sharing. A form of shared property ownership in which a purchaser acquires the right to occupy a piece of property, such as a condominium in a resort area, for a specific period of time, typically two weeks, each year.

time window. The period of time before and after a desired departure time that a customer will accept a flight should the ideal flight not be available.

Titanic, The. Supposedly unsinkable British luxury liner that sank on its maiden voyage in 1914 after striking an iceberg.

TKNO. *CRS.* Ticket number.

tkt, tktd. *Abr.* Ticketed (qv).

TKTL. *CRS.* Ticket time limit.

TN. *CRS.* Telephone number.

TNA. *Abr.* Thermal neutron analysis (qv).

TO. *CRS.* Tour order.

TOE. *CRS.* Ticket order exception.

toll call. Any phone call other than one to the local dialing area. A long-distance call.

toll road. A highway system charging a fee, typically based on type of vehicle and total miles traveled.

tonnage. The carrying capacity of a ship.

TOP. *Abr.* Tour Operator Program (qv).

torrid zone. *See* tropics, the.

TOTL. *CRS.* Total.

touch-tone phone. A telephone on which push buttons produce a distinct tone for each number. As distinct from a rotary phone (qv).

tour. A travel product in which several elements are bundled together and sold as a unit. Tours typically involve the use of a guide, host, or escort by groups (as opposed to packages (qv) which do not).

tour conductor. 1. An employee of or contractor to a tour operator who accompanies and is in overall charge of a tour. 2. A member of a group taking a tour who is designated as that group's leader and who might have played a key role in bringing the group together for the tour.

tour conductor pass. A free passage, as on a cruise, awarded for a specific number of bookings. Typically, a tour conductor pass is controlled by the travel agent responsible for the bookings and can be used at the agent's discretion for personal use or for the tour conductor (see def. 2, above).

tour desk. A counter at a hotel where local tours can be booked.

tour documents. A packet of tickets, vouchers, itineraries, instructions, and other information sent to a passenger by a tour company.

tour escort, tour leader, tour manager. *See* tour conductor.

tour operator. A company that assembles the various elements of a tour.

Tour Operator Program. An endorsement program administered by ASTA (qv) which certifies that a participating travel agency or tour operator meets certain consumer protection standards.

tour organizer. Any individual who finds people to go on tours. Distinct from a tour operator (qv).

tour wholesaler. *See* tour operator.

tour-based fare. *See* inclusive tour fare.

tourism. 1. The activity of travel for pleasure. 2. The industry based on such travel.

tourist. 1. A leisure traveler. 2. The economy class on an airline. Also referred to as "economy" or "coach." 3. The section of the plane designated for this class of passenger.

tourist card. A document issued in lieu of a visa for a short visit to a country. Typically, a tourist card does not require the person to whom it is issued to have a passport.

tourist trap. 1. Derogatory term for any attraction appealing to tourists but considered to be in bad taste or to give poor value for the money. 2. An area of a tourist destination that has become over-commercialized.

tpl. *Abr.* Triple (qv).

TPM. *CRS.* Ticketed point mileage (qv).

tracker. A person skilled in locating animals in the wild.

trade mission. 1. A quasi-governmental office of one country, located in another, created to encourage trade between the two nations. 2. An organized trip made by business representatives to explore trade opportunities in another country.

trade name. The legally protected name of a company's product or by which the company does business.

Traffic Conference Area. Divisions of the world used for the purposes of fare construction. There are three traffic conference areas (TCs): TC1 comprises North and South America; TC2 comprises Europe, Africa, and the Middle East; TC3 comprises Asia and the Pacific.

training fare. Airline fare negotiated by a corporation for the use of employees traveling for the purposes of training.

tram. A streetcar (qv).

tramp steamer. A cargo vessel with no set route, sometimes carrying passengers.

tramway. A streetcar line.

trans-canal. Referring to a cruise or other sea traffic that passes through the Panama Canal.

transcon. *Abr.* Transcontinental (qv).

transcontinental. Spanning a single continent.

transfer. 1. The transportation of a passenger between two points, such as from the airport to a hotel or vice versa, often included as an element of a tour. 2. A chit or similar device allowing a passenger to transfer from one vehicle or form of transport to another without paying an additional fare.

transient. Any person who is not a permanent resident. In some hotels, a guest who is not renting by the month.

transit point. An intermediate stop on a journey, typically one made only to change planes or mode of transportation.

transit visa. A limited-term visa issued solely to allow passage across or through the issuing country's territory.

transparency. 1. A piece of clear acetate containing an image which can be projected onto a screen; used in making presentations to groups. 2. A photographic slide.

trattoria. *It.* A restaurant or cafe.

travel advisory. A formal warning, issued by the United States Department of State, advising caution in traveling to specific countries due to political unrest, natural disaster, or other cause.

travel agency. 1. Usually used in the travel industry to refer to an ARC-appointed storefront retailer. 2. Any business that refers to itself as a travel agency.

travel agent. 1. Any person who sells travel products on a commission basis. 2. A person selling travel who meets certain minimum qualifications, which can vary widely according to who uses the term or sets the standards.

travel agent arbiter. *See* arbiter, travel agent.

travel bureau. *See* travel agency.

travel consultant. 1. An alternative term for travel agent (qv). 2. A person with specific knowledge of the travel industry hired on a contract basis to provide advice, guidance, or services to a company.

travel counselor. An alternate term for travel agent (qv).

travel manager. *See* corporate travel manager.

travel partner. A travel supplier that participates in a frequency marketing program (qv) operated by another travel supplier.

traveler's diarrhea. A usually mild intestinal condition caused by adjustment to microorganisms in the water of another geographical destination or by other causes associated with travel.

travelog, travelogue. A documentary film or video extolling the attractions of a specific travel destination or group of destinations.

Travelshopper®. A simplified version of the Worldspan® CRS (qv).

trawler. A pleasure boat based on the design of a type of fishing vessel.

trek. A hike, often with backpacks and typically lasting a number of days.

trekking. A category of adventure travel, typically involving visits to remote areas, with overnight lodging in tents or other minimal accommodation.

trip. In the travel industry, any journey of more than 100 miles from a person's home, regardless of whether an overnight stay is involved.

triple. A hotel room for three people.

trolley. A streetcar (qv).

tropical storm. A weather disturbance originating in the tropics (qv), with sustained winds of less than 75 mph.

tropics, the. 1. Any area where it is hot year-round. 2. The area of the globe between the Tropic of Cancer on the North and the Tropic of Capricorn on the South.

troupe. A theater group, especially one that travels from place to place.

TRPB. *CRS.* Triple with bath.

TRPN. *CRS.* Triple without bath.

TRPS. *CRS.* Triple with shower.

trundle bed. A bed that rolls out from under another bed.

trunk carrier. A major airline carrier, as evidenced by its extensive system of routes.

trust territory. A semi-autonomous territory that is administered by a member of the United Nations Trusteeship Council.

truth-in-advertising. A principle, sometimes enacted into law, requiring companies to be scrupulously honest in their advertising, providing accurate descriptions of products and services and omitting no material details.

TS. *Abr.* Twin-screw. Turn screw.

TSEA. Trade Show Exhibitors Association.

TSI. *Abr.* Travel Service Intermediary.

TSI card. A photo ID issued by IATAN (qv) to those who work in

IATAN-approved firms but who do not issue airline tickets (e.g. cruise-only agents).

TSS. *Abr.* Turbine steam ship.

TST. *CRS.* Transitional stored ticket record.

tsunami. Japanese term for tidal wave (qv).

TTGAC. Travel and Tourism Government Affairs Council.

TTRA. Travel and Tourism Research Association.

tube. *Brit.* 1. Subway. 2. The London Underground.

tug boat. A utility vessel, used in harbors to tow or move much larger vessels.

turbulence. Rough, sometimes violent, atmospheric conditions encountered by airplanes.

turista. *Sp.* Literally, "the tourist." Slang term for traveler's diarrhea (qv).

turnaround. The process of refueling and reprovisioning a plane to ready it for another flight. Also applied to ships.

turnaround point. The geographical location at which outbound travel becomes inbound travel, as on a cruise.

turndown service. In hotels, the practice of folding back the blanket and sheet of the bed in the evening, sometimes accompanied by putting a mint on the pillow or a cordial on the night stand.

turnover. 1. The periodic change of staff, as employees are dismissed, resign, or retire. 2. The periodic change of a customer base, as some customers stop doing business with a company and others start. 3. The rate at which such change takes place.

turnpike. *See* toll road.

turnstile. A rotating device through which passengers or customers pass after paying their fare or admission. Some unattended turnstiles may be unlocked only by the insertion of the correct fare or price of admission.

TV. *Abr.* 1. Turbine vessel. 2. Television.

TWB. *CRS.* Twin room with bath.

twin. A hotel room containing two single beds.

TWNB. *CRS.* Twin room with bath.

TWNN. *CRS.* Twin room without bath.

TWNS. *CRS.* Twin room with shower.

TWOV. *CRS.* Transit without visa.

TWR. *CRS.* Tower.

typhoon. A hurricane occurring in the Eastern hemisphere.

– U u

UATP. Universal Air Travel Plan. *See* Air Travel Card.

UBOA. United Bus Owners of America.

UC. *CRS.* Unable to accept request (not waitlisted). *See also* US.

UCCCF. *CRS.* Universal credit card charge form.

U-drive. *Brit.* A rental car.

UFO. *Abr.* Unidentified flying object.

UFTAA. Universal Federation of Travel Agents Associations.

UK. *Abr.* United Kingdom.

UM. *CRS.* Unaccompanied minor.

UMNN. *CRS.* Unaccompanied minor, where NN denotes the child's age.

UMNR. *CRS.* Unaccompanied minor.

UN. 1. *CRS.* Unable. 2. *Abr.* United Nations.

UNA. *CRS.* Unable.

unchecked baggage. Baggage which a traveler retains in his or her personal control. An important distinction when liability for loss or damage is to be determined. *See also* checked baggage.

undercurrent. *See* undertow.

underdeveloped. Not having a sufficiently modern infrastructure.

undertow. A dangerous coastal current that can drag swimmers out to sea.

undeveloped. Without amenities or infrastructure, as a camping area or tourist destination.

uninterrupted international air transportation. Any airline flight that does not include a schedule stop of more than twelve hours in the United States.

Union Jack. The flag of the United Kingdom.

Universal Air Travel Plan. *See* Air Travel Card.

UNK. *CRS.* Unknown.

unlimited mileage. In a rental car, the absence of any per mile charge for miles driven.

unrestricted fare. A higher fare for a ticket offering maximum flexibility. Typically, unrestricted fares require no advance purchase, no Saturday night stay, no roundtrip purchase, and are fully refundable without penalty or fee.

unscheduled. Not on or according to a timetable.

unspoiled. Term used to describe tourist destinations that, in theory, have not been discovered by or overrun with tourists.

upgrade. 1. *v.* To move to the next higher category, as to upgrade a passenger from tourist to business class. 2. *n.* A coupon entitling someone to an upgrade. 3. *n.* The act of upgrading.

upper/lower. A designation indicating the use of bunk beds or berths, as in a ship's cabin or railway compartment.

upscale. Appealing to or designed for a more affluent clientele.

upwind. Toward the direction of the wind.

URL. *Abr.* Universal resource locator. The address of a web site (qv).

US. *CRS.* Unable to accept request (waitlisted). *See also* UC.

user friendly. Designed in such a way as to be easy to use or operate, especially of computers and computer software.

U-shape setup. In a meeting, a configuration in which tables are formed in the shape of a U, with chairs on the outside of the U and the front of the room at the open end of the U.

USS. *Abr.* United States ship.

USTDC. United States Travel Data Center.

USTOA. United States Tour Operators Association.

USTS. United States Travel Service. Now USTTA (qv).

USTTA. United States Travel and Tourism Administration.

usury laws. Legislation restricting the amount of interest that may be charged.

UTC. 1. *CRS.* Unable to contact. 2. *Abr.* Coordinated universal time.

UTDN. *Abr.* Unattended ticket delivery network.

utilization rate. In the car rental industry, the percentage of vehicles in use during a specified period of time, figured on a system-wide or local basis.

UTR. *CRS.* Unable to reach.

UTV. *Abr.* Universal travel voucher.

UU. *CRS.* Unable.

_ Vv

vacancy. An empty room at a hotel or motel. By extension, any available space.

vaccination. An inoculation given to produce immunity to a disease.

valet. 1. *n.* A personal servant. 2. *adj.* Describing services such as those provided by a personal servant, as in valet parking.

validation. 1. Approval or issuance, as of travel documents. 2. The marking of a document to indicate validity or payment.

validator. A machine used to imprint tickets or other documents.

validity dates. The inclusive dates for which a fare or other offer is valid.

valise. A small piece of luggage.

value added tax. A form of taxation in which taxes are added cumulatively as a product changes hands. A common tax in Europe, which, upon application, can often be refunded to foreign visitors after their visit.

value season. 1. Shoulder season (qv). 2. Low season (qv). 3. Any period during which lower fares or rates are offered.

van. Any of a number of forms of motorized transportation larger than a car but smaller than a bus.

VAT. *Abr.* Value added tax (qv).

VDT. *Abr.* Video display terminal.

vector. The direction of motion, as of an airplane, often expressed in degrees of the compass.

veldt. The savannas of southern Africa.

velocity. Speed.

velodrome. A stadium designed for bicycle racing.

vending. In a hotel, an area containing vending machines.

vendor. In the travel industry, any supplier of travel products or services.

venture capital. Financial capital provided to fund the creation or expansion of a business, especially a highly speculative business with a high potential payback.

veranda, verandah. A roofed porch.

verboten. *Ger.* Forbidden.

verification. The process of authenticating or confirming, as of a reservation.

vertigo. A dizzy sensation brought on by an inner-ear condition or a fear of heights.

vessel. A generic term for any boat or ship.

VFR. *CRS.* Visiting friends and relatives.

VGML. *CRS.* Vegetarian meal.

via. *Lat.* By way of.

VIA Rail. Also, VIA Rail Canada, the Canadian railway system.

VICE. *CRS.* Instead of. (From the Latin.)

Victorian. Characteristic of the Victorian era or the late 1800s, used to describe architecture and interior decor.

videoconference. A meeting in which some or all of the participants are in different locations, linked by video transmitted by satellite.

villa. *It.* A country-home. Sometimes used in the hotel industry to describe a small, separate suite or cottage.

vintage. The year in which a wine was bottled.

VIP. *CRS.* Very important person.

virus. In computers, a malicious and destructive program designed to be passed unwittingly from machine to machine via floppy disks, downloading, or other means.

visa. A document or, more frequently, a stamp in a passport authorizing the bearer to visit a country for specific purposes and for a specific length of time.

visa expediter. A person or company charging a fee to procure visas an other travel documents.

vis-à-vis. *Fr.* Literally, "face to face." 1. In regard to. 2. Compared with.

visitor's visa. A tourist visa.

vistadome. A car on a train featuring a glassed-in, domed ceiling, offering a view of the passing countryside.

VLA. *CRS.* Villa.

volume incentive. An extra commission or other inducement offered by a supplier to a travel agency to increase sales.

voucher. 1. A coupon or other document, either prepaid or given free, entitling the bearer to certain goods, services, or discounts upon presentation. 2. An exchange order (qv).

V-shape setup. *See* chevron setup.

VUSA. *CRS.* Visit USA fare.

– *W w*

Wagon-Lits. European company providing sleeping car services on trains.

wait list, waitlist. 1. *n.* A roster of names of those wishing passage on a full flight or other trip, usually honored in order in case of cancellations. 2. *n.* A group of people waiting for cancellations. 3. *v.* To place someone on such a list.

waiver. 1. A written acknowledgment by a passenger of his or her declining something, as insurance coverage. 2. A document used by a travel agency and signed by the customer indicating that certain forms of insurance or other protection has been advised or offered. 3. The formal acknowledgment of dismissal of a requirement.

wake. The trail of waves left by a ship.

walked. *adj.* In the hotel industry, term used to refer to a guest lodged in another property at the hotel's expense because no room was available for his or her use.

walkie-talkie. A portable radio communication device with limited range.

walk-in. In a hotel, a guest who arrives without a reservation. In a travel agency, a customer who arrives unannounced, especially a new customer.

walkout. A labor strike.

walk-up. In the airline industry, a passenger who purchases a ticket shortly before flight time.

wanderlust. A desire to travel.

WAPTT. World Association for Professional Training in Tourism.

WATA. World Association of Travel Agents.

water closet. Toilet.

water table. A point below the surface of the land, below which the earth is saturated with water.

waterfront. The section facing the sea. A harbor area.

waterline. 1. The line on a ship's hull to which the sea reaches. 2. Any of a number of lines drawn on a ship's hull indicating the point to which the sea will reach when the vessel is fully loaded.

watershed. The area drained by a system of rivers. The crest of a ridge or mountain range, marking the point at which water will flow in the opposite direction.

WATS. *Abr.* Wide area telephone service. A form of long-distance telephone service which is purchased in bulk at lower rates.

way station. An intermediate or less-important station, especially on a railroad.

WB. *CRS.* Westbound.

WC. *Abr.* Water closet (toilet).

w/c. *Abr.* Will call.

WCHC. *CRS.* Wheelchair (passenger immobile).

WCHR. *CRS.* Wheelchair.

WCHS. *CRS.* Wheelchair (passenger cannot negotiate stairs).

web. Informal term for the World Wide Web (qv).

web browser. A software program enabling users to navigate the World Wide Web and the Internet.

web site. Informational or commercial computer files posted on the Internet and viewable from remote computers.

webmaster. The person designated to maintain a web site.

wet bar. In a hotel room, a bar or counter area with running water, used for preparing drinks.

wet lease. Rental of a crewed and provisioned boat or vessel.

w/fac. *Abr.* With facilities.

wharf. A dock.

whistle stop. 1. Traditionally, a very brief stop on a railroad. By extension, any brief stop. 2. A very small town.

white cap. A wave with a frothy top, especially one whipped up by the wind.

white-knuckle flyer. A person nervous about flying.

WHO. World Health Organization.

wholesaler. Any company that sells to retailers as opposed to the general public. A tour operator.

wide-body. An aircraft designed for increased passenger load by expanding the number of seats in each row and adding an aisle.

widow's walk. A raised platform or high porch on the roof of a house, usually in a coastal town, originally designed to provide a view of ships far out to sea.

wind chill, wind chill factor. A calculation that takes into account the effect of the wind to provide a reading of the apparent temperature (as opposed to the actual temperature as registered on a thermometer).

wind shear. A violent and sudden downdraft of wind which can be fatal to a landing airplane.

windjammer. 1. A sailing ship. 2. A type of sailed cruise ship designed to resemble the merchant ships of the late 1800s.

windward. In the direction of the wind.

WK. *CRS.* Was confirmed.

WL. *CRS.* Waitlist (qv).

w/o fac. *Abr.* Without facilities.

WOAG. Worldwide Official Airline Guide.

workshop. Seminar.

World Wide Web. A global network of computers using hypertext technology to create a world-wide depository of information.

Worldspan®. A computerized reservation system (qv).

write off, write-off. 1. *v.* Deduct, as from one's income tax. 2. *v.* Regard as hopelessly lost or damaged. 3. *n.* An expenditure that can be deducted from one's income tax.

WTCIB. Women's Travellers Center and Information Bank.

WTO. World Tourism Organization.

WTRVW. *CRS.* Water view.

WTTC. World Travel and Tourism Council.

—*X x*———————————————————

X. *CRS.* Connection.

XBAG. *CRS.* Excess baggage.

xenophobia. Fear or hatred of foreigners or things foreign.

XF. *CRS.* Cancelled phone.

XL. *CRS.* Cancel. Cancel waitlist.

XLD. *CRS.* Cancelled.

Xmas. *Abr.* Christmas.

XN. *CRS.* Cancelled name.

XO. *CRS.* Exchange order.

XR. *CRS.* Cancellation recommended.

x-ray. A baggage screening technology.

XS. *CRS.* Cancelled segment.

XSEC. *CRS.* Extra section (qv).

XTN. *CRS.* Extension.

XX. *CRS.* Cancelled.

— Y y

Y discount fare. *See* selling fare.

yacht. A luxury sail or powered vessel.

yaw. A deviation in a ship's course, such as that caused by a storm or heavy seas.

yield. Revenue per statistical unit. For example, an airline's yield would be stated as the average revenue per mile per paying passenger.

yield management. The practice of adjusting prices up or down in response to demand in order to control yield. This process is usually computerized.

YMCA. *Abr.* Young Men's Christian Association.

YMHA. *Abr.* Young Men's Hebrew Association.

yogwan. A traditional Korean inn.

youth fare. A fare for young people. The definition of "youth" varies among suppliers but generally ranges from 12 years of age to 22 or 25 years of age.

youth hostel. *See* hostel.

yurt. A dome-shaped Mongolian dwelling. Any construction patterned on such a dwelling.

YWCA. *Abr.* Young Women's Christian Association.

YWHA. *Abr.* Young Women's Hebrew Association.

Zz

zebra. *Brit.* Parallel white lines on a road indicating that oncoming traffic must yield to pedestrians.

zenith. The highest point.

zephyr. A gentle breeze.

zeppelin. 1. A blimp (qv). 2. One of a now obsolete class of lighter-than-air passenger airships.

zero-zero. Used to describe weather conditions of no ceiling (qv) and no visibility.

zip code. A five- or nine-digit number used to facilitate the delivery of mail. "Zip" is an acronym for zone improvement plan.

zoning. Municipal laws or regulations regulating the type and size of buildings that can be erected and activities undertaken in specific areas.

zoo, zoological park. A park displaying wild (as opposed to domesticated) animals.

Sources of Additional Information

Travel Trade Publications

The Airfare Report
7709 Queen Avenue North
Minneapolis, MN 55444
612-569-9950
Monthly.
Terry Trippler plays the CRS like
Heifetz played the violin. He publishes
two complementary monthly newsletters. *The Consumer's Guide to the High
Fare Airlines* ($24/year) and *The
Buyer's Guide to the Low Fare Airlines*
($48/year). Or subscribe to both for $65/
year, plus a free guide to the major airlines' rules.

Annals of Tourism Research
Elsevier Science
P.O. Box 945
New York, NY 10010
212-989-5800
Quarterly; $385/year.
This scholarly journal brings a "multi-
disciplinary approach" to studying the
social sciences aspects of tourism in an
effort to develop "theoretical con-
structs," whatever that means.

Association Meetings
The Laux Company
63 Great Road
Maynard, MA 01754
508-897-5552
Bi-monthly; free to qualified subscribers, $42/year to others.

ASTA Agency Management
Pace Communications, Inc.
1301 Carolina Street
Greensboro, NC 27401
919-378-6065
800-828-2712
Monthly; free to ASTA members, $36/
year to others.
This is the magazine for members of
the American Society of Travel Agents
who receive it as part of their membership dues. Covers travel industry
trends (the ecological impact of increased tourism, what's new in automation, etc.) and agency issues (why
agents are cutting back on fam trips).
Also features how-they-did-it success
stories that might fire your imagina-
tion.

*ASU Travel Guide: The Guide for Air-
line Employee Discounts*
1525 East Francisco Boulevard
San Rafael, CA 94901
415-459-0300
Quarterly; $34.95/year.
Features paid listings by hotels, tour
operators, airlines and others offering
discounts and other deals to airline employees.

Bank Travel Management
401 West Main Street
Lexington, KY 40507
606-253-0455
Bi-monthly; $20/year.

Aimed at banks that offer travel incentive programs for their senior (50+) depositors.

Bus Tours Magazine
9698 West Judson Road
Polo, IL 61064
815-946-2341
Bi-monthly; $10/year.
Provides information on destinations and attractions for an audience of motorcoach tour operators.

Canadian Travel Press Weekly
310 Dupont Street
Toronto, Ontario M5R lV9
CANADA
416-968-7252
Weekly; $85.60/year.
Provides general industry coverage of interest to travel agents.

Corporate and Incentive Travel
Coastal Communications
2600 North Military Trail
Boca Raton, FL 33431-6309
561-989-0600
Monthly; free to qualified subscribers, $60/year for others.
Targeted at corporate meeting planners and those who serve the industry.

Corporate Meetings and Incentives
The Laux Company
63 Great Road
Maynard, MA 01754
508-897-5552
Monthly; $60/year.

Cruise & Vacation Views
25 Washington Street
Morristown, NJ 07960
201-605-2442
Bi-monthly; $48.
Covers the leisure market, with an accent on cruising. Also contains helpful articles on selling techniques and industry issues.

Cruise Week
620 South Elm Street
Greensboro, NC 27406
910-378-1290
Weekly; $99/year.

A one-page faxed newsletter "covering the top cruise-related news items of the week."

The Destination Series
Stamats Communications
550 Montgomery Street
San Francisco, CA 94111
800-358-0388
415-788-1905 fax
http://www.funtrips.com
Quarterly; free to travel agents
A glossy magazine with a different theme each quarter — Romantic, Family, Senior, or Adventure. Regional survey articles are followed by annotated lists of properties.

Destinations
American Bus Association
1100 New York Avenue NW
Washington, DC 20005-3934
800-283-2877
Monthly; $25/year.
This sleek magazine tracks trends and tour destinations and attractions for a primary audience of motorcoach operators.

The Fam Connection
15170 Amaral Road
Castroville, CA 95012
888-249-5627
$39/year; $69/two years.
A regularly updated on-line or email service that lists "hundreds of fam trips and industry discounts for Travel Professionals."

Group Travel Leader
401 West Main Street
Lexington, KY 40507
606-253-0455
Monthly; free to qualified subscribers, $39/year to others..
"National newspaper for senior group travel." The organ of Group Leaders of America (GLAMER).

GTC Fam Facts
717 St. Joseph Drive
St. Joseph, MI 49085
800-522-2093
Monthly; $60/year; $89.95/two years.

A newsletter listing familiarization trips, agent incentives, contests, complimentary hotel rooms, and such. The price of the subscription includes a directory of "over 200 pages and updated annually."

Independent Travel Seller
4742 Liberty Road South
Suite 239
Salem, OR 97302-5000
888-448-7624
Bi-monthly; $36/year.
A glossy magazine covering issues of interest to the growing market of home-based and independent travel agencies.

Industria Turistica
P.O. Box 521898
Miami, FL 33152-1898
305-551-8493
305-551-0141 fax
Bi-monthly; free to qualified subscribers, otherwise, $30/year, $40 overseas.
A trade magazine with some articles in Spanish and some in English. The main audience is Spanish-speaking travel agents in Florida and the American southeast.

Insurance Meetings Management
Coastal Communications
2600 North Military Trail
Boca Raton, FL 33431-6309
561-989-0600
Bi-monthly; free to qualified subscribers, $40/year for others.
Aimed at the senior insurance company executive.

Jax Fax Travel Marketing Magazine
397 Post Road
P. O. Box 4013
Darien, CT 06820-1413
203-655-8746
203-655-6257 fax
Monthly; $15/year, $24/two years.
A thick, information-packed monthly that focuses on what's available from various travel suppliers. A gold mine of information on deep-discount consolidator fares. Just look up the destination you (or your client) wants and find

out who's offering the best deal. Also features information on the latest in cruises, tours, and fam trips.

Les Romantiques
E&M Associates
211 East 43rd Street, #1404
New York, NY 10017
800-223-9832
212-599-8280
Published three times a year, this newsletter highlights "the best romantic hotels" around the world. Aimed at travel agents (it's free to agents with IATA numbers), the publication features only properties paying at least 8% commission and reachable through an 800 number.

Meeting News
Miller Freeman, Inc.
1 Pennsylvania Plaza
New York, NY 10119
212-714-1300
18 times/year; free to meeting planners.
"The newspaper for meeting, convention, incentive and trade show professionals."

Outbound Traveler
Travel Review Publishing
22 School Street
Marblehead, MA 01945
617-631-1690
617-631-0203 fax
Monthly; $25/year
Subtitled "for agents specializing in international travel," this sleek publication carries news of fams, spiffs, and commission deals, along with short, punchy articles designed to improve your product knowledge of popular international destinations.

Recommend
5979 NW 151 Street
Miami Lakes, FL 33014
800-447-0123
305-828-0123
Monthly; free to qualified subscribers.
"Helping travel agents sell travel" is the subtitle to this publication.

Southeast Travel Professional
1200 NW 78th Avenue
Suite 216
Miami, FL 33126
305-592-6133
Monthly; $12/year.
A tabloid newspaper covering activities, personalities, and issues of interest to the region's travel agent community.

Tour and Travel News
Miller Freeman, Inc.
1 Pennsylvania Plaza
New York, NY 10119
212-714-1300
Weekly; free to qualified travel agents, $95/year otherwise.
This "newspaper for the retail travel industry" offers a mix of articles on what's going on in the travel biz, from fare wars to agency bankruptcies, coupled with destination stories highlighting new tours.

Travel a la Carte
Interpress Inc.
1200 Eglinton Avenue East
Suite 404
Don Mills, Ontario, M3C 1H9
CANADA
416-444-3633

TravelAge East
500 Plaza Drive
Secaucus, NJ 07094
201-902-2000
Weekly; free to qualified agents, $63/year otherwise.
Published in regional editions, this magazine-sized weekly features general travel industry news, with a regional focus. One nice feature is the Discount Corner, listing discounts available to travel agents. There is also a separate listing of fam trips as well as seminars being offered around the country.

TravelAge MidAmerica
625 North Michigan Avenue
Chicago, IL 60611
312-346-4952

TravelAge West
49 Stevenson Street
San Francisco, CA 94105
415-905-1155

Travel Agent
801 Second Avenue
New York, NY 10017
212-370-5050
Weekly; free to the trade, otherwise $79/year.
Slick, weekly newsmagazine in the mold of *Time* or *Business Week*. Bills itself as "The National Newsweekly of the Travel Industry." Provides a good overview of the industry and its trends with an emphasis on reporting (as opposed to reprinting press releases). Profiles of agencies sometimes provide good how-to tips.

Travel Agents Marketplace
1515 Broadway
New York, NY 10036
212-869-1300
Essentially an advertising vehicle consisting of "bounce-back" cards that allow travel agents to request information from resorts, cruise lines, and other advertisers.

Travel Counselor
Miller Freeman, Inc.
1 Pennsylvania Plaza
New York, NY 10119
212-714-1300
Quarterly.
This magazine is "directed solely to the graduates of ICTA," Certified Travel Counselors (CTC) and Destination Specialists (DS). It describes itself as dedicated to "the continuing education of Travel Counselors, covering marketing communications, career growth, legal issues, research, and travel counseling opportunities."

Travel Expense Management Newsletter
American Business Publishing
3100 Highway 138
Wall Township, NJ 07719-1442
908-681-1133
Twice monthly; $427/year.
Aimed at corporate travel managers,

this eight- to ten-page newsletter covers a range of issues of importance to people overseeing the corporate travel function. It is of little use to agencies, unless they are into the corporate travel scene in a major way. The *Travel Expense Management Guide*, is published periodically for approximately $85, and is available to non-subscribers.

Travel Industry Indicators
P.O. Box 6627
Miami, FL 33154
305-868-3818
Monthly; $95/year.
Tracks and analyses statistical trends in the travel industry with easy-to-read graphs in no-nonsense newsletter format.

Travel Management Daily
1155 15th Street NW
Suite 510
Washington, DC 20005
202-467-8087
Daily (with special convention issues); $735/year, $420 for six months.
This two-page newsletter is faxed or e-mailed daily and contains much the same nitty-gritty industry information you will read next week in the trade magazines, if at all.

Travel Management Newsletter
1155 15th Street NW
Suite 510
Washington, DC 20005
202-467-8087
Twice weekly; $370/year, $205/six months.
A four-page, less frequent version of *Travel Management Daily*.

Travel New England
256 Marginal Street
East Boston, MA 02128
617-561-4000
Monthly; free to qualified subscribers, $50/year to others.
"For the New England travel professional, including wholesalers, hotels, and leisure and business travel professionals."

Travel Trade
15 West 44th Street
New York, NY 10036
212-730-6600
Weekly; $10/year.
A no-nonsense business-oriented weekly tabloid — it likes to call itself "the business paper of the travel industry." Among its better features are a lively Letters to the Editor column and the "Business Features Showcase" with tips and suggestions from industry pros.

Travel Weekly
500 Plaza Drive
Secaucus, NJ 07094.
800-360-0015
Twice weekly; $21.50/year, $32.25/two years.
A lively, glossy, tabloid style publication that combines travel industry news (who's doing what) with regular features on specific destinations (which can alert you to tours and cruises you might want to sell). There are regular supplements that give extended attention to various destinations (Hawaii and Europe are the most frequent, but less familiar areas like the Maya region of Central America are covered, too). Occasionally carries classified ads from agencies looking for outside reps. A good, cheap way to get a feel for the business.

Travel World News
One Morgan Avenue
Norwalk, CT 06851-5017
203-853-4955
Monthly; free to qualified subscribers, $25/year to others.
Similar to *Jax Fax* in look, feel, and layout. Covers the usual mix of industry news, new tours by region of the world, consolidator fares, cruises, fams, and so forth.

Consumer Travel Publications

The Affordable Caribbean
330 West Canton Boulevard
Winter Park, FL 32789
800-783-4903
407-628-4802
Monthly; $39/year.
For the cost-conscious island lover,
with an emphasis on budget packages
and off-season specials.

Andrew Harper's Hideaway Report
P.O. Box 300
Whitefish, MT 59937
Monthly; $100/year.
The granddaddy of luxury travel newsletters. Harper (not his real name)
tours super-luxury resorts, hotels, and
spas and writes unbiased and highly
opinionated critiques. The circulation
of this 8-pager is held to 15,000 to
heighten the exclusivity of the letter
and there is sometimes a waiting list
for new subscribers. The articles can
serve as useful sales aids when dealing
with well-heeled clients.

Belize First
Equator Travel Publications
280 Beaverdam Road
Candler, NC 28715
704-667-1717 fax
Quarterly; $24/year.
"The ad-free guide to travel and life in
Belize and other parts of the 'Carib-
bean coast' of Central America and
Mexico." An additional "Best of Belize"
issue is published annually.

Best Fares
245 Greenmont Circle
Alpharetta, GA 30201
800-228-7956
Monthly; $59.90/year.
Tom Parsons is the guru of the travel
deal. His monthly magazine tracks every promotion and plays every angle to
give readers the lowest fares possible.

Better Business Traveling
25115 West Avenue Stanford

First Floor
Valencia, CA 91355-3922
805-295-1250
Bi-monthly; distributed free through
consortiums.
Articles on business travel featuring
products that are commissionable to
travel agents.

Business Traveler International
51 East 42nd Street
Suite 1806
New York, NY 10017
212-697-1700
Monthly; $12/year.
News and tips of interest to the fre-
quent business traveler.

Caribbean Travel and Life
330 West Canton Boulevard
Winter Park, FL 32789
800-588-1689
407-628-4802
Bi-monthly; $23.95/year.
A glossy magazine covering the Caribbean area in much the same way as
Travel & Leisure covers the world.

Conde Nast Traveler
P.O. Box 57018
Boulder, CO 80322-7018
800-777-0700
Monthly; $18/year.
A glossy monthly with an emphasis on
the upscale travel experience. Appeals
to the well-to-do traveler and the not-
so-well-to-do dreamer.

Consumer Reports Travel Letter
P.O. Box 53629,
Boulder CO 80322-3629
Monthly; $37/year.
Geared to the up-scale penny-pincher,
this no-nonsense newsletter gives the
low-down on the best deals in travel,
covering things like consolidators,
travel clubs, round-the-world fares, frequent flyer programs, and so forth.

Cruise Travel
990 Grove Street
Evanston, IL 60201-4370
847-491-6440
Bi-monthly; $11.97/year.
A magazine for the frequent cruiser.
Each issue features a cruise, ship, and
port of month. A directory issue is published in January.

Currents
International Voyager Media
77 East Street
South Salem, NY 10590
914-533-6830
Three times a year; $7.99/year.
A general interest travel magazine,
published by Carnival Cruises and
mailed to their past customers.

The Discerning Traveler
504 West Mermaid Lane
Philadelphia, PA 19118-4206
800-673-7834
215-247-5578
Bi-monthly; $50/year.
This newsletter is a labor of love by a
husband-wife team. Each issue focuses
in-depth on one vacation area on the
East Coast. Back issues (which come
with updated information, when available) may be ordered separately.

EcoTraveler
2535 NW Upshur Street
Portland, OR 97210-2549
503-224-9080
Bi-monthly;
"Travel with an emphasis on environmentally and culturally-sensitive
trips."

The Educated Traveler
P.O. Box 220822
Chantilly, VA 22022
703-471-1063
Bi-monthly; $48/year.
A newsletter covering group tours for a
wide variety of special interests. Sub-
scription price includes a copy of their
Directory of Special Interest Travel.

Endless Vacation
P.O. Box 80260

Indianapolis, IN 46280-0260
317-876-1692
800-338-7777
Monthly; free with membership.
A travel magazine for members of Resort Condominiums International, an
association of time share owners.

Escape
3205 Ocean Park Boulevard
Suite 160
Santa Monica, CA 90405
310-392-5235
Quarterly; $18/six issues.
A glossy "spirit of the road" travel
magazine, with an emphasis on adventure travel and global cultures.

First Class Executive Travel
3255 Wilshire Boulevard
Los Angeles, CA 90010
213-382-3335
Bi-monthly.
Aimed at the upscale business traveler.

Freighter Travel News
3524 Harts Lake Road
Roy, WA 98580
Monthly; $18/year.
Readers of this newsletter provide first-
hand accounts of trips aboard passenger-carrying freighters. Interesting look
at an off-beat corner of the travel world
but of limited use to the travel agent.

Frequent Flyer
2000 Clearwater Drive
Oakbrook, IL 60521-8809
630-574-6000
Monthly; $24/year.
"Consumer news and business develop-
ments for upscale executive travelers."

Gemütlichkeit
UpCountry Publishing
2892 Chronicle Avenue
Hayward, CA 94542
800-521-6722
Monthly; $67/year.
An 8-page newsletter covering Ger-
man-speaking Europe (primarily Germany, Austria, and Switzerland), with
an emphasis on itineraries and hotel/
restaurant suggestions.

Golf Travel
P.O. Box 3485
Charlottesville, VA 22903-0485
800-225-7825
804-295-1200
Monthly; $79/year, $135/two years.
An 8-page newsletter that anony-
mously covers the better golfing resorts
around the world.

Hawaii: Big Island Update
Kauai Update
Maui Update
Paradise Publications
8110 SW Wareham
Portland, OR 97223
503-246-1555
Quarterly; $10 each/year.
Three separate 4-page newsletters with
an emphasis on restaurant reviews and
accommodations updates.

The International Railway Traveler
P.O. Box 3000
Denville, NJ 07834
Bi-monthly; $39.95/year.
A 16-page newsletter with an emphasis
on foreign train itineraries and rail
pass updates.

International Travel News
520 Calvados Street
Sacramento, CA 95815
916-457-3643
Monthly; $16/year.
On a pennies-per-word basis, *ITN* has
to be the best buy in travel magazines.
Printed on cheap newsprint-like paper,
this 100-pager appeals primarily to
older, more adventurous travelers.
Written largely by its readers, each issue contains short tips on (mostly) budget accommodations. There are also in-
depth reviews of moderate-to-luxury
tour packages and cruises and many
small advertisements from offbeat tour
companies. A good source of first-hand
information.

Islands
Island Publishing Company
3886 State Street
Santa Barbara, CA 93105
805-682-7177

The Italian Traveler
Cognoscenti Publications
P.O. Box 32
Livingston, NJ 07039
201-535-6572
11 times a year; $59/year.
An 8-page newsletter covering primarily upscale hotels and restaurants
with tips on itineraries, attractions,
and events.

La Belle France
P.O. Box 3485
Charlottesville, VA 22903
800-225-7825
804-295-1200
Monthly; $87/year, $145/two years.
An 8-page newsletter covering luxury
hotels and restaurants in France, with
the emphasis on Paris.

Las Vegas Advisor
5280 South Valley View Boulevard
Las Vegas, NV 89118
Monthly; $45/year.
A 12-page newsletter with an emphasis
on "deals" in the gambling capital of
the world.

National Geographic Traveler
P.O. Box 64112
Tampa, FL 33664
800-NGS-LINE
Monthly; $25/year.
Covers the world, much in the style of
Conde Nast Traveler or *Travel & Lei-
sure*, although with perhaps more of an
outdoorsy sensibility.

Net News for the Thrifty Traveler
P.O. Box 8168-K
Clearwater, FL 33758
800-532-5731
Monthly; $29/year.
"How to find travel bargains on the Internet, keep up with the latest technology and surfing techniques, all in a
user-friendly format."

Northwest Travel
P.O. Box 18000
Florence, OR 97439
503-997-8401
Bi-monthly; $16.95/year.

A glossy travel magazine featuring articles on vacation spots in the Pacific Northwest. The same company publishes *Oregon Coast Magazine, Northwest Parks & Wildlife,* and *Oregon Parks.*

Our World
1104 North Nova Road
Suite 251
Daytona Beach, FL 32117
904-441-5367
904-441-5604 fax
Ten times a year; $35/year.
Our World describes itself as "the travel magazine for gays and lesbians" and "the best source of reliable gay travel information by both consumers and travel professionals."

Out And About
542 Chapel Street
New Haven, CT 06511
800-929-2268
Ten times a year; $49/year.
A 16-page newsletter offering "the unbiased truth" about destinations and attractions of interest to gays and lesbians. The newsletter claims a circulation of 500 among travel agencies.

Out West
408 Broad Street
Nevada City, CA 95959
800-274-9378
Quarterly; $11.95/year.
An offbeat tabloid with an emphasis on back-road, off-the-beaten-path sightseeing in the Old West.

The Over 50 Thrifty Traveler
P.O. Box 8168-K
Clearwater, FL 33758
800-532-5731
Monthly; $29/year.
This sister publication to *The Thrifty Traveler* (see below), focuses on the budget-conscious senior market.

Passport Newsletter
401 North Franklin Street
3rd floor
Chicago, IL 60610
800-542-6670

Monthly; $75/year.
A 20-page newsletter with an emphasis on brief reviews of upscale hotels and restaurants. Each issue contains a removable Special Report on a single destination.

Sports Traveler
167 Madison Avenue
New York, NY 10016-5430
212-686-6480
"Everything of interest to the active woman."

The Thrifty Traveler
P.O. Box 8168-K
Clearwater, FL 33758
800-532-5731
Monthly; $29/year.
This 8-page newsletter focuses on money-saving tips for the world traveler that you might want to use yourself or pass along to clients. Some coverage of low-priced packages.

Travel and Leisure
1120 Avenue of the Americas
New York, NY 10036
800-888-8728
212-382-5600
Monthly; $35/year.
A slick, thick, luxurious look at the world of (generally) luxury travel, with an accent on good writing and honest appraisals.

Travel America
990 Grove Street
Evanston, IL 60201-4370
847-491-6440
Bi-monthly; $11.97/year.
Covers a broad range of tourist destinations and activities in the United States. Each issue features a tour, city, and resort of month. Formerly *Tours & Resorts.*

Travel Books Review
P.O. Box 191554
Atlanta, GA 31119-1554
404-634-5874
Bi-monthly; $21.95/year.
This 12-page newsletter reviews 20 to 30 travel books in each issue. Typically,

each issue will feature one themed group of reviews (e.g. family travel or train travel in Europe), two pages of U.S. travel books, one page of travel literature reviews and one review each of a photography book and a general interest book.

Travel Books Worldwide
2510 S Street
P.O. Box 162266
Sacramento, CA 95816-2266
916-452-5200
Ten times a year; $36/year.
This 14- to 24-page newsletter lists a hundred or more travel books (with complete publisher information) received for review each month and reviews between 12 and 25.

Travel Companions
Travel Companion Exchange
P.O. Box 83
Amityville, NY 11701
516-454-0880
Bi-monthly; $48/year.
Travel safety and health tips for single travelers with hundreds of listings of those seeking travel companions and partners.

Travel Holiday
1633 Broadway
New York, NY 10019-6708
212-767-6000
10 times a year; $12.97/year, $25.94/ two years.
A somewhat less glamorous version of *Conde Nast Traveler* and *Travel & Leisure*, with an accent on how-to information and tips.

Travel News
Travel Agents International
111 Second Avenue NE
15th floor
St. Petersburg, FL 33701
813-895-8241
Monthly; free to qualified subscribers.
A consumer-oriented travel magazine put out by the TAI franchise to drum up business for its franchisees. Consumers can ask to be put on the mailing list through a local TAI branch.

Travel Smart
40 Beechdale Road
Dobbs Ferry, NY 10522
914-693-8300
Monthly; $37/year.
Newsletter offering short bits of information on travel tips, low fares, hotel discounts, last-minute deals, and the like. Also runs what to do-see-eat features on destinations, with an emphasis on the U.S.

Traveling Times
25115 West Avenue Stanford
First Floor
Valencia, CA 91355-3922
805-295-1250
Quarterly; distributed free through consortiums.
Focuses on domestic and international travel that is commissionable to travel agents.

TravLtips
P.O. Box 188
Flushing, NY 11358
718-939-2400
Bi-monthly; $20/year, $35/two years.
Reports on freighter trips and other long-term, low per diem cruises by some of the 28,000 subscribers who've taken them. TravLtips is also a retailer and wholesaler of freighter cruises.

Voyager International
7 Northgate
P.O. Box 277
Westport, CT 06880
203-226-1647
voyagerint@aol.com
Bi-monthly; $38/year.
A 32-page newsletter with an emphasis on hotels and restaurants in major European and Asian tourist destinations, with spotty coverage of other areas.

Travel Industry Reference Books

Adventure Travel North America
Adventure Guides, Inc.
800-252-7899
Annual; $18.

Alternative Travel Directory
Transitions Abroad Publishing
800-293-0373
Annual; $23.95.

Business Travel Planner
Reed Travel Group
800-342-5634
Quarterly; $142/year.

Caribbean Travel Directory - Gold Book
Caribbean Hotel Association
787-725-9139
Semi-annual.

Directory of Travel Agencies for the Disabled
Twin Peaks Publishing
360-694-2462
Annual; $20.

Ferrari Guides' Gay Travel A-Z
(also *Men's Travel in Your Pocket* and
Women's Travel in Your Pocket)
Ferrari International
602-863-2408
Annual; $16.

Ford's Deck Plan Guide
Ford's Travel Guides
818-701-7414
Annual; $75.

Ford's Freighter Travel Guide
Ford's Travel Guides
818-701-7414
Semi-annual; $24.

Ford's International Cruise Guide
Ford's Travel Guides
818-701-7414
Quarterly; $40/year.

Guide to Academic Travel
Shaw Guides

212-787-6021
Annual; $20.

Hotel & Travel Index
Reed Travel Group
800-360-0015
Quarterly; $50/copy.

Index to Air Travel Consolidators
Travel Publishing
800-241-9299
Annual, with updates; $49.50.

International Golf Resort Directory
Travel Publishing
800-241-9299
Annual; $39.50

International Ski Resort Directory
Travel Publishing
800-241-9299
Annual; $39.50

OAG Agent's Gazetteer
Reed Travel Group
800-342-5634
(several separate editions)
Annual.

OAG Cruise and Ferry Guide
Reed Travel Group
800-342-5634
Quarterly.

OAG Flight Guides
Reed Travel Group
800-342-5634
(Various editions, frequencies, and formats, print and electronic.)

OAG Guide to International Travel
Reed Travel Group
800-342-5634
Quarterly.

OAG Travel Atlas
Reed Travel Group
800-342-5634
Semi-annual.

OAG World Airways Guide
Reed Travel Group
800-342-5634
(two editions)
Monthly.

Official Cruise Guide
Reed Travel Group
800-360-0015
Annual; $95.

Official Hotel Guide
Reed Travel Group
800-360-0015
Annual; $250.

Official Meeting Facilities Guide
Reed Travel Group
800-360-0015
Semi-annual; $59/year.

Official Railway Guide
K-III Directory Group
212-714-3100
Quarterly; $172/year.

Official Travel Industry Directory
Travel Agent Magazine
212-370-5050
Annual; $19.95.

Personnel Guide to Canada's Travel Industry
Baxter Publishing
416-968-7252
Semi-annual; $54/year.

Single-Friendly Travel Directory
Connecting Newsletter
604-737-7791
Annual; $8.

Specialty Travel Index
800-442-4922
Annual; $10.

Travel 800
Travel
818-990-3509
Quarterly; $30/year.

Travel Agencies
American Business Information
402-331-5481
Annual; $1,275.

Travel Industry Personnel Directory
Fairchild Publications
800-247-6622
Annual; $30.

Travel Source Directory
Intelligentsia Publications
800-979-4433
Annual; $400.

World Travel Guide
Columbus Press
800-322-3834
Annual; $159.

Worldwide Brochures
800-852-6752
Annual; $39.

Worldwide Travel Information Contact Book
Gale Research
800-877-4253
Annual; $175.

Books About the Travel Industry

Anolik, Alexander, *The Law and the Travel Industry*. San Francisco: Anolik, 1990.

Boe, Beverly, and Phil Philcox *How You Can Travel Free as a Group Tour Organizer.* Babylon, NY: Pilot Books, 1987.

Boniface, Brian G. and Christopher P. Cooper, *The Geography of Travel and Tourism.* 2nd ed. Newton, MA: Butterworth-Heinemann, 1994.

Boyd, Wilma, *Travel Agent*. Upper Saddle River, NJ: Prentice Hall, 1989.

Bravos, Brooke Shannon, *Cruise Hosting*. Sausalito, CA: Travel Time, 1992.

Bryant, Carl L., et. al., *Travel Selling Skills*. Albany: Delmar Publishers, 1992.

Burke, James, *Marketing and Selling the Travel Product*. Albany: Delmar Publishers, 1991.

Cassidy, Maggie B., *Taking Students Abroad: A Complete Guide for Teachers*. Rev. ed. Brattleboro, VT: Pro Lingua Associates, Inc., 1988.

Cournoyer and Marshall, *Hotel, Restaurant, and Travel Law*. 5th ed. Albany: Delmar Publishers, 1997.

Dallas, Melissa, and Carl Riegel, *Hospitality and Tourism Careers*. Upper Saddle River, NJ: Prentice Hall, 1997.

Davidoff, Doris, and Philip Davidoff, *Air Fares and Ticketing*. 3rd ed. Upper Saddle River, NJ: Prentice Hall, 1995.

Davidoff, Doris, and Philip Davidoff, *Financial Management for Travel Agencies*. Albany: Delmar Publishers, 1986.

Davidoff, Doris, and Philip Davidoff, *Sales and Marketing for Travel and Tourism.* 2nd ed. Upper Saddle River, NJ: Prentice Hall, 1994.

Davidoff, Doris, and Philip Davidoff, *Worldwide Tours: A Travel Agent's Guide to Selling Tours*. Upper Saddle River, NJ: Prentice Hall, 1990.

Davidoff, Philip G., et. al., *Tourism Geography*. 2nd ed. Upper Saddle River, NJ: Prentice Hall, 1995.

DeSouto, Martha Sarbey, *Group Travel Operations Manual*. 2nd ed. Albany: Delmar Publishers, 1993.

Dervaes, Claudine, *Careers in Travel* (video). Tampa: Solitaire, 1996.

Dervaes, Claudine, *Travel Dictionary. 8th ed.* Tampa: Solitaire, 1996.

Dervaes, Claudine, *Travel Training Series, The.* 6 vol., 9th ed. Tampa: Solitaire, 1997.

Enggass, Peter M., *Tourism and the Travel Industry: An Information Sourcebook.* Phoenix: Oryx Press, 1988.

Fay, Betsy, *Essentials of Tour Management*. Upper Saddle River, NJ: Prentice Hall, 1992.

Fee, Gary, and Alexander Anolik, *Official Outside Sales Travel Agent Manual, The.* 3rd ed. San Francisco: Dendrobium, 1996.

Foster, Dennis L., *Business of Travel, The: Agency Operations and Administration.* New York: Macmillan, 1990.

Foster, Dennis L., *Destinations: North American and International Geography*. New York: Macmillan, 1994.

Foster, Dennis L., *First Class: An Introduction to Travel and Tourism*. 2nd ed. Westerville, OH: Glencoe, 1993.

Foster, Dennis L., *Sales and Marketing for the Travel Professional*. New York: Macmillan, 1990.

Fremont, Pamela, *How to Open and Run a Money-Making Travel Agency*. New York: Wiley, 1983.

Friedheim, Eric, *Travel Agents: From Caravans and Clippers to the Concorde*. New York: Universal Media, 1992.

Fuller, Gerald, *Travel Agency Management*. Albany: Delmar Publishers, 1994.

Gagnon, Patricia J., et. al., *Travel Career Development*. 5th ed. Burr Ridge, IL: Times Mirror, 1993.

Godwin, Nadine, *Complete Guide to Travel Agency Automation*. 2nd ed. Albany: Delmar Publishers, 1987.

Gold, Hal, *The Cruise Book: From Brochure to Bon Voyage*. Albany: Delmar Publishers, 1990.

Goldsmith, Carol, and Ann Waigand, *Building Profits with Group Travel*. San Francisco: Dendrobium, 1990.

Gregory, Aryear, *The Travel Agent: Dealer in Dreams*. 4th ed. Upper Saddle River, NJ: Prentice Hall, 1993.

Hayes, Greg, and Joan Wright, *Going Places: The Guide to Travel Guides*. Boston, MA: Harvard Common Press, 1988.

Heckler, Helen, *Directory of Travel Agencies for the Disabled*. Vancouver, WA: Twin Peaks Press, 1993.

Hoosen, Chris, and Francis Dix, *Travel Agent Training Series*. 15 vol. Clinton Turnpike, MI: Travel Text Associates, 1989.

Howell, David, *Passport: An Introduction to the Travel and Tourism Industry*. Albany: Delmar Publishers, 1993.

Howell, David W., *Principles and Methods of Scheduling Reservations*, 3rd ed. Upper Saddle River, NJ: Prentice Hall, 1992.

Hudman, Lloyd, and Richard Jackson, *Geography of Travel and Tourism*. 2nd ed. Albany: Delmar Publishers, 1994.

Jung, Gerald, *A Practical Guide to Selling Travel*. Upper Saddle River, NJ: Prentice Hall, 1993.

Landry, Janice L., and Anna H. Fesmire, *The World Is Waiting Out There: An Introduction to Travel and Tourism*. Upper Saddle River, NJ: Prentice Hall, 1994.

Makower, Joel, ed., *The Map Catalog*. New York: Random House, 1992.

Mancini, Marc, *Conducting Tours*. 2nd ed. Albany: Delmar Publishers, 1996.

Mancini, Marc, *Selling Destinations: Geography for the Travel Professional*. Albany: Delmar Publishers, 1995.

Maxtone-Graham, John, *Crossing & Cruising: From the Golden Era of Ocean Liners to the Luxury Cruise Ships of Today*. New York: Scribner's, 1993.

Middleton, Victor T. C., *Marketing in Travel and Tourism*. 2nd ed. Newton, MA: Butterworth-Heinemann, 1994.

Mill, Robert C., *The Tourism System: An Introductory Text*. Upper Saddle River, NJ: Prentice Hall, 1992.

Mill, Robert C., *Tourism: The International Business*. Upper Saddle River, NJ: Prentice Hall, 1990.

Miller, Capt. Bill, *Insiders' Guide to Cruise Discounts*. St. Petersburg, FL: Ticket to Adventure, 1990.

Mitchell, Gerald E., *How to Be a Cruise Counselor*. Englewood, FL: G.E. Mitchell & Associates, 1992.

Mitchell, Gerald E., *How to Be a Destination Manager*. Englewood, FL: G.E. Mitchell & Associates, 1992.

Mitchell, Gerald E., *How to Be an International Tour Director*. Englewood, FL: G.E. Mitchell & Associates, 1992.

Mitchell, Gerald E., *How to Be a Tour Guide*. Englewood, FL: G.E. Mitchell & Associates, 1992.

Mitchell, Gerald E., *How to Design and Package Tours*. Englewood, FL: G.E. Mitchell & Associates, 1992.

Mitchell, Gerald E., *The Travel Consultant's On-Site Inspection Journal*. Englewood, FL: G.E. Mitchell & Associates, 1990.

Monaghan, Kelly, *Air Courier Bargains*. 6th ed. New York: The Intrepid Traveler, 1997.

Monaghan, Kelly, *Consolidators: Air Travel's Bargain Basement*. New York: The Intrepid Traveler, 1996.

Monaghan, Kelly, *Home-Based Travel Agent*. New York: The Intrepid Traveler, 1997.

Monaghan, Kelly, *Shopper's Guide to Independent Agent Opportunities, A*. New York: The Intrepid Traveler, 1997.

Morrison, Alastair, *Hospitality and Travel Marketing*, 2nd ed. Albany: Delmar Publishers, 1996.

Nickerson, Norma P., *Foundations of Tourism*. Upper Saddle River, NJ: Prentice Hall, 1994.

Nwanna, Gladson I., *Americans Traveling Abroad: What You Should Know Before You Go*. 2nd ed. Baltimore, MD: World Travel Institute Press, 1996.

Nyy, Linda, *Vacation CounSELLing*. Upper Saddle River, NJ: Prentice Hall, 1992.

Ogg, Tom, *How To Buy or Sell a Travel Agency*. Valley Center, CA: Ogg & Associates, 1988.

Payette, Douglas A., *So You Want To Be a Travel Agent*. Upper Saddle River, NJ: Prentice Hall, 1995.

Poynter, James M., *Corporate Travel Management*. Upper Saddle River, NJ: Prentice Hall, 1990.

Poynter, James, *Foreign Independent Tours*. Albany: Delmar Publishers, 1989.

Poynter, James, *Travel Agency Accounting Procedures*. Albany: Delmar Publishers, 1991.

Poynter, James, *Tour Design, Marketing & Management*. Upper Saddle River, NJ: Prentice-Hall, 1993.

Reiff, Annette, *Introduction to Corporate Travel*. Albany: Delmar Publishers, 1994.

Reilly, Robert T., *Travel and Tourism Marketing Techniques*. 2nd ed. Albany: Delmar Publishers, 1988.

Reilly, Robert T., *Effective Communication in the Travel Industry*. Albany: Delmar Publishers, 1990.

Reilly, Robert T., *Handbook of Professional Tour Management*. 2nd ed. Albany: Delmar Publishers, 1991.

Rice, Susan, and Ginger Todd, *Travel Perspectives: A Guide to Becoming a Travel Agent*. 2nd ed. Albany: Delmar Publishers, 1996.

Roberts, Graeme, compiler, *Computerized Reservations System Words and Phrases*. Holmes Beach, FL: Wm. W. Gaunt & Sons, 1991.

Schmidt, Gary, *101 Ways to Sell Travel*. St. Paul, MN: Travel Publishing, 1997.

Semer-Purzicki, Jeanne, *A Practical Guide to Fares and Ticketing*. 2nd ed. Albany: Delmar Publishers, 1994.

Sorensen, Helle, *International Travel and Tourism*. Albany: Delmar Publishers, 1997.

Starr, Nona, and Sybil Norwood, *The Traveler's World: A Dictionary of Industry and Destination Literacy*. Upper Saddle River, NJ: Prentice Hall, 1996.

Stevens, Laurence, *Guide to Travel Agency Security*. Albany: Delmar Publishers, 1982.

Stevens, Laurence, *Your Career in Travel, Tourism, and Hospitality*. 6th ed. Albany: Delmar Publishers, 1988.

Stevens, Laurence, *Guide to Starting and Operating a Successful Travel Agency*. 3rd ed. Albany: Delmar Publishers, 1990.

Stevens, Laurence, *Travel Manager's Personnel Manual, The*. 2nd ed. Albany: Delmar Publishers, 1990.

Tepper, Bruce, *Incentive Travel, The Complete Guide*. San Francisco: Dendrobium, 1992.

Thompson, Douglas, *How to Open Your Own Travel Agency*. 4th ed. San Francisco: Dendrobium, 1992.

Thompson, Douglas, *Profitable Direct Mail for Travel Agencies*. San Francisco: Dendrobium, 1992.

Thompson, Douglas, and Alexander Anolik, *Personnel and Operations Manual for*

Travel Agencies, A. San Francisco: Dendrobium, 1993.

Thompson-Smith, Jeanie M., *Travel Agency Guide to Business Travel.* Albany: Delmar Publishers, 1988.

Todd, Ginger, *Selling Travel 1-2-3.* Indianapolis, IN: Travel Careers, 1996.

Travel Industry Association of America, *Discover America Package Tour Handbook.* Washington, DC: TIAA, 1993.

Trooboff, Dr. Stevan K., et.al., *Travel Sales and Customer Service.* Burr Ridge, IL: Times Mirror, 1995.

Ward, Douglas, *Berlitz Guide to Cruising and Cruise Ships.* New York: Berlitz, 1997.

Webster, Susan, *Group Travel Operating Procedures.* 2nd ed. New York: Van Nostrand Reinhold, 1993.

WHO staff, *International Travel and Health: Vaccination Requirements and Health Advice.* World Health Organization, c/o Chicago: ASCP Press, 1993.

Woodring, Carol, and Gail S. Huck, *Reservations and Ticketing: Apollo.* Albany: Delmar Publishers, 1991.

Zvoncheck, Juls, *Cruises: Selecting, Selling & Booking.* 2nd ed. Upper Saddle River, NJ: Prentice Hall, 1994.

Major Publishers of Travel Guides

Access Guides
Access Press
10 East 53rd Street
New York, NY 10022
212-207-7094

Baedeker's Guides
See Frommer's

Berkeley Guides
See Fodor's

Berlitz Publishing Company, Inc.
257 Park Avenue South
New York, NY 10010
212-598-2499
Publishes *Berlitz Pocket Guides*, *Berlitz Travellers,* and *Discover* guides, along with an extensive line of foreign language phrase books.

Birnbaum Travel Guides
Harper Perrennial
10 East 53rd Street
New York, NY 10022
212-207-7094

Cadogan Guides
Leets House, London
distributed by The Globe Pequot Press
P.O. Box 833
Old Saybrook, CT 06475
800-243-0495
Cheap Eats and Cheap Sleeps
Chronicle Books
275 5th Street
San Francisco, CA 94103
415-777-7240

Eyewitness Travel Guides
Dorling Kindersley Publishing, Inc.
95 Madison Avenue
New York, NY 10016
212-684-0404

Fielding Guides
Fielding Worldwide, Inc.
308 South Catalina Avenue
Redondo Beach, CA 90277
310-372-4474

Fodor's Guides
Fodor's Travel Publications, Inc.
201 East 50th Street
New York, NY 10022
212-572-8756
Publishes *Fodor's Guides*, *Berkeley Guides*, *Compass American Guides*, *Exploring Guides*, and regional *Bed & Breakfasts and Country Inns* guides.

Frommer's Travel Guides
Prentice Hall Travel Books
Macmillan USA
15 Columbus Circle
New York, NY 10023
Holiday Islands Visitor's Guides
Moorland Publishing
Ashbourne, Derbyshire
distributed by The Globe Pequot Press
P.O. Box 833
Old Saybrook, CT 06475
800-243-0495

Insight Guides
Houghton Mifflin Company
222 Berkeley Street
Boston, MA 02116-3764
617-351-5000
Publishes *Insight Guides* and *Insight Pocket Guides with Maps*.

Karen Brown's Guides
P.O. Box 70
San Mateo, CA 94401
415-342-9117
Guides to hotels, B&Bs, and inns of Europe and California.

Knopf Guides
Alfred A. Knopf
201 East 50th Street
New York, NY 10022
212-751-2600
Let's Go Guides
St Martin's Press Inc.
175 Fifth Avenue
New York, NY 10010
212-674-5151

Lonely Planet Guides
Lonely Planet Publications
155 Filbert Street
Suite 251
Oakland, CA 94607
510-893-8555
Publishes the *Travel Survival Kit* and
on a Shoestring series as well as walk-
ing guides, city guides, and
phrasebooks.

Michelin Guides
Michelin Travel Publications
P.O. Box 19001
Greenville, SC 29602-9001
803-458-6470

Moon Travel Handbooks
Moon Publications
P.O. Box 3040
Chico, CA 95927-3040
916-345-5473

Off The Beaten Track Guides
Moorland Publishing
Ashbourne, Derbyshire
distributed by The Globe Pequot Press
P.O. Box 833
Old Saybrook, CT 06475
800-243-0495

Passport's Guides
Passport Books
NTC Publishing Froup
4255 West Touhy Avenue
Lincolnwood, IL 60646-1975
708-679-5500

Publishes Passport's *Trip Planners, Essential Travel Guides, European Regional Guides, Handbooks of the World,*
and *Illustrated Travel Guides from
Thomas Cook.*

Rough Guides
375 Hudson Street
New York, NY 10014
212-366-2331

Time Out Guides
Penquin Books
375 Hudson Street
New York, NY 10014
212-366-2000

A Traveller's History of . . .
Interlink Publishing Group
99 Seventh Avenue
Brooklyn, NY 11215
718-797-4292

2 to 22 Days In . . .
John Muir Publications
P.O. Box 613
Santa Fe, NM 87504
505-982-4078

Virago Woman's Travel Guides
Ulysses Press
The Berkeley Publishing Group
200 Madison Avenue
New York, NY 10016

Mail order sources for travel books

These travel-oriented catalogs will be most helpful in locating guidebooks and general travel books.

Bon Voyage!
2069 West Bullard Avenue
Fresno, CA 93711-1200
800-995-9716

Book Passage
51 Tamal Vista Boulevard
Corte Madera, CA 94925
800-321-9785
415-927-0960
415-924-3838 Fax

The Complete Traveller Bookstore
By Mail
199 Madison Avenue
New York, NY 10016
212-685-9007

Travellers' Bookstore
75 Rockefeller Plaza
(22 West 52nd Street)
New York, NY 10019
212-664-0995

The following sources carry specialized books about the travel business or travel industry directories and reference works.

The Intrepid Traveler
P.O. Box 438
New York, NY 10034
212-569-1081
212-942-6687 Fax
http://www.intrepidtraveler.com
Offers a free catalog with a selection of books for the travel professional.

Publications For Less
P.O. Box 916452
Longwood, FL 32791-6452
800-665-9067
407-786-2333
407-786-3689 Fax
travelpubs@aol.com
Claims to have the lowest prices on travel trade magazine subscriptions and standard industry reference books.

Resources for the Intrepid Traveler
More Money-Saving Books from
"The Intrepid Traveler"

Home-Based Travel Agent —
How To Cash In On The Exciting NEW World Of Travel Marketing
Kelly Monaghan $24.95   ©1997   400 pages

Here's your chance to join the growing number of people who are earning good money and FREE trips just by sharing their love of travel with their friends and neighbors. Recent changes in the travel marketplace have created unparalleled opportunities for you to grab a piece of the $30,000,000,000 (*thirty billion*) travel market. What once was available only to a closed shop of "travel professionals" is now open to all.

YOU can become a Home-Based Travel Agent
— *INSTANTLY* —
and start earning $50, $100, $200 (*or more*)
for every trip you book!

This book reveals the secrets you need to:

- Open your own home-based travel agency.
- Avoid high start-up costs and limit your initial investment to pocket change.
- Book air travel, tours, cruises, hotels, and car rentals like a pro — and make money every time you do.
- Gain access to the airlines' sophisticated computerized reservations systems for just $15 a month.
- Buy a $1,200 airline ticket for $800 — and then resell it for whatever the traffic will bear.
- Work part-time for pocket change or forge a full-time career.
- Take tax-deductible cruises for a fraction of their normal cost.
- Get FREE trips from tour operators eager for your business.
- Earn FREE trips just by getting as few as four people to go with you.
- Get FREE magazines and travel info to help you build your business.

This is not a once-over-lightly treatment, but a COMPLETE, easy-to-use business system. You get detailed instructions on how to set up your business, how to legally earn a commission on all travel you sell (even to yourself!), how to make your first bookings, how to find (and keep) customers, how to take advantage of the many benefits available to travel professionals, and MUCH, MUCH MORE!

FREE, with every order of $20 or more — *Ticketing Ploys:*
How To Beat the Airlines at Their Own Game — a $4.00 value

Whether you just want to save some money on your own travel, start a fun part-time business out of your home, or become a six-figure, full-time travel agent, this book will tell you how. You'll save several times the cover price on the next family vacation you book using the tips contained in *Home-Based Travel Agent — How To Cash In On The Exciting NEW World Of Travel Marketing.*

"A definitive guide to getting in on the travel business. Kelly's book will tell you more than any of those mail-order deals about starting on a legitimate, part-time basis. And for lots less money."

Rudy Maxa, National Public Radio's 'Savvy Traveler'

"A gold mine of infomation for the independent contractor who wants to get his or her home-based travel business started on the right foot to success."

Gary M. Fee, Chairman, Outside Sales Support Network

"Finally, someone has written a travel agent book that tells it like it is. Kelly Monaghan's knowledge explodes off every page."

Donna M. Scherf, former Executive Director,
National Association of Commissioned Travel Agents

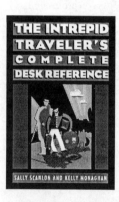

The Intrepid Traveler's Complete Desk Reference

Sally Scanlon and Kelly Monaghan
$16.95   ©1997   375 pages

What's an arunk? If you're flying into AUA, where are you going? The answers to these and thousands of other questions will be found in *The Intrepid Traveler's Complete Desk Reference*, an indispensable reference work for anyone who is really serious about travel. And if you're buying *Home-Based Travel Agent: How To Cash In On The Exciting NEW World Of Travel Marketing*, this book can help you look like a pro almost overnight! Here you'll find not just the definitions of common and obscure travel terms, but the kind of industry information a travel agent needs handy every day:

- The three-letter codes for every airport in the world that make booking reservations a snap.
- Codes for hotels and rental cars.
- An extensive directory of toll-free numbers for suppliers — airlines, hotels, rental cars, tour operators, and cruise lines.
- Complete listings of travel organizations and publications.
- Detailed information on how to get passports and visas.
- Time zones around the world at a glance.
- The currency of every country in the world.
- Sources of FREE travel information, across the nation and around the world.
- A complete glossary of travel-related terms, acronyms, and abbreviations.

FREE, with every order of $20 or more — *Ticketing Ploys: How To Beat the Airlines at Their Own Game* — a $4.00 value

A Shopper's Guide To Independent Agent Opportunities

Kelly Monaghan $39.95   ©1997   79 pages

There are a growing number of outfits offering you the chance to become a travel agent — overnight — and start reaping the many benefits available to the travel industry insider. But which one is right for you?

This information-packed Special Report, containing in-depth profiles of more than 60 companies, provides you with straightforward, *unbiased* information about the current crop of offerings.

In this no-holds-barred report, you will learn . . .

- How to evaluate an outside agent opportunity.
- What the glossy brochures *don't* tell you.
- How to find the best deals.
- The hard questions to ask before signing up with any company.
- Which companies charge *no sign-up fees whatsoever.* (And which ones charge the most!)
- What you get from each company. And just as important, what you *don't* get.
- The truth about travel industry benefits and why many companies offering outside agent opportunities don't want to tell you about it.

Get past the hype and the salesmanship. Get the straight information from someone who's been there. This insider information — not available anywhere else — will save you weeks of research time and let you narrow your search for an outside agent relationship that will work for you. It can also save you thousands of dollars in sign-up charges and annual fees.

THIS INSIDE INFORMATION IS
NOT AVAILABLE ANYWHERE ELSE!

Air Courier Bargains —
How To Travel World-Wide For Next To Nothing. (Sixth Edition)
Kelly Monaghan $14.95   ©1997   232 pages
New York to London for $99 roundtrip! San Francisco to Bangkok for $148!
L.A. to Tokyo for **free!**
Sound impossible? It's not. Every day, hundreds of people take off to exotic
ports of call as air couriers. An air courier is someone who accompanies time-
sensitive cargo shipped as passengers' baggage on regularly scheduled
airlines. Sometimes these people are employees of air freight companies.
Most of the time, they are "freelancers," ordinary people — like you! — who
perform a valuable service for the air freight company in exchange for a deep,
deep discount on their round-trip air fare.
Being an air courier requires no training, no advanced degrees, no special
knowledge of the air freight business. **Anyone can be an air courier.** All it takes
is a yen for low-cost travel, a taste for adventure, and the right insider contacts
— contacts that *Air Courier Bargains* provides in abundance.

Consolidators: Air Travel's Bargain Basement
Kelly Monaghan
$6.95   © 1995, 1996   73 pages
In this exciting book, Kelly Monaghan unlocks the secrets of the world of
"consolidators" — travel specialists who buy huge blocks of seats from the
airlines at deep discounts and then pass those savings on to you. Lists over 300
consolidators across the U.S., both those who deal directly with the public and
those you can work with through your travel agent. Learn how to ...
  • Get "super-saver" fares, even when the deadline has passed!
  • Get an additional 5% off any flight you book yourself!
  • Book by phone and receive your tickets in the mail!

Ticketing Ploys: How To Beat the Airlines at Their Own Game
Kelly Monaghan
$4.00   ©1996   Special Report
The airlines have a bewildering number of ticket rules, all designed to insure that
you pay a premium for your ticket. Savvy travelers have devised a number of ways
around these rules — back-to-back ticketing, hidden city ploys, bulk purchases,
and others. Some can get you in trouble if you're caught and should be avoided. But
the airlines' rules differ widely. What one airline says is a no-no is perfectly okay
with another. And many of the best ploys are perfectly legal. This Special Report
reveals the secret strategies for playing hardball with the airlines, while protecting
yourself against reprisals. A must-have for the serious business traveler or the travel
agent who *always* wants to get the best deal possible.
      FREE with your order of $20 or more! See coupon on last page.

FREE, with every order of $20 or more — *Ticketing Ploys:*
How To Beat the Airlines at Their Own Game — a $4.00 value

How To Get Paid $30,000 A Year To Travel (Without Selling Anything)

Craig Chilton

$24.95   ©1997   340 pages

Have you ever seen a Winnebago transported on the back of a truck? Or an ambulance? A hearse? A fire truck? Or a UPS truck? Chances are you never have. Craig Chilton, author of *HOW TO GET PAID $30,000 A YEAR TO TRAVEL (Without Selling Anything)*, will tell you why the delivery of recreational and specialty vehicles is America's greatest "sleeper" travel lifestyle. There are about 50,000 people throughout the USA and Canada who do this all the time, on a full-time or part-time basis, working for more than 1,000 manufacturers and transporter companies.

Here are some basic facts:

- In all states and provinces, all you need is an ordinary driver's license to deliver RVs. (Larger specialty vehicles require a chauffeur's license.)
- All companies provide full insurance coverage for vehicles and their drivers.
- All vehicles are new, so they're covered by manufacturer's warranty in case of breakdown.
- Companies pay all road expenses and return transportation, apart from earnings. (Earnings normally are based on the number of miles driven per trip.) Drivers who fly home normally get to keep all their frequent flyer miles.
- This lifestyle is nothing like trucking. No freight. Very few regulations. It's like getting paid to drive your own car.
- College students (18 and over) are needed during the summer months to supplement the regular work force. They typically earn $8,000-$12,000 during that season.
- 30 percent are retired people over age 65 who never worry about a "fixed income." (There's no upper age limit. As long as a person is a safe driver, he's in demand, due to his experience and maturity.)

Craig Chilton has appeared on more than 500 talk shows to inform the public about this profitable and fun lifestyle. This **NEW, COMPLETELY REVISED, 1997 EDITION** reveals Craig's system for maximizing this exciting lifestyle and lists more than 4,000 potential employers throughout the US, Canada, Europe, and Australia!

Who hasn't dreamed of getting paid to travel?
Now you can find out how.

A COMPLETE CAREER SYSTEM FOR JUST $24.95

FREE, with every order of $20 or more — *Ticketing Ploys: How To Beat the Airlines at Their Own Game* — a $4.00 value

Orlando's OTHER Theme Parks

What To Do
When You've Done Disney

Kelly Monaghan

$14.95   © 1997   480 pages

Orlando's not a one-mouse town. There's a whole 'nother 'World' outside the 'Kingdom'

The Orlando area abounds in attractions of every sort — from thrill rides to pristine wilderness, paintball games to ballet. But general guidebooks have to devote so much space to Disney's multitude of attractions that the wealth of things to see and do outside Mickey's portals gets short shrift or not a single word. Now, *Orlando's OTHER Theme Parks* provides in-depth guidance to the abundance of other attractions in the greater Orlando area. Imagine:

- ❏ Nearly 100 pages devoted just to Universal Studios Florida.
- ❏ Over 50 pages on Sea World.
- ❏ Reviews of every non-Disney dinner attraction.
- ❏ Complete chapters on Cypress Gardens, Kennedy Space Center, Busch Gardens Tampa, Church Street Station, Gatorland, Splendid China, and Cypress Island.
- ❏ Individual reviews of a legion of other attractions ranging from the area's spectacular miniature golf courses to airboat rides, amazing things to do and see — even the smallest go kart track.
- ❏ The "real Florida" of pristine wilderness walks and unspoiled canoe trails, just minutes from the tourist bustle.
- ❏ Extensive coverage of Orlando's burgeoning arts and sports scenes.
- ❏ Water parks, animal attractions, botanical gardens, museums, and much, much more.

Plus insider tips to help you get the most out of your Central Florida vacation — or the precious few hours you have free from your meeting or convention.

Don't leave for Orlando without it!

FREE, with every order of $20 or more — *Ticketing Ploys: How To Beat the Airlines at Their Own Game* — a $4.00 value

YOUR TICKET TO SAVING *BIG* MONEY ON TRAVEL

☐ **YES!** I want to succeed in my own home-based travel marketing business! Send me the Complete Home-Based Travel Agent System for just $59.95. (Counts as 3 books)	

I prefer to order separately:

☐ *Home-Based Travel Agent: How To Cash In On The Exciting NEW World of Travel Marketing* $24.95	
☐ *The Intrepid Traveler's Complete Desk Reference* $16.95	
☐ *A Shopper's Guide To Outside Agent Opportunities* $39.95	
☐ I need a copy of *Air Courier Bargains*, for just $14.95, so I can learn how to travel the world and save big bucks as an air courier.	
☐ I want to see more than the Mouse! Send me *Orlando's OTHER Theme Parks* so that I'll be sure of getting the most out of my Central Florida trip. And it's just $14.95.	
☐ I want to learn *How To Get Paid $30,000 A Year To Travel (Without Selling Anything)!* Send me Craig Chilton's blockbuster 1997 edition for just $24.95.	
☐ I never want to pay full fare again. Send me *Consolidators: Air Travel's Bargain Basement* for just $6.95.	
☐ My order totals more than $20, send me my *FREE* copy of *Ticketing Ploys.* ($4.00 if less than $20 or ordered by itself.)	**FREE**

Delivery Options: For regular postage (Special 4th Class Book Rate), add $3.50 for the 1st book and $.50 for each additional book ordered. Postage is $.75 for Ticketing Ploys ordered alone. Allow 3 to 4 weeks for delivery. For faster UPS delivery, add $5.00 for the 1st book and $1.00 for each additional book. For foreign delivery (except Canada), add 15% to "Total" for surface mail; for air mail costs fax 212-942-6687. **U.S. funds only.**	Book total	
	NY tax (8.25%)*	
	Regular postage	
	UPS delivery	
	TOTAL	

*NY residents only

Name: _____

Address: _____
UPS can deliver only to street addresses (no P.O. boxes) in the continental US.

City: _____ State: _____ Zip: _____
(Zip + 4 speeds your order!)

Visa / MC / Amex: _____ Exp: _____

Phone: _____

Make checks payable to:

The Intrepid Traveler • Box 438 • New York, NY 10034-0438

Fax credit card orders to 212-942-6687

☐ **I'm not ordering but put me on your mailing list.**

cdr2   Prices & availability subject to change without notice.